The
Postnational
Self

PUBLIC WORLDS

Dilip Gaonkar and Benjamin Lee, Series Editors

ULF HEDETOFT AND METTE HJORT, EDITORS

The

Postnational

Self

Belonging

and Identity

PUBLIC WORLDS, VOLUME 10
UNIVERSITY OF MINNESOTA PRESS
MINNEAPOLIS   LONDON

An earlier version of chapter 3 appeared as "Changing Spaces of Political Communica-tion: The Case of the European Union," *Political Communication* 16, no. 3 (1999): 263–79; reprinted by permission of Taylor & Francis, http://www.tandf.co.uk/journals. An earlier version of chapter 6 appeared as "Citizens, Residents, and Aliens in a Changing World: Political Membership in the Global Era," *Social Research* 66, no. 3 (Fall 1999): 709–44; reprinted with permission. An earlier version of chapter 8 appeared as "Limits of Citi-zenship: Migrants and Post National Membership in Europe," *Ethnic and Racial Studies* 23, no. 1 (2000): 1–15; reprinted by permission of Taylor & Francis, http://www.tandf.co. uk/journals. Chapter 9 was first published as chapter 10 in *The Demands of Citizenship*, edited by Catriona McKinnon and Iain Hampsher-Monk (London and New York: Continuum, 2000); reprinted by permission of Continuum. An earlier version of chap-ter 14 appeared as "Crossing Borders: The Nationalization of Anxiety," *Ethnologia Scandinavica: A Journal for Nordic Ethnology* 29 (1999). Passages from chapter 15 were pre-viously published in *Divided Memory: The Nazi Past in the Two Germanys*, by Jeffrey Herf (Cambridge: Harvard University Press, 1997); copyright 1997 by the President and Fellows of Harvard College; reprinted by permission of Harvard University Press.

Published by the University of Minnesota Press
111 Third Avenue South, Suite 290
Minneapolis, MN 55401-2520
http://www.upress.umn.edu

Library of Congress Cataloging-in-Publication Data

The postnational self : belonging and identity / Ulf Hedetoft and Mette Hjort, editors.
    p.   cm. — (Public worlds ; v. 10)
    Includes bibliographical references and index.
    ISBN 0-8166-3936-1 (HC : alk. paper) — ISBN 0-8166-3937-X (PB : alk. paper)
    1. Nationalism.   2. Group identity.   3. Globalization.   4. Citizenship.
  I. Hedetoft, Ulf.   II. Hjort, Mette.   III. Series.
    JC311 .P673 2002
    320.54—dc21

                            2002007556

Printed in the United States of America on acid-free paper

The University of Minnesota is an equal-opportunity educator and employer.

12 11 10 09 08 07 06 05 04 03 02   10 9 8 7 6 5 4 3 2 1

Contents

Ulf Hedetoft
and Mette Hjort

Introduction

Home and Belonging: Meanings, Images, and Contexts

At first blush, the concepts of "home" and "belonging" are as innocuous as they are semantically interdependent. Our home is where we belong, territorially, existentially, and culturally, where our own community is, where our family and loved ones reside, where we can identify our roots, and where we long to return to when we are elsewhere in the world. In this sense, belonging is a notion replete with organicist meanings and romantic images. It is a foundational, existential, "thick" notion. In the sense that it circumscribes feelings of "homeness" (as well as homesickness), it is also a significant determinant of identity, that elusive but still real psychosociological state of being in sync with oneself under given external conditions. Most important, "home" and "belonging," thus conceived, are affectively, rather than cognitively, defined concepts; the indicative, seemingly neutral, and very simple statement "home *is* where we belong" really means "home is where we *feel* we belong."

But what, for instance, if where we feel we belong (our "cultural" or "ethnic" home) does not match objective ascriptions of membership (our "political" or "civic" home), because "belonging" separates into its two constituent parts: "being" in one place, and "longing" for another? This is where the web starts to get tangled, where ostensible simplicity is supplanted by complexity, permanence by mutability, clear-cut boundaries by fluid images of self and other. In one sense, therefore, the preceding amounts to a false start, for at best it delineates the contours of an ideal state of affairs, a Herderian dream of many different "homes," and, congruously, as many configurations of "belonging," existing peacefully and permanently side by side. Let's try again, on a less pacific note.

"Identity and belonging plainly are potentially divisive," argues Anthony Giddens (1999, 129), because "nationalism can become belligerent." For though belonging does not, *eo ipso*, belong to nationalism, it is nationalism which in our world has appropriated and reconfigured most people's sense of belonging and identity in ways that deeply affect the harmonious portrayal given above. Think of it in the following way: People may feel that they belong to a piece of territory, to a community, or to a state. Normally they will also have a good idea who else rightfully belongs to this their own authentic context, their home, in other words how their primary "in-group," their "gemeinschaft" (Tönnies 1957), and their "organic solidarity" (Durkheim 1965) are constituted. But, as routinely, they will know and feel who is not part of this in-group, and who for that reason does *not* belong—not really at least, though some of these *others* may well be tolerated, sometimes even as co-citizens of the same state.

People, in other words, may find themselves living and breathing in their own home, their privileged community space, with people of "their own kind," in more or less pronounced "ethnic purity." But they may also find themselves elsewhere, in voluntary or enforced exile, as part of a so-called minority, being treated miserably, decently, or possibly even quite well by the ethnonational core (Brubaker 1996)—in which case be-longing more often than not turns into a question of longing-to-be . . . at home. This condition will typically produce images and memories, often quite out of touch with contemporary realities, of these their authentic roots (spatially or temporally)—and sometimes a matching politics of identity as well (e.g., the Rastafarian movement in Britain, Native Americans in North America, Turks in Germany, Germans abroad [*Volksdeutsche*], German speakers in northern Italy, Hungarians in Rumania, and hosts of other groups in Eastern Europe that have suffered displacement, deportation, redrawing of maps, and state attempts to blot out identities and memories of belonging). In some cases (though increasingly rarely), this mental condition will even engender plans for an eventual return to them.

Yet others may find that even though they *are* living in the place and the space where they prefer to be, their home is less than pure because "others" have taken up residence there. These others may, as indicated, be more or less reluctantly recognized, or they may be ostracized, marginalized, forcibly assimilated (a feature of empires), locked up, killed off, or "repatriated"—either to where they do, culturally and ethnically, belong, at least in the eye of the majority wielding the big stick, or deported "out of territory," so that the home, soil, and culture of the dominant *ethnies* can again become exclusively theirs (a feature of homogeneous nationalisms).[1]

But if we turn the mirror on this scenario, the view we get is different still: here people are also breathing their own air in their own (national) home, but this home has either been inundated by a mass of "others" who are now in the majority as well as in power, or it is being ruled from a political center that is neither in nor of the relevant ethnic group, which will therefore be fighting to reclaim its territory through the creation of its own state.

Once this condition has been achieved, one way or another (and the roads to national homogeneity are many and diverse), people may start to feel so much at home that their primary belongingness never really becomes a fully conscious issue, because the convergence of ethnonationality, state territory, and "homogeneous" cultural practices is now normality and can be taken for granted, providing people with a commonsense, consensual context for their activities, dreams, and aspirations (Billig 1995). In fact, the national context and its identity-shaping power can become so "banal," so inconspicuous, that it may cause people to imagine that it has disappeared, that they are cosmopolitan and global *rather than* national, and that nationalism is alive (but not well) only in the Balkans and other foreign hot spots, but not in "our" part of the civilized world.

Finally, people may feel that they have several belongings, several places and cultures they belong to and that determine their identity as multiple, nested, situational, or fluid, whereas others react to the uncertainties and erosions of belonging following either from nomadic existences in the global village or from the impact of globalizing forces on handed-down sites of loyalty by developing new attachments, to belongings (in the sense of material possessions), familiar surroundings, close-knit localities, or the intimacy of personal relationships. Still others choose to abandon all collective solidarity in favor of pursuing individualism or elitism, in whatever guise.

Thus, the English word *belonging* is a fortuitous compound of *being* and *longing*, of existential and romantic-imaginary significations and associations, shaped and configured in multiple ways by the international system of nationalism as simultaneously a political and a cultural ordering principle. Hence belonging can constitute an important element of identity, and not just can but does lead to manifold forms of identity politics, across the political spectrum, not just on the right—where the politics of belonging has always spelled unadulterated racism and national chauvinism. But this traditionally rightist confine of discourse and power has now been invaded by a motley gathering of "ethnic" groups, who "from below" tirelessly seek recognition of their status of rightful belonging (either to an existing or a would-be state: blacks in the United States, Maoris in New Zealand, Palestinians in the Middle East, Republicans in Northern Ireland); organizations and political parties arguing their right to secede in order to reclaim their authentic, sovereign space of belonging and action (Taiwan, Quebec, Flanders, Kosovo, East Timor); and states finding or refinding each other in old-new configurations of common identity or civilizational collaboration (Germany and the European Union, respectively).

Today, belonging constitutes a political and cultural field of global contestation (anywhere between ascriptions of belonging and self-constructed definitions of new spaces of culture, freedom, and identity),[2] summoning a range of pertinent issues concerning relations between individuals, groups, and communities. It raises questions about cultural, sociological, and political transformative processes and their impact on imagined and real boundaries, notions of citizenship and cultural hybridization, migration and other forms of mobility, displacements and so-called ethnic cleansing, and of course also on the extent and nature of perceived normalcies of national belonging, in a world seemingly turning more fluid, aided and abetted by increasingly transnational flows of speculative capital, information, entertainment, and ideas.

This, then, is a somewhat different picture of belonging than the utopian one we started out with: more confused, more bristly, and much harsher. Indeed, as Giddens argues, nationalism *can* become belligerent, though it does not have to. It is *plainly* divisive, though only *potentially* so. Like forms of belonging, it is an ambiguous and contradictory construction, exclusive and international, hostile and friendly, ethnic and civic, conservative and liberal, backward-looking and progressive, all at the same time (Hedetoft 1999). It structures belonging along all these parameters. But so does, to an increasing extent, globalization as an independent force in its own right. Let us take a closer look at these interlocking, and partly competing, determinants of belonging and identity—the national and the global.

Home as Belonging: The Prepolitical and the Political as One

In an interesting recent article, Judith Lichtenberg discusses the "moral ambiguity of sources of identity based on belonging" (Lichtenberg 1999, 171), because belonging (meaning national belonging in this context) is both egalitarian and not based on accomplishment (but on ascribed membership), but, on the other hand, for precisely this reason also clashes with modern notions of the individual freedom to choose: "there is also something 'illiberal' in basing membership on something over which people have no control. This is, after all, part of the reason we condemn racism and other forms of prejudice and discrimination" (ibid.).

Toward the end of this section of her article, Lichtenberg resolves the ambiguity by abandoning the entire arsenal of analytic and moral distinctions, only to take note of the fact that

> for most people cultural belonging is very important. It is hard to say a great deal about this in analytical (as opposed to poetic or literary) terms, perhaps because it is basically so very simple: for most of us, our native culture provides us with a sense of being at home in the world. . . . we can recognize the superior virtues of other cultures, but still feel the attachment bred of familiarity our own culture affords. The features of a culture that produce this sense of familiarity and well-being are its language and folkways, its sounds and smells, the innumerable subtle and, in the scheme of things, trivial customs and practices and ways of life we grow up with. (Ibid., 173)

This account no doubt would meet with the approval of many simply because it corresponds well with both commonsense perception and emotionally based orientation: we feel we belong to our culture, because it constitutes a home of natural embeddedness and unthinking attachment— "familiarity" *tout court*. Somehow it is beyond the grasp of analytic understanding, defies rationality, and has to be accepted for what it is. There is something alluringly attractive about this reference to the "banality" of belonging, and it does have its merits.

For one thing, it takes us beyond the most barren forms of dedication to the idea of a constitutional, totally rational form of patriotism and belonging (see Keitner 1999 and Yack 1999 for critiques of this notion), an idea that often overlooks the fact that national attachment and identity, in whatever form, are inconceivable and inexplicable without recourse to a certain measure of irrationality, emotionality, sentiment, and unselfish dedication. All the apparently rational principles of government, citizens' rights, and collective solidarity that are routinely invoked in discussions about civic nationalism "tend to say much more about the way in which we should order lives within *given* national communities than about why the boundaries of these communities should take one shape rather than another" (Yack 1999, 111; emphasis in the original); or, differently put, why there should be any national boundaries at all.

For another, it rightly identifies the unconscious and very powerful nature of (national) belonging and some of the immediate objects of reference and justification most of us use when asked to explain our sense of "home(sick)ness." In other words, in anthropological terms, Lichtenberg's account faithfully reflects the "organicist," or, one might say, prepolitical, dimension of our feelings of belonging to a national "gemeinschaft."

In the process, however, this account tends to reify "culture" by assuming a direct, uncomplicated link between this concept and "nation." In fact, the national element of culture is simply elided, the implicit argument being the following: Cultures (as homogeneous units) produce nations, which in turn engender strong feelings of attachment and belonging on account of the cultural homogeneity underpinning them. Culture equals nation equals home equals identity.[3] Thus cultures become "native" cultures, taken-for-granted and matter-of-course frames of reference and action. No matter how seductive the argument, then, it overlooks the fact that to the extent we can reasonably talk about cultural homogeneities in national terms (and often this is very difficult), such homogeneity is the outcome rather than the cause of both historical processes and mental reconstructions; of oblivion as much as memory; of elite efforts to nationalize the masses in the transition from different kinds of empire to an international order based on nation-states; of selective perception in the process, which all individuals must go through, of forming a homogeneous image of their national communities (in spite of the fact that most nations are culturally and ethnically "mongrel," as Giddens [1999, 131] calls them) and creating mental boundaries that match the borders of the state in which they live—here the national education systems play an invaluable role.

In other words, this kind of explanation overlooks national belonging in the form both of Renan's "daily plebiscite" (Renan 1882) and of the symbolic and historical construction of roots ("native culture") as identical with the limits of the national—in imperative, top-down, discursive terms *and* as popular transformations of such official discourse into second-order naturalness and axiomatic referentiality. In such terms, national belonging follows from neither nature nor culture in any simple forms—though this is how it is often experienced and more often discursivized—but is the result of complex social and historical processes whereby the political, sovereign communities that we know as nation-states reinvent themselves as prepolitical, simplistic, and "ethnic," partly in the mirror of selective histories of glory, heroism, and destiny, partly by drawing on anthropological paradigms of kinship, blood, and territorial rootedness.

Ulf Hedetoft and Mette Hjort

In these communities, therefore, it requires more than just legal citizenship really to belong and therefore to be a true native with a genuine and universally recognized nationality.[4] Features and images of the political (civic) and the prepolitical (ethnic) community must merge for a nation-state to be experienced and recognized as the authentic, cultural home of any individual living inside or outside its politically given borders. In other words, the state must appear as nation and the nation as ethno-culturally given and historically continuous. Identity and belonging must seem to derive organically from such prepolitically given homogeneity, though in the real world there is no such transparent, innocent, and immediate relationship, and whatever cultural-national homogeneity there is more often than not is the outcome of decades, sometimes centuries, of cultural honing, ethnic mixing, and social assimilation or exclusion.

One problem, of course, is that in spite of such long-standing efforts, frequently homogeneity amounts to little more than official discourse, a thin veneer of a common identity covering up the coexistence of a multiplicity of cultures and, sometimes, identities too (take, for instance, the cases of Belgium, the United Kingdom, and Switzerland as different types of illustration of such scenarios). In this sense, most territorial states are not proper nation-states, but "multiethnic" in one way or another. Citizenship, culture, and identity tend to part ways and to reassemble in new and multiple configurations of belonging. In the case of the United States, it has now even become the quasi-official credo to celebrate Americanness as multicultural and the United States as the prototype of an immigrant nation with ethnic roots all over the world and little common history to show for itself—a fact that for some bodes ill for the cohesion of the country (for example, Schlesinger 1992), but for others signals the strength of this (post)modern identity formation, which has managed to create unity out of diversity or where homogeneity is simply configured in ways that are different from what we have come to expect based on the European model of cultural exclusivism and ethnic cleansing (Hall and Lindholm 1999).

Whichever take one prefers, for many the United States embodies the liberal, civic nation-state in almost pure form and reintroduces the question of how identity and belonging are structured in plural states that seem to defy the logic of ethnic uniformity as the basis for societal cohesion and loyalty. Membership in a republican order with clear constitutional principles will not do, because it does not explain the emotional attachment and overt manifestations of sacrifice and sentiment that clearly characterize the patriotism of U.S. citizens—nor does it account for the multiplicity of ethnic groups that, whatever their distinctiveness, all conduct a politics of recognition *as Americans* (and not, say, as humans or cosmopolitans). In fact, as Hall and Lindholm rightly argue (1999, 3), no other state makes such a claim to "exceptionalism" and "manifest destiny" as the United States, and feelings of belonging to this country and its history and myths of independence and conquest are obviously no less forceful and deep-seated than in other national contexts. The "home of the brave" presents itself to the American imagination (though this comes in infinite subvarieties) as basically one, not many, and this oneness is not primarily political or civic, though many of the ingredients thrown into the cauldron are undoubtedly of a deliberative, rational origin.

In spite of the fact, therefore, that, on the face of it, the United States seems to diverge radically from the ethnic, European blueprint of nation-states, the fact of the matter is rather that it has reworked and modernized the model in order to assimilate patriotic identity (homogeneity) to individualism and cultural pluralism, allowing different groups to seek out their own avenue toward American identity, exceptionalism, and pride, and thus to reconfigure forms of belonging as national, subnational, and cosmopolitan at the same time.

Where in Europe political communities pose as prepolitical and ethnic, in the United States the situation is reversed: feelings of common ethnicity and organic solidarity, shaped no less arduously than in the rest of the world and drawing on a wealth of myths (of the West, of nature, of frontiers, of the self-made man, of golden opportunities, of war and heroism . . .), consistently pose as political or civic, ethnicity *eo ipso* being universally recognized and officially celebrated only in its plural form and as "hyphenated" Americanness. But, as Yack succinctly argues, "were Americans . . . to make citizenship contingent upon commitment to political principles instead of the mere accident of birth (to citizen parents or on American territory), they might become considerably more suspicious of their fellow citizens' declarations of political loyalty. Birthright citizenship can promote toleration precisely by removing the question of communal membership from the realm of choice and contention about political principles" (1999, 116). In other words, an American "nation-state" genuinely based on civic, political principles would not be particularly tolerant or all-inclusive, but would draw borderlines between "us" and "them" based on formulated, "rational" distinctions and assimilate nonnationals in different ways than through oaths of allegiance to the flag.

The result, therefore, is much the same in the two kinds of nation-states: home as belonging to nation is a structured set of emotions and attitudes, shaped by an imagined oneness of political and prepolitical, contemporary and historical, rational and cosmological orientations. Liberal nationalism and internationalism, however open-minded, do not basically alter this fact (see the next section for further reflections on this), and even cosmopolitans—in spite of their assumption of belonging everywhere and nowhere in particular—arguably base their outlook, confidence, and global interventionism on embeddedness in particular national contexts and the possession of a national passport and national citizenship rights (Ignatieff 1993). However, what *has* tended to alter the basic conditions for national homogeneity—by imposing new conditions for "homeness" and belonging—are European, transnational, and globalizing processes and the new types of identity formation, boundary confusion, and ethnic politics that follow in their wake.

Belonging in Conditions of Postnationality: One Home or Many?

"Globality"—for want of a better term—spells significant changes in the cultural landscapes of belonging, not because it supplants the nation-state and the forms of homeness outlined so far, but because it changes the contexts (politically, culturally, and geographically) for them, situates national identity and belonging differently, and superimposes itself on "nationality" as a novel frame of reference, values, and consciousness, primarily for the globalized elites, but increasingly for "ordinary citizens" as well. In this context, notions of liberal and civic nationalism assume new implications. Their real news value lies less in the theoretical assumptions as such— which have been known and debated since the nineteenth century—and more in the widespread interest they have recently attracted, inside as well as outside academic circles.

The pervasiveness of this interest reflects two points worth noting: first, the organicism and essentialism of national identities are no longer just taken for granted, but are being universally challenged by forces (whether "rational" or not) claiming forms of loyalty and allegiance that are not readily assimilable to the nation-state context; and second, this state of affairs has given rise to attempts to rescue the nation-state— as "civic," "liberal," "cosmopolitan," or whatever—by rethinking its basic parameters and proposing a rational trajectory (for example, in the form of Jürgen Habermas's "constitutional patriotism," or sometimes even a political program, as in the case of the European Union) for its practical transformation, a "third way" between rampant globalization and conservative nationalism.

This double scenario reconfigures belonging reflexively by introducing wedges of uncertainty and impermanence into the imagined oneness of political and prepolitical orientations that underpin national identity. On the one hand, globality can only constitute "belonging" in the most flimsy and liminal of senses; on the other, nationality increasingly appears to be no longer a sufficient, though maybe still a necessary, linchpin of identity and belonging. This state of affairs, often compounded by new forms of individualism and migration, leads to feelings of uprootedness, identity loss, or the construction of multiple homes and hybrid senses of belonging (in other words, new cosmopolitanisms or the advocacy of multicultural states)—though it might also imply reaffirmations of old-style nationalism in nostalgic, secessionist, or "new racist" forms. In any event, it strengthens and reinvents the politics of identity as an increasingly transnational phenomenon, in the double sense of finding its way into all national contexts as a fairly uniform occurrence, and playing itself out as a substantively transnational politics of organization, platform, support, and discourse: a "McDonaldization" of cultural and political differences, one might call it, exacerbated by declining trust in national politicians on a global scale.

Thus, the oxymoron of "civic nationalism" and its pervasive popularity are a fairly precise reflection of a state of affairs where the nature and context of nationalism are being transformed by globalization.[5] Where the age of nationalism and the nation-state demanded that the political and the prepolitical community, citizenship and ethnicity/identity, be imagined as one, the postnational era threatens to disaggregate the two, either by propagating a wholly rational kind of nationalism as the ideal end goal while relegating ethnic nationalism to the dustheap of a belligerent history (or to less civilized parts of the world!); by transposing the "political" dimension of identity and loyalty to a supranational level (e.g., the European Union, or some ideal cosmopolitan setup) while conceding that people's ethnicity (or cultural identity) may remain nationally bound; or by building "civic" allegiances to the country one happens to live in while remaining "ethnically" tied to one's country of origin (the case of many Turkish "guest workers" in Germany, for instance).

Although examples of such cleavages have been around for many years, the difference today is that they used to be exceptions, but now they are more like the rule: all-pervasive, institutionally organized, and the subject of public and private debates. It is becoming widely acknowledged that hybrid identities, several homes, and multiple attachments are a fact of life in most nation-states. Where dual or multiple citizenship used to be seen as a remote and esoteric concern, relevant only to highly privi-

leged elites, such issues are now widely debated (though not always con-
doned) in contexts increasingly recognized as multicultural. Cosmopolitan
or global citizens today are not to be recognized by the lack of passports
(as was the case in the nineteenth century), but far more by the number of
passports they can legitimately show for themselves.

From being conceived as a fact of nature, "belonging" has come to be
treated as a property of the rational mind, as a particular kind of "politics,"
situating subjects between individual freedom, collective rights, and negotiated identities, and confronting states with difficult choices between
transnationalized policies and communicative strategies aimed at convincing their national populations of their primary belonging in and loyalty to
their particular nation-state. Increased mobility and virtual universes have
added to this movable feast of symbolically and deliberately constructing
our roots as we go along, amid perceived chaos and more seriously liminal
borders. An interesting case in point is the following statement from a
Pole living in the United States:

> Contrary to what you may have thought, we will stay put for the holidays
> because we will have to move out of our current apartment at the end of
> the month. We are experiencing the "real thing"—American mobility;
> every four months at a different address! I got so mad that I arranged for a
> P.O. box to get all my mail there. A simple P.O. box will give me some
> roots in this soil and will keep me sane—or so I hope. Although I do recog-
> nize certain Americanisms in me, I *refuse* to be integrated into this culture.
> During my college years, I had zero American friends. My attitude hasn't
> changed much since. I've just had to be stronger in alienating myself from
> Americans because there were so many of them around, and not enough
> foreigners. Have I succeeded? I don't know, but I must leave the U.S. in
> 2000 at the latest. By then, it will have been a decade for me, and that is
> definitely enough.[6]

This brief excerpt from a much longer set of reflections on the tribulations
of *feeling* Polish while *being* in the United States is a telling illustration of
the changes modern individuals experience as far as their self-image, identity, and sense of belonging are concerned, and the affective as well as
cognitive processes these changes activate as regards reconfiguring existential components such as roots, community, and stability in a global age,
which this person clearly identifies as "American." In this setting, "roots"
shrinks into an unimaginable fixed point, a post office box address, identity being sought in a rationally pursued and implemented outsider existence (hankering for many more "foreigners"), and security residing in

images of future mobility, across state borders, back to (hopefully) authentic roots and a (wistfully imagined) genuine ethnic community—in order to escape the consequences of the mobility that life in America currently imposes.

For such reasons, the state of voluntary exile from one's imagined roots—and its attendant forms of consciousness—is one of the precise emblems of the reactive patterns that modern national cosmopolitans resort to in order to cope with (as well as rationalize) their existence in societies that apparently offer them ever-diminishing possibilities for collectivity, adaptation, tradition, and belonging of a more stable "national" kind. Benedict Anderson's "imagined political communities" are facing tremendous difficulties when, for substantial numbers of people, the world appears as complex, liminal, lacking in clearly demarcated borders and commonly accepted values. The reverse side of exile and marginalization—for the individual in the American "melting pot" or the small-nation collectivity in the European integration process—then frequently reappears as a longing for authentic values and a journey back (or forward) to a country, a culture, and a citizenship that are less hybrid, where politicians are trustworthy, and the language sounds right.

Other reactions are possible and pervasive too: the pursuit of constitutional patriotism, the development of civilizational identities, the forging of security communities, joining inter- and transnational organizations, and the cultivation of cosmopolitan stances (including the championing of a global human-rights regime) being just a few of them. However, as indicated, globality—or, for that matter, Europeanness—is not an emotionally convincing substitute for nationality, no matter how intellectually and morally appealing such wider identifications might be (Weiler 1997). "Belonging" requires, as far as identity goes (rather than vaguer and more noncommittal attachments), territorial and historical fixity, cultural concreteness, and ethnic exceptionalism, in addition to the existence (at least potentially) of a political superstructure with which one can identify and which is the provenance and safeguard of passport, citizenship, and a sense of communal solidarity. "The globe" does not qualify in those respects, not even for the most liberal-minded elites—at least not yet. People can develop a sense of multiple homes (often functionally differentiated and spatially wide apart). The most affluent elites can even afford to set up house in different parts of the world and can use this as a substitute for genuine "global belonging." For these elites, such conditions might well figure *as* such a truly postnational situation, materially and identity-wise.

Nevertheless, these cases highlight the significance of observing a basic distinction inherent in the concept of "belonging": that there is a world of difference between imagining that "the globe," like material possessions, memories, and ideas, belongs to "us" (or, rather, "me")—and that "we" belong to "the globe" and "globality." The images of home that we all carry around with regard to national identity, and our linguistic way of speaking to them, are in the latter category. The question is: what national entity do "we" belong "to"? In our perceptions and conceptions of this type of homeness, we routinely objectify ourselves, make ourselves into a part and a property of a given nation-state. We somehow adhere to it, are organically bound up with it, and spring from it, by virtue of birth, blood, race, history, culture, or customs.

In fact, the basic organicism of national belonging manifests itself in our reified way of talking about it, and dispels any thoughts of constructing a wholly civic, rational nationalism. It is not our nation that belongs to us—it is we who belong to our nation, even though we might imagine it as our choice. But even so, it is a freely chosen relationship of interdependence in which we all imagine ourselves as the dependent variable.

This is all very different in the case of images and discourses of "global belonging." Here the world appears as a terrain of opportunities, mobility, networking, moneymaking, and so forth: it turns into a means for the achievement of particular goals, and does not appear as the end goal of ideal belonging and identity formation, as "roots." Potentially, the world is ours, it does not own us. It opens up possibilities but does not require sacrifices that we abide by because we belong to it. Or it allows us to cultivate myths and reveries of having our real roots elsewhere than where we happen to be, or of eventually finding real happiness somewhere else.

In such terms, "the globe" is a material and utopian tax haven, a site of (imagined) benefits, but very little belonging, in the sense in which this concept has been employed so far. Only in the cases of ardent universal religiosity, global environmentalism, or the idealism of helping needy people on a global scale can we identify traces of an ideology of belonging to the globe, based on programmatic ideas of global responsibility; but even here the point of departure, more often than not, is a firm rootedness in a specific national identity, and the global position, including its cosmopolitan virtues, is ideologically rather than existentially defined.[7]

Thus, globalization—while certainly making inroads on the contexts and natural assumptions of national rootedness and homeness—does not offer a global substitute for them, despite much discourse to the contrary. The forms and perceptions of belonging that it engenders are, if not incompatible with those of the national, then at best their extension and complement. The new awareness of the difference between political and prepolitical components of national identity that globalization and Europeanization have spawned has led to new configurations for the most globally minded, for whom nationality has come to represent their prepolitical, ethnic, "banal" site of belonging, whereas globality or Europeanness has taken over as the main locus of their political orientations and identifications.[8] For the rest, belonging in globality is either a curse (globality as rootlessness), a blessing (globality as help against repression), or an opportunity (globality as freedom and progress); but in none of these cases is globality imagined as something people belong *to*. Our home may be open to the globe (liberal, tolerant, sensitive, multicultural), but the globe is not our home. "Belonging" spells different assumptions and implications in the two settings and the ever more crucial interaction between them.

Contributions

As these framing reflections indicate, there is a great need for detailed scholarly work on the different processes that are instrumental in reconfiguring the contexts, meanings, and objects of belonging in the contemporary world. Ideally, this would be imaginative, interdisciplinary, and innovative, drawing on insights and methodologies from sociology, political science/international relations, philosophy, cultural and literary studies, and anthropology and ethnography.

The essays in this volume, individually and collectively, meet such demanding standards and shed new light on home, belonging, and identity. The contributions have been subdivided into three main parts, each reflective of an important dimension of the general problematic. Part I, "Nationalism and Postnationality," addresses aspects of the larger contextual changes of the national and global environment that impinge on forms and substances of belonging. Part II, "Self and Community," engages with new forms of interaction (politically and sociologically) among individuals, groups, and larger communities in the context of globalization. Part III, "Images of Home, Belonging, and Exile," investigates transformative processes of memory, culture, and identity in different social and historical circumstances.

In "The Paradox of Nationalism in a Global World," Mark Juergensmeyer seeks to explain why the erosion of the nation-state and secular nationalism effected by globalization has been accompanied by the emergence of new, ethnoreligious nationalisms. His central claim is that these new nationalisms respond to specific needs that are created by globalizing forces and should be thought of not as "anomalies in the homogeneity of globalization, but as further examples of its impact." Globalization, Juergensmeyer claims, is a multifaceted phenomenon and particular communities are typically affected in only some of the possible ways. Indeed, in many cases, what is salient is a process of economic globalization that is perceived as undermining local cultures and social identities, which appear, as a result, to require protection. What is striking about the ethnoreligious movements arising in such contexts is their creativity; that is, while the relevant ideologies resuscitate "ancient images and concepts," they do so in order to meet specific, contemporary, social, and political needs generated by aspects of globalization. It is Juergensmeyer's contention that globalization and the new nationalisms it provokes together constitute a "global confrontation," a "new cold war." Juergensmeyer concludes his discussion by pointing out that some of the ethnoreligious nationalisms involve globalizing, transnational aspirations. What these movements oppose, then, is secular globalization, not globalization per se. As a result, ethnoreligious nationalism in a global world is likely to involve transnationalizing activities as well as overt hostility and sublime indifference to globalization.

The influential idea that nationalism in a bipolar world is the dominant source of destabilization in international politics is subjected to critical scrutiny in Ray Taras's essay, "The Nationalizing International System and the National Collective Self." Taras contends that what emerged toward the end of the millennium was a "nationalizing international system"; that is, the current salience of ethnonationalist conflict is in large measure a result of the international system's tendency to construe a wide variety of problems, including many of the international disputes of the past, in nationalist terms. The true source of instability is not nationalism as such, but the inconsistent way in which nations' claims to self-determination are dealt with by the international system. Taras identifies some of the consequences of the nationalizing system, especially for U.S. foreign policy. In this context, he considers differences between advocates of interventionism and isolationism in an attempt to determine which approach best fosters a denationalized and stable international order. Taras argues that the nationalizing paradigm serves the specific interests of international organizations by allowing them largely to ignore the conflicts that have no direct implications for the major powers. Selective intervention, he claims, is justified in terms of key differences between interstate and intrastate conflict and the kinds of responses they require at the international level. More specifically, interstate conflict is typically held to call for international intervention inasmuch as the sovereignty of nation-states is at issue. The situation is rather different, however, in the context of intrastate conflict, for here the principle of sovereignty would appear to dictate a noninterventionist stance. Taras concludes by noting that nationalists do indeed pose a threat to the new world order, but he insists that it is the U.S.-dominated international system that determines who the nationalists in fact are in a process involving the reframing of a wide variety of conflicts as intrastate ethnonationalist disputes.

In "Media and Belonging: The Changing Shape of Political Communication in the European Union," Philip Schlesinger explores the implications of this supranational entity for the nation-state's tendency to define itself in terms of communicative specificities that effectively equate politico-communicative space with national space. Following Schlesinger, there is evidence to suggest that the media initiatives accompanying European integration at the political level are generating a supranational communicative space capable of providing the conditions of possibility for new, transnational loyalties and belongings. At the same time, he points out that participation in the relevant communicative space remains the prerogative of an elite composed primarily of executives and politicians. The kinds of mass-mediated affiliations that constitute the supranational arrangement as a site of belonging are, in other words, very much a reflection of class. Schlesinger's assessment of the current situation is accompanied by a more speculative account of future developments. He situates his remarks in relation to the tradition of social communications theory more generally and develops his views with particular reference to Jürgen Habermas's theory of the public sphere and Manuel Castells's concept of an information society. Schlesinger accepts Habermas's contention that the Union's evolving communicative dimensions cannot be construed in terms of a unified public sphere because no single, defining mode of address is likely to emerge. At the same time, he rejects Habermas's suggestion that the envisaged communicative spaces are best thought of as constituting an *unbounded* network. Schlesinger's claim is that if supranationality is to be a matter of loyalty, and more than a purely formal arrangement, then the Union's emerging communicative spaces will have to be circumscribed by at least some communicative specificities. He concludes by evoking some of the ways in which supranational communication can strengthen the Union's civil society and significantly extend the sense of belonging that national publics invest in individual member states.

John A. Hall's aim, in "Transatlantic Images of Belonging," is to call into question some of the standard accounts of globalization. More specifically, he contests the idea that the nation-state and related national identities are being undermined by globalizing tendencies. He develops his point by drawing a distinction between two senses of transatlantic belonging, the one involving membership in a transatlantic political entity, the other some kind of deep attachment to a nation-state other than the one in which one lives. His claim is that the modern world in fact involves a significant decline in the first kind of transatlantic belonging, and not the inverse, as globalizers would have it; that is, belonging has become increasingly "national, nationalist and international rather than transatlantic." To support this general line of argument, Hall refers to historical developments in Canada, especially the repatriation of the constitution. Hall goes on to consider informal transatlantic identities and his aim is to determine the extent to which we should be swayed by influential ideas of postnationality and multiculturalism. Referring to the case of the United States, Hall contends that multiple attachments and complex, transnational identities by no means have replaced the classical immigrant experience, which is based on assimilation. Diversity, he argues, was once far greater in the United States than it is today, and what is striking, then, is precisely the ability of this particular nation-state to function as a veritable engine of "nationalizing homogeneity." Hall concludes by invoking trading patterns, the structure of corporations, research and development in the corporate world, and restrictions on labor as counterevidence against recurrent claims about the nature and extent of globalization.

In "Transnational Corporations? Perhaps. Global Identities? Probably Not!" Richard Jenkins argues that transnational corporate activities do foster certain transnational identities. It is his contention, however, that these identities do not necessarily qualify as properly global. Transnational activities of the kind likely to encourage collective identities are not, for example, distributed around the globe, but are firmly rooted in the privileged sites of the world's economic system. What is more, inasmuch as transnational corporations are governed by the logic of capitalism they are more likely ultimately to obstruct rather than contribute to the emergence of "transcendent global identities." Jenkins situates his views in relation to standard accounts of globalization as a recent development involving an internationalized economic order, an internationalized political system, individual and collective mobility, rapid information transfers, and sociocultural convergence. He claims that any serious thinking about the relation between transnational corporations and collective identities must take account of the diverse nature of the relevant corporate arrangements. To this end, he proposes a typology of transnational corporations. He also points to the difficulties involved in determining what exactly is meant by the term *global identity*. Global identities, he claims, may be a matter of identities that are comparable at an institutional level, but not at the level of existential meaning. The teaching profession is, for example, a transnational phenomenon, but what it means to be a teacher varies from one country to another. The situation is different in the case of professions such as that of scientist or international businessman, for here the relevant identities can be compared transnationally, at the level of both institutional form and existential content. Finally, Jenkins points to the kinds of global identities imagined by proponents of universalizing religions, feminisms, and workers' movements. It is perhaps here, he claims, that we find properly globalized identities. At the same time, he points out, it is important to remember that the relevant identities are merely utopic projections with little or no chance of realization.

The thrust of Seyla Benhabib's argument in "Citizens, Residents, and Aliens in a Changing World: Political Membership in a Global Era" is that political philosophers' normative concepts of citizenship require critical examination in light of the changing sociological and institutional realities of political membership in an increasingly globalized world. Global integration, she remarks, has been accompanied by sociocultural disintegration and the eruption of ethnic nationalisms fueled by the idea that national identities can be preserved only through the suppression of difference and otherness. In this context, the task of articulating a properly democratic, transnational conception of citizenship capable of accommodating difference assumes considerable urgency. Benhabib argues that dominant conceptions of citizenship in the West involve a number of false premises and contradictions. More specifically, the "closed society" with nonporous borders postulated by influential political thinkers is held to be at odds with the development of a global civil society and with the moral rights of exit and entry that are defining features of democratic societies. Citizenship in democratic Western societies, Benhabib claims, is predicated on notions of active consent and participation, yet political membership is determined in practice by a passive criterion of belonging having to do, for example, with blood, birth, and lineage. Finally, whereas ideals of consent and participation militate in favor of making active involvement in civil society a condition of political membership, citizenship continues to be largely determined by abstract criteria administered at the level of the state. Benhabib's rethinking of citizenship in the light of globalizing tendencies involves an attempt to trace a *via media* between two extremes: a radical universalism aimed at a politics of open borders, on the one hand, and a communitarian approach focused excessively on ideas of deep cultural belonging, on the other. The challenge, she claims, is to ensure that democratic societies properly reflect their two constitutive concepts: popular sovereignty and universal human rights. For this to be the case, it is necessary to see the right to exit and the right to entry as perfectly symmetrical, while recognizing that the criteria for admittance cannot coincide exactly with the criteria for political membership. The specific focus for Benhabib's discussion is provided throughout by the European Union and the prospect of Union citizenship.

In "Citizenship and Belonging: Beyond Blood and Soil," Riva Kastoryano examines the implications of identity politics for the concept and reality of the modern nation-state, which postulates as an ideal the perfect harmony and even conflation of nationality and citizenship. This conflation, she claims, is increasingly challenged by *practices* of citizenship that are nourished by the complex identities and multiple attachments of immigrants, who are at pains to distinguish between national communities and particularist, identity-based communities. The key issue to be negotiated between immigrant groups and the state is thus precisely that of complex identity, for what urgently needs to be determined is the extent to which particularist, nonnational identities can or will be *officially* recognized and accommodated. The current situation, Kastoryano claims, is one in which full-fledged inclusion and participation ultimately are made possible only by *legal* citizenship, which continues to stress and institutionalize a link between nationality and citizenship by means of ethnic or civic conceptions, or some combination thereof. In Kastoryano's mind, then, postnational citizenship is a project that has yet to be realized, rather than an existing reality that already reflects a transformation of the modern nation-state. Kastoryano's attempt to chart the relevant political landscapes foregrounds the importance of seeing the state not merely as a punctual administrative and juridical entity, but as an institutional reality marked by history and ideology. Her claim is that the larger traditions supporting specific state formations must be carefully considered if we are to understand the specificity of civil and civic citizenship in a given national context. It is for this reason that she develops her arguments contrastively and with reference to republican and ethnic models of the state in France and Germany, respectively.

Yasemin Nuhoğlu Soysal's "Citizenship and Identity: Living in Diasporas in Postwar Europe?" further develops some of the central claims made in her *Limits of Citizenship*, which outlines a model of postnational citizenship based on comparative studies of a range of Western countries. Soysal is primarily concerned with the dimensions of citizenship that fall outside the scope of formal or legal citizenship; that is, on Soysal's view, citizenship is not reducible to agents' formal belonging to a national citizenry, as reflected in their right to vote in national elections, but is also a matter of the rights and duties associated with various forms of participation in civil society. Inasmuch as inclusion in civil society effectively extends social and economic rights to nonnationals, thereby making it possible for them indirectly to exercise a certain degree of political influence, postnational citizenship is construed as an already existing reality in postwar Europe, rather than as a purely regulative ideal. Expanded conceptions and practices of citizenship emerge as a result of the abilities of nonnationals to frame certain demands for recognition in the terms provided by host country discourses, including, for example, universalist discourses of human rights and personhood. Soysal thus argues that patterns of immigrant behavior cannot be derived in any straightforward manner from a prior attachment to certain national or ethnic identities. Instead, immigrant behavior is held to reflect the enabling conditions and particular constraints associated with the host society's key institutions, discourses, and practices. Soysal's account of the dynamics of postnational citizenship in postwar Europe can thus be seen as usefully taking issue with certain primordialist conceptions of nations, nationality, and citizenship.

James Tully's contribution extends the arguments developed in his *Strange Multiplicity: Constitutionalism in an Age of Diversity*. Whereas the latter focuses on the way in which belonging is constituted by the formal recognition of various cultural and national identities that are worthy of respect, the present essay foregrounds the constitutive role played by forms of positive freedom generated by citizen participation. Tully contends that the fact of being able to participate in public dialogues over identity-related issues itself engenders a sense of belonging based on an implicit acknowledgment of the participants' favored self-understandings as worthy of respect. Tully's suggestion, then, is that acknowledgment be viewed as a more important factor than recognition in generating social cohesion in multicultural and multinational societies. Agonic public exchanges over identity-related issues serve a cathartic function and help to generate self-respect and self-esteem among those demanding recognition even in those cases in which no formal recognition ultimately is granted. As a result, claims Tully, the sense of self-respect and self-esteem that are important features of belonging are not based only on recognition as some theorists have claimed. Tully identifies some of the defining traits of identity politics and related demands for recognition in multiethnic societies. He underscores that decisions about which identities are worthy of recognition and on what grounds ultimately are a matter not of theoretical reason, but of practical reason; that is, ideally citizens would determine the relevant evaluative criteria in the course of deliberative processes aimed at mutual understanding and mutual agreement. In multiethnic societies, he claims, a sense of belonging and commitment hinges on the cultivation of an identity-diversity awareness and not on the actual recognition of specific identities; for in multicultural societies, the very identities for which recognition is claimed are likely to change significantly in the course of the discursive exchanges.

In "Working Men's Imagined Communities: The Boundaries of Race, Immigration, and Poverty in France and the United States," Michèle Lamont examines the way in which working-class men in France and the United States define social membership in the imagined communities to which they belong. Unlike many studies of identity-related issues, Lamont's essay is governed by a properly inductive approach and is based on two-hour interviews with 150 working-class men living in suburbs surrounding New York and Paris. Lamont's interview questions enable her to assess the role played by status cues having to do with color, class, and immigrant origins in the construction of imagined communities in the countries in question. Lamont concludes that whereas the French model of inclusion/exclusion emphasizes strong external boundaries and weak internal boundaries, the American model insists on strong internal boundaries and weak external boundaries; that is, in the French case notions of universalism, solidarity, and equality have the effect of granting social membership to blacks and the poor, and of erecting strong external boundaries in relation especially to Muslim immigrants whose culture is deemed to be incompatible with French traditions. The situation is quite the opposite in the United States, where inclusive attitudes are expressed with respect to immigrants, but not in relation to the poor or African-Americans. Lamont suggests that comparisons between the French and American models of inclusion/exclusion may help to shed light on the "narrowing of bonds of solidarity" that is entailed by ongoing racist and neoliberal developments. In this sense, her contribution urges critical reflection not only on the categorical frameworks underwriting a number of specific imagined communities, but on the relation between these frameworks and larger political tendencies.

Michael Herzfeld's focus in "Cultural Fundamentalism and the Regimentation of Identity: The Embodiment of Orthodox Values in a Modernist Setting" is on identity formation in Greece, with special emphasis on the role played by nativist ideas (or what he calls Neo-Orthodoxy) in current social imaginings. It is Herzfeld's assumption that an analysis of the emergence of nativist tendencies in Greece will help to challenge stereotyped thinking about NATO's war against Serbia and the dynamic governing the Balkans more generally. The claim is that international powers and Western politicians and journalists continue to rest their accounts of developments in the Balkans on discredited anthropological theories, on what Herzfeld refers to as "cultural fundamentalism." His point, more specifically, is that Western discourses regularly ascribe essential and unchanging traits to the Balkan peoples, thereby mirroring precisely the ethnonationalist mentalities that are held to be the key, enduring sources of conflict in the region. Herzfeld contends that the Western discourse of cultural fundamentalism has a performative dimension and effectively produces the very realities it describes. He goes on to account for the emergence of Neo-Orthodoxy in Greece, and here the central claim is that the equation of the modern with the classical that was largely imposed on Greece by the West has had the effect in the long run of provoking a resentful modernity that emphasizes a quite different past. Having identified the defining features of Neo-Orthodoxy, Herzfeld concludes that it provides a religious antidote to the cultural fundamentalism that Milosevic's ethnic cleansers share with the policymakers who are attempting to impose a new world order.

In "Where We Are and Who We Want to Be," Ulf Hannerz explores a range of relations between identity and space, focusing in particular on the impact of globalization on home and belonging. Home, Hannerz says, is essentially a contrastive concept linked to some notion of what it means to be away from home. As a result, the many meanings of "home" range from a deep sense of rootedness in a given sociogeographic site to an intensely imagined affiliation with a distant locale held to be capable of providing the conditions for self-realization. Hannerz takes issue with the prevalent claim that globalization entails a form of deterritorialization or a "homeness deficit." Globalization, he argues, is more accurately thought of as encouraging "biterritorialization" or "multiterritorialization," an ability to imagine two or more sociogeographic sites as home. Hannerz revisits the debate over the role played by the mass media in configuring relations between what is home and what is away from home. The effect of the mass media, he claims, is by no means uniform. In some instances, intensive media coverage may make the unhomely homely through a process of familiarization, but it may also have the effect of underscoring the undesirability of what is elsewhere, thereby contributing to xenophobia and the tightening of borders. Hannerz also argues that the role of the mass media has been overemphasized at the expense of the small-scale, personal media that are increasingly eroding distinctions between home and its Other. He concludes by considering the specificity of home and belonging in the context of cosmopolitanism. He distinguishes between aesthetic and political cosmopolitanism, the former being construed as involving an interest in cultural diversity and the latter a range of activities aimed at transnational political organizing. He finds it illuminating to think of these two kinds of cosmopolitanism in connection with two types of nationalism, the one ethnic, the other civic. Much like civic nationalism, political cosmopolitanism suffers from a certain cultural deficit, an inability to command loyalty and commitment. Aesthetic cosmopolitanism, on the other hand, resembles ethnic nationalism in one respect: it involves "thick" and deeply felt, imagined affiliations. Hannerz contends that the elaboration of a cosmopolitan, transnational culture is urgent in a globalizing world where global problems frequently require global solutions. He further argues that transnational culture need not be shallow, superficial, or somehow artificial, as skeptics have claimed. Transnational culture can be a matter of deep affective responses prompted by ideas of home and belonging, especially if it emerges through the kind of spontaneous personal networking that is a salient feature of aesthetic cosmopolitanism.

Benjamin Lee, in "The Subjects of Circulation," is concerned with a specific aspect of globalization, namely, the emergence of new forms of abstraction allowing for the transnational circulation of money and goods, people, images, and ideas. He is interested in foregrounding the way in which circulation in an increasingly globalized world is a matter not simply of the movement of ideas and objects, for example, but of the emergence of cultures marked by the semiotic forms of what is actually being circulated. Lee draws on Benedict Anderson's account of nationalism as a phenomenon involving acts of the imagination and a widespread circulation of print culture in an attempt to clarify the issue of performativity and its relation to what Arjun Appadurai has called "imagined worlds." Lee is interested, in other words, in the way in which the complicated philosophical and linguistic problems of self-reference and self-reflexivity are reflected in the very founding moments of the imagined communities of modern nation-states, transnational arrangements, and identity politics.

In "The Nationalization of Anxiety: A History of Border Crossings,"

Orvar Löfgren targets certain tendencies characteristic of globalization studies and discussions of the nation-state. He argues that what is required is not abstract generalizations, but detailed studies that chart the material dimensions of the relevant phenomena. On Löfgren's view, an analysis of diverse border-crossing practices can help to identify the specificities of various state formations. Whereas, for example, early states emphasized porous borders, the modern nation-state, which provides the focus for Löfgren's discussion, tends to insist on the visibility of national borders. Löfgren's point is that the crossing of national borders is a heavily choreographed and emotionally charged activity that helps to reproduce the nation-state by making manifest and further entrenching categories of belonging and exclusion. In such contexts, he argues, border crossing is not only a matter of regulated motion, but of intense emotions reflecting larger socio- and geopolitical realities. His account of the emotions prompted by various border-crossing rituals serves to highlight a salient feature of the modern nation-state, namely, the extent to which it has been imagined and constructed in terms of metaphors of home and homelessness. Löfgren illustrates his key points by means of examples drawn from the straits of Øresund, a region where border crossing and notions of belonging are being reconfigured following the completion of the historic bridge connecting Denmark and Sweden in the year 2000.

Diverging traditions of public memory of the Holocaust from the postwar years to the present provide the focus for Jeffrey Herf's "Traditions of Memory and Belonging: The Holocaust and the Germans since 1945." The traditions in question, he claims, are a matter of linking a nation's past to its present concerns, for in postwar West Germany, as well as in East Germany after 1989, preferred imaginings of the nation were understood to depend on an honest confrontation with the Nazi past. This link between past and present was forged in a properly postnational manner, particularly in West Germany, and it is this feature of the relevant tradition that is worth contemplating carefully at a time when nationalism is generating conflicts around the world. Herf contrasts the way in which *Vergangenheitsbewältigung* was understood in the East and West and his aim throughout is to respond to two guiding questions: What are the historical bases for a tradition of public memory of the Holocaust in postwar Germany? And why does this tradition arise in the West rather than the East? It is Herf's contention that public memory involving the restoration of a number of anti-Nazi, German traditions ultimately finds its conditions of possibility in an unconditional military victory over Germany, the dismantling of the Nazi government, the occupation, and the Nuremberg trials. Herf's account of the role played by key figures such as Konrad Adenauer, Kurt Schumacher, and especially Theodor Heuss suggests that public memory of Nazi atrocities was inaugurated in West Germany, not in the 1960s, as historians have suggested, but in the 1940s and 1950s. He further examines the way in which post-Nazi governments in the German Democratic Republic (GDR) marginalized the Holocaust and revived anti-Semitic discourses in their various celebrations of antifascist resistance fighters within the larger context of the cold war. His point is that in the former GDR, fighting the cold war emerged as the dominant form of *Vergangenheitsbewältigung*.

Notes

1 It must be emphasized that the distinction employed here between empires and nation-states often is easier to deal with analytically than in the real world: assimilating empires might want to assimilate precisely in order to reinvent themselves as nation-states, and ethnic nationalisms often operate in conditions that are de facto imperial, dynastic, or at least multinational. Assimilation strategies in France have been successful, hence France is now recognized as a nation-state. They failed in the USSR, which is therefore thought of as an empire, whereas the many new states of the Newly Independent States (NIS) area see themselves and are recognized as ethnic, in spite of the fact that almost all of them have retained sizable contingents of other "ethnicities," notably Russians, who are often less than welcome. See Beissinger 1995 and Motyl 1999 for pertinent reflections on this problematic.

2 See, for example, Bell 1999 for interesting analyses of new forms of belonging.

3 For a thorough critique of this proposition of homogeneity, see Hedetoft 1995, Part I, chapter 5.

4 This distinction between citizenship and nationality is one that not least colored "immigrants" in old colonial states such as Britain and France have been confronted with, for example, in the forms of Powellism and Le Penism. It was Enoch Powell, for instance, who in the 1960s talked about the "legal fiction of British citizenship" as regards these people and further claimed that "you do not become British by being born in Britain." This is the credo that has since defined the ideologies of rightist nationalist movements in most European countries.

5 The oxymoronic nature of the concept of "civic nationalism" is nicely captured by Bernard Yack, who argues that "the idea of the civic nation defends the Enlightenment's liberal legacy by employing the very concept—that of the political community by voluntary association—whose plausibility has been undermined by the success of nationalism" (1999, 115).

6 This statement derives from a letter to one of the authors from a Polish-American acquaintance.

7 See Gubert 1999 for noteworthy contributions to the discussion of territorial belonging in the context of culture and ecological concerns.

8 For an interesting example of such interactions between matter-of-course national identity and self-proclaimed cosmopolitanism, see Michael Billig's analysis of the American nature of Richard Rorty's political philosophy (Billig 1995, chapter 7).

Works Cited

Beissinger, Mark R. 1995. "The Persisting Ambiguity of Empire." *Post-Soviet Affairs* 11:2: 149–84.

Bell, Vikki, ed. 1999. *Performativity and Belonging.* London: Sage.

Billig, Michael. 1995. *Banal Nationalism.* London: Sage.

Brubaker, Rogers. 1996. *Nationalism Reframed.* Cambridge, Mass.: Cambridge University Press.

Durkheim, Émile. 1965. *The Elementary Forms of Religious Life.* New York: Free Press.

Giddens, Anthony. 1999. *The Third Way: The Renewal of Social Democracy.* Cambridge: Polity Press.

Gubert, Renzo, ed. 1999. *Territorial Belonging between Ecology and Culture.* Trento: University of Trento (Sociology Series).

Hall, John A., and Charles Lindholm. 1999. *Is America Breaking Apart?* Princeton, N.J.: Princeton University Press.

Hedetoft, Ulf. 1995. *Signs of Nations.* Aldershot: Dartmouth.

———. 1999. "The Nation-State Meets the World." *European Journal of Social Theory* 2:1: 71–94.

Ignatieff, Michael. 1993. *Blood and Belonging.* London: Chatto and Windus.

Keitner, Chimène I. 1999. "The 'False Promise' of Civic Nationalism." *Millennium* 28:2: 341–51.

Lichtenberg, Judith. 1999. "How Liberal Can Nationalism Be?" In *Theorizing Nationalism,* ed. Ronald Beiner, 167–89. New York: State University of New York Press.

Motyl, Alexander J. 1999. *Revolutions, Nations, Empires: Conceptual Limits and Theoretical Possibilities.* New York: Columbia University Press.

Renan, Joseph Ernest. 1882. "Qu'est-ce qu'une nation?" [lecture at the Sorbonne]. English translation by Martin Thom, "What Is a Nation?" In *Nation and Narration,* ed. Homi K. Bhabha, 8–22. London: Routledge, 1990.

Schlesinger, Arthur. 1992. *The Disuniting of America.* Knoxville, Tenn.: Whittle Direct Books.

Tönnies, Ferdinand. 1957 [1887]. *Community and Society.* Trans. C. P. Loomis. East Lansing: Michigan State University Press.

Weiler, Joseph. 1997. "Belonging in Europe—Eros and Civilization." Paper presented to Nobel Symposium on the topic "Nationalism and Internationalism in the Post–Cold War Order," Stockholm, September 7–10.

Yack, Bernard. 1999. "The Myth of the Civic Nation." In *Theorizing Nationalism,* ed. Ronald Beiner, 103–19. New York: State University of New York Press.

PART I

Nationalism and

Postnationality

Mark Juergensmeyer

1

The Paradox of Nationalism in a Global World

Several years ago when I interviewed Sheik Ahmed Yassin, spiritual leader of the Palestinian Islamic movement Hamas, in his home near Gaza City, I noticed that the bare interior of his living room contained only two pictures. One was a kind of cartoon showing the Qur'an superimposed on a map of the world. The Muslim holy book was portrayed as if it had hands stretching from Algeria to Indonesia. The other picture was more specific: a photograph of the Jerusalem holy site the Dome of the Rock, which marks the spot where the prophet Muhammad is said to have ascended to heaven during his extraordinary Night Journey. Although revered throughout the Muslim world, the shrine is a particular source of pride to Palestinians, who regard themselves as its caretakers. Its portrayal in Gaza homes, therefore, is as much a symbol of Palestinian identity as drawings of the global Qur'an are of transnational Islam.

Therein lies a paradox: the resurgence of national identities in a global world. Why have limited loyalties and parochial new forms of ethno-religious nationalism surfaced in today's sea of postnationality? History seems poised on the brink of an era of globalization, hardly the time for new national aspirations to emerge. In fact, some observers have cited the appearance of ethnic and religious nationalism in such areas as the former Yugoslavia and the former Soviet Union, Algeria and the Middle East,

South Asia, Japan, and among right-wing militia movements of the United States, as evidence that globalization has not reached all quarters of the globe. But is this really the case? Is it possible to see these quests for local identities and new nationalisms not as anomalies in the homogeneity of globalization, but as further examples of its impact?

This is what I would like to explore in this essay. It seems to me that the paradox of new nationalisms in a global world can be explained, in part, by seeing them as products of one or more of several globalizing forces. In many cases, the new ethnic and religious movements are reactions to globalization. They are responses to the insufficiencies of what is often touted as the world's global political standard: the secular, Westernized constructs of nationalism that are found not only in the West, but also remain in many parts of the former Third World as vestiges of colonialism.

This essay will examine the responses to old secular nationalisms, which are under seige precisely at a time when they have themselves been weakened by globalization. Their vulnerability has been the occasion for a new ethnoreligious politics to step into the breach and shore up national identities and purposes in their own distinctive ways. Yet, as the al Qaeda network of Osama bin Laden has demonstrated, these new ethnoreligious identities often have international and supernational aspects of their own. Some forms of ethnoreligious politics are global, some are virulently antiglobal, and yet others contend with creating ethnoreligious nation-states. Thus, as the pictures on Sheik Ahmed Yassin's wall indicate, these new forms of ethnic and religious politics remain paradoxical: sometimes aligned with nationalism, sometimes with transnational ideologies, and in both cases standing in an uneasy relationship with the globalizing economic and cultural forces of the post–cold-war world.

Globalization's Assault on Nationalism

It should not be surprising that new sociopolitical forms are emerging at this moment of history because globalization is redefining virtually everything on the planet. This includes especially those social and political conventions associated with the nation-state. Among other things, global forces are undermining many of the traditional pillars on which the secular nation-state has been based, such as national sovereignty, economic autonomy, and social identity. As it turns out, however, these aspects of the nation-state have been vulnerable to change for some time.

Born as a stepchild of the European Enlightenment, the idea of the modern nation-state is profound and simple: the state is created by the people within a given national territory. Secular nationalism—the ideology that originally gave the nation-state its legitimacy—contends that a nation's authority is based on the secular idea of a social compact of equals rather than on ethnic ties or sacred mandates. It is a compelling idea, one with pretensions of universal applicability. It reached its widest extent of worldwide acceptance in the mid-twentieth century.

But the latter half of the century was a different story. The secular nation-state proved to be a fragile artifice, especially in those areas of the world where nations had been created by retreating colonial powers—in Africa by Britain, Portugal, Belgium, and France; in Latin America by Spain and Portugal; in South and Southeast Asia by Britain, France, the Netherlands, and the United States; and in Eurasia by the Soviet Union. In some cases, boundary disputes led to squabbles among neighboring nations. In others, the very idea of the nation was a cause for suspicion.

Many of these imagined nations—some with invented names such as Pakistan, Indonesia, and Yugoslavia—were not accepted by everyone within their territory. In other cases, the tasks of administration became too difficult to perform in honest and efficient ways. The newly created nations had only brief histories of prior colonial control to unite them, and after independence they had only the most modest of economic, administrative, and cultural infrastructures to hold their disparate regions together.

By the 1990s, these ties had begun to fray. The global economic market undercut national economies, and the awesome military technology of the United States and NATO reduced national armies to border patrols. More significantly, the rationale for the nation-state came into question. With the collapse of the Soviet Union and the postcolonial, post-Vietnam critique of Western democracy, the secular basis for the nation-state seemed increasingly open to criticism. In some instances, as in Yugoslavia, when the ideological glue of secular nationalism began to dissolve, the state fell apart.

The effect of what I have elsewhere called "the loss of faith in secular nationalism" was devastating (Juergensmeyer 1993). Throughout the world, it seemed, nationalism was subject to question, and the scholarly community joined in the task of trying to understand the concept in a post–cold-war and transnational era (Anderson 1983; Gottlieb 1993; Kotkin 1994; Smith 1995; Tamir 1993; Young 1993).[1] One of the reasons for nationalism's shaky status was that it was transported to many parts of the world in the cultural baggage of what Jürgen Habermas has called "the project of modernity" (Habermas 1987, 148)—an ascription to reason and a progressive view of history that many thought to be obsolete. In a multicultural world where a variety of views of modernity are in competition, the very concept of a universal model of secular nationalism became a matter of lively debate.

Globalization challenges the modern idea of nationalism in a variety of ways. These challenges are varied because globalization is multifaceted: the term, after all, refers not to any one thing but to a series of processes. The term embraces not only the global reach of transnational businesses, but also their labor supply, currency, and financial instruments. In a broader sense, it also refers to the planetary expansion of media and communications technology, popular culture, and environmental concerns. Ultimately, it also includes a sense of global citizenship and a commitment to world order, as demonstrated in this list of aspects of globalization:

1 globalization of production, ownership, market
  · transnational businesses and labor in shifting venues of production (i.e., "commodity chains") and distribution
2 globalization of currency and financial instruments
  · increased reliance on the U.S. dollar around the world, replacement of cash with electronic transactions
3 globalization of political alliances, law, world order
  · regional alliances (e.g., European Union), expansion of authority of international courts and regulations
4 globalization of military justification and intervention
  · U.S., NATO, and UN peacekeeping forces playing role of global police, mediating local conflict
5 globalization of environmental concerns and protection
  · development of multilateral alliances to protect environment
6 globalization of media and communications
  · satellite technology and Internet, allowing for rapid communications, "E-mail ethnicities," virtual communities
7 globalization of culture and ideology
  · universal availability of television, film, and higher education; transnational popular culture, values
8 globalization of citizenship and identity
  · demographic shifts and emergence of global cities of varied ethnic backgrounds; growth of transnational urban professional elites

When one speaks of "globalization," therefore, it is useful to specify which aspect of it one has in mind. It is possible that people in a particular region of the world will experience one kind of globalization but not others.

For instance, countries that are brought into contact with economic globalization—by supplying labor for the commodity chains of global-ized production—may not experience the globalization of culture and citi-zenship. In fact, the advent of economic globalization may threaten local identities in such a way as to encourage the protection of local cultures and social identities, sometimes in hostile and defensive ways. This is the contradiction observed by Benjamin Barber, who noted that the "McWorld" of contemporary Westernized culture has assaulted the public conscious-ness in various parts of the world. In extreme forms it has triggered the "jihad" of militant tribalism (Barber 1995).

My own studies have demonstrated that some of the most intense movements for ethnic and religious nationalism arise in nations where local leaders have felt exploited by the global economy—as in Iran and Egypt—or believe that somehow the benefits of economic globalization have passed them by (Juergensmeyer 1993, 2000). The global shifts in economic and political power that occurred following the breakup of the Soviet Union and the sudden rise and subsequent fall of Japanese and other Asian economies have had significant social repercussions. The pub-lic sense of insecurity that has come in the wake of these changes has been felt especially in areas economically devastated by the changes, including those nations and regions that had been under the dominance of the Soviet Union.

These shifts led to a crisis of national purpose in less developed nations as well. Leaders such as India's Jawaharlal Nehru, Egypt's Gamal Abdel Nasser, and Iran's Reza Shah Pahlavi once tried to create their own ver-sions of the United States—or, in some cases, a cross between the United States and the Soviet Union. But a new, postcolonial generation no longer believed in the Westernized vision of Nehru, Nasser, or the shah. Rather, it wanted to complete the process of decolonialization by asserting the le-gitimacy of their countries' own traditional values in the public sphere and constructing a national identity based on indigenous culture (Chatterjee 1993). This eagerness was made all the more keen when they observed the global media assault of Western music, videos, and films that satellites beam around the world, and that threaten to obliterate local and tradition-al forms of cultural expression.

In other cases, it has been a different kind of globalization—the emer-gence of multicultural societies through global diasporas of peoples and cultures, and the suggestion of global military and political control in a "new world order"—that has elicited fear. Perhaps surprisingly, this re-sponse has been most intense in the most developed countries, which in other ways seem to be the very paradigm of globalization. In the United States, for example, the Christian Identity movement and militia organizations have been fueled by fears of a massive global conspiracy involving liberal American politicians and the United Nations. In Japan, a similar conspiracy theory motivated leaders of the Aum Shinrikyo movement to predict a catastrophic World War III, which the group's nerve gas assault in the Tokyo subways was meant to emulate (Asahara 1995).

As far-fetched as the idea of a "new world order" of global control may be, there is some truth to the notion that the integration of societies, communication among disparate peoples, and the globalization of culture have brought the world closer together. Although it is unlikely that a cartel of malicious schemers has designed this global trend, its effect on local societies and national identities has nonetheless been profound. It has undermined the modern idea of the nation-state by providing nonnational and transnational forms of economic, social, and cultural interaction. The global economic and social ties of the inhabitants of contemporary global cities are linked together in a way that supersedes the Enlightenment notion that peoples in particular regions are naturally linked together in a social contract. In a global world, it is hard to say where particular regions begin and end. For that matter, it is hard to say how one should define the "people" of a particular nation.

This is where religion and ethnicity step in to redefine public communities. The fading of the nation-state and old forms of secular nationalism has produced both the opportunity for new nationalisms and the need for them. The opportunity has arisen because the old orders seem so weak; and the need for national identity persists because no single alternative form of social cohesion and affiliation has yet appeared to dominate public life the way the nation-state did in the twentieth century. In a curious way, traditional forms of social identity have helped to rescue the idea of national societies. In the increasing absence of any other demarcation of national loyalty and commitment, these old staples—religion, ethnicity, and traditional culture—have become resources for national identification.

Ethnicity and Religion to the Rescue of Nationalism

In the contemporary political climate, therefore, religious and ethnic nationalisms provide a solution to the problem of Western-style secular politics in a non-Western and multicultural world. As secular ties have begun to unravel in the post-Soviet and postcolonial era, local leaders have searched for new anchors to ground their social identities and political loyalties. Many have turned to ethnicity and religion. What is ideologically significant about these ethnoreligious movements is their creativity. Although many of the framers of the new nationalisms have reached back in history for ancient images and concepts that will give them credibility, theirs are not simply efforts to resuscitate old ideas from the past. These are contemporary ideologies that meet present-day social and political needs.

In the modern context, this is a revolutionary notion—that indigenous culture can provide the basis for new political institutions, including resuscitated forms of the nation-state. Movements that support ethnoreligious nationalism are, therefore, often confrontational and sometimes violent. They reject the intervention of outsiders and their ideologies and, at the risk of being intolerant, pander to their indigenous cultural bases and enforce traditional social boundaries. It is no surprise, then, that they get into trouble with each other and with defenders of the secular state. Yet even such conflict with secular modernity serves a purpose for these movements: it helps define who they are as a people and who they are not. They are not, for instance, secularists.

Because secularism is often targeted as the enemy, that enemy is most easily symbolized by things American. The United States has taken the brunt of religious and ethnic terrorist attacks in recent years, in part because it so aptly symbolizes the transnational secularism that the religious and ethnic nationalists loathe, and in part because it does indeed promote transnational and secular values. For instance, the United States has a vested economic and political interest in shoring up the stability of regimes around the world. This often puts it in the position of being a defender of secular governments. Moreover, it supports a globalized economy and a modern culture. In a world where villagers in remote corners of the world increasingly have access to MTV, Hollywood movies, and the Internet, the images and values that have been projected globally have often been American.

So it is understandable that the United States would be disdained. What is perplexing to many Americans is why their country would be so severely hated, even caricatured. The demonization of the United States by many ethnoreligious groups fits into a process of delegitimizing secular authority that involves the appropriation of traditional religious images, especially the notion of cosmic war. In such scenarios, competing ethnic and religious groups become foes and scapegoats, and the secular state becomes religion's enemy. Such satanization is aimed at reducing the power of one's opponents and discrediting them. By humiliating them—by making them subhuman—ethnoreligious groups assert the superiority of their own moral power.

During the early days of the Persian Gulf War in 1991, the Hamas movement issued a communiqué stating that the United States "commands all the forces hostile to Islam and the Muslims," and singled out then President George Bush, who, it claimed, was not only "the leader of the forces of evil" but also "the chief of the false gods."[2] As late as 1997, Iranian politicians, without a trace of hyperbole, described the United States as the "Great Satan." This rhetoric first surfaced in Iran during the early stages of the Islamic revolution when both the shah and President Jimmy Carter were referred to as "Yazid" (in this context an "agent of Satan"). "All the problems of Iran," the Ayatollah Khomeini elaborated, are "the work of America" (Khomeyni 1977, 3). By this he meant not only political and economic problems, but also cultural and intellectual ones, fostered by "the preachers they planted in the religious teaching institutions, the agents they employed in the universities, government educational institutions, and publishing houses, and the Orientalists who work in the service of the imperialist states" (Khomeini 1985, 28). The vastness and power of such a conspiratorial network could only be explained by its supernatural force.

The Global Agenda of Ethnic and Religious Nationalism

Although the members of many radical religious and ethnic groups may appear to fear globalization, what they distrust most are the secular aspects of globalization. They are afraid that global economic forces and cultural values will undercut the legitimacy of their own bases of identity and power. Other aspects of globalization are often perceived by them as neutral, and, in some instances, useful for their purposes.

Some groups have a global agenda of their own, a transnational alternative to political nationalism. Increasingly, terrorist wars have been waged on an international and transnational scale. When the World Trade Center was demolished in the dramatic aerial assaults of September 11, 2001, it was not just the United States that was targeted, but also the power of the global economic system that the buildings symbolized. Osama bin Laden's al Qaida network was itself a global structure. The Gamaa i-Islamiya, a group related to al Qaeda, literally moved its war against secular powers abroad when its leader, Sheik Omar Abdul Rahman, moved from Egypt to Sudan to Afghanistan to New Jersey. It was from the Jersey City location that his followers organized the 1993 bombing attack on the World Trade Center that killed six and injured a thousand. Osama bin Laden's operative, Ramzi Youssef, also convicted of complicity in the 1993 World Trade Center bombing, masterminded the "Bojinka Plot" that would have destroyed a dozen American airliners over the Pacific during the mid-1990s; Youssef moved from place to place throughout the world, including Pakistan and the Philippines. Algerian Muslim activists brought their war against secular Algerian leaders to Paris, where they have been implicated in a series of subway bombings in 1995. Hassan Turabi in Sudan has been accused of orchestrating Islamic rebellions in a variety of countries, linking Islamic activists in common cause against what is seen as the great satanic power of the secular West. Osama bin Laden, from his encampment in Afghanistan, was alleged to have ordered many of these acts of terrorism around the world.

These worldwide attacks may be seen as skirmishes in a new cold war, or, more apocalyptically, a "clash of civilizations," as Samuel Huntington termed it (Huntington 1996). It is possible to imagine such a clash if one assumes that Islam and other religions are civilizations comparable to the modern West, or if one regards secular nationalism to be, in the words of one of the leaders of the Iranian revolution, "a kind of religion" (Banisadr 1981, 40). He went on to explain that it was not only a religion, but one peculiar to the West, a point that was echoed by one of the leaders of the Muslim Brotherhood in Egypt (el Arian 1989).

Behind this image of a clash of cultures and civilizations is a certain vision of social reality, one that involves a series of concentric circles. The smallest are families and clans; then come ethnic groups and nations; the largest, and implicitly most important, are religions. Religions, in this sense, are not just bodies of doctrine and communities of believers, but shared worldviews and cultural values that span great expanses of time and space: global civilizations. Among these are Islam, Buddhism, and what some who hold this view call "Christendom" or "Western civilization" or "Westernism" (Shitta 1989). The so-called secular cultures of places such as Germany, France, and the United States, in this conceptualization, stand as subsets of Christendom/Western civilization. Similarly, Egypt, Iran, Pakistan, and other nations are subsets of Islamic civilization. From this vantage point, it is both a theological and a political error to suggest that Egypt or Iran should be thrust into a Western frame of reference. In this view of the world, they are intrinsically part of Islamic, not Western, civilization, and it is an act of imperialism to think of them in any other way. Proponents of Islamic nationalism, therefore, often see themselves as a part of a larger, global encounter between Western, Islamic, and other cultures. This view of a "clash of civilizations" is not confined to the imaginations of Samuel Huntington and a small number of Islamic extremists, but underlies much of the political unrest at the dawn of the twenty-first century.

An even more extreme version of this global cultural clash is an apocalyptic one, in which contemporary politics is seen as fulfilling an extraordinary religious vision. Some Messianic Jews, for instance, think that the biblical age that will be ushered in at the time of the return of the Messiah is close at hand. It will occur when the biblical lands of the West Bank are returned to Jewish control and when the Jerusalem temple described in the Bible is restored on its original site—now occupied by the Muslim shrine the Dome of the Rock. Several of these activists have been implicated in plots to blow up the shrine in order to hasten the coming of the kingdom. One who served time in prison for his part in such a plot said that the rebuilding of the temple was not just a national obligation but a critical moment for the sake of the redemption of the world (Lerner 1995).

Religious activists who embrace traditions such as millenarian Christianity and Shi'ite Islam, which have a strong sense of the historical fulfillment of prophecy, look toward a religious apocalypse that will usher in a new age. American Christian political activists such as Jerry Falwell and Pat Robertson are animated by the idea that the political agenda of a righteous America will help to usher in an era of global redemption. The leader of Aum Shinrikyo, borrowing Christian ideas from the sixteenth-century French astrologer Nostradamus (Michel de Nostredame), predicted the coming of Armageddon in 1999 in the form of World War III, after which the survivors—mostly members of his own movement—would create a new society in the year 2014, led by Aum-trained "saints" (Asahara 1995, 300).

Activists in other religious traditions may see a righteous society being established in a less dramatic manner, but some Sunni Muslims, Hindus, and Buddhists have, in their own ways, articulated hopes for a political fulfillment of a religious society. They believe that "dhammic society can be established on earth," as one activist Buddhist monk in Sri Lanka put it, by creating a religious state (Thero 1991). These forms of religious politics are more than nationalist, therefore, because they envision the world as caught up in a cosmic confrontation, one that will ultimately lead to a peaceful world order constructed by religious nations. The result of this process is a form of global order radically different from secular versions of globalization, yet it is an ideological confrontation on a global scale.

The Future of Religious and Ethnic Politics in a Global World

Emerging movements of ethnic and religious politics are therefore ambivalent about globalization. To the extent that they are nationalistic, they often oppose the global reach of world government, at least in its secular form. But the more visionary of these movements also at times have their own transnational dimensions, and some dream of world domination shaped in their own ideological images. For this reason, one can project at least three different futures for religious and ethnic nationalism in a global world: one where religious and ethnic politics ignore globalization, another where they rail against it, and yet another where they envision their own transnational futures.

NONGLOBALIZATION: NEW ETHNIC AND RELIGIOUS STATES

The goal of some ethnic and religious activists is the revival of a nation-state that avoids the effects of globalization. Where new religious states have emerged, they tend to be isolationist. In Iran, for instance, the ideology of Islamic nationalism that emerged during and after the 1979 revolution and that was propounded by the Ayatollah Khomeini and his political theoretician, Ali Shari'ati, was intensely parochial. It was not until some twenty years later that new, moderate movements in Islamic politics encouraged political leaders to move out of their self-imposed international isolation (Wright 2000). The religious politics of Afghanistan during the reign of the Taliban was even more strongly isolationist. Led by members of the Pathan ethnic community who were former students of Islamic schools, the religious revolutionaries of the Taliban established a self-contained autocratic state with strict adherence to traditional Islamic codes of behavior (Marsden 1998).

Other movements of religious nationalism have not been quite as isolationist, however. In India, when Hindu nationalists in the Bharatiya Janata Party (BJP), "Indian People's Party," came to power in 1998—a victory that was consolidated in the national elections of 1999—some observers feared that India would become isolated from world opinion and global culture as a result. The testing of nuclear weapons as one of the BJP's first acts in power did little to dispel these apprehensions. But in many other ways, including its openness to economic ties and international relations, the BJP has maintained India's interactive role in the world community. Credit for this may be owing, in part, to the moderate leadership of the BJP prime minister, Atal Bihari Vajpayee, one of the country's most experienced and temperate politicians.

If other movements of religious and ethnic nationalism come to power, will they behave like the Taliban or the BJP? Observers monitor developments in Pakistan, Egypt, Algeria, and elsewhere for signs of antiglobal sentiment should the considerable strength of religious politics in those regions lead to the establishment of religious states. When Abdurrahman

Wahid, a Muslim cleric, edged past the daughter of Indonesia's founder to become the country's prime minister in 1999, observers wondered whether he would usher in an era of religious nationalism. In this case, however, the fears were unfounded. The actions of his government showed Wahid's brand of Islam to be moderate and tolerant, and committed to bringing Indonesia into the world community and the global economic market.

GUERRILLA ANTIGLOBALISM

In other regions of the world, it is not the creation of new religious states that is at issue but the breakdown of old secular states with no clear political alternative. In some instances, religious and ethnic activists have contributed to these anarchic conditions. In the former Yugoslavia, for instance, the bloodshed in Bosnia and Kosovo was caused by the collapse of civil order as much as by the efforts to create new ethnic and religious regions. Because these situations have been threats to world order they have provoked the intervention of international forces such as NATO and the United Nations.

It is, however, world order that many of these religious and ethnic nationalists oppose. They note that the increasingly multicultural societies of most urban communities around the world have undermined traditional cultures and their leaders. They have imagined the United States and the United Nations to be agents of an international conspiracy, one that they think is hell bent on forming a homogeneous world society and a global police state. It was this specter—graphically described in the novel *The Turner Diaries*—that one of the novel's greatest fans, Timothy McVeigh, had hoped to forestall by attacking a symbol of federal control in the U.S. heartland. His assault on the Oklahoma City federal building, and other terrorist attacks around the world—including Osama bin Laden's alleged bombing of U.S. embassies in Africa in 1998 and of the USS *Cole* in Yemen in 2000, and the attack on the World Trade Center in New York and the Pentagon in September 2001—were acts of what might be considered "guerrilla antiglobalism."

TRANSNATIONAL RELIGIOUS AND ETHNIC ALLIANCES

Ultimately, however, it seems likely that despite these efforts to ignore or reject the forces of globalization, transnational cultures will expand, and among them will be elements of religion and ethnicity. One future form of religious transnationality may emerge from the international relations of kindred religious states. According to one theory of global Islamic politics that circulated in Egypt in the 1980s and 1990s, local movements of

Muslim politics were meant to be only the first step in creating a larger Islamic political entity—a consortium of contiguous Muslim nations. In this scenario, religious nationalism would be the precursor of religious transnationalism. Transnational Islam would lead to Islamic versions of such secular consortia as the North American Free Trade Agreement (NAFTA) and the European Union. In the Islamic model, however, the divisions among states would eventually wither away once a greater Islamic union is formed.

A second kind of transnational association of religious and ethnic activists has developed in the diaspora of cultures and peoples around the world. Rapid Internet communication technologies allow members of ethnic and religious communities to maintain a close association despite their geographic dispersion. These "E-mail ethnicities" are not limited by any political boundaries or national authorities. Expatriate members of separatist communities—such as India's Sikhs, and both Sinhalese and Tamil Sri Lankans—have provided both funding and moral support to their compatriots' causes. In the case of Kurds, their "nation" is spread throughout Europe and the world, united through a variety of modern communications technologies. In some cases, these communities long for a nation-state of their own; in other cases, they are prepared to maintain their nonstate national identities for the indefinite future.

Identity, Power, and Globalization

Each of these futures contains a paradoxical relationship between the national and globalizing aspects of ethnoreligious politics. This suggests that there is a symbiotic relationship between certain forms of globalization and religious and ethnic nationalism. It may appear ironic, but the globalism of culture and the emergence of transnational political and economic institutions enhance the need for local identities. They also create the desire for a more localized form of authority and social accountability.

The crucial problems in an era of globalization are identity and control. The two are linked, in that a loss of a sense of belonging leads to a feeling of powerlessness. At the same time, what has been perceived as a loss of faith in secular nationalism is experienced as a loss of agency as well as identity. For these reasons, the assertion of traditional forms of religious and ethnic identities is linked to attempts to reclaim personal and cultural power. The vicious outbreaks of religious and ethnic terrorism that occurred around the turn of the century can be seen as tragic attempts to regain social control through acts of violence. Until there is a surer sense of citizenship in a global order, therefore, ethnoreligious visions of moral order will continue to appear as attractive, though often disruptive, solutions to the problems of identity and belonging in a global world.

Notes

1 The renewed academic interest in nationalism has spawned two new journals, *Nations and Nationalism* and *Nationalism and Ethnic Politics*, both launched in 1995. Other journals have devoted special issues to the topic: "Reconstructing Nations and States," *Daedalus* 122:3 (summer 1993); "Ethnicity and Nationalism," *International Journal of Comparative Sociology* 33:1–2 (January–April 1992) (Anthony D. Smith, guest editor); and "Global Culture," *Theory, Culture, and Society* 7:2–3 (June 1990).
2 Hamas communiqué, January 22, 1991, quoted in Jean-François Legrain, "A Defining Moment: Palestinian Islamic Fundamentalism," in Piscatori 1991, 76.

Works Cited

Anderson, Benedict. 1983. *Imagined Communities: Reflections on the Origin and Spread of Nationalism.* London: Verso.

Asahara, Shoko. 1995. *Disaster Approaches the Land of the Rising Sun: Shoko Asahara's Apocalyptic Predictions.* Tokyo: Aum Publishing Company.

Banisadr, Abolhassan. 1981. *The Fundamental Principles and Precepts of Islamic Government.* Trans. Mohammad R. Ghanoonparvar. Lexington, Ky.: Mazda Publishers.

Barber, Benjamin R. 1995. *Jihad vs. McWorld.* New York: Times Books.

Chatterjee, Partha. 1993. *The Nation and Its Fragments: Colonial and Postcolonial Histories.* Princeton N.J.: Princeton University Press.

el Arian, Essam. 1989. Author's interview with Dr. Essam el Arian, member of the National Assembly, Cairo, January 11.

Gottlieb, Gidon. 1993. *Nation against State: A New Approach to Ethnic Conflicts and the Decline of Sovereignty.* New York: Council on Foreign Relations.

Habermas, Jürgen. 1987. "Modernity—An Incomplete Project." Reprinted in *Interpretive Social Science: A Second Look,* ed. Paul Rabinow and William M. Sullivan. Berkeley: University of California Press.

Huntington, Samuel P. 1996. *The Clash of Civilizations and the Remaking of World Order.* New York: Simon and Schuster.

Juergensmeyer, Mark. 1993. *The New Cold War? Religious Nationalism Confronts the Secular State.* Berkeley: University of California Press.

———. 2000. *Terror in the Mind of God: The Global Rise of Religious Violence.* Berkeley: University of California Press.

Khomeini, Imam [Ayatollah]. 1985. *Islam and Revolution: Writings and Declarations,* Translated and Annotated by Hamid Algar. London: Routledge and Kegan Paul (orig. pub. by Mizan Press, Berkeley, 1981).

Khomeyni, Imam [Ayatollah]. 1977. *Collection of Speeches, Position Statements.* Translations from "Najaf Min watha 'iq al-Imam al-Khomeyni did al-Quwa al Imbiriyaliyah wa al-Sahyuniyah wa al-Raj'iyah" ("From the Papers of Imam Khomeyni against Imperialist,

Zionist and Reactionist Powers"). Translations on Near East and North Africa, Number 1902. Arlington, Va.: Joint Publications Research Service.

Kotkin, Joel. 1994. *Tribes: How Race, Religion and Identity Determine Success in the New Global Economy.* New York: Random House.

Lerner, Yoel. 1995. Author's interview with Yoel Lerner, member of the Yamini Israel political party, Jerusalem, August 17.

Marsden, Peter. 1998. *The Taliban: War, Religion and the New Order in Afghanistan.* London: Zed Books.

Piscatori, James, ed. 1991. *Islamic Fundamentalisms and the Gulf Crisis.* Chicago: The Fundamentalism Project, American Academy of Arts and Sciences.

Shitta, Ibrahim Dasuqi. 1989. Author's interview with Prof. Ibrahim Dasuqi Shitta, Professor of Persian Literature and adviser to Muslim students at Cairo University, January 10.

Smith, Anthony D. 1995. *Nations and Nationalism in a Global Era.* London: Polity Press.

Tamir, Yael. 1993. *Liberal Nationalism.* Princeton, N.J.: Princeton University Press.

Thero, Rev. Uduwawala. 1991. Author's interview with Rev. Uduwawala Chandananda Thero, member of the Karaka Sabha, Asgiri chapter, Sinhalese Buddhist Sangha, in Kandy, Sri Lanka, January 5.

Wright, Robin. 2000. *The Last Great Revolution: Turmoil and Transformation in Iran.* New York: Knopf.

Young, Crawford, ed. 1993. *The Rising Tide of Cultural Pluralism: Nation-State at Bay?* Madison: University of Wisconsin Press.

2

The Nationalizing International System

and the National Collective Self:

Paradigms in Conflict

Until the terrorist attacks on the United States in September 2001, the most recurrent and intractable challenge facing the international system was identified as nationalism. In retrospect, this explanation served as a surrogate for the real crisis in international politics—the absence of a world order capable of regulating conflicts, providing incentives for peaceful state behavior, creating regional equilibriums, and managing and promoting global development.

Rather than examining the often-repeated thesis that after the cold war nationalist conflicts became the principal cause of instability in international politics, I wish to consider a contrary proposition—that in the post-bipolar world, a "nationalizing" international system emerged. It made the nationalism of peoples salient as an *international* problem while at the same time treating expressions of the national collective self inconsistently. Put differently, the international community regarded nationalism as a pathology even as it recognized certain people's collective self, but not that of others. Dissonance between the two approaches in large measure explained the international disorder of the 1990s. After September 2001, the unofficial "attack on nationalism" was, of course, replaced by the declared war on terrorism.

Few would disagree that the pivotal actor giving shape to the present international order is the United States. In many respects, a new global order can only be constructed with U.S. support. In this essay, I consider the debate within the U.S. foreign-policy establishment prior to September 2001 on the choice between interventionism and isolationism. Especially influential during the Clinton presidency, supporters of an activist American foreign policy stressed the significance of "belonging" to an international system. Some interventionists went further and emphasized the need not merely for belonging, but for American leadership, whether in the form of a liberal hegemony or of a more imperial project. Those who advocated an isolationist foreign policy, prominent under George Bush's administration and initially influential in his son's administration, rejected the value of belonging and instead stressed apartness. Paradoxically, the purported pervasiveness of ethnic conflicts in the world was invoked by all sides to support their preferred foreign-policy course. The essay concludes by proposing that a denationalized, more coherent international order can only be constructed by discarding the nationalizing paradigm.

After Bipolarity, a World of Nationalisms?

A decade after the collapse of the Soviet Union, it remained unclear what kind of political order capable of anchoring the community of nations was emerging. In its time, superpower rivalry had engendered many proxy wars, Soviet-backed "popular" revolutions, U.S.-inspired military coups, and, above all, a terrifying arms race. Its end provided an opportunity structure for the establishment of a new international order based on peace and democracy. Since then countervailing tendencies in international politics have instilled both hope about prospects for peace and fears about the inevitability of conflict. At the beginning of the twenty-first century, the most that can be said about an emergent world order is that it resembles another Pax Americana; harsher critics would call it a *bellum americanum*.

After World War I, national self-determination was held up as the panacea for the ills of the world system. Today, ironically, nationalism is regarded as the malaise that has infected that system. As Scottish writer Tom Nairn put it, anticommunist demonology has been replaced by the "Devil of Nationalism . . . Armageddon has been replaced by the ethnic Abyss" (1997, 61).[1] Is nationalism invariably to blame for today's international disorder?

Apart from the failure of global peace to materialize, other post-bipolar disappointments included the inability to finalize peace agreements in several regional conflicts that had originally begun as proxy wars of the superpowers. These included the Israeli–Palestinian conflict in the Middle East, civil wars in Afghanistan and Angola, even the United States' Cuba problem. Furthermore, NATO–Russian disagreement on conflict-resolution measures in the region making up the former Yugoslavia originates in that country's nonaligned status under bipolarity. The former Yugoslavia was supposedly a locus for the clash of civilizations, but we should recall that continuously since 1945 it had been the backdrop for the clash of contending political orders. Many Russians see it this way. One article published in a leading Russian newspaper in February 1994, before NATO took military action in Bosnia, stated:

> By its very nature, because of its intrinsic genetic code, NATO has been, and is now and will continue to be designed exclusively for the military-political containment of the USSR and now Russia. . . . Whereas in the past it was a matter of containing Soviet expansion, now the tasks that have been set up are the perpetuation of the breakup of the Soviet Union, weakening Moscow's military-political position and bringing its foreign and military policies under Western control. (Chernov 1994, 263)

To be sure, ethnic conflicts in the Balkans are nothing new, but neither is great-power rivalry. Nationalism in the region is inextricably linked to power balances and spheres of influence. What is novel is not the internationalization of nationalist conflicts, but the process of nationalizing the international disputes of the past.

Even the supposed unique "ethnic" brutality of the Balkan wars of the 1990s needs to be contextualized: "raping, looting and aimless games with death have always accompanied war. An explanation of this requires the psychology of war rather than the political or cultural analysis of the ethnic groups of former Yugoslavia" (Dijkink 1996, 118).

Apart from regional rivalries, other reasons exist why impediments to the construction of a more peaceful democratic world order derive less from nationalism than from balance of power. Wars between states may not be as numerous as wars within states, but this is part of a longer-term trend rather than a sudden outburst of ethnonationalist conflicts within countries (Small and Singer 1982, 271, table 16.8). Regional conflicts still flare up, as evidenced by Iraq's attempt to annex Kuwait in 1990, the ebb and flow of tensions between India and Pakistan over the status of Kashmir and of a general arms race on the subcontinent, and the power vacuum created in Central Africa by the collapse of Zaire. Mass poverty in most parts of the globe, disunity and fragmentation of central authority in many states of the third world and former Soviet lands, and the clash of modernity with tradition in much of the Islamic world compound the difficulties of establishing a post-bipolar international order. Ethnonationalist conflicts often follow from rather than precede these problems.

Finally, the rise of transnational terrorist networks pronouncing an Islamic jihad, Russia's chronic political and economic instability, the growing strength of anti-immigrant movements across Western Europe, trade disputes involving the European Union, the United States, and Japan, and the friction between the United States and China over issues such as human rights, nuclear technology, copyright laws, and arms exports, seriously undermine the effectiveness of international cooperation among the major powers in defusing tensions and promoting stability around the world. These problems, too, can only tenuously, if at all, be connected to the rise of nationalism.

Given the number and nature of crises facing the international order, it is surprising that many political leaders and scholars ascribe the world's problems to the phenomenon of nationalism. Longtime U.S. senator and scholar Daniel Patrick Moynihan exemplified this approach in his landmark study of international disorder *Pandaemonium: Ethnicity in International Politics* (1994). We can agree that post-bipolar pandemonium is rife, but can we really equate it with the ethnicization of international politics?

It is true that the politics of identity and belonging have been ubiquitous for more than a decade. In the democratic West, "ethnic revival" and growing assertiveness characterized various national minority groups such as the Basques and Catalans in Spain, the Bretons and the Corsicans in France, the Walloons and the Flemish in Belgium, the Scots, Welsh, and Irish in the United Kingdom, African-Americans and Hispanics in the United States, and French-speaking Quebecers in Canada. Peoples in northern democracies—Sami and Inuit (along with Sakha in the Russian Federation)—have demanded greater autonomy. Partially in response to rising anti-immigrant sentiments, immigrant communities display growing assertiveness whether in France (Berbers and other North Africans), Germany (Kurds and Turks), England (South Asians), or elsewhere. The reemergence of right-wing anti-immigrant nationalism on the streets of Germany, at the ballot boxes in Austria and France, and in political parties in Denmark and Italy is evidence of the growing exclusionary character of nationalism within ethnic majorities.

Rapid transformations in the old communist Second World have triggered a rebirth of ethnonationalist movements. At the top of the list of trouble spots here has been the former Yugoslavia. But the rights of ethnic minorities, such as the Hungarians, have also been undermined in Romania and Slovakia, where discriminatory policies were pursued by nationalist parties representing the ethnic majorities. Hungary's political leaders have themselves embraced nationalism to counter their neighbors' policies. The Czech Republic has been criticized for failing to extend citizenship to its Roma population. Serious ethnonationalist violence occurred within such former Soviet republics as Georgia (between majority Georgians and breakaway Abkhazians), Armenia and Azerbaijan (over the territory of Nagorno-Karabakh), Tajikistan (where minority Uzbeks were aligned against Tajiks), and, of course, Russia (the 1994–96 and 1999 onward war in Chechnya). Except for the latter, where the West implicitly acknowledges Russia's exclusive sphere of influence (a consideration of Realpolitik rather than a product of ethnic pandemonium), all of these conflicts were to one degree or another internationalized with third parties intervening either to mediate between or, in some cases, to tip the balance in favor of one of the adversaries.

In most countries of the Third World, ethnonationalism is inextricably tied to colonialism, which first created artificial borders that ignored cultural divisions and popular aspirations. In their postcolonial histories, many of these states witnessed increased nationalist assertiveness by minorities that had come to regard the dominant cultural groups as new colonizers. Very few of these ethnically driven conflicts have been peacefully resolved. They occur in the Middle East, sometimes caused by an exaggerated differentiation between peoples (Arabs and Israelis), sometimes by, inter alia, the denial of ethnic differentiation (the case of Iraqis toward Kuwaitis, or Turks toward Kurds). In Central Africa, Nigeria, South Asia, and the Indonesian archipelago, armed conflict between rival ethnic and communal groups has produced much bloodshed. Often, Islamic identity is the axis along which conflict arises, for example, fundamentalist groups seeking to preserve it and rival groups rejecting its political salience.

Competing constructions of the collective self are, therefore, an ongoing source of friction. For the international system, defining the collective self entails an additional problematic: it must determine *which* national groups are to be given the legitimate right to define a political self. After the French Revolution, collective selves were allowed to emerge if they were *antidynastic* in nature. In the latter half of the nineteenth century, in the era of liberal nationalism, modern "nation-states" came into being where, paradoxically, *the parts were made into a whole,* as in the cases of Germany and Italy. Perhaps from the outset these were not truly multinational states, but they illustrated the unification ideology underpinning the international system. This changed after World War I with a paradigm shift—limited to Central Europe—toward national self-determination. The parts *were* the whole, they represented the collective self. After World War II, anticolonial struggles revealed a new set of collective selves, albeit appearing within the *administrative borders* drawn by the colonial powers. The result was the freezing of the political map of the world when the decolonization process was over.

After the cold war, the problem of determining the legitimacy of the claims and counterclaims of various groups for self-determination resurfaced. The principle was applied that the *communist parts were to become the postcommunist wholes.* The international community sanctioned the breakup of communist federations—the Soviet Union, Yugoslavia, and Czechoslovakia—and refused to contemplate that there could be other collective selves struggling for political recognition. Consequently, the system found it difficult to arbitrate or weigh competing claims in such places as Abhazia, Bosnia-Herzegovina, Chechnya, Kosovo, Trans-Dniester. Shadow states expressing collective selves have emerged in some of these areas but have been largely ignored by intergovernmental organizations, if not by international nongovernmental ones.

The inconsistent standards applied by the international system were especially transparent in the 1990s Balkan wars. Recognition of a Bosnia-Herzegovina confederation "belonging" to the international community was extended precisely because it did *not* represent a collective self. But on the future of Kosovo (a more ethnically homogeneous area), the international system reached a stalemate. Its nationalizing paradigm was exposed as internally contradictory. The paradigm was unable to suggest whether a protectorate, outright national independence, or autonomy within the state of Serbia was the most logical outcome of a war defined in ethnonationalist terms.

The Nationalizing Paradigm: The U.S. Variant

Ours is a kaleidoscopic world characterized by changing identities and affiliations. Fatima Mernissi, a cultural theorist from Morocco, observed how "Our fin-de-siècle era resembles the apocalypse. Boundaries and standards seem to be disappearing. Interior space is scarcely distinguishable from exterior" (1992, 8). The nationalizing international system acknowledges that nationalism cannot be confined solely to interior space. Determining the role that a state should play in the kaleidoscopic system requires fresh thinking. Where the distinction between interior and exterior political space is fading and boundaries are increasingly permeable, it becomes difficult to formulate a foreign policy that has fixed, consistent parameters. No country is faced with as great a responsibility in identifying the role it should play in the system as the sole remaining superpower, the United States.[2]

The argument can be made that in the 1990s American foreign policy, too, viewed many conflicts occurring in the international arena as "ethnic," while in practice it acted strategically—to promote its national interest in the Balkans, Africa, and Asia. Was the notion of nationalism-engendered global pandemonium a pretext for imposing a twenty-first-century Pax Americana under the guise of liberal internationalism? Samuel Huntington's much-cited clash-of-civilizations thesis prepares the theoretical ground supporting such an interpretation. In his view, the world has been moving from nation-state conflict to ideological conflict to cultural conflict: "differences among civilizations are not only real; they are basic" (1993, 25–26). Huntington predicted that in the future interlocking conflicts would occur among Hindu, Muslim, Slavic Orthodox, Western, Japanese, Confucian, Ibero-American, and possibly African civilizations. Admittedly, "The central axis of world politics in the future is likely to be . . . the conflict between 'the West and the Rest'" (ibid., 41). But Huntington concluded that by concentrating on civilizations' fault lines, American foreign policy could meet the challenges of building a new world order.

As with the British Empire, then, a (post)modernized U.S. world order is likely to be grounded in—but also camouflaged by—ethnonationalist and normative conflicts worldwide (Knutsen 1999). Thus the U.S. foreign-policy establishment, long committed to containing and combating communism, recognized the strategic advantages after 1989 of the self-determination of peoples in the communist world. The principle served as a formula for partition of ex-communist states. But, in their forward planning, U.S. leaders may have underestimated the strength of the demonstration effect on other nations seeking independence from multiethnic states. They also were divided over the U.S. role following partitions. Explaining the reticence of the United States to act as global gendarme, Michael Ignatieff contended that "The Americans may be the last remaining superpower, but they are not an imperial power: their authority is exercised in the defense of exclusively national interests, not in the maintenance of an imperial system of global order" (1993, 12).

The sense of belonging to an international community has ebbed and flowed throughout recent U.S. history. Today, given the unique status of the United States as an economic and political juggernaut, when it feels no strong sense of belonging it has serious consequences for many of the world's peoples. As Ignatieff concisely phrased it, "huge sections of the world's population have won the 'right of self-determination' on the cruelest possible terms: they have been simply left to fend for themselves" (ibid., 13). The ripple effects of *American apartness* can exacerbate international instability.

The converse, that what happens in distant lands does affect U.S. national interest, also holds true. American writer Robert Kaplan persuasively demonstrated the linkage between political crises in developing states and U.S. foreign-policy priorities. Generalizing on the experience of Sierra Leone, he pointed to

> the withering away of central governments, the rise of tribal and regional domains, the unchecked spread of disease, and the growing pervasiveness of war. West Africa is reverting to the Africa of the Victorian atlas. It consists now of a series of coastal trading posts . . . and an interior that, owing to violence, volatility, and disease, is again becoming, as Graham Greene once observed, "blank" and "unexplored." (1994, 45; see also 2001)

Kaplan believed that the elemental threat that Africa faced—"nature unchecked"—would confront other countries:

> The coming upheaval, in which foreign embassies are shut down, states collapse, and contact with the outside world takes place through dangerous, disease-ridden coastal trading posts, will loom large in the century we are entering. . . . Africa suggests what war, borders, and ethnic politics will be like a few decades hence. (1994, 75)

Here we find another example of the nationalizing paradigm. The borders, wars, and conflicts involving Sierra Leone are Europe's and the United States' own future. A nationalizing determinism is at work that the West cannot escape—unless, the inference is, the United States as a superpower intervenes selectively, picking its fights and opponents and time lines that maximize its advantage. This has been the U.S. approach to an even greater extent after September 11, 2001.

Variants of the U.S. Variant: From Bush to Bush

American thinking about nationalism, ethnic conflict, and self-determination in the 1990s developed an obsession about how international problems were engendered by these factors alone. Resistance to the processes of U.S.-managed globalization could have no other source, it was widely assumed, than the anachronistic appeal of ethnonationalisms. The nationalizing paradigm was an essential corollary, therefore, of the globalization model. Hostage taking by the Serb military and Kashmiri militants, terrorist attacks by Algerian and Egyptian fundamentalists on Western tourists, civil wars from Algeria to Angola, insurgency and counterinsurgency in Afghanistan, Chechnya, Kurdistan, and Sri Lanka, were all classified as ethnonationalist or ethnoreligious conflicts. Little or no reference was made to the political conditions in these states that produced armed confrontations between incumbent and opposition groups, or to the economic conditions that made these states too backward to benefit from globalization. Ignoring these background conditions, the head of the CIA, R. James Woolsey, cautioned that "This world that we are beginning to see looks more and more like a more lethal version of the old world that existed before 1914 when a range of nationalist sentiments produced the holocaust of World War I" (Clarke 1994, 13).

Different presidential administrations advanced different versions of the nationalizing paradigm, however. During President George Bush's administration in the years of the "Great Transition" in international politics (1989–92), reading a conflict in ethnonationalist terms provided a justification for the United States to stay out of it. In early August 1991, just prior to the failed putsch in Moscow that sealed the fate of the USSR, Bush visited the Ukraine capital to lecture on political concepts: "Freedom is not the same as independence," he lectured the independence-minded Ukrainian parliament. "Americans will not support those who seek independence in order to replace a far-off tyranny with a local despotism. They will not aid those who promote a suicidal nationalism based upon ethnic hatred" (quoted in Moynihan 1994, 166). This was to become known as Bush's "chicken Kiev" speech, for, by the end of the year, Ukraine had achieved both independence and greater freedom in spite of Washington's temerity.

Other members of Bush's administration also cautioned against involvement in ethnonationalist pandemonium. Paul Goble, a State Department specialist on ethnic relations in Soviet space, warned that the USSR could melt down unpredictably into more than fifteen constituent republics. This helps explain why the United States lagged behind other Western democracies in recognizing Baltic independence. Bush's last secretary of state, Lawrence Eagleburger, stressed how the different character of every ethnonationist struggle would not permit any one formula to address every contingency. "There is no rule or strategy that can be applied across-the-board as a remedy to this kind of problem," he stated. "Each instance of trouble in a multiethnic nation, whether it's Yugoslavia or whatever, has its own historical, political, economic and cultural context and has to be approached on a case-by-case basis" (cited in Goshko 1991). The combination of going to war against Saddam Hussein in 1991 for strategic reasons with equivocation in the face of early Serb ethnic aggression in the Balkans in 1991–92 encapsulates Bush's foreign-policy legacy.[3]

A continuity in the foreign-policy approach of Bush and his successor, Bill Clinton, was the fixation with ethnonationalism. Its uniqueness was believed to reside in the different tactics used by nationalist and secessionist groups in different regions to attack the international state system. This required crafting a defensive, flexible American foreign policy to meet its challenges. Because ethnonationalism could not be met head-on, as in the case of Stalin's Soviet Union after World War II, the United States had to draw crucial distinctions when deciding on a measured response to each ethnic conflict. One distinction was between humanitarian intervention and balance-of-power concerns, a second between peacekeeping and peacemaking, and a third between protecting the helpless and punishing the aggressor.

A case where these distinctions were blurred was the Somalian intervention of 1993 to 1995. Under the aegis of the United Nations, President Clinton approved a U.S. humanitarian mission to bring food relief to the famine-afflicted African state. But this initially well-defined mission became obscured when Somali warlords, with, apparently, the connivence of Saudi extremist Osama bin Laden, turned against the American presence. The ensuing conflict was interpreted as taking on an ethnonationalist dimension. Colin Powell, then chairman of the Joint Chiefs of Staff, expressed concern about the "nation-building" mission his troops were assuming in Somalia. The so-called Mogadishu line in U.S. foreign policy that was elaborated following the withdrawal of American forces after they had suffered serious casualties in Somalia emphasized the difference between humanitarian efforts enjoying broad consensual endorsement and zero-sum intervention in complex ethnic and clan rivalries where any type of aid to one side was perceived as hostile activity by the rival party.[4]

The nebulous connection among U.S. foreign policy, ethnic conflict, and morality was a constant dilemma for President Clinton. The fundamental issue he had to consider had been succinctly posed by scholar Adam Roberts: "If international politics consists largely, not of a Manichean struggle of right versus wrong, but of impossibly competing ethnic identities and mutually incompatible dreams of national self-determination, might this not reinforce American disenchantment, not just with the supposed New World Order, but with all involvement in a hopelessly benighted world?" (Foreword, in Moynihan 1994, x).

The Clinton administration was aware that intervention in a non-Manichaean world was perilous. In 1993, his national security affairs adviser, Anthony Lake, laid out the groundwork for interventionism: "A major challenge to our thinking, our policies and our international institutions in this era is the fact that most conflicts are taking place within rather than among nations." Moreover, "These conflicts are typically highly complex; at the same time, their brutality will tug at our consciences. We need a healthy wariness about our ability to shape solutions for such disputes, yet at times our interests or humanitarian concerns will impel our unilateral or multilateral engagement" (Lake 1993).

Lake explained why the United States should remain engaged in world affairs. Throughout the twentieth century, "As we fought aggressors and contained communism, our engagement abroad was animated both by calculations of power and by this belief: to the extent democracy and market economics hold sway in other nations, our own nation will be more secure, prosperous and influential, while the broader world will be more humane and peaceful." By contrast, the approach to "backlash states"—those refusing to join the community of multiplying democracies and ruled by lawlessness, violence, racism, ethnic prejudice, religious persecution, xenophobia, and irredentism—should be to isolate them diplomatically, militarily, economically, and technologically.

Lake's successor as national security affairs assistant, Sandy Berger, reiterated this approach in the last year of the Clinton presidency. Arguing that local conflicts can have global consequences, he singled out the urgency for peacemaking "in regions containing major fault lines of ethnicity, faith, or ideology." Under Clinton, the rationale for U.S. activism was clear: "We have used diplomacy where possible, force where absolutely necessary, not pretending we can solve all the world's problems, but rejecting the idea that because we can't do everything, we must, for the sake of consistency, do nothing" (Berger 2000, 29).

But critics of Clinton's foreign policy protested that his administration went beyond simple diplomatic isolation of backlash states and that military missions had multiplied exponentially, best seen in the case of Yugoslavia. One analysis summarized how "The Clinton administration and the foreign policy community generally have viewed the Balkan crisis as a crucial test of America's leadership in creating order in the post–Cold War world" (Layne and Schwarz 1993, 6). The president had asserted that the Balkans would set "the standard for addressing other ethnic conflicts and the effectiveness of vital international institutions, including the European Community, the Atlantic Alliance, and the United Nations itself." For Clinton, the choice was "between unstable, highly nationalistic states with centralized and potentially oppressive governments, on the one hand, and democratic states . . . on the other" (cited in ibid., 6–7). Advocates of American activism identified imperial understretch—a shrinking of U.S. global commitments— not imperial overstretch, as the most serious post–cold-war miscalculation. Clinton's defense secretary, William Perry, explained why understretch was counterproductive: "America's prosperity depends upon international economic interdependence and the precondition for economic interdependence is the geopolitical stability and reassurance that flow from America's security commitments" (ibid., 10–11).

The case against interventionism rested on rejecting a modified version of the domino theory that assumed chain reactions to political events: "in the world of statecraft crises are usually discrete happenings—not tightly linked events. The outcome of events in potential hot spots like Nagorno-Karabakh, Moldova, the Baltics, Ukraine, Transylvania, and Slovakia will be decided by local conditions, not by what the United States does or does not do in the Balkans" (ibid., 16). Although almost all disorder in international politics was still attributed to nationalism (as can be seen from the examples cited), anti-interventionists contended that their nationalizing perspective provided the reason why the United States should disengage from international security commitments.

A senior U.S. foreign-policy specialist, George F. Kennan, listed other grounds for nonintervention. He referred to John Quincy Adams's 1823 speech—at a time when the United States was tempted to become involved in the conflict between Spain and its colonies in Latin America— to argue against interventionism in a new period of collapsing empires: "America . . . well knows that by once enlisting under other banners than her own, were they even the banners of foreign independence, she would involve herself beyond the power of extrication, in all the wars of interest and intrigue, of individual avarice, envy, and ambition, which assumed the colors and usurped the standards of freedom" (cited in Kennan 1995, 118).

In their study of the real world order of the 1990s, Max Singer and Aaron Wildavsky drew attention to the conflicting objectives inherent in any intervention:

In Yugoslavia, none of the following principles gave us a clear answer about what to do: preventing ethnic conflict, self-determination, preservation of national borders and stability of government, support for democracy, encouragement of negotiated solutions for conflict, prevention or punishment of aggression, neutrality, or preserving or restoring peace. (Singer and Wildavsky 1993, 163)

Ranking these principles was a near-impossible task. But in assailing Serb leader Slobodan Milosevic, President Clinton revealed his hand: the "grand vision" of a freer, more peaceful world in the twenty-first century "is threatened by the oldest demon of human society: our vulnerability to hatred of the other—those who are not like us" (Babington 1999). Rooting out ethnic hatreds was a prerequisite for a new international order and the United States had to play a part in seeing that this was achieved. To be sure, hatred of the other was the explanation also given for why a war on terrorism had to be initiated in the fall of 2001.

By the time that George W. Bush took office, nationalist pandemonium and ethnic hatreds were viewed as largely peripheral to international politics. This did not signal a policy of complete U.S. disengagement; the mantras of a "new American internationalism" advanced by Bush and "a uniquely American internationalism" outlined by his secretary of state, Colin Powell, were intended to demonstrate the dimension of continuity in American foreign policy. Powell's speech on his nomination to his new post seemingly reflected continuity in extremis; it could have been delivered a decade earlier: "The old world map as we knew it, of a red side and blue side that competed for something called the Third World, is gone. And the new map is a mosaic, a mosaic of many different pieces and many different colors spreading around the world" (*New York Times*, December 17, 2000). Yet there was no reference to ethnic conflicts among the international problems he identified. Furthermore, for Bush and Powell, the "nation-building" mission that the United States had undertaken in Somalia under Clinton was now a target of scorn. The promise that "There will be no more nation building" appeared to be a euphemism for no more American involvement in ethnonationalist conflicts. Powell's well-known opposition to U.S. military intervention in both Iraq and the Balkans, and his concerns for "force protection" (making U.S. troops posted abroad invulnerable) and "exit strategies" (not engaging American forces abroad without knowing when and how to extricate them) seemed to assure the marginalization of ethnic conflict management (Judt 2000, 98–99).

Were U.S. foreign policymakers discarding the nationalizing paradigm even before the events of September 2001, then? It did seem that Bush advisers were originally arguing against American activism regardless whether it involved mediation and peacekeeping in ethnic conflicts or even the level of American troop deployment in Western Europe. National Security Assistant Condoleezza Rice had mocked "The belief that the United States is exercising power legitimately only when it is doing so on behalf of someone or something else" that "was deeply rooted in Wilsonian thought" and had shaped Clinton foreign policy (Rice 2000, 47). Indeed, the Clinton "administration began deploying American forces abroad at a furious pace—an average of once every nine weeks. As it cut defense spending to its lowest point as a percentage of GDP since Pearl Harbor, the administration deployed the armed forces more often than at any time in the past fifty years" (ibid., 51). It is ironic, of course, that the new Bush administration soon made a commitment to using the armed forces for an indeterminate period and throughout the world as a response to the threat of terrorism.

Rice's critique of internationalism did not spare humanitarian interventions that most commonly target areas hit by nationalist conflict. She asked: "What if our values are attacked in areas that are arguably not of strategic concern? Should the United States not try to save lives in the absence of an overriding strategic rationale?" She replied: "'Humanitarian intervention' cannot be ruled out a priori. But a decision to intervene in the absence of strategic concerns should be understood for what it is. Humanitarian problems are rarely only humanitarian problems; the taking of life or withholding of food is almost always a political act" (ibid., 53).

The two key foreign policymakers under George W. Bush—Powell and Rice—concurred that "uniquely American internationalism" signified embedding U.S. national interests above humanitarian ones. In its war against Taliban-led Afghanistan, the United States did invoke some humanitarian concerns, especially for the plight of Afghani women (the fact that many were turned into destitute widows because of the war was not mentioned). But the Bush administration brashly announced that promoting U.S. national interests was its overriding objective. In doing this, the primacy of Realpolitik in international relations was underscored, and the decade-long paradigm of a nationalizing world order was cast aside.

Conclusion

The United States and the international system that it anchors do not determine who the victors and victims will be in every contemporary conflict. But they can decide who will be *recognized* as victors and who as rogues. Under the nationalizing paradigm, nationalists were the enemy of a new world order. Who the nationalists were—who the enemy was—was a construct of the U.S.-dominated international system. In the cold-war era, it was a relatively straightforward task to identify the communist other. But during the 1990s, the task of identifying the nationalist "other" was neither simple nor consistent nor fair to the genuine national collective selves possessing moral grounds for sovereignty but lacking support among international actors.

Nationalisms exist. They did not disappear after the events of September 2001. They are kindled by regional ethnic entrepreneurs and transformed into malignancies. They are occasionally fanned by *international* entrepreneurs who stand to gain from the eruption of an ethnonationalist conflict. They are sometimes discernible in the shape of pan-nationalisms that mobilize people living in different states; Islam is often cited as a pan-nationalist movement.[5]

An international system guided by a nationalizing paradigm needs extreme nationalists to stigmatize. Meciar, Milosevic, and Mugabe play indispensable roles so that the nationalizing paradigm can function. How can any effort to obtain some form of institutionalized recognition of national identity—not necessarily taking the form of statehood—undertaken by Kurds, Chechens, Zulus, or Quechua speakers succeed when the international system stigmatizes nationalism?

A denationalized, more coherent international order has eclipsed the nationalizing paradigm that dominated thinking about international politics in the 1990s. As never before, the United States squarely aspires to be the hegemon of this order. Most paradigms have their moment in time and then fade away, to be replaced by another one. This is the case for the nationalizing model as well. Greater international stability and prosperity could be promoted by adopting a model positing a more inclusive and democratic world order, one that would institutionalize at the international-system level the idea of belonging that has been promoted within individual states. Instead, however, the international model accepted by the United States in the new century appears in many ways to be as exclusionary and undemocratic as the nationalist regimes that were condemned by the previous nationalizing paradigm. Unlike the latter, however, it is not one that enjoys a broad consensus among the principal actors of the international system.

Notes

1 Nairn was referring to issues of the *New Statesman* (June 1, 1990) and *Time* (August 6, 1990), which, respectively, had cover stories titled "Nationalities on the Loose" and "Nationalism: Old Demon."

2 For the argument that other great powers will emerge to balance unchecked American power, see Layne 1993.

3 On the response to the Balkan crisis, see Danner 2001, Gow 1999, Ullman 1996.

4 For a more positive appraisal of intervention in Somalia, see Crocker 1995.

5 The extent to which Islam can be viewed as a pan-nationalist movement is considered in Taras 2002.

Works Cited

Babington, Charles. 1999. "Clinton Defends NATO Air Campaign." *Washington Post*, April 16.

Berger, Samuel R. 2000. "A Foreign Policy for the Global Age." *Foreign Affairs* 79:6: 22–39.

Chernov, Vladislav. 1994. "Moscow Should Think Carefully." *Nezavisimaia gazeta* February 23. In Ilya Prizel, *National Identity and Foreign Policy: Nationalism and Leadership in Poland, Russia, and Ukraine*. Cambridge: Cambridge University Press, 1998.

Clarke, Jonathan G. 1994. "American Foreign Policy Must Evaluate New Priorities." *USA Today Magazine* (July).

Crocker, Chester A. 1995. "The Lessons of Somalia: Not Everything Went Wrong." *Foreign Affairs* 74:3: 2–8.

Danner, Mark. 2001. *The Saddest Story: America, the Balkans, and the Post–Cold War World*. New York: Pantheon Books.

Dijkink, Gertjan. 1996. *National Identity and Geopolitical Visions: Maps of Pride and Pain*. London: Routledge.

Goshko, John. 1991. "Ethnic Strife Replaces Cold War Rivalries." *Washington Post*, July 14.

Gow, James. 1999. *Triumph of the Lack of Will: International Diplomacy and the Yugoslav War*. New York: Columbia University Press.

Huntington, Samuel P. 1993. "The Clash of Civilizations?" *Foreign Affairs* 72:3: 22–49.

Ignatieff, Michael. 1993. *Blood and Belonging: Journeys into the New Nationalism*. New York: Farrar, Straus and Giroux.

Judt, Tony. 2000. "The White House and the World." *New York Review of Books* 47:20: 98–99.

Kaplan, Robert D. 1994. "The Coming Anarchy: How Scarcity, Crime, Overpopulation, Tribalism, and Disease Are Rapidly Destroying the Social Fabric of Our Planet." *The Atlantic* 273:2: 44–76.

———. 2001. *The Coming Anarchy: Shattering the Dreams of the Post Cold War*. New York: Vintage Books.

Kennan, George F. 1995. "On American Principles." *Foreign Affairs* 74:2: 116–26.

Knutsen, Torbjorn L. 1999. *The Rise and Fall of World Orders*. Manchester: Manchester University Press.

Lake, Anthony. 1993. "From Containment to Enlargement." Speech at Johns Hopkins University School of Advanced International Studies, Washington, D.C., September 21. www.fas.org/news/usa/1993/usa-930921.htm.

Layne, Christopher. 1993. "The Unipolar Illusion: Why New Great Powers Will Rise." *International Security* 17:4: 5–51.

Layne, Christopher, and Benjamin Schwarz. 1993. "American Hegemony—without an Enemy." *Foreign Policy* 92: 5–23.

Mernissi, Fatima. 1992. *Islam and Democracy: Fear of the Modern World.* New York: Addison-Wesley.

Moynihan, Daniel Patrick. 1994. *Pandaemonium: Ethnicity in International Politics.* New York: Oxford University Press.

Nairn, Tom. 1997. *Faces of Nationalism: Janus Revisited.* London: Verso.

Rice, Condoleezza. 2000. "Promoting the National Interest." *Foreign Affairs* 79:1: 45–62.

Singer, Max, and Aaron Wildavsky. 1993. *The Real World Order: Zones of Peace/Zones of Turmoil.* Chatham, N.J.: Chatham House Publishers.

Small, Melvin, and David J. Singer. 1982. *Resort to Arms: International and Civil Wars, 1816–1980.* Beverly Hills, Calif.: Sage.

Taras, Raymond. 2002. *Liberal and Illiberal Nationalisms.* Basingstoke, England: Palgrave.

Ullman, Richard H., ed. 1996. *The World and Yugoslavia's Wars.* New York: Council on Foreign Relations Press.

Philip Schlesinger

3

Media and Belonging:

The Changing Shape of Political Communication

in the European Union

Political and economic integration in the European Union (EU) is bringing about significant change in the conceptualization of public spaces for debate and discussion. The EU—a regional grouping of fifteen member states[1]—increasingly presents a challenge to conventional thinking both about political organization and communicative space and about collective identities and a sense of belonging.

The EU's drive toward the creation of common political institutions is distinctive and far-reaching when compared to other trading blocs around the world (Katzenstein 1996). Hirst and Thompson (1996, 153–54) consider the EU to be "the most ambitious project of multinational economic governance in the modern world" and suggest the Union may be seen as "a complex polity made up of common institutions, member states, and peoples" that combine their efforts in governance. The long-term impact of collaborative practices inside the EU is gradually modifying the ways in which political life is conducted. The scope and nature of political communication is bound to change in line with the reconfiguring EU political economy.

In the contemporary world, the key framework for the practice of democratic politics and the exercise of citizenship is the nation-state. Conventionally, politico-communicative space is taken to be coextensive with national space. But this functional fit is disrupted by the emergence of a supranational polity such as the EU. The shift to a supranational formation begins to tranform the established communicative relations between national publics and state-centered systems of power. I shall illustrate theoretical shifts that try to address these changing realities by reference to the social communications tradition of thinking about nations and states, in particular by considering the work of Jürgen Habermas and Manuel Castells.

Inasmuch as a media-sustained, supranational communicative space is emerging because of EU integration, this is class-inflected and predominantly the domain of political and economic elites, not that of a wider European public. The skew of the news market in favor of the powerful and influential is congruent with the EU's widely acknowledged "democratic deficit," which derives from the predominantly executive and bureaucratic style of its governing institutions (the European Commission and the Council of Ministers), coupled with their weak accountability to the legislature (the European Parliament).

Beyond the "National" Public Sphere

Theoretical thinking about the "public sphere" has shifted in line with the transforming political space on the European continent. Jürgen Habermas (1989) and his followers see the public sphere as an arena that exists outside the institutions of the state in which a range of views and opinions can be developed in relation to matters of public concern. Although fruitful for media research, Habermas's ideal-typical conception of the classical bourgeois public sphere has been subjected to a range of criticisms, notably, its exclusionary and limited character in respect of women, the working class, and people of color (Calhoun 1994).

That debate is well known and does not need to be reviewed here. It should be emphasized, though, that Habermas's early theory took the European *nation-state* addressed as a political community as its framework. Likewise, Leon Mayhew's (1997) contemporary development of public-sphere arguments unselfconsciously takes the United States as its political space. Although the historical formation of the public sphere has been closely connected to the process of creating nation-states, that relationship is a contingent one (Eley 1994, 296).

The view that communicative processes delineate the boundaries of a political community is central to the "social communications" approach in the theory of nationalism. Nations are distinguished from other collectivities by the special nature of their internal communications, their "communicative complementarity," in Karl Deutsch's (1966) phrase. Influential writers of this school variously emphasize the role of education, standardized languages, the nationally charged routines of everyday life, and a common collective history (Anderson 1983; Billig 1995; Castells 1996, 1997, 1998; Gellner 1983; cf. Schlesinger [2000] for a critical discussion of these authors).

The early Habermas depicted the national polity as a *single* public sphere with a sole authoritative center. In fact, this is a limiting case that suggests a degree of cultural homogeneity to be found in few societies, if any. Rather, as Nancy Fraser (1994, 126) has argued, the ideal of equal participation in public debate is better served by imagining a *plurality* of competing publics. This lays stress on a diversity of interests and backgrounds while postulating the possibility of "interpublic discursive interaction." Craig Calhoun (1995, 242) has suggested that we therefore think in terms of "spheres of publics," conceptualizing these as "multiple intersections among heterogeneous publics, not only as the privileging of a single overarching public." By this account, public life in late-capitalist democracies involves a plurality of discourses competing for position in national space. Of course, this presupposes a democratic order that permits diverse groups to wage the battle for public opinion, and it certainly does not necessarily mean that they do so on equal terms.

But this revised approach still treats public space as protoypically bounded by a nation-state. Consider, instead, political discourse in the space of the European Union, which is neither a nation-state nor a conventional polity. Both national and European discourses coexist. "Europe" is *inside* the nation-state as part of the domestic political agenda and also as a constitutive part of the broader politico-economic framework; yet, it is also still another place, a different political level and locus of decision making that is *outside*. In the EU, given this ambiguity, the national, state-bounded context no longer completely defines the scope of communicative communities. To analyze the emergent European communicative spaces, the focus needs to shift to the new, supranational arenas and their constituent publics.[2]

The European Union's Communicative Dimension

Is a distinct sphere of publics emerging at the European level? Habermas (1994, 21–23) has observed that in Europe the "classic form of the nation-state is at present disintegrating" in the face both of global economic pressures and of multiculturalism. Instead of traditional factors such as a common ethnicity or language, Habermas proposes that "the political culture must serve as the common denominator for a constitutional patriotism which simultaneously sharpens an awareness of the multiplicity and integrity of the different forms of life which exist in a multicultural society" (ibid., 27). "Political culture" here refers to legal principles and political institutions, norms and practices that are diffused throughout a given polity; in short, the rules of the game.

Habermas assumes that networks will stretch across national boundaries and sees an ideal interplay between "institutionalised processes of opinion and will formation" and "informal networks of public communication" (ibid., 31). He postulates a radical form of broadly based popular involvement in public affairs as an essential corrective to professionalized politics. Parliamentary democracy, therefore, "demands a discursive structuring of public networks and arenas in which anonymous circuits of communication are detached from the concrete level of single interactions"— to put it plainly, a communicative space (Habermas 1997, 171).

Latterly, Habermas has partially dethroned the single public sphere and written instead of "a highly complex network that branches out into a multitude of overlapping international, national, regional, local and subcultural arenas" (ibid., 1997, 373–74). Yet, an underlying conception of "the" public sphere does remain. It is within this logically presupposed integrative frame that "hermeneutic bridge building" between different discourses occurs.

Habermas also now portrays the public sphere as potentially unbounded, as having shifted from specific locales (such as the nation) to the virtual copresence of citizens and consumers linked by public media. We must conclude that a European public sphere would therefore be open-ended, with communicative connections extending well beyond the Continent. This makes sense because contemporary communication flows and networks ensure that no—or hardly any—political community can remain an island. But how does the suggestion that we all really belong to a global village sit alongside the postulate of a European identity? We still have to ask which communicative boundaries matter most for the development of a distinctive political identity and political culture in the EU. In other words, how might communicative processes contribute to the Union's social cohesion? A European polity without at least some distinctive communicative boundary markers simply cannot be imagined as a sociological possibility.

For Habermas, the potential impact of communications technologies on communities is subordinate to how an appropriate new communicative space might be constituted in the European Union. He touches on the concept of the network. But this idea is much more developed in the work of Manuel Castells (1996, 1997, 1998), for whom the new communications technologies contribute to the formation of an altogether new kind of society, the "informational."

Like Habermas, Castells considers the European Union to be of especial interest. He regards the EU as the precursor of a new political order, of new forms of association and loyalty: the emerging Euro-polity epitomizes what he terms "the network state." The EU is assessed not just as a political-economic zone but, because of its network character, is also seen as a specific kind of communicative space.

For Castells, the EU has different "nodes" of varying importance that together make up a network. Regions and nations, nation-states, European Union institutions, together constitute a framework of shared authority. Castells (unlike Habermas) holds the "stateless nation" to be a prototype of potentially innovative forms of post–nation-state affiliation—an exemplar of flexible networking that offers multiple identities and allegiances to its inhabitants. Nations (as distinct from states) are characterized as "cultural communes constructed in people's minds by the sharing of history and political projects" (1997, 51).

This fits Castells's more general contention that "[b]ypassed by global networks of wealth, power and information, the modern nation-state has lost much of its sovereignty" (ibid., 354). The result is a "dissolution of shared identities," ostensibly producing a split between global elites that consider themselves to be citizens of the world and those without economic, political, and cultural power who "tend to be attracted to communal identities" that either crosscut the nation-state or operate below that level (ibid., 356). The EU is an instance of the former, Catalonia and Scotland examples of the latter. For Castells, European integration represents "at the same time a reaction to the process of globalization and its most advanced expression" (1998, 318).

Much as with Habermas, we might ask what gives boundaries to the putative European communicative space invoked by Castells? The answer resides in the nexus of political institutions that constitute Union Europe, the dealings between them, and the growing "subsidiary" horizontal links across the member states (ibid., 330–31). This coincides exactly with Habermas's argument. In short, a form of Deutschian "communicative complementarity" emerges out of the informal processes of state making. The potentially globalizing pull of communications technologies is countered by emergent patterns of social interaction in the European Union's space. These are polyvalent: simultaneously, they knit together diverse actors economically, politically, and communicatively. It is implied that the EU is developing a special interactive intensity that favors internal communication and creates a referential boundary that coexists with global networking.

The Euro-polity and Communicative Space

The impact of the EU's institutional framework on political and media discourse (as well as on the theories discussed thus far) is not surprising. Since 1950, the developing supranational European space has had a major impact on its member states (Millward 1994). Today, considered as a quasi polity, the EU consists of four main institutions: the European Commission; the Council of Ministers; the European Parliament; and the European Court of Justice. Together, these constitute a unique institutional arrangement. Although the EU is a political space, it is also the junction point of communications activities that range from policy dissemination, through lobbying, to reporting and commentary. The interplay between the communicative and political dimensions is central to the development of my overall argument.

The Commission is the "motor of the integration process" (Christiansen 1996, 78). A supranational institution led by twenty commissioners, it is a bureaucratic body that formulates policy and implements European Union legislation. The Commission is the EU's main focus for lobbying and other forms of private political communication. There has been mounting debate about the existence of a "democratic deficit"— namely, a lack of accountability by the Commission both to elected representatives in the European Parliament and to the wider public. An unprecedented crisis occurred in March 1999, when the Commission resigned over allegations of fraud and mismanagement.

While the Commission pushes the political and legislative agenda, the Council of Ministers (drawn from all the member states) is the key forum for interstate bargaining and the representation of national interests. The Council's procedures are, however, more secretive than those of the Commission owing to the intergovernmental nature of negotiations and there has been serious resistance to offering wider public access to information (Edwards 1996, 143). This makes the Council less amenable to lobbying groups than the Commission (Mazey and Richardson 1992). What we learn of these opaque decision-making processes comes primarily through

national news media, a process of framing that allows national governments to emphasize their victories and play down compromises reached
with other member states.

The European Parliament is the only directly elected body in the EU.
Since the Single European Act of 1987, and even more so since the Treaty
on European Union of 1991, its powers have expanded. Latterly it has had
an increased role in "co-deciding" legislation with the Council of Ministers
(Earnshaw and Judge 1996). Its increased political power has made it more
of a focus for lobbying activities.

The European Court of Justice (ECJ) is perceived by many analysts as
having made a substantial contribution to the process of European integration by its decisions on the interpretation of EU legislation, challenges
to member states over the nonimplementation of regulations, and also the
resolution of legal arguments between the institutions. National courts as
well as citizens and interest groups from the member states have taken
cases to the ECJ. The Court's interaction with other institutions and interests in developing both Community law and policy has been crucial for
European integration (Wincott 1996, 183).

Communication about the EU is most obviously shaped by national
political and cultural frameworks during European Parliament election
campaigns and when referenda are held. Elections for the Parliament do
not take place among a single European electorate. Rather, they focus on
national political issues, are almost exclusively fought by national political
parties, and are reported through national media using the reporting conventions used for national elections (Blumler 1983; Wober 1987; Leroy
and Siune 1994). Analogously, the information campaigns of the European Union have addressed national and regional political, media, and PR
structures.

The "Europeanization" of governmental processes is reflected in the development of a truly transnational European political community. The EU's
institutions have long been the target of organized lobbying by bodies
such as the Union of Industries in the European Community (UNICE), the
elite club of managing directors who gather as the European Round Table
(ERT) and the European Trade Union Confederation (ETUC) (Bartak
1998, 12–13). There is also the burgeoning army of EU-based European
public-affairs professionals, think tanks, and consultants, as well as a large
cohort of outside interests, especially from the United States and Japan
(Mazey and Richardson 1996; Miller and Schlesinger 2000). Although a
supranational public space has indeed evolved around the policy-making

actors in the various institutions, much activity still ultimately derives from national or regional interests.

"Europeanized" political communication processes such as policy consultation, lobbying, public affairs, and interest representation reflect the "multilevel governance" of the European polity. The complexity of political society in Europe means that—in line with recent retheorizations—we can think neither of political space as contained within the nation-state nor of the role of information as adequate if limited to assisting the conduct of the citizen within the national democratic polity. As the EU's policy making and political direction impinge increasingly on member states, the European dimension increasingly shapes the content and sets the agenda of the mediated political discourse of national polities (Fundesco 1997; Morgan 1995, 323; Schlesinger 1998, 58–60).

In member states, national editorial values influence coverage and national governmental sources are still of key importance for journalists covering European Union issues. Morgan (1995, 327) has argued that most journalists "report with a highly developed sense of the domestically acceptable so far as EU news is concerned." Current reporting styles mean that citizens are more likely to learn about decisions and legislation than the policy process itself. Reporting patterns tend to obscure where, and by whom, influence has been exerted, as well as shrouding the compromises made by national representatives.

Elements of a European civil society have begun to emerge, organized through the mobilization of diverse and often competing interests, and oriented toward the political institutions of the EU. Political communication—broadly understood—while focused on the Euro-polity, is at the same time complexly mediated by national and regional political actors. To the extent that information about, and the interpretation of, EU activities is disseminated outwards from the Union's administrative heartlands, it characteristically flows along the grooves of established national and regional networks of communication.

The EU does not constitute a single public sphere. Multilevel governance, and the continuing tensions and divergences between the supranational level and those of the member states and regions, now require us to think in terms of overlapping spheres of publics.

It is this very complexity that has driven the search for a common public sphere capable of transcending Europe's diversity. First, there has been the attempt to develop a "European audiovisual space" by promoting cross-border film and television production; and second, there has been the drive to create a "European information area" based on the convergence of telecommunications, computing, and media. Each of these policy initiatives presupposed a common communicative space. The one emphasized cultural value and heritage, whereas the other stressed the image of a wired society and informational exchange.

Neither approach was really driven by a direct concern with political communication as such. However, to the extent that they have embodied conceptions of either cultural or, alternatively, informational aspects of citizenship, they clearly bear on the construction of a political space in which communication is important.

The relationship between media and political citizenship has been more evident in efforts to devise a common framework for assuring media pluralism in the EU. However, so far this has foundered on the opposed interests of those who want a single EU marketplace where large media conglomerates can operate with minimal constraints and those who wish to protect consumer interests in the member states. The level at which pluralism is to be secured is a moot point: should it be that of the member state or of the Union itself? This dilemma neatly encapsulates the ambiguous politico-communicative status of the EU.

As public communication inside the EU is still largely produced for national markets bounded by states, there is little scope for pan-European modes of address. The short history of attempts to fashion Europe-wide public-service satellite television channels has been above all a tale of casualties (Collins 1993). Nor, with exceptions considered later in this essay, have there been good grounds for thinking that a European market exists for print media. Without the broad mass of European media consumers organized transnationally as common audiences or readerships there is no basis for talking about a single European public for political communications.

Public policy on media and communication at the EU level, therefore, has been fragmented and inconsistent in its attempts to create a common communicative space. In fact, the contemporary dynamics of the transnational market for news have had more impact on political communication than has official intervention.

In the European communicative space today some news media are in effect creating specialized audiences and readerships by way of seeking markets. An incipient change is taking place in the collectivities to be addressed, ultimately owing to the EU's development as a novel political form. We may think of such emergent media audiences as occupying a transnational space. Although driven by profit seeking, some Europe-wide media are creating new possibilities for collective debate, albeit a highly restricted one. This contrasts strongly with the policymakers' failure to create a new European public in the face of the deep-rooted barriers of language, culture, ethnicity, nation, and state that make Europe into such a mosaic (Schlesinger 1993, 1994).

In this connection, it is essential to distinguish between information made available to elites engaged in the policy process or economic decision making and that produced for mass publics. The press is preferred by elites, whereas television is the most used mass medium. That said, television is increasingly capable of finding pay-per-view niche markets. The growth of digital technology means that this medium, too, is capable of targeting elites. Top professionals are increasingly gravitating to the Internet for specialist information seeking, and their use of the World Wide Web and of E-mail is now taken as an index of elite status in business surveys.

Supranational Mediation

Although the press remains an almost exclusively national medium, there are newspapers and magazines that do self-consciously address a European (as well as a global) elite audience composed of political and economic decision makers. In television, too, related developments may be illustrated by the case of Euronews.

A PRESS FOR THE POLITICO-BUSINESS ELITE

Economic elites are a key battleground for the printed press. How media enterprises and their journalists regard the European arena plainly depends greatly on their vantage point. We need to distinguish an "internal" perspective from an "external" one. Inside the EU, the key concerns of elites are with the ramifications of creating a common economic and political order supported by law and regulation. Outsiders see the European space quite differently. From the standpoint of external capitalist interests, Europe is a region about which intelligence is needed. What happens in the interior is interesting because it affects the political stability of the Continent, the sharpness of economic competition between blocs and states, and the attractiveness of investment conditions.

Europe is a distinct regional market. Its specificity is underlined when we consider its attraction for a daily newspaper with worldwide distribution such as the *Financial Times* (*FT*). The *FT* sells itself as "the best source of world-wide business," claiming its authoritativeness against "a background of increasing globalisation of markets," and using a reporting perspective represented as "international." Its circulation is more than three hundred thousand, the readership more than 1 million, and distribution takes place in 140 countries (http://www.FT.com, January 27, 1999). According to one authoritative trade survey, the *FT*—with a 9 percent share of the elite's "important business reading"—is the most widely read daily in the fifteen EU countries, Norway, and Switzerland. For these purposes, Europe's elite is defined as "the top 4 per cent in terms of income and executive activity" (Research Services Ltd. 1996, 17).

The *FT* is owned by Pearson plc and headquartered in London. But the paper has globalized its marketplace. Like Britain itself, Europe is undoubtedly a crucial regional market for the *FT*, which publishes in the United Kingdom, France, Germany, Sweden, and Spain. Within Europe, among senior people in the Continent's largest businesses in seventeen countries the newspaper outstrips key daily competitors that include *Die Frankfurter Allgemeine Zeitung (FAZ)*, *Das Handelsblatt*, *Der Spiegel*, the *International Herald Tribune*, and the *Wall Street Journal*.

In Brussels, journalists report that the *FT* is "usually cited as being favoured by official sources" because of its "European-wide readership" (Morgan 1995, 333). Despite its global reach and ambitions, the *FT*'s European edition contributes to a common agenda for a fraction of Europe's elite. Pertinently, on February 9, 1998, when 155 German economists wrote to the press calling for a delay in the implementation of European Monetary Union, they sent their letter to both the *FT* and the *FAZ*.

Along with the Benelux countries, France and Germany are also the continental states of greatest interest to *The Economist*, owned by the London-headquartered Economist Newspaper Ltd., in which Pearson has a 50 percent share. Like the *FT*, but in the weekly market, *The Economist* is the most widely read paper of its category across Europe, taking 3 percent of the possible readership. Inside the company it is held that there is "a pan-European business-government elite . . . speaking English on a daily basis, using it in business and personal life." Certainly, survey figures bear this out: of the top 4 percent of employees across fourteen of the richest European countries examined (a mere 5.7 million people), 68 percent speak or read English (with French at 42 percent, and German at 23 percent, way behind). Of these, more than 38 percent use some English at work, albeit with major variations between countries (Research Services Ltd. 1995, 11). For *The Economist*, the EU's development offers "transnational cultural opportunities" for selling its product (personal communication, *The Economist*, April 21, 1998).

The company has also tapped into the special Brussels marketplace, launching *European Voice* in October 1995 on the model of Washington, D.C.'s *Roll Call. European Voice* is a weekly newspaper with a "village feel" to it aimed at all the top people in the Brussels micropolity. This publication has "the exclusive co-operation of the European Commission, the Council of Ministers and the European Parliament, who circulate 7,000 individually addressed copies of the newspaper to Commissioners, their Cabinets, MEPs [Members of the European Parliament] and A grade civil servants." Other targets are registered lobbyists, the business community, and the press, with total circulation reaching sixteen thousand (URL: http://www. european-voice.com/advertise/2.p15, January 27, 1999; personal communication, *The Economist,* April 21, 1998).

The short, eight-year life of *The European* (launched in May 1990, closed down in December 1998) may well be instructive about the risks involved in relying largely (if not exclusively) on the European market, as well as in letting a political agenda strongly critical of the EU predominate.

The European began as a weekly broadsheet intended to contribute to European unity under the aegis of the U.K.-based Mirror Group Newspapers, then run by the late Robert Maxwell. It ended as a weekly tabloid-style news magazine with a "Euro-skeptical" vocation, owned by the Barclay Brothers' European Press Holdings. In its last, anti-EU incarnation, the editor in chief aspired to reach the status of *The Economist,* namely, to offer an "essential read for the people ruling Europe" (Neil 1997). The paper's executives believed that "The true Europeans now are the business-men . . . people who might be operating in one, two, or three different countries at one time" and that U.S. decision makers needed a "one-stop shop" when reading about Europe (personal communication, European Press Holdings, February 4, 1998).

Although *The European's* business elite target audience did exist, the magazine had to fight against established titles and its Euro-skeptical editorial policy was disastrous, leading to a downturn in sales from some 155,000 to around 133,000 in 1997. The paper's eventual collapse is of less interest than the fact that, for some years, it did hold a modest share of a cross-national readership. Although one-third of sales were in the United Kingdom, its home base, a more than negligible presence was achieved in the big EU states and in Belgium, principal home of the EU institutions. Insiders told this author that in political terms it was "before its time," that Europe had yet to become a political entity. If correct, the implication is that as the EU's politico-communicative space develops, a successor venture of this kind will not be out of the question.

Euronews was launched in January 1993 in an attempt to produce a distinctive news agenda for a broader, European, public. It came in the wake of a number of failed experiments in pan-European television. Supported by a consortium of eighteen European public-service broadcasters and the European Parliament, the Euronews project reflected the desire in some quarters (notably the French government) to produce a "European" perspective on world news (Hjarvard 1993).

Pressure to enter the marketplace was especially marked after the Gulf War in 1991, when CNN's success both in reporting from the front line, and in acting as a vehicle for television diplomacy, marked out new territory subsequently also entered by the BBC's World Television News. Although global in reach, the Anglo-American companies are firmly rooted in their national journalistic cultures, with distinctive corporate identities and brand recognition.

By comparison with Euronews, which has always broadcast in five major European languages (English, French, German, Italian, and Spanish) and also since 1997 in Arabic, both CNN and BBC World are monolingual channels, transmitting solely in English. As a transnational broadcaster, Euronews reflects major features of the linguistic and national diversity of the European cultural space.

Despite major financial losses, Euronews has twice proved attractive to firms rethinking their strategies in the European communications market. Its operating company was purchased in 1995 by a subsidiary of the French telecommunications giant, Alcatel-Alsthom, because of the weak public-sector finance provided by the European broadcasters and the EU. Alcatel sought to combine its communications distribution capacity and the information services offered by Euronews (Machill 1998).

The French telecommunications enterprise's acquisition of news-producing capacity was short-lived. Alcatel's shares were purchased by ITN, the British television news provider, in November 1997. By finding a new niche product—Europe-wide broadcasting in the public-service tradition—ITN diversified, breaking into broadcasting after forty years as a news supplier. Multilanguage broadcasting was seen as providing a competitive edge in the European marketplace, with added potential for international sales. The strategy assumes that over time, and especially with a single European currency, the EU's national publics will gradually develop a sense of a common news agenda (personal communication, ITN, April 20, 1998).

Euronews is the only pan-European broadcaster to transmit in more than two languages. Audience research indicates that the channel reaches 90 million households via cable, satellite, or terrestrial broadcasting, three times the reach of BBC World. Euronews is the number two pan-European news broadcaster after CNN, compared to whose 28.1 percent share of the Continent's viewing in one month Euronews has 21.3 percent ("Euronews," ITN Information Pack, 1998; http://www.euronews.net/en/about/about.htm, January 21, 1999). Widespread distribution, however, does not equate to actual viewing and transnational news of this kind reaches very small audiences indeed by comparison with those of news broadcasters aiming at specific national audiences (Sparks 1998, 117).

Moreover, although the figures do not tell us what audiences make of the news programs that they view, Euronews has its highest distribution by far in the largest media markets of the continental EU member states: France (20.9 million viewers), Italy (20.2 million), Germany (12.9 million), Spain (11.7 million). These are the main non-Anglophone states in whose languages Euronews broadcasts. In the United Kingdom, in sharp contrast, the potential viewership is a mere 1.2 million, far exceeded by both Belgium and Finland, with much smaller populations.

Euronews is attempting to harness linguistic diversity to commercial advantage. Digital distribution offers the means to meet specific audience tastes in a fragmenting marketplace where viewer choices can be more directly expressed. ITN believes that there is a growing market for news about Europe among those dissatisfied with increasingly parochial national news programs and is aiming for upmarket viewers who prefer to have the news in their own languages (personal communication, April 20, 1998). The company has sought the financial support of the European Commission and the European Parliament, recognizing the need for political sentiment to sustain this kind of venture over the longer term, and anticipating that digital technology will eventually make a European Union public-affairs channel possible.

It remains to be seen whether this niche audience for news can provide a route to creating a transnational public. The original French government policy of pushing back "Anglo-Saxon" dominance in the international news market failed on two counts. First, effective control shifted to London, although production is still located in Lyons in France. Second, ITN reshaped the company along the lines of what its British managers see as good journalism. Will British-influenced practice therefore increasingly provide the common idiom for increasingly large segments of the continental European viewing public, competing with national stations?

The European Communicative Space

How might we now think about the EU's changing communicative space? First, the core of the emergent European political class and the business elite do have a number of print media that they use intensively and variously. Second, despite the well-known complexities of language politics in the European Union, English already functions to a considerable extent as a lingua franca among elites. Third, a transnational market for information about the European space does exist—and not just in Europe. Arguably, that is because global business and political elites see the EU, and Europe more generally, as a distinct region within a global economy.

A distinct, complex Euro-polity that is generating multilevel forms of political communication that encompass lobbying, official information campaigns, and news reporting has emerged. There is no single, coherent European public arena, but rather an often contradictory field of political forces. Rather than imagine a European public sphere as the outcome of economic and political integration, we should think about the growth of interrelated spheres of European publics. How these will evolve is open to conjecture. However, what Keith Middlemass (1995) has called the "Euro-civilising" process may, in due course, knit these discursive spaces together. In the *longue durée*, a distinctive Euro-political culture that offers a potential focus for a new layer of political identity may develop. A necessary precondition for this, however, would be broad public engagement in European public affairs. Presently, at best, some European elites have begun to constitute a restricted communicative space.

Ideal-typically, Europe's *transnational citizens* would have (1) an equal and widespead level of communicative competence; (2) relatively easy access to the full range of the means of communication; and (3) a generalized communicative competence that embodies sufficient background knowledge, interest, and interpretative skills to make sense of the EU and its policy options and debates.

A hypothetical *European sphere of publics* would, among other things, (1) involve the dissemination of a European news agenda; (2) need to become a significant part of the everyday news-consuming habits of European audiences; and (3) require that those living within the EU have begun to think of their citizenship, in part at least, as transcending the level of the member nation-states.

In reality, in the process of media reception, any common European public agenda will be diversely "domesticated" within each distinctive national or language context (Gurevitch, Levy, and Roeh 1991). This does not foreclose the question of how national audiences might—in some significant respects—still be oriented toward a "European" frame of reference. We already have some nascent forms of "European" journalism. For this to contribute to the creation of a European public, it needs to find a mass, transnational audience that recognizes it as offering something distinct from national forms of reporting, with a different institutional focus and agenda from that of the individual member states. This journalism will have to interest and be significant for large numbers of Europe's citizens.

Public policy intervention to create a common European media space, or attempts to engage the public via official information, have not been a notable success. If pan-European media have begun to emerge in the press and in television—and these are still rare birds indeed—their market-seeking behavior has been the driving force. And if the news market is taking a "European" shape, and thereby helping to build a restricted communicative space for some, this has occurred because of the institutional framework of the European Union. The very existence of the emergent Euro-polity has created conditions for a transnational, elite media to develop. The result is that an elite conversation is now under way in the European space—and much of it is taking place in English.

Notes

This essay was originally published at greater length in *Political Communication* 16, no. 3 (1999). My thanks to the journal's editor, David Swanson, and to Alison Labatte of Taylor and Francis for permission to republish here. I am grateful to the UK's Economic and Social Research Council, whose grant no. L126251022 funded this research.

1 These are Austria, Belgium, Denmark, Finland, France, Germany, Greece, Ireland, Italy, Luxembourg, the Netherlands, Portugal, Spain, Sweden, and the United Kingdom.

2 It is also necessary to address the level *below* that of the nation-state that is being politically redefined by the EU's regional dynamic. For an analysis of Scotland, see Schlesinger (1998).

Works Cited

Anderson, Benedict. 1983. *Imagined Communities*. London: Verso.
Bartak, Karel. 1998. "Les institutions européennes sous influence." *Le Monde Diplomatique* 45: 12–13.
Billig, Michael. 1995. *Banal Nationalism*. London: Sage Publications.
Blumler, Jay G. 1983. *Communicating to Voters: Television in the First European Parliamentary Elections*. London: Sage Publications.
Calhoun, Craig. 1995. *Critical Social Theory*. Oxford: Blackwell.

————, ed. 1994. *Habermas and the Public Sphere.* Cambridge: MIT Press.

Castells, Manuel. 1996. *The Rise of the Network Society.* Malden, Mass.: Blackwell Publishers.

————. 1997. *The Power of Identity.* Malden, Mass.: Blackwell Publishers.

————. 1998. *End of Millennium.* Malden, Mass.: Blackwell Publishers.

Christiansen, Thomas. 1996. "A Maturing Bureaucracy? The Role of the Commission in the Policy Process." In *European Union,* ed. Jeremy Richardson. 77–95.

Collins, Richard. 1993. "Public Service Broadcasting by Satellite in Europe: Eurikon and Europa." *Screen* 34: 162–75.

Deutsch, Karl W. 1966. *Nationalism and Social Communication.* Cambridge: MIT Press.

Earnshaw, David, and David Judge. 1996. "From Co-operation to Co-decision: The European Parliament's Path to Legislative Power." In *European Union,* ed. Jeremy Richardson. 96–126.

Edwards, Geoffrey. 1996. "National Sovereignty vs Integration? The Council of Ministers." In *European Union,* ed. Jeremy Richardson. 127–47.

Eley, Geoff. 1994. "Nations, Publics and Political Cultures: Placing Habermas in the Nineteenth Century." In *Habermas and the Public Sphere,* ed. Craig Calhoun, 289–39.

Fraser, Nancy. 1994. "Rethinking the Public Sphere: A Contribution to the Critique of Actually Existing Democracy. In *Habermas and the Public Sphere,* ed. Craig Calhoun. 109–42.

Fundesco/AEJ. 1997. *The European Union in the Media 1996.* Madrid: Fundesco.

Gellner, Ernest. 1983. *Nations and Nationalism.* Oxford: Blackwell.

Gurevitch, Michael, Mark R. Levy, and Itzhak Roeh. 1991. "The Global Newsroom: Convergence and Diversities in the Globalisation of Television News." In *Communication and Citizenship,* ed. Peter Dahlgren and Colin Sparks. 195–216. London: Routledge.

Habermas, Jürgen. 1989. *The Structural Transformation of the Public Sphere.* Cambridge: Polity Press.

————. 1994. "Citizenship and National Identity." In *The Condition of Citizenship,* ed. Bart van Steenbergen, 20–35. London: Sage Publications.

————. 1997. *Between Facts and Norms.* Cambridge: Polity Press.

Hirst, Paul, and Grahame Thompson. 1996. *Globalization in Question.* Cambridge: Polity Press.

Hjarvard, Stig. 1993. "Pan-European Television News: Towards a European Public Sphere?" In *National Identity and Europe: The Television Revolution,* ed. P. Drummond, R. Paterson, and J. Willis, 71–94. London: British Film Institute.

Katzenstein, Peter J. 1996. "Regionalisation in Comparative Perspective." Working Paper 95/1. Oslo: ARENA.

Leroy, Pascale, and Karen Siune. 1994. "The Role of Television in European Elections: The Cases of Belgium and Denmark." *European Journal of Communication* 9: 47–69.

Machill, Marcel. 1998. "Euronews: The First European News Channel as a Case Study for Media Industry Development in Europe and for Spectra of Transnational Journalism Research." *Media, Culture and Society* 20: 427–50.

Mayhew, Leon H. 1997. *The New Public: Professional Communication and the Means of Social Influence.* Cambridge: Cambridge University Press.

Mazey, Sonia, and Jeremy Richardson. 1992. "British Pressure Groups in the European Union." *Parliamentary Affairs* 45: 92–107.

————. 1996. "The Logic of Organization: Interest Groups." In *European Union,* ed. Jeremy Richardson. 200–215.

Middlemass, Keith. 1995. *Orchestrating Europe: The Informal Politics of European Union, 1973–1995.* London: Fontana Press.

Miller, David, and Philip Schlesinger. 2000. "Public Relations and the EU: Changing Configurations." In *The Handbook of Public Relations*, ed. R. Heath, 675–83. London: Sage Publications.

Millward, Alan. 1994. *The European Rescue of the Nation-State.* London: Routledge.

Morgan, David. 1995. "British Media and European News." *European Journal of Communication* 10: 321–43.

Neil, Andrew. 1997. "The European: A Brief History [press release]." London: *The European*, June 12.

Research Services Ltd. 1995. "The Pan European Survey 6: The Results of the 1995 Fourteen Country Survey." Harrow: RSL.

———. 1996. "The European Business Readership Survey 1996." Harrow: RSL.

Richardson, Jeremy, ed. 1996. *European Union: Power and Policy-Making.* London and New York: Routledge.

Schlesinger, Philip. 1993. "Wishful Thinking: Cultural Politics, Media and Collective Identities in Europe." *Journal of Communication* 43: 6–17.

———. 1994. "Europe's Contradictory Communicative Space." *Daedalus* 123: 25–52.

———. 1998. "Scottish Devolution and the Media." In *Politics and the Media: Harlots and Prerogatives at the Turn of the Millennium*, ed. J. Seaton, 56–75. Oxford: Blackwell Publishers.

———. 2000. "The Nation and Communicative Space." In *Media Power, Professionals and Policies*, ed. H. Tumber, 99–115. London and New York: Routledge.

Sparks, Colin. 1998. "Is There a Global Public Sphere?" In *Electronic Empires: Global Media and Local Resistance*, ed. D. K. Thussu, 108–24. London and New York: Arnold.

Wincott, Daniel. 1996. "The Court of Justice and the European Policy Process." In *European Union*, ed. Jeremy Richardson. 170–99.

Wober, J. Mallory. 1987. "Voting in Europe: Television and Viewers' Involvement in the 1984 European Parliamentary Election." *European Journal of Communication* 2: 473–89.

4

Transatlantic Images of Belonging

Belonging needs to be reimagined because the world has changed. The nation-state is being hollowed out by global forces, making traditional national identities less and less adequate. That one response to such globalization has been the creation of narrow and vicious nationalisms lends to the task of reimagining considerable moral urgency. There is a good deal of sense to this implicit sociology, so reminiscent of Benjamin Barber's contrast between jihad and McWorld (Barber 1996), although vicious nationalism has perhaps been the norm rather than the exception within European history. In these circumstances, it makes sense to think about transatlantic images of belonging. Vast movements of people and capital, membership of international regimes, and the legacies of a single civilization almost dictate thinking about identities other than the national.

Basic mapping of the terrain to do with transatlantic images of belonging suggests considerations that run counter to the assumptions identified. Much depends on drawing a distinction between two senses of transatlantic belonging: on the one side is membership in a transatlantic political entity, whether formal or informal; on the other is a sense of belonging to a society other than that of the nation-state in which one resides. The first two parts of this essay offer some consideration of these two topics, with evidence being drawn from North America. Concluding comments offer more general reflections on global processes, the putative decline of the nation-state, and the position of the United States within the world's political economy.

Two conceptual points should be borne in mind. First, particular attention is paid to a broad range of social identities. The vast majority of social interactions in the historical record has been *local;* the creation of *national* patterns of interaction is accordingly quintessentially modern. Where national identity is passive, *nationalist* identity is active, especially because it has ideas about the proper conduct of geopolitics. The determination to establish that the nation has its proper "place in the sun" has led to conflict with those with *internationalist* identities. In late-nineteenth-century Europe, nationalists sought to control and cage foreign-policy-making elites whose behavior was held to be altogether too internationally responsible. International interaction and identity are—although this is not always appreciated—different from the truly *transnational* (Mann 1993). Second, a warning is in order about the celebrated notion of social construction. Everything in social life, and not just nationalism, is socially constructed. But to leave matters at this point can lead to licentious voluntarism, that is, to the implicit belief that anything can be constructed at any time. Nothing could be further from the truth: social structures limit and select ideological innovation. Attention here will be given to structural as much as to ideological forces.

Membership in Transatlantic Entities

The broad claim to be defended here is simple: membership within transatlantic political entities has declined quite markedly in the modern world. Let us consider formal transatlantic entities to begin with, in general terms and by means of a single example, and then turn to more recent, novel, informal arrangements. The latter have considerable importance but they need to be characterized properly.

Historians now pay much attention to the Atlantic society and economy of the early eighteenth century (e.g., Langley 1996). The first British empire was, unlike its later successor, very profitable, and the same was true for the early years of French and Spanish transatlantic structures of domination. The British case is especially interesting in the key matter that concerns us. The inhabitants of the colonies were distinctively British. This can be seen, for example, in the cultural patterning of the United States. Bernard Bailyn has demonstrated ideological continuity, whereas David Hackett Fischer's monumental work shows the re-creation in the

New World of very varied social patterns, from architecture and familial life to political attitudes and leadership styles (Bailyn 1968; Fischer 1989). More important, rebellion occurred in large part because of colonial loyalty to the ideals of the homeland. The move from being the best Englishmen to becoming Americans took place as the result of the conflict; it was consequence, not cause. The destruction of the Spanish and British transatlantic empires is generally best explained in terms of the limit to the logistics of rule imposed by geography and composite construction—although accidents (Britain fought without allies, Spain was debilitated by Napoleon) played some part. But the precise cause does not matter here. The analytic point is that belonging became national, nationalist, and international rather than transatlantic. Bluntly, this must be true: without this development, the novels of Henry James—to take an obvious example—would simply not make sense.

This point can be made with more force and sophistication by considering the history of Canada, certainly from Confederation in 1867 to the First World War and perhaps even to the 1960s. Here was a country with a state but without a national identity of its own. This is not to say that there was no sense of identity present within Canada. If Québécois identity was in large part inward-looking, the same is not true for the rest of Canada. Here identity had a predominantly transatlantic character, as firmly as was the case for the members of the American colonies in the early eighteenth century. The proof of loyalty was, of course, paid in blood, in the Boer War and still more so in two world wars. Three points are worth making about the working of this transatlantic entity (Cannadine 1997). First, the economic development of Canada, the shipping lines and the railways, depended on capital provided by London. More than 70 percent of the 500 million pounds sterling absorbed between 1900 and 1914 came from Britain. Second, Canada provided job opportunities for the highest level of the metropolitan aristocracy. One governor-general, Lord Lorne, was Queen Victoria's son-in-law, another, the Duke of Connaught, was her favorite son. Third, the imperial connection allowed for quite remarkable social mobility for colonials within the metropolis. Two examples make this point. Consider first Donald Alexander Smith, who arrived in Canada a penniless Scot in 1838. For twenty-six years he worked in the Hudson's Bay Company. He then moved to Montreal and became a major figure in the Canadian Pacific Railway and in national politics. In 1895, already long past seventy, he became the official representative of Canada in London, where he died in 1914—to the considerable irritation of Sir Frederick Borden, the famous

Minister of Militia and Defence who had sought to succeed him (Miller 1997). Smith piled up colossal wealth, was ennobled as Lord Strathcona and Mount Royal, and lived in great state on both sides of the Atlantic. He was chancellor of McGill University; he equipped at his own cost a troop of horses during the Boer War; he presided in London at an annual banquet each July 1 to celebrate Canadian Confederation; and he spent forty thousand pounds sterling to celebrate his Lord Rectorship of Aberdeen University. A second case is that of William Maxwell Aitken. Within a decade of his arrival in Britain, Aitken was a member of Parliament, a baronet, a peer, the owner of *Express* newspapers, and the friend and confidant of that other Canadian, Andrew Bonar Law—who became prime minister (in contrast to Aitken himself, whose highest political post was that of Minister of Aircraft Production in 1940). The causes to which Aitken was attracted—empire free trade in the 1930s and opposition to entry into the Common Market, together with deep antipathy to Lord Mountbatten on the grounds that he gave away India, the jewel of the empire as a whole—were characteristic of this transatlantic world. Bluntly, he loved the British empire more than did the British themselves.

The historic pattern has scarcely completely ended. An old joke about Pierre Trudeau had it that the history of Canada would have been very different had he taken his theory of nationalism from Ernest Gellner rather than from Elie Kedourie while he was a student at the London School of Economics. Equally, such contemporary public intellectuals as Michael Ignatieff and James Tully gained much of their intellectual capital at the University of Cambridge. Still, the analytic point to be made remains the same as for the first British and the Spanish Atlantic empires. This transatlantic entity has by and large come to an end. There is at least a Canadian national anthem (or, rather, two of them), the constitution has (at last for every province except Quebec) been repatriated, and it would not be surprising were a republican movement to arise in the future to echo the one that is now making inroads in Australia. Perhaps the general point is best made with reference to two contemporary figures. James Tully— another contributor to this volume—is not a Briton who happens to be living in Canada. Although he doubtless has multiple identities, it looks as if his strongest desire is to create a new, sophisticated, open, and tolerant Canadian national identity; in the final analysis, his identity is not transatlantic, but international, national, and occasionally nationalist. Conrad Black, the owner of Britain's *Daily Telegraph*, illuminates matters by sheer contrast. His status as Aitken's presumptive heir seemed assured in 1999 when the British government offered him a peerage. But the Canadian government (whose prime minister has reason to dislike the newspaper tycoon) refused to allow him, as a Canadian citizen, to accept this honor. National identity has trumped this transatlantic political entity.

Informal transatlantic identities have made an impact on the historical record. International relations scholars like to point to the transfer of power between Britain and the United States at the end of the nineteenth century as perhaps the sole example of a peaceful hegemonic transition within the history of the world polity. This transition was certainly eased by geography, but it depended on shared liberal norms (Doyle 1983)—and perhaps still more on shared Anglo-Saxon habit (Mann 1993). Kipling lived in Vermont for a long period, knew Mahan and Teddy Roosevelt, and eventually felt as at home with the key figures in Great Britain's military apparatus, Lords Fisher and Esher. This background transatlantic identity did a great deal to allow for the creation of a strategy to counter imperial Germany. A division of military labor meant in particular that Britain could concentrate on designing plans to bottle up the German fleet so as to starve the German population into submission (Offer 1989).

Is there any more recent equivalent to this situation? The least that can be said about the Atlantic community was that an attempt was made to create an extensive transatlantic identity (see Schaeper and Schaeper 1998). All those CIA-funded Congresses for Cultural Freedom sought to cement a shared identity, an enterprise in a sense personified in the vigorous figure of Edward Shils, resident for most of his life half a year in Chicago and half a year at the University of Cambridge. Still, how extensive and deep was this identity? Identities habitually involve some sort of mix between interest and affect. Is emotional attachment as strong in the Atlantic community as it was among Anglo-Saxons at the turn of the last century? Let us consider the most powerful transatlantic link—the "special relationship" between the United States and Great Britain—before characterizing the nature of the Atlantic community as a whole.

One of the earliest architects of the special relationship was Winston Churchill. The fact that his mother was American lends authenticity to the notion of a transatlantic identity. Still, his behavior as First Lord of the Admiralty and as prime minister had at its core the pragmatic desire to extend *British* power by means of the American connection. Calculation seems stronger still in Harold Macmillan's celebrated words to Richard Crossman while attached to Eisenhower's headquarters in Algiers in 1942: "[We] are the Greeks in this American empire. You will find the Americans much as the Greeks found the Romans—great big, bustling people, more vigorous than we are and also more idle, with more unspoiled virtues but also more corrupt. We must run [this headquarters] as the Greek slaves ran the operations of the Emperor Claudius" (Horne 1988, 160). This same vein was struck by Keynes, when commenting to his staff before beginning meetings about the British loan, "they may have all the money, but we've got all the brains."[1]

If we turn to continental European cases, the air of calculation rather than of shared identity comes to the fore. As an intellectual, Raymond Aron, despite his intelligence and carefully nurtured American relationships, was first and foremost French. In more political terms, the "empire by invitation" that is NATO resulted from the famous calculation, coined by Lord Ismay, that it was necessary "to keep the Russians out, the Americans in and Germany down" (Lundestad 1986). A similar point must be made about the nature of transatlantic relations in general, to whose characterization we can now turn.

Nationalist geopolitics in the period from 1870 to 1945 produced genuine anarchy in the international system. In these conditions, it made sense to grab territory; nationalism became inextricably linked with imperialism, for only extensive territory could secure supplies and markets. The resolution of Europe's security dilemma after 1945 broke this connection. A very particular transatlantic society was created. There are now frequent meetings of the leaders of the Atlantic states, but key transatlantic (and international) institutions are dominated in the last resort by the leading power. This is obviously true of NATO, whose commanding officer is, has been, and, it is safe to say, always will be an American. Europeans have realized that the United States has solved its security dilemma, has occasionally shared anticommunist attitudes, and is well aware that the benefit of being geopolitically supine is its considerable affluence. Nonetheless, the fact that interest in international cooperation is not any automatic or unquestioning transatlantic identity can be seen in endless quibbles and in pervasive anti-Americanism. Still, the pretense is that of community, and so it hurts—especially in London—when the United States acts unilaterally, as it does whenever anything of consequence to its own interests is at stake.

The most striking recent portrait of American–European relations, that of Steven Walt's "The Ties That Fray" (1998–99), suggests that interests have now diverged to such an extent as to destroy any continuing sense of community. It is certainly true that trade between the United States and Europe is not great (with the United States alone having the option of isolationism), and that economic interests, both in agriculture and in communicative technologies, diverge sharply. All of this will lead, and in the eyes of commentators in addition to Walt, to an economic challenge spearheaded by the new euro. Further, Europeans calculate the threats in the Middle and Near East in a manner all their own, and clearly resent being subject to American meddling—with the same applying with still greater force in cultural affairs. Despite the cogency of these points, Walt seems to me to be quite wrong. Given that calculation rather than community ruled in the first instance, there is more evidence of continuity than he allows. There is no sign of any real challenge to the United States, and a good deal to suggest the exact opposite. Who would have predicted, for example, that France would effectively rejoin NATO—a move calculated to balance united Germany by strengthening the American involvement? Does anybody really think it likely that Europe's status as economic giant and military worm will change? Has not the timing of actions in the former Yugoslavia been dependent, for better and for worse, on what happens in Washington? And is it really likely that the euro, which at this writing seems so weak, can triumph over the dollar, when the United States remains the provider of geopolitical security?

Transatlantic political entities are weaker than they once were. On the one hand, formal political entities have disappeared. On the other hand, the large element of calculation in transatlantic relations means that the taken-for-granted quality inherent in the very notion of identity is somewhat lacking.[2] Still, this diminished condition looks, in the absence of any alternative, rather durable. But this is a first approximation; more will be said about the United States in the next section.

Belongings beyond One's Nation-State

A proper investigation of images of belonging to social worlds outside one's own state or nation-state would, of course, be vast. An enormous amount could be said about the images of the other held by people, differentially divided by class, religion, and ethnicity, on different sides of the Atlantic. Much has little to do with belonging. Still less prominent is accuracy of perception. One can only feel loathing, for instance, for much BBC drama, so often featuring effete members of the aristocracy, that is produced for American consumption. This makes a good deal of money, and justifies American views of the backwardness of Britain—but at the expense of any sense of what actually happens in that country. Other images do have much more to do with a sense of belonging, not least among American intellectuals who dream of the Café Flore. However, rather than concentrate on such images, let me raise the bar higher and ask not just about dreams, but about what might be called networks of interaction—by which is meant those belongings that affect actions rather than dreams.

There is nothing novel about the presence of networks of interaction that transcend borders. In medieval Europe, the larger identities of feudalism and of Christianity for centuries transcended states; similar points can be made about most of the world religions, and intellectuals often have more allegiance to their fellows than to the state in which they live. Still, the standard generalization of historical sociology has been that the rise of the nation-state has increasingly caged social interactions within its borders. This has overwhelmingly been true of the means of violence: there have been few Wallensteins since the seventeenth century, although it is true that the career of Juan Perón cannot be understood without knowledge of his period of residence in fascist Europe. In the period between 1870 and, say, 1958, capitalists were similarly caged, although I will argue later that their subsequent release is not as great as is often imagined—and that, at least in Europe, it results less from the defeat of the state than from deliberate state design. Bearing these points in mind, let us concentrate on peoples. Is it the case that the classical immigrant experience—in which one assimilated, at considerable cost, to the host national culture—has come to an end? Are diasporas now so well connected by cheap travel and the Internet that homogeneous national entities can no longer be created? This brings us to key theoretical debates. How much of the ideas of postnationalism and of multiculturalism should we accept?

Certainly there are cases where the extensive search of a diaspora matters for very practical reasons, as most obviously was and is true for the overseas Chinese—many of whom live in genuinely multicultural settings. Is there any transatlantic equivalent? Let us consider Europe and the United States.

At the end of the nineteenth century, the United States was the stuff of which dreams were made, both for peasants in Central and southern Europe and for the persecuted from regions further to the east. Histories of immigration show that there was much more movement back than we now realize, with perhaps 50 percent of Italians who came to the United States returning when economic conditions proved too adverse. This is evidence of an extensive network before the era of modern communications, although it is far from sure that this amounted to a genuine transatlantic identity. Irish immigration to the United States since the 1970s has had a similar character. But the fact is that Europe no longer provides the bulk of immigrants to the United States. American racism, of course, closed off southern and eastern Europe in 1924. More important, most of the nation-states of Europe have made themselves attractive places in which to live, with industrialization now capable of absorbing populations once forced to migrate. Tourism to the United States from across the Atlantic booms, but a transatlantic identity based in Europe does not seem in the cards.

Certainly there are cases in North America where an image of transatlantic belonging matters. Capital, the human capital of the young trained in computer technology, and political leadership have come, with varying degrees of benefit, to the Baltics and to the Balkans from the United States. But we need to be careful before saying that transatlantic belongings are generally strong and on the increase. First, what is at issue at times is longing rather than belonging: for instance, the Québécois often feel rejected and jilted by the French, who rarely go to live in Quebec—often preferring to make jokes about the Québécois accent. Second, the images of belonging are imaginary, and the process of imagining distinctively reflects American culture rather than any primordial identity. The spaghetti with meatballs that marks Italian-American culture is unknown in Italy; more important, the support given by Irish-Americans to NORAID was often an extreme embarrassment to Irish citizens, among them the members of the rock band U2—who famously and very bravely criticized their "fellows" in this regard. Third, transatlantic identities are simply not present at all in key circumstances. That is true, for instance, with the emergence of nonethnic white Americans, present in striking numbers in the Midwest, who no longer make any pretense at having a transatlantic identity. More controversially, it is worth pointing out the huge difference that exists between African-Americans and Afro-Americans. Except for some very striking exceptions, it is by and large true to say that Afro-Americans have no particular loyalty or link to Africa. Evidence shows that Afro-Americans share mainstream American values, and wish for nothing more than to be full members of their own society— making it all the more cruel, of course, that they cannot gain proper entry into mainstream American society.

Let us consider the United States in more detail, not least as this society, the largest and most powerful in the transatlantic world, is the source of recent claims about multiculturalism and postnationality. Diversity was once much greater in the United States than it is today. On the one hand, the United States in 1920 boasted 276 newspapers in German, 118 in Spanish or Portuguese, 111 in Scandinavian languages, 98 in Italian, 76 in Polish, 51 in Czech or Slovak, 46 in French, 42 in Slovenian, and 39 in

Yiddish—together with the genuinely different culture of the solid South (Lind 1995, 75). All of this has of course disappeared. On the other hand, Mary Waters has demonstrated both that ethnicity is no longer a cage, but rather an option—one, it should be noted, that has astonishingly little actual substance (Waters 1990). This is not to say that the constructed identity is not somehow real and important: to the contrary, to have an ethnic identity is now almost a constitutional right. But the point about the politics of difference is that so many people are demanding recognition: that so many ask for the same thing is a demonstration of the continuing powers of American nationalizing homogeneity—for all but Afro-Americans (Hall and Lindholm 1999). Furthermore, difference is entertained only so far as it is, so to speak, toilet-trained and American: it is fine to express one's Asian background by wearing a sari when graduating from high school—but only on the condition that one does not take caste seriously. As this view is contentious, not to say unpopular, it is worth justifying. Research on Hispanics, for example, shows that they are no different from previous immigrants: Cuban-Americans in Florida have out-marriage rates of above 50 percent within a single generation, together with a set of attitudes in tune with those of the larger society.[3] Perhaps this should not be surprising. It remains the case that immigrants are attracted to the United States because of the opportunities for social mobility that an ever more powerful and nationally integrated capitalist culture offers. If that is to say that the immigrants who come to the United States are self-selected in such a way as to reinforce core American beliefs, there should be no gainsaying of the other side of the picture. A stump speech directed against Ann Richards when she was running to be governor of Texas had it that "If English is good enough for Jesus Christ, it is good enough for Texas." Poll evidence shows high levels of opposition in the United States to any general recognition of a second official language; the votes against such recognition in California are thus entirely representative of strong external pressures placed on immigrants (Wolfe 1998). All of this can be summarized in the starkest possible terms: no real transatlantic identity will develop from the United States, which will remain a great engine for creating Americans.

Conclusion: The Globe, the Nation-State, and the United States

This essay began by noting the prominence of a general sociological view in which the nation-state is held to have been hollowed out both from above and from below. It may be useful to end by making some general points about this, not least in view of my own skepticism about this position. Some cursory comments about the globe, the nation-state, and the United States should give cause for thought.

We should not all be globalizers now for a number of reasons (Hall 2000). First, trading patterns go against any naive view of the globe as the key economic unit (Wade 1996). World trade has only just regained the level of 1913, with most of the increase since 1945 resulting most of all from the removal of tariffs within Europe. Further, between 1970 and 1990 the share of the North within world trade increased from 81 percent to 84 percent; importantly, the United States trades only 12 percent of its GDP—with only 3 percent of its GDP being involved with the developing world. Second, foreign direct investment patterns show both that external investments—small as a proportion of home capital—go largely to the North rather than to the South. Third, the most striking research on firms suggests that we should speak of NFIOs rather than TNCs or MNCs—of national firms with international operations rather than transnational or multinational corporations. Profits are still repatriated to the home base, with management reflecting national ownership more and more strongly as one mounts the corporate ladder. Fourth, technological innovation, measured by research and development spending and the taking of patents, continues to reflect the historical differences of nation-states. Fifth, restrictions on labor, to some extent in the United States, but much more so in Europe, look set to increase, while those of Japan do not look as if they are about to diminish: it is this evidence that makes me doubt the case for postnationalism. To be set against all this, of course, is the undoubted speed with which money now flows around the world. But here too reservations are in order: stock markets remain very largely national, while the floating of currencies reflects the interests of the United States quite as much as any global logic of its own.

We should be equally cautious when assessing the powers of the nation-state. States within capitalism have rarely had and have rarely sought total control over their destinies. Historical awareness makes one realize that states are very adaptable, with the loss of power in one arena often being compensated for by an increase elsewhere—as is the case now, for the penetrative power of the state is increasing for all that some monetary powers are being abandoned. Are European states less powerful now that they have been humbled by the attempts made between 1870 and 1945 to become total power containers? Is not less more? Exactly how many states are really challenged seriously from below? Were not the great secessionist drives of the last years directed only against the last great empire, that of the Soviet Union? The European Union has depended at all times on the motor of the Franco-German alliance—something that suggests that the future of the Union is likely to remain international rather than trans-national (Milward 1992). If the nation-state is still present in Europe, where one can at least argue about new forces, there is little likelihood of it suddenly collapsing in the case of the United States or Japan. The only place where states are collapsing is in sub-Saharan Africa. This demon-strates how provincial much Western commentary is when speaking about the state: much of the world needs the powers of the state to increase.

The final general point is implicit in much of what has been said al-ready. A measure of order in the world comes from the re-creation of inter-national society. But behind that remains the huge powers of the most powerful state the world has yet seen. In retrospect, it is clear that the de-bate about American decline was utterly misconceived. Only the United States has military, cultural, monetary, economic, and ideological force of primary weight in the contemporary world. One sign of the supremacy of the United States is the fact that it has the ability to run a continual trade imbalance with the rest of the world. The current account of the United States is balanced by borrowing most of the excess capital of the world economy. Such capital is available, it has been argued (Wade and Veneroso 1998), because of the American insistence on the opening of financial markets—an opening, it should be noted, that helped to cause, and certainly to exacerbate, the Asian crisis of the late 1990s. This suggests a final thought. The inhabitants of the Beltway do not really possess any transatlantic iden-tity, thereby making traditional realist concepts all too relevant. But the fact that much of the motion of modernity is now determined, for better or worse, in Washington means that it behooves Europeans to have a trans-atlantic awareness (and much of the rest of the world to have international awareness)—even though they lack much sense of transatlantic belonging.

Notes

1 I heard this story from James Meade. Though I have learned a great deal from Kevin Phillip's *The Cousins Wars* (1999), the thesis of that book—that there is a unit-ed Anglo-America—is not convincing for a simple reason, namely, that there have been many occasions when the United States has chosen to act alone. This was true of the shaping of the postwar architecture of the international economy with which Keynes was involved. Equally, Margaret Thatcher was apparently only told about the bombing raid on Libya when American planes were airborne.
2 It should be emphasized that pure affective identity can and does matter in contem-porary Europe. The most obvious example is the desire of many citizens in Central Europe to "rejoin Europe."

3 This figure is drawn from the unpublished research of Elizabeth Arias, Department
of Sociology, State University of New York at Stony Brook.

Works Cited

Bailyn, Bernard. 1968. *The Origins of American Politics.* New York: Vintage Books.
Barber, Benjamin. 1996. *Jihad vs. McWorld: How Globalism and Tribalism are Reshaping the World.* New York: Ballantine Books.
Cannadine, David. 1997. "Imperial Canada: Old History, New Problems." In *Imperial Canada, 1867–1917,* ed Colin Coates, 1–19. Edinburgh: Centre for Canadian Studies.
Doyle, Michale. 1983. "Kant: Liberal Legacies and Foreign Affairs." *Philosophy and Public Affairs* 12:3–4: 205–35 and 323–53.
Fischer, David Hackett. 1989. *Albion's Seed.* Oxford: Oxford University Press.
Hall, John A. 2000. "Nationalism and Globalization." *Thesis 11* 63: 63–79.
Hall, John A., and Charles Lindholm. 1999. *Is America Breaking Apart?* Princeton, N.J.: Princeton University Press.
Horne, Alastair. 1988. *Harold Macmillan.* Vol. 1, *1894–1956.* New York: Viking Press.
Langley, David. 1996. *The Americas in the Age of Revolution, 1750–1850.* New Haven: Yale University Press.
Lind, Michael. 1995. *The Next American Nation: The New Nationalism and the Fourth American Revolution.* New York: Free Press.
Lundestad, Geir. 1986. "Empire by Invitation? The United States and Western Europe, 1945–1952." *Journal of Peace Research* 23: 263–77.
Mann, Michael. 1993. *The Sources of Social Power.* Vol. 2, *The Rise of Classes and Nation-States.* Cambridge: Cambridge University Press.
Miller, Carman. 1997. "Sir Frederick Goes to London: Money, Militia and Gentlemanly Capitalists." In *Imperial Canada, 1867–1917,* ed. Colin Coates, 155–65. Edinburgh: Centre for Canadian Studies.
Milward, Alan. 1992. *The European Rescue of the Nation-State.* Berkeley: University of California Press.
Offer, Avner. 1989. *The First World War: An Agrarian Interpretation.* Oxford: Oxford University Press.
Phillips, Kevin. 1999. *The Cousins Wars: Religion, Politics and the Triumph of Anglo-America.* New York: Basic Books.
Schaeper, Thomas, and Kathleen Schaeper. 1998. *Cowboys and Gentlemen: Rhodes Scholars, Oxford and the Creation of an American Elite.* Leamington Spa: Berg.
Wade, R. 1996. "Globalization and Its Limits: Reports on the Death of the National Economy Are Greatly Exaggerated." In *National Diversity and Global Capitalism,* ed. S. Berger and R. Dore, 60–88. Ithaca, N.Y.: Cornell University Press.
Wade, R., and Frank Veneroso. 1998. "The Gathering World Slump and the Battle over Capital Controls." *New Left Review* 231: 13–42.
Walt, Steven. 1998–99. "The Ties That Fray: Why Europe and America Are Drifting Apart." *National Interest* 54: 3–11.
Waters, Mary. 1990. *Ethnic Options.* Berkeley: University of California Press.
Wolfe, Alan. 1998. *One Nation, After All.* New York: Viking Press.

5

Transnational Corporations? Perhaps.

Global Identities? Probably Not!

This essay considers the impact of globalization on social life, and its implications for social identification. Putting to one side questions about the antiquity or novelty of globalization—although on balance those arguments that emphasize its premodern historical roots seem to be the most plausible (Frank and Gills 1993; Robertson 1992; Waters 1995)—there is considerable consensus among social scientists and other commentators about what globalization means.

Regardless of whether it is understood as abrupt and very recent, or gradual and longer term, globalization represents at least a partial qualitative break with past social experiences and social realities. In this respect, as a package of developments it is generally understood as one of the characteristic features of late modernity (or even, depending on one's tastes in this matter, postmodernity). It is also important to emphasize that it is a package. Globalization, rather than a single process, is the cumulative interaction of a number of analytically distinct, but utterly interrelated, developments.

The earliest of these was probably the emergence of an internationalized economic order, encompassing finance, trade, production, marketing, and ownership or control. This was followed by the development of an internationalized political system in response to problems and risks that transcended the interests of individual states. Technological, economic, and political changes led to an increase in the volume, speed, and reach of individual and collective spatial mobility. With rapid technological innovation there has been a dramatic expansion of the power, speed, and volume of information transfers. Finally, there has been burgeoning sociocultural homogeneity or convergence, particularly with respect to consumption patterns, media of communication, and institutions and policies.

The recent academic discourse that might be called "globalization studies" attaches particular significance to the last three developments as marking the qualitative break between what went before, and what is happening now. Thus globalization does not just mean the greater geopolitical compression of the world, or the increased interdependence of its component parts—political economists and students of international relations have, after all, been talking about both for decades—but an increasing awareness, everywhere, of compression and interdependence, and of their snowballing everyday significance. Even political economists of globalization recognize the significance of these developments:

> If, previously, global integration in the sense of a growing unification and interpenetration of the human condition was driven by the logic of capital accumulation, today it is the unification of the human condition that drives the logic of capital accumulation. (Hoogvelt 1997, 121)

When the political economists of the 1960s first began to elaborate models of a world system (Baran and Sweezy 1966; Cockcroft, Frank, and Johnson 1972; Wallerstein 1974), one of their central concerns was the place of multinational corporations in the international political and economic order. The subsequent shift in emphasis, from "the political economy of the world-system" to "globalization," was in part the result of a marked cultural turn in critical social science, and in part a recognition—pace Marshall McLuhan—of the rapidity and significance of the information technology revolution. However, a concern with, and about, multinational—or, in recent globalization-speak, *transnational*—corporations has remained. Of particular interest for this discussion is the suggestion that transnational corporations, and organizations more broadly defined, may be a significant institutional arena within which globalized identities are beginning to be established.

In this vein, Reich (1991), while making a strong case for the continued importance of the nation, observed that although every transnational corporation has a "nominal nationality"—a historical homeland, a head office, a flag of convenience, or whatever—their strategies and everyday activities exhibit determined "transnationality." Castells, noting the same trend, offered an interpretation that suggested the gradual development of new institutional arenas (1996, 192):

> Multinational enterprises seem to be still highly dependent on their national basis. The idea of transnational corporations being "citizens of the world economy" does not seem to hold. Yet the networks formed by multinational corporations do transcend national boundaries, identities and interests. . . . as the process of globalization progresses, organizational forms evolve from *multinational enterprises* to *international networks*, actually by-passing the so-called "transnationals" that belong more to the world of mythical representation (or self-serving image-making by management consultants) than to the institutionally-bounded realities of the world economy.

Although even the most plausible candidates for authentic transnationality—Murdoch's media empire, for example (Castells 1997, 254–59)—*have* to pay attention to the national contexts in which they operate, perhaps the most important point is that all capitalist organizations are only contingently confined within nation-states: "From its very beginnings capitalism is international in scope" (Giddens 1990, 57). Capitalism, by its nature, is no respecter of national boundaries or sentiments. Whether this implies internationality, multinationality, or transnationality depends on one's point of view, and may be more a matter of terminology than of substantial theoretical disagreement.

That organizational membership is an important dimension of collective and individual social identification (Jenkins 1996, 139–53) has some interesting possible implications. Hannerz, for example, contemplating the possible "withering away of the nation," asks whether transnational corporations can become a source of transnational identities (1996, 81–90). He suggests that face-to-face relationships are among the most likely sources of emergent transnational identities, and that relationships with colleagues and business associates are among the more significant of these relationships. The organization of employment also contributes: "Transnational cultures today tend to be more or less clear-cut occupational cultures (and are often tied to trans-national job markets)" (ibid., 106).

Hannerz is envisaging the commercial or industrial equivalent of Friedman's cosmopolitan intellectual elite of cultural theorists and commentators (Friedman 1997), or the worldwide "epistemic communities" of technical and other specialists who are increasingly employed in identifying "global" problems and formulating responses to them (Haas 1990). Some reflexivity about our own participation in these transnational communities or networks, and the distorting impact it might have on our analytic perspectives, seems appropriate.

With respect to whether we are witnessing a movement toward a *global* community or culture, supporting authentically global identities, Hannerz seems to conclude with a no, but also, perhaps more significantly, a cautious yes:

> The nation and its culture, however, is not being replaced by any single "transnational culture.". . . But I think it is a process of the piecemeal, the disjointed, and the frequently unplanned (but sometimes planned), on variously large and small scales, which we can already observe. (1996, 90)

Taking a slightly different tack, Sklair, addressing the decline of the nation-state and the emergence of transnational practices "that cross state boundaries but do not necessarily originate with state agencies or actors" (1998b, 2), is less tentative. He identifies an emergent but nonetheless definite global identity in the shape of an elite "transnational capitalist class," a socially interlocking network of transnational corporation executives, commercial elites, and globalizing bureaucrats and politicians, whose members move in and out of, and between, business and government. As the "transnational managerial class," this social network was originally identified, although not mapped out in detail, by Cox, more than fifteen years earlier (1981, 147–48).

Organizational membership is not, however, the only possible contribution that capitalist corporations can, in principle, make to the globalization of identification. They are, for example, the major producers and suppliers of the trademarked and designered accessories of identification— everything from clothes to soft drinks to cars—that constitute perhaps the most visible dimension of global cultural homogeneity and convergence. "Grunge" youth styles are no less diagnostic here than the international chic of airport duty-free shopping centers. Inasmuch as individual and collective identification occurs "in the head" as well as on the body or the street, the globalization of the mass media of information and entertainment is of major significance. Among the other things that these media do is place styles such as grunge and international chic in the widest possible circulation. Finally, large-scale capitalism exports its distinctive ways of working—I nearly said "relations of production"—as well as its products. These ways of working include packages of occupations, jobs, and positions and hierarchies, all of which are in themselves constitutive of social identification. Selling burgers in Boise, Idaho, has much in common these days with selling burgers in Red Square or Soweto (Ritzer 1993, 1997).

However, and firmly against any suggestion that cultural convergence and homogenization constitute an unproblematic procession toward a single global culture-identity complex, identification is not a top-down process of imposition, but always a dialectic involving agency, imagination, and resistance (Jenkins 1996). People do not passively accept and consume either style or message. That the reality of the situation is likely to be resistant to simplification,

> should not suggest to us that cultural power does not exist, or that the American-dominated international media have no effect whatever—rather it should alert us to the complexity of the modes in which cultural power is both exercised and resisted. (Morley and Robins 1995, 224)

With respect to the ubiquitous burger, McDonald's, for example, does not have everything its own transnational way: the years 1999–2000 saw a vigorous popular campaign of direct action against new McDonald's restaurants in provincial France. Furthermore, ethnographic studies from East Asia document how local practices and values influence the reception and utilization of franchised, apparently standardized fast-food outlets, their employment practices, and, necessarily, their menus and marketing (Watson 1997). Meaning is not as easily imposed as method.

Transnational Corporations?

Even so, it appears that transnational corporations may encourage the formation of global identities. However, is there a meaningful generic category of the "transnational corporation," in any other than the broadest of senses, such as the United Nations' definition: "an enterprise which controls assets such as factories, mines, sales offices and so on in two or more countries" (Bougrine 1999, 1176)? This seems to be little more than an old-fashioned multinational. Transnationality, if it is to mean anything, ought to imply more than that, something genuinely transcending the nation-state. As Castells argues, it is not clear that "transnational" is a useful expression at all, that there is a species of inter-national corporation that is "more multinational" than the multinational. For this reason, I will sidestep definitional distinctions between multi- and transnational corporations, and use the two expressions interchangeably.

Furthermore, to talk about corporations in general, rather than the details of what specific corporations are up to, can encourage a neglect of the social processes and historical contexts within which these organizations and organs of economic life—effectively capitalism—operate and develop, and from which they acquire their meaning and *their* identities. Acknowledging that identity is really a process—*identification*—rather than a thing, further encourages this point of view. It may, therefore, be useful to typologize multi- or transnational corporate *activity* (rather than organizational form or structure), according to historical and social context, and the enterprise—in the sense of project—in question.

Colonial or imperial commerce offers perhaps the earliest model. The expansionist states of Western Europe used commercial companies—in the British case, the East India Company and the Hudson's Bay Company (not to forget the London Company during the Plantation of Ulster) come immediately to mind—as a means of offsetting the economic risks of empire while maintaining some political control and imperial presence. These were corporations to which government and empire were effectively subcontracted. A version of this system persists today, in modern corporate monopolies on primary extractive industries or large-scale monocultural agriculture in what is still euphemized as "the developing world"; witness recent U.S. trade disputes with the European Union—remember the expression "banana republic"?—or the controversial relationship between Shell Oil and the Nigerian state.

Transport presents another kind of distinctive transnational business opportunity. In premodern Europe and Asia, mercantile houses had some interest in organizing travel and transport, but it was only from the nineteenth century onwards that one sees, frequently in various imperial contexts, the increasing conglomeration and actual incorporation of international shipping in particular. The development of railways and, in the twentieth century, practical aviation opened up further markets and possibilities that capitalism rushed to exploit. From the earliest period, the movement of goods and people offered potential for international investment and organization. Through companies such as American Express and Thomas Cook's, it also organized tourism as a particular perspective on the world (Urry 1990).

One of the characteristic ways in which transnational transport was incorporated was through *foreign direct investment*, one of the defining hallmarks of the "classic" multinational firm. Money with its corporate source in state A is exported, to establish plant or other moneymaking facilities, managed by locally incorporated subsidiaries, in state B (the income reverting, of course, to the home organization in state A). The management personnel of the local subsidiaries are also, to some extent, exported. This very basic definition does not, for example, capture subtleties such as getting state B to underwrite a large slice of the costs of the plant or facility in question, but it will do for the moment. The end product is a hierarchical international network of corporate subsidiarity and control organized around the repatriation of investment and the expropriation of profit. The origins of this form of multi- or transnational enterprise can be dated to the second half of the nineteenth century: Singer, for example, established its first overseas sewing machine factory in Glasgow in 1867.

Along with all of this went the *internationalization of finance*. Indeed, without successful international finance—in the first place, the capacity to transcend national currencies through mechanisms of secure transfer and exchange—large-scale travel and foreign direct investment would probably never have developed. Small-scale international finance did exist in the premodern world, and the present system can trace some of its origins to those merchant and banking houses, but from the eighteenth century onwards came the development of modern banks, and eventually of an international system that not only guaranteed exchange, but also treated money as tradable in its own right. This system, spectacularly encouraged by recent developments in information technology, has allowed an exponential expansion of transnational markets and finance corporations. There is a perpetual and growing tension between these globalized markets and corporations and the role of national governments as guarantors of sound money, perhaps best epitomized by the 1992–93 exchange-rate mechanism crisis.

In the late twentieth century, the McDonaldization thesis began to make sociological headlines (Ritzer 1993, 1997; Smart 1999). Building on Weber and Mannheim's theoretical discussions of rationalization and modernity, and the literature on Fordism and post-Fordism, Ritzer argues that social life globally is increasingly being organized according to principles of standardization, low-quality predictability, time management, control, and organizational flexibility that have reached their apex in the American mass fast-food industry. The relevance of the thesis here is that, globally, the kind of enterprise that Ritzer identifies has, typically, proliferated via *franchising systems*. Although McDonald's did not invent franchising, it has refined it into a system of control and mutual self-interest that has allowed it to offer a degree of product uniformity, and, most important, to garner fairly uniform profits, on a genuinely global basis without the need for massive foreign direct investment. McDonald's and similar companies are transnational corporations that lease expertise and product identities, in the shape of trademarks, to local subordinate partners globally. That these are their primary stocks-in-trade explains the considerable lengths they will go to in order to control their use and to defend customer confidence in them.

Finally, corporations can also function in international *coalition* or *federation* with each other. Here we return to the international networks identified by Castells: independent enterprises, engaged in similar or complementary activities in different nation states, cooperate in the global exploitation of markets or the satisfaction of reciprocal and mutual requirements, without merging identities, capital, or management. This has a history in transport—it has become a common strategy for airlines—but it can also be seen elsewhere. Other good examples can be found in financial services, aerospace, and automobile manufacture.

The preceding discussion is not an exhaustive guide to the varieties of transnational corporate activity, but it does cover the important bases (see Waters 1995). Looking at these activities, one might wish—along with Castells, and others—to question the degree to which the multinational has become the transnational. Are these corporations truly transcending the national? The answer is, probably no . . . and probably yes: in terms of the impact on their activities of national state powers, not yet; in terms of patterns of majority ownership and control, not yet, certainly in most cases; in terms of national loyalties, perhaps the best answer is that for most of these corporations, the matter has yet to be rigorously tested (although the attachments of individual senior executives—members of the transnational capitalist class identified by Sklair—may well be very flexible). But in terms of supply sourcing, production, marketing, financing, recruitment, and communication—in other words, many core corporate activities—nations, and all that they entail, have become probably not much more than one significant aspect of the wider business environment.

This, however, prompts further questions: *Which* nations? Does *transnational* corporate activity—even if the notion is taken at its most ambitious face value—equal *global*? Are transnational corporate activities evenly and ecumenically distributed around the globe? Or is the capitalist world-system effectively only part of the globe? Is "global" more an imaginative, ideological, or marketing expression than a spatial reality?

The answer depends on whether one focuses on the economic flows underwriting the corporate system or on its broader consequences. In economic terms, there seems little doubt that, rather than increasing and expanding global interdependence and connectedness, what is in fact happening is the steady deepening and widening of the gulf between core and periphery (Hirst and Thompson 1999). The great bulk of transnational corporate economic activity takes place between the nations of the core (which, although it has expanded slightly to accommodate new members, still includes a minority of the world's population). What is more, the evidence suggests that economic globalization may actually have gone into reverse since the apex of imperialism in the nineteenth century:

> An ambitious net of capitalist catchment may have been thrown during the colonial era, but having caught the fish it has pulled back and settled comfortably on the shores of a relatively small part of the world. (Hoogvelt 1997, 76–77)

However, in terms of the wider consequences of transnational corporate activity commonly described as "social" or "cultural," the picture is much less clear-cut. The globalizing impacts of travel and information technology are disproportionately enjoyed by the affluent populations of the metropolitan core: those who can afford them and have the leisure to enjoy them. Even so, what this *means* is unclear: neither tourism nor satellite television necessarily—or even often—broaden, let alone globalize, the mind. Nor is their contribution to the complexities of identification necessarily clear or straightforward. Most writers about globalization agree that

> Globalization and heightened localization . . . are inter-linked: the world is becoming smaller and larger at the same time, cultural space is shrinking and expanding. Localism and ethnicity are . . . two sides of the same coin, and each may (re)assert itself as a defensive reaction to, or a result of, the increasing global context of social life. (Jenkins 1997, 43)

Nor are business and tourist class the only ways to travel. Bauman (1998) has distinguished between *tourists* and *vagabonds*, between "moving through the world" and "the world moving by." If only in terms of numbers of bodies, labor migration is probably the most important human transfer between core and periphery. One of its consequences is the gradual establishment of what are becoming known as "transnational communities," linking core and periphery (Portes, Guarnizo, and Landolt 1999).

It is nonetheless true that versions—albeit impoverished versions— of Western consumerist culture can be encountered no matter where one travels. Cultural diffusion, to use an anthropologically old-fashioned term, is a reality (and analogies with the cargo cults of Melanesia and Micronesia might not be out of place: desire as well as harsh economic necessity are at work here). The arrival of Coca-Cola and McDonald's may not mean very much, but it does mean something. The arrival of the CNN crew means something too: "The whole world is watching" is more true today, although not necessarily more significant, than it was during the 1968 Democratic Convention in Chicago. The invasion of satellite dishes may be even more important, although the local meanings of exposure—

access is probably not the best word here—are a matter about which it is difficult to be confident.

Thus there is no easy equivalence between the *transnational* and the *global*, with respect to corporate activity. Although it appears that economic, political, and interpersonal relationships among the affluent 25 percent of the world's population are becoming ever more dense, multiplex, and *shared*, the same is not true for the other 75 percent, or between the richer and the poorer ends of the global spectrum. It might, therefore, be sensible to distinguish the *internationally extensive*—in whatever sphere of activity— from the *global*. Globalization is a complex of processes that are worked out, and have their meaning, at the local level, in the lives and networks of real people. And those real people in their local lives are still worlds apart.

Global Identities?

If it is important to look at the varieties of transnational corporate activity, and avoid reifying a gross category of "transnational corporations," it is no less necessary to take care in talking about "global identities." The expression trips easily off the tongue, but what might it actually mean? In the most general sense, there are two very different alternatives here.

The first encompasses the kinds of identities that Hannerz seems to have in mind as transnational. These are identifications that have currency and more or less cognate meanings all over the world. Many occupational identities are cases in point: teachers, police officers, and lawyers, for example, are recognizable job titles pretty much everywhere. This reflects the functional institutional convergences of nation-states around the world:

> nation-states have come to resemble each other more and more in their cultural forms. Which state today does not have certain standard political forms: a legislature, a constitution, a bureaucracy, trade unions, a national currency, a school system? . . . Even in the more particularistic arena of art forms, which country does not have its songs, its dances, its plays, its museums, its paintings, and today its skyscrapers? And are not the social structures that guarantee these art forms increasingly similar? (Wallerstein 1991, 93)

However, what it is to be a teacher, or a police officer, or a lawyer varies dramatically from nation-state to nation-state—sometimes even within states—in terms of status, economic reward, gender, the mundane tasks and responsibilities of the job, professional bodies of knowledge, occupational ideologies, and so on. We are talking about comparability of *institutional form* rather than *meaning*. All those who bear these titles do not necessarily identify with each other, inter- or transnationally, in anything other than the most superficial sense. These are typically social *categories* rather than self-conscious social *groups* (Jenkins 1996, 80–89).

With regard to transnational corporations, cosmopolitans, and epistemic communities, at least four occupations have some claim to global currency and scope, and where the meaning of the form is not specifically local. Let us call the first the *scientist*. Since the Enlightenment gave birth to it, science has always made claims to transnational universalism. It has also always cultivated a range of relationships with, and memberships in, the institutions of power and money. In the modern world, transnational corporations own, whether directly or indirectly, much science (and many scientists).

The second is the *international businessperson*. Largely transcending the local specificities of profession and status, the world of meetings, deals, contracts, schedules, delivery dates, and interpersonal confidence is virtually the same everywhere. The hotels—the most important environments for this kind of transnational practice—certainly are. These members of the transnational capitalist class constitute an emergent *self-conscious* social network and community of shared interests:

> Having its own ideology, strategy and institutions of collective action, [the transnational managerial class] is both a class in itself and for itself. (Cox 1981, 147)

These are networks of people who, especially at the top end of the organizational hierarchies, know each other in more than a casual way. And although national or ethnic differences and misunderstandings may get in the way, "business is business." (Not coincidentally, the word for business in most languages is, increasingly, just that . . . *biznezz*.) It is no coincidence that combining science and business produces the third global identity: the *engineer*.

The fourth is the *employee of a global corporate family*. Although the nature of organizational membership varies from corporation to corporation, some stress vertical corporate integration—"belonging"—on a truly global scale. This is the *corporation-as-a-global-family* approach to the management of industrial relations. The Toyota Motor Manufacturing North America (TMMNA) Web site (http://www.toyota.com) offers some insights into this. To be part of TMMNA involves membership in "a team made up of individuals from around the world," part of "the Toyota family worldwide." Thus, one imagines that working for Toyota in North America has much in common with working for Toyota in Japan or the United Kingdom. The *family* metaphor is central:

> The entire Toyota organization is strongly focused on families and understands their needs . . . we don't just build fine cars, we're committed to working with our team members to build fine families too. . . . The Toyotas built in Georgetown, Kentucky are "family cars" in more ways than one. Although team members and their families represent great diversity in age, background and interests, they also share a sense of "family."

The emphasis throughout is on the coming together of a diverse workforce through *teamwork*:

> Everyone including the president wears casual business attire, shares common benefits and works in an open office concept. There are no separate executive parking places or dining areas.

Finally, the company emphasizes its *global identity*, stressing its "leadership in protecting the Earth's climate," while graduate recruitment to its technical center offers placements outside North America and a "global perspective."

It is tempting to regard this as just rhetoric in the service of public relations and staff recruitment. However, "belonging" has consequences: the Toyota family may be an imagined community, but it is far from imaginary for those who join it. Membership in this global family is somewhat exclusive, and it involves both responsibilities and, crucially, benefits:

> job security is important to morale. We maintain lean staffing levels, focus on good attendance and cross-train team members to make them as flexible as possible. This staffing system is designed to hire only as many team members as needed to avoid employment fluctuations often found in the auto industry.

To return to global identities, being a scientist, an international businessman, an engineer, or an employee of a global corporate family such as Toyota is relatively comparable, wherever it is found. Locality is subsidiary to occupation or corporation. There are transnationally shared meanings, as well as forms. Crucially, these are all memberships in *meaningful international social networks*, if not necessarily face-to-face communities.

These are, however, elite and privileged occupational identities that are inaccessible to all but a few. They are disproportionately located within the world economic core. They are also, in terms of their significance for individuals, in competition with, if not utterly subordinate to, a wide range of national and other identities. Occupational and corporate identities are undoubtedly important, but *how* important depends on what they are worth, to real people in real contexts. Although money is among the yardsticks of value—and the closest to a universal one (which is, after all, its whole point)—it is not the only arbiter of what things are worth. Whether it really makes sense to call these global identities is still, therefore, moot.

The second alternative with regard to global identities, as mentioned earlier, involves the utopian universalism of dreams of "world culture" (Wallerstein 1991) and "world society." These are collective social identities that have the potential to transcend the national and other identities just discussed. Among the earliest transcendent global identities are those that declare allegiance to the great universal religions (which are not called "world religions" for nothing). Religion as a world-saving or -conquering corporate transnational business is at least as old as the medieval Roman Catholic Church and as recent as the Unification Church or the Brahma Kumaris World Spiritual University.

The next potentially global identity was conjured up by the opening call to arms of *The Communist Manifesto* in 1848: "Workers of the world, unite!" The dream of international socialism and the millennium of communism may seem tarnished in retrospect, but the vision was and is authentically global. When the *Internationale* comes round to the line, "Arise, ye wretched of the earth," it is not only the proletariat that is being addressed, it is the entire world of the dispossessed, the poor, and the exploited. The complete constituency of revolution. Different revolutions may, however, aim to overturn different existing orders, for the benefit of different constituencies: the transcendentally global does not necessarily include everyone. Even though women hold up (only) half the world, if all women *are* sisters under the skin, this is, potentially at least, a sufficient basis for a genuinely global identification and mobilization. In stronger or weaker senses, this has been the consistent dream of feminism.

The most ambitious possibility of all is the emergence of shared humanity as *the* meaningful collective identification. This is a utopia that explicitly negates race, nationality, ethnicity, and other differences. It is invoked in references as diverse as the words of a pop song ("What we need is a great big melting pot"), the "giant step for mankind" that took Neil Armstrong from the Apollo 11 module to the surface of the Moon, and the marketing campaign that wanted to buy the world a Coke (and presumably sold millions of cans). More soberly, it has informed the establishment of the United Nations, the Universal Declaration of Human Rights, and the work of many other international organizations.

So far at least, these global identities remain dreams of utopia. Even the most successful world-conquering universal religions can claim extensive partial coverage at best. And, to return to the theme of this essay, transnational corporations are relevant to the existence and prosperity of those dreams largely in their capacity to undermine, subvert, and frustrate them. Transnational corporate practices are, in the main, confined within the privileged economic core of the world system. That they might expand significantly, let alone take in the underprivileged rest of the world, seems unlikely. The global and the transnational corporations are at their closest in the marketplace, but the limited market for consumer goods in the economic periphery suggests that they are likely to remain distant from each other.

With respect to consumption, its intimate connection to identification is sociological conventional wisdom (e.g., Mackay 1997). Consumerism may also be the core culture and ideology of world capitalism:

> The notions of men and women as economic or political beings are discarded by global capitalism, quite logically as the system does not even pretend to satisfy everyone in the economic or political spheres. People are primarily consumers. (Sklair 1998b, 3)

However, most people in the world are *not* primarily consumers, they are primarily—and urgently—precarious subsisters (Hirst and Thompson 1999; Hoogvelt 1997). Thus, while capitalist consumerism is a culture and ideology with undoubted implications for individual projects of personal identity, it is of limited everyday relevance to more than half the globe's population. It is a luxury they simply cannot afford.

People can be workers, as well as consumers. The *corporation as a global family* is a direct and oppositional response to the identificatory potential of organized labor, and its potential to disrupt capital accumulation. Foreign direct investment—the capacity to shift production and other economic activities from global location to global location in response to labor cost differentials—is another response, more likely to breed international competition between workers than global solidarity. On balance, transnational corporations seem more likely to profit from international and other differences (although overt conflict between nations is generally not in their interests) than from the evolution of effective global collective identifications (which could mean effective global collective activity—political organization—and, horror of horrors, might open the door to effective global regulation).

Thus it is no surprise that perhaps the only social and organizational context where one can discern the *beginnings* of something that *might* develop into a kind of authentically globalized collective social identity is that of transnational business and corporate activity: "The old Marxist argument that the workers have no nation has to be turned on its head. Today it is globalising capitalists who have no nation" (Sklair 1998a, 142). The possibilities are real, and may be nearly endless:

> all senior members of the TCC will occupy a variety of interlocking positions, not only . . . interlocking directorates . . . but also connections outside the direct ambit of the corporate sector, the civil society as it were servicing the state-like structures of the corporations. . . . Business, particularly the transnational corporation sector, then begins to monopolise symbols of modernity like free enterprise, international competitiveness and the good life and to transform most, if not all, social spheres in its own image. (Sklair 1998b, 6)

Transnational Corporations and Global Identities

Transnational corporations come in different shapes and sizes, doing different things, and these have different implications for any discussion of the possibility of truly global identifications. Transnational corporate activities *may* encourage the formation of *some* occupational and organizational identities on an internationally extensive—if not a global—scale, but they are likely to discourage and obstruct the emergence of transcendent global identities.

The existing "cultural" emphases in the globalization literature can only go so far in analyzing these processes. If the logic of the argument about globalization and transnationality in this essay is even partly correct, then one needs to appreciate some of the more free-floating and unsentimental realities of moneymaking on such a grand scale. Transcending institutional and ethical local constraints is, in part, precisely the point of the enterprise and a motivation driving globalization. This is not to suggest that one can neglect the meaning of things, whether local or more extensive, but that political economy, as well as a "cultural" approach, is needed if one is to understand the social construction of identities in the transnational, let alone the global, field.

Acknowledgments

In addition to useful feedback from fellow participants at the "Reimagining Belonging" conference in Aalborg, I am enormously grateful to my

Sheffield colleagues, Bob Deacon, Ankie Hoogvelt, and Nick Stevenson, for their helpful criticisms of a draft of this essay.

Works Cited

Baran, Paul, and Paul M. Sweezy. 1966. *Monopoly Capital*. New York: Monthly Review Press.

Bauman, Zygmunt. 1998. *Globalization: The Human Consequences*. Cambridge: Polity Press.

Bougrine, Hassan. 1999. "Trans-national Corporations." In *Encyclopedia of Political Economy*, ed. Phillip Anthony O'Hara, 1175–1180. London: Routledge.

Castells, Manuel. 1996. *The Information Age: Economy, Society and Culture*. Vol. 1, *The Rise of the Network Society*. Malden, Mass.: Blackwell.

———. 1997. *The Information Age: Economy, Society and Culture*. Vol. 2, *The Power of Identity*. Malden, Mass.: Blackwell.

Cockroft, James D., Andre Gunder Frank, and Dale L. Johnson. 1972. *Dependence and Underdevelopment: Latin America's Political Economy*. New York: Doubleday Anchor.

Cox, Robert W. 1981. "Social Forces, States and World Orders: Beyond International Relations Theory." *Millennium: Journal of International Studies* 10: 126–55.

Frank, Andre Gunder, and Barry K. Gills, eds. 1993. *The World System: Five Hundred Years or Five Thousand Years?*. London: Routledge.

Friedman, Jonathan. 1997. "Global Crises, the Struggle for Cultural Identity and Intellectual Porkbarrelling." In *Debating Cultural Hybridity*, ed. Pnina Werbner and Tariq Madood, 70–89. London: Zed.

Giddens, Anthony. 1990. *The Consequences of Modernity*. Cambridge: Polity Press.

Haas, Peter M. 1990. "Obtaining International Protection through Epistemic Consensus." *Millennium: Journal of International Studies* 19: 347–64.

Hannerz, Ulf. 1996. *Trans-national Connections: Culture, People, Places*. London: Routledge.

Hirst, Paul, and Graham Thompson. 1999. *Globalization in Question*. 2d ed. Cambridge: Polity Press.

Hoogvelt, Ankie. 1997. *Globalisation and the Postcolonial World: The New Political Economy of Development*. London: Macmillan.

Jenkins, Richard. 1996. *Social Identity*. London: Routledge.

———. 1997. *Rethinking Ethnicity: Arguments and Explorations*. London: Sage.

Mackay, Hugh, ed. 1997. *Consumption and Everyday Life*. London: Sage.

Morley, David, and Kevin Robins. 1995. *Spaces of Identity: Global Media, Electronic Landscapes and Cultural Boundaries*. London: Routledge.

Portes, Alejandro, Luis E. Guarnizo, and Patricia Landolt, eds. 1999. "Trans-national Communities." Special issue of *Ethnic and Racial Studies* 22:2.

Reich, Robert B. 1991. *The Work of Nations: Preparing Ourselves for Twenty-first Century Capitalism*. New York: Knopf.

Ritzer, George. 1993. *The McDonaldization of Society*. Thousand Oaks, Calif.: Pine Forge.

———. 1997. *The McDonaldization Thesis: Explorations and Extensions*. Newbury Park, Calif.: Sage.

Robertson, Roland. 1992. *Globalization: Social Theory and Global Culture*. London: Sage.

Sklair, Leslie. 1998a. "The Transnational Capitalist Class." In *Virtualism: A New Political Economy*, ed. James G. Carrier and Daniel Miller, 135–59. Oxford: Berg.

————. 1998b. "Trans-national Practices and the Analysis of the Global System." *ESRC Trans-national Communities Research Programme Working Paper* 4.

Smart, Barry, ed. 1999. *Resisting McDonaldization.* London: Sage.

Urry, John. 1990. *The Tourist Gaze: Leisure and Travel in Contemporary Societies.* London: Sage.

Wallerstein, Immanuel. 1974. *The Modern World-System.* New York: Academic Press.

————. 1991. "The National and the Universal: Can There Be Such a Thing as World Culture?" In *Culture, Globalization and the World System,* ed. Anthony D. King, 91–105. London: Macmillan.

Waters, Malcom. 1995. *Globalization.* London: Routledge.

Watson, James L., ed. 1997. *Golden Arches East: McDonald's in East Asia.* Stanford, Calif.: Stanford University Press.

PART II

Self and

Community

6

Seyla Benhabib

Citizens, Residents, and Aliens in a Changing World:

Political Membership in the Global Era

Our contemporary condition is marked by the emergence of new forms of identity/difference politics around the globe. As globalization proceeds at a dizzying rate, as a material global civilization encompasses the earth from Hong Kong to Lima, from Pretoria to Helsinki, worldwide integration in economics, technology, communication, armament, and tourism is accompanied by the collective and cultural disintegration of older political entities, in particular of the nation-state (Benhabib 1997a). India and Turkey, which are among the oldest democracies of the Third World, are in the throes of struggles that call into question the very project of a secular, representative democracy. Need one mention in this context ethnic wars, cleansings, and massacres in the former Yugoslavia, the Russian destruction of Chechnya, the simmering nationality conflicts between Azerbaijan and Armenia, Macedonia and Greece, the rise of militant Islamic fundamentalism, and the continuing tribal massacres in the central African states of Rwanda, Uganda, and the Congo? Displaying a social dynamic that we have hardly begun to understand, global integration is proceeding alongside sociocultural disintegration and the resurgence of ethnic, nationalist, religious, and linguistic separatisms (Ignatieff 1994; Barber 1995; Friedman 1995; Mendes and Soares 1996).

With globalization and fragmentation proceeding apace, human rights and sovereignty claims come into increasing conflict with each other (Heiberg 1994). On the one hand, a worldwide consciousness about universal principles of human rights is growing; on the other hand, particularistic identities of nationality, ethnicity, religion, race, and language in virtue of which one is said to belong to a sovereign people are asserted with increasing ferocity. Globalization, far from creating a "cosmopolitical order," a condition of perpetual peace among peoples governed by the principles of a republican constitution (Kant [1795] 1963), has brought to a head conflicts between human rights and the claim to self-determination of sovereign collectivities. Because sovereignty means the right of a collectivity to define itself by asserting power over a bounded territory, declarations of sovereignty more often than not create distinctions between "us" and "them," those who belong to the sovereign people and those who do not. Historically, there is no convergence between the identity of all those "others" over whom power is asserted because they happen to reside in a bounded state territory and the sovereign people in the name of whom such power is exercised. The distinction between citizens, on the one hand, and residents and foreigners, on the other, is central to the theory and practice of democracies. In this regard, Hannah Arendt's astute observations, although formulated in a different context and with respect to the difficulties of protecting human rights in the interwar period in Europe, are more perspicacious than ever: "From the beginning the paradox involved in the declaration of inalienable human rights was that it reckoned with an 'abstract' human being who seemed to exist nowhere. . . . The whole question of human rights, therefore, was quickly and inextricably blended with the question of national emancipation; only the emancipated sovereignty of the people, of one's own people, seemed to be able to insure them" (Arendt [1951] 1979, 291).

The citizenship and naturalization claims of foreigners, denizens, and residents within the borders of a polity, as well as the laws, norms, and rules governing such procedures, are pivotal social practices through which the normative perplexities of human rights and sovereignty can be most acutely observed. Sovereignty entails the right of a people to control its borders as well as to define the procedures for admitting "aliens" into its territory and society; yet, in a liberal-democratic polity, such sovereignty claims must always be constrained by human rights, which individuals are entitled to, not in virtue of being citizens or members of a polity, but insofar as they are human beings *simpliciter*. Universal human rights transcend the rights of citizens and extend to all persons considered as moral beings. What kinds of immigration, naturalization, and citizenship practices, then, would be compatible with the commitments of liberal democracies to human rights? Can claims to sovereign self-determination be reconciled with the just and fair treatment of aliens and others in our midst?

In debates around these issues, two approaches dominate: the radical universalist argument for open borders and the civic republican perspective of "thick conceptions of citizenship." Radical universalists argue that, from a moral point of view, national borders are arbitrary and that the only morally consistent universalist position would be one of open borders. Joseph Carens, for example, uses the device of the Rawlsian "veil of ignorance" to think through principles of justice from the standpoint of the refugee, the immigrant, the asylum seeker (Carens 1995, 229ff.; see Carens 2000 for modifications of these early arguments). Are the borders within which we happen to be born, and the documents to which we are entitled, any less arbitrary from a moral point of view than other characteristics such as skin color, gender, and genetic makeup? Carens's answer is "no." From a moral point of view, the borders that circumscribe our birth and the papers to which we are entitled are arbitrary because their distribution does not follow any clear criteria of moral worth, achievement, and compensation. Therefore, claims Carens, liberal democracies should practice policies that are as compatible as possible with the vision of a world without borders.

Opposed to Carens's radical universalism are a range of communitarian and civic-republican positions, articulating more or less "thick" conceptions of citizenship, community, and belonging (see Galston 1991; Sandel 1996; Kessler 1998). These theories of citizenship, though not precluding or prohibiting immigration, will want to articulate stricter criteria of incorporation and citizenship of foreigners than the universalists. Only those immigrants who come closest to the model of the republican citizen envisaged by these theories will be welcome; others will be spurned (Honig 1998, 2001). Of course, given how contested such thick conceptions of citizenship inevitably are, communitarian theories can easily lend themselves to the justification of illiberal immigration policies and the restricting of the rights of immigrants and aliens.

This essay will steer a middle course between the radical universalism of open borders politics, on the one hand, and sociologically antiquated conceptions of thick republican citizenship, on the other. Instead, stressing the constitutive tension between universalistic human rights claims and democratic sovereignty principles, it will analyze the contemporary practices of political incorporation into liberal democracies. The essay will focus on dilemmas of citizenship and political membership in contemporary

Western Europe against the background of these larger theoretical concerns. Current developments in citizenship and incorporation practices within the member states of the European Union in particular are the primary focus. There are a number of compelling historical as well as philosophical reasons for choosing European citizenship and incorporation practices as the focal point for these concerns.

Insofar as they are liberal democracies, member states of the European Union cannot form a "fortress Europe." No liberal democracy can close its borders to refugees and asylum seekers, immigrants and foreign workers. The porousness of borders is a necessary, though not sufficient, condition of liberal democracies. By the same token, no sovereign liberal democracy can lose its right to define immigration and incorporation policies.

I will distinguish conditions of entry into a country (e.g., the permission to visit, work, study, and buy property) from conditions of *temporary residency*, and both in turn from *permanent residency* and *civil incorporation*, the final stage of which is naturalization and *political membership*. These are different stages of political incorporation, very often collapsed into one another in theoretical discussions, but analytically distinguishable. At each of these stages, the rights and claims of foreigners, residents, and aliens will be regulated by sovereign polities; but these regulations can be subject to scrutiny, debate, and contestation, as well as protest by those to whom they apply, their advocates, and national and international human-rights groups. No step of this process can be shielded from scrutiny by interested parties. Democratic sovereignty in immigration and incorporation policy is not an unlimited right. The right to self-assertion of a particular people must be examined and evaluated in the light of the commitment of this very same people to universal human rights. Developments of citizenship and immigration practices within contemporary Europe reflect some of the deepest perplexities faced by all nation-states in the era of globalization.

Dilemmas of Citizenship in the European Union

Since 1989 and the fall of authoritarian communism, the worldwide trend toward material global integration and ethnic and cultural fragmentation has coincided with another set of epochal developments on the Continent: the end of the cold war, the unification of Germany, and the transformation of the European Union from a monetary and financial organization—a customs union—into a political entity with a European Parliament, a European Council of Ministers, a European Court of Justice, and, since January 2002, a European currency—the euro, adopted by twelve out of the fifteen states. But what is Europe? (Benhabib 1997b). For some, Europe is not a continent, a mere geographical designator, but an ideal, the birthplace of Western philosophy and the Enlightenment, of democratic revolutions and human rights. For others, Europe is a fig leaf behind which big finance capital and in particular the German Bundesbank hide in order to dismantle the social-welfare states of the Union. These sentiments were particularly strong in the mid-1990s, after the Maastricht Treaty (1993) and the requirement that national governments cut their annual budget deficits to 3 percent. Member states forced their own populations to accept fiscal stability over full employment, and to place the shared confidence that international financial markets show in their national economies above the quality of life of these countries. Europe ceased to be an ideal; for some it became an illusion. Tony Judt gives voice to the Euro-pessimist position with the following words: "we shall wake up one day to find out that far from solving the problems of our continent, the myth of 'Europe' has become an impediment to our recognizing them. We shall discover that it has become little more than the politically correct way to paper over local difficulties, as though the mere invocation of the promise of Europe could substitute for solving problems and crises that really affect the place" (Judt 1996, 140).

Whether as ideal or as illusion, "Europe" is moving toward an ever-closer union since the new millennium, but it is also being invoked to define a new set of boundaries. During the time of the cold war, the terms *east* and *west* came to designate a geopolitical division of regimes. Whereas once the term *east*, or the *Orient*, would have been reserved for that border which separated Europe from the Ottoman Empire, after 1945 and the division of Germany, the line separating "east" from "west" ran through the heart of Europe, that is, the city of Berlin. The communist regimes of Europe became, oddly enough, part of the Orient; "Eastern Europe" designated differences in types of political regime by making communism appear as part of "them," the East, as opposed to "us," "the free West." This conversion of geopolitics into physical geography was a political subterfuge through which one rendered the unfamiliar familiar. The term *Eastern Europe*, which conveniently hid the fact that Prague is to the west of Vienna, rendered communism—the unfamiliar—familiar, by marking it as "oriental," or as "eastern." The revolutions of 1989 showed how illusory it was to mark political, cultural, and historical differences through purportedly neutral geographical designators.

Contemporary Europe is facing the danger that its moral and political boundaries will be redefined via geographical borders. Geography once again will be used to cover the tracks of complex processes of political and moral inclusion and exclusion. Where are Europe's borders after 1989? How can these borders be justified as boundaries? Europe, whether as an ideal or an illusion—whom does it include and whom does it exclude? After the cold war, who are Europe's "others"?

According to statistics provided by the Council of Europe, between 1950 and 1992–93 the foreign population in the countries of Western Europe grew as follows: whereas foreigners made up 1.1 percent of the population in Germany in 1950, in 1992–93 this number rose to 8.6 percent. During the same period, the foreign population of France increased from 4.2 percent to 6.6 percent; of Belgium from 4.1 percent to 9.1 percent (in 1994, the foreign population of Belgium stood at 10.7 percent); of Holland from 1.0 percent to 5.1 percent, and of Luxembourg from 9.8 percent to 29.1 percent (in 1994 this figure stood at 34 percent for Luxembourg). On the whole, the foreign population of Europe increased from 1.3 percent in 1950 to 4.9 percent in 1992–93.[1]

The year 1993 marks a turning point in immigration trends in European countries. After the increase in immigration flows during the 1980s and the beginning of the 1990s, a reduction in the number of immigrant entries occurred. The decline in the number of asylum claims during this period was offset by the predominance of flows linked to family reunion and the importance of highly skilled workers (SOPEMI Publications 1998, 15).

Despite leveling off at 8.5 percent of the total population in 1993, the foreign population of Germany rose to 8.9 percent between 1996 and 1999. According to Rainer Muenz, "in 1999 Germany had 82 million inhabitants: 74.7 were German citizens—including those holding dual citizenship—and 7.3 million residents did not have German citizenship. The share of the foreign nationals was therefore just below 9 percent of the total population" (Muenz 2001, 1). During the same period, the Netherlands' foreign population declined from 5.1 percent in 1993 to 4.4 percent in 1996; France has remained steady at about 6.3 percent and Belgium at about 9.1 percent. The foreign population in Denmark increased from 3.6 percent in 1993 to 4.7 percent in 1996. As of 1998, the percentage of the foreign-born population in Denmark remains at about 5. Among the European Union countries, only Austria, Germany, and Luxembourg have foreign populations higher than the 2.5 to 6 percent range that is characteristic of Ireland, the United Kingdom, Denmark, Sweden, and the Netherlands (as well as Norway, which is not an EU member). In Luxembourg, the foreign population increased from 31.8 percent in 1993 to 34.1 percent in 1996; during this same period, Austria's foreign population went from 8.6 percent to 9.0 in 1996 (SOPEMI Publications 1998, 224).

These figures are not broken down according to different geographical regions and countries of origin. Foreigners from former East European countries are included in these figures along with guest workers from Turkey and refugees from the former Yugoslav countries.[2] A more precise breakdown shows that ethnic Turks and ethnic Kurds are the largest group of foreigners, not only in Germany, but in Western Europe in general. In 1993, they numbered 2.7 million. Of that number, 2.1 million live in Germany and, as of 1999, made up 2.8 percent of the population.[3] The second-largest group of foreigners are members of former Yugoslav states, many of whom enjoy either full or temporary refugee status: 1.8 million Croats, Serbs, Bosnian Muslims, and Albanians. As of 1998, for example, there were 719,500 former Yugoslavs resident in Germany (Serbs, Montenegrins, and Kosovo Albanians), 283,000 Croatians, and 190,100 citizens of Bosnia-Herzegovina (SOPEMI Publications 2000, 339). By the year 2000, the number of Bosnians living in Germany, including war refugees living under temporary protection, increased to 281,000 (Muenz 2001, 8).

Among the EU countries most affected by the breakup wars of the former Yugoslavia, and the resulting inflow of migrants, refugees, and asylum seekers, are the Netherlands, where, as of 1998, citizens of the former Yugoslavia numbered 47,500; Sweden, where the corresponding figure is 70,900; and Italy, in which 40,800 former citizens of Yugoslavia, as well as 91,500 Albanians, have settled. Since 1996, Sweden has also given refuge to about 48,000 Bosnia-Herzegovinians.

This picture is complicated by the increasing migration of EU residents from one country to another. Already in 1993, Italians working outside their home country numbered 1.5 million; they are followed by the Portuguese, of whom about 900,000 work and live outside Portugal; Spaniards, who are members of the EU, and Algerians, who are not, each number around 600,000. As of the 1990 census, France counted 614,200 Algerian-born individuals among its population, and 572,200 Moroccans.

After the fall of communism in East and Central Europe, a slow but increasing tide of immigration from the former East bloc countries to the EU also began. In 1998, 66,300 Poles entered Germany, about 10,400 France, and about 14,000 the Netherlands. In 1998, there were 20,500 members of the Russian Federation resident in Finland; Greece is host to about 5,000 Russians, 3,000 Bulgarians, and 2,700 Albanians.

Against the juridical and political background of European unification, these developments are bringing a two-tiered status of foreignness throughout Europe. Different rights and privileges are accorded to different categories of foreigners within the fifteen member states.

The Maastricht Treaty makes provisions for a "Union citizenship."[4] Nationals of all countries who are members of the European Union are also citizens of the European Community. What does being a citizen of the Union mean? What privileges and responsibilities, what rights and duties does this entitle one to? Is citizenship of the Union merely a status category, just as being a member of the Roman Empire was? Does membership in the Union amount to more than possessing a passport that allows one to pass through the right doors at border crossings?[5]

Clearly, Union membership is intended to be much more than that. It is intended to designate not just a passive status, but an active civic identity. Members of the Union states can settle anywhere in the Union, take up jobs in their chosen countries, and vote, as well as stand for office, in local elections and in elections for the European Parliament. As the process of European monetary and economic integration progresses, debates are occurring over whether Union citizenship should also entail a package of social rights and benefits, such as unemployment compensation, health care and old-age pensions, that members of EU states could enjoy wherever they go.[6]

The obverse side of membership in the Union is a sharper delineation of the conditions of those who are not members. The agreements of Schengen and Dublin intended to uniformize practices of granting asylum and refugee status throughout member states (Neuman 1993).[7] Referred to as "legal harmonization," these agreements have made the granting of refugee and asylum status in the Union increasingly difficult. A person who seeks refugee or asylum status in one member country is not permitted to apply in another country of the Union until the first application is resolved. Although it is left unsaid, the presumption is that once an application has been denied in one member country, it is unlikely to succeed in another. The decision of the European Council of Ministers to erect a Union-wide office to deal with refugee and asylum issues, while creating legal and bureaucratic homogenization and standardization, by the same token intends to make Europe's borders less and less porous by disallowing individuals in need of multiple venues of aid and rescue.

As Union citizenship progresses, in each member country discrepancies are arising between those who are foreigners and third-country nationals, and those who are foreign nationals but EU members. A two-tiered status of foreignness is thus developing: on the one hand, there are third-country national foreign residents of European countries, some of whom have been born and raised in these countries and who know no other homeland; on the other hand, there are those who may be near-total strangers to the language, customs, and history of their host country but who enjoy special status and privilege in virtue of being nationals of a state that is an EU member (Klusmeyer 1993). Members of the fifteen EU countries who are residents in countries different from those of their nationality can vote and can run for and hold office in municipality elections and in elections for the European Parliament. These rights are as a rule not granted to third-country nationals, though, as I shall argue later, some EU countries (e.g., Denmark, Sweden, Finland, and Holland) permit foreigners who have fulfilled certain residency requirements to vote in local, and even in some cases regional, elections.

Partially in response to the growing pressures created by this situation, Germany on May 7, 1999, reformed its 1913 citizenship law. The German parliament agreed by a two-thirds majority to supplement the principle of *jus sanguinis* by *jus soli* in the acquisition of German citizenship (see Benhabib 1999b). From January 1, 2000, on, children born to foreign parents who have resided in the country for eight years acquire German citizenship without forfeiting other passports they hold. When they reach the age of twenty-three, they must decide for one passport or another. In addition to the *jus soli* regulation, the new law expedites the acquisition of German citizenship by foreigners by reducing the transition period from residency to citizenship from fifteen to eight years. The decision of the German parliament is, of course, to be applauded, but its significance can only be understood in a larger conceptual and institutional context.

Since the Treaty of Amsterdam signed on May 1, 1997, there has been growing awareness as well as desire among EU member countries to harmonize the citizenship and naturalization laws of member countries, and to reduce discrepancies between the juridical and political status of EU citizens and third-country nationals. According to the Treaty of Amsterdam, naturalization, immigration, refugee, and asylum policies within the EU are placed in the Third Tier. The First Tier refers to EU-wide laws and regulations; the Second Tier concerns common security and cooperation measures, particularly those pertaining to fighting criminality and drug trafficking; the Third Tier is defined as "intergovernmental law" and is subject to discretionary agreement and cooperation as well as the conventions of international public law. In these areas, a unanimous decision procedure will hold till the year 2004 (see de Jong 2000, 21–25). In other words, although EU member countries retain sovereign discretion over their immigration and asylum policies, "the Treaty of Amsterdam firmly embeds immigration and asylum policies within an EC framework" (ibid., 25).

The resolutions of the European Council, reached in Tampere, Finland, October 15–16, 1999, reiterate the commitment to European integration based on respect for human rights, democratic institutions, and the rule of law. The Council emphasizes, however, that these principles cannot be seen as the exclusive preserve of the Union's own citizens. "It would be in contradiction with Europe's traditions to deny such freedoms to those whose circumstances led them justifiably to seek access to our territory. This in turn requires the Union to develop common policies on asylum and immigration, while taking into account the need for a consistent control of external borders to stop illegal immigration and to combat those who organize it and commit related international crimes" (cited in van Krieken 2000, 305).

Despite these wishes and guidelines for a coherent immigration and asylum policy at the intergovernmental level of EU institutions, legal and institutional conditions for immigrants and persons granted asylum vary widely among member countries. There is no clarity among the public or among politicians as to how these issues are related to the foundations and well-being of liberal democracies; potentially, immigration and asylum issues remain nondiffused time bombs in the hands of demagogues and right-wing politicians, ready to explode on short notice. Not only politically, but theoretically as well, the incorporation and acceptance of immigrants, resident aliens, and foreigners into liberal democracies touch on fundamental normative and philosophical problems concerning the modern nation-state system.

Dilemmas of citizenship in contemporary Europe thus have implications for debates around citizenship in contemporary political philosophy. In discussions throughout the 1980s and 1990s, and particularly under the influence of the "liberal-communitarian" debate, the concept and practice of citizenship were analyzed largely from a normative perspective (Galston 1991; Macedo 1990; Kymlicka and Norman 1995). Usually, one aspect—the privileges of political membership—was in the foreground.[8] This normative discussion, largely about the duties of democratic citizenship and participatory democratic theory, was carried out in a sociological vacuum. Political philosophers paid little attention to citizenship as a sociological category and as a social practice that inserts people into a complex network of privileges and duties, entitlements and obligations. Political philosophy and the political sociology of citizenship went their separate ways. But privileges of political membership are only one aspect of citizenship. Collective identity and the entitlement to social rights and benefits are others. We need to disaggregate the theory and practice of citizenship into these various dimensions and broaden our focus to include conditions of citizenship in sociologically complex, decentered, welfare-state democracies. Through the unprecedented movement of peoples and goods, capital and information, microbes and communication across borders, individuals no longer enter their societies at birth and exit them at death, as John Rawls counterfactually assumed (see Rawls 1993, 41; and Kleger 1995).

To underscore how constitutive the movement of peoples back and forth across borders has become in the contemporary world, Rainer Bauböck has observed:

> On the one hand, immigrants who settle in a destination country for good may still keep the citizenship of the sending society and travel there regularly so that the sending country rightly regards them as having retained strong ties to their origins. . . . Temporary migrants, on the other hand, often find it difficult to return and to reintegrate. Some migrants become permanent residents in destination countries without being accepted as immigrants and without regarding themselves as such; others develop patterns of frequent movement between different countries in none of which they establish themselves permanently. . . . Contemporary migration research should go beyond these narrow national views and conceive of migration as a genuinely transnational phenomenon, not only at the moment of border crossings but also with regard to the resulting social affiliations. International migration transnationalizes both sending and receiving societies by extending relevant forms of membership beyond the boundaries of territories and of citizenship. (Bauböck 1998, 26; see also Cohen 1999)[9]

Citizenship as Social Practice

Sociologically, the practice and institution of "citizenship" can be broken down into three components: collective identity, privileges of political membership, and social rights and benefits.

COLLECTIVE IDENTITY

Citizenship implies being a member of a political entity that has been formed historically, that has certain linguistic, cultural, ethnic, and religious commonalties, and that can be distinguished from other such entities.

The precise form of such an entity, whether it is a multinational empire or a national republic, a commonwealth or a federation, varies historically. Viewed analytically, though, the concepts of "citizenship" (in the sense of being a member of a political community) and "nationality" (in the sense of being a member of a particular linguistic, ethnic, religious, and cultural group) are to be distinguished from each other. Political communities are not composed of nationally and ethnically homogeneous groups. Historically, this was just as little the case in the multinational and multiethnic Hapsburg and Ottoman empires as it is the case today in the United States, Canada, Australia, or New Zealand.

PRIVILEGES OF POLITICAL MEMBERSHIP

The oldest meaning of citizenship is that of the privileges and burdens of self-governance. For the ancient Greeks, the *politos* is the member of the *polis*, the one who can be called to military service as well as jury duty, who must pay taxes and serve in the *Ecclesia* in his capacity as member of his *Demei* at least one month of the year. The link between the city and the citizen is retained in the etymology of *civitas* and *citoyenne*, on the one hand, and *Buergher* and *Burgh* on the other.

Citizenship confers upon its holders the right of political participation, the right to hold certain offices and perform certain tasks, and the right to deliberate and decide upon certain questions. Aristotle writes in the *Politics:* "The state is a compound made of citizens; and this compels us to consider who should properly be called a citizen and what a citizen really is. The nature of citizenship, like that of the state, is a question which is often disputed: there is no general agreement on a single definition: the man who is a citizen in a democracy is often not one in an oligarchy" (Aristotle 1941, 1274b–75a). In making the identity of the citizen dependent on the type of political regime, Aristotle is emphasizing the contingent nature of this concept. It is not nature but the city and its conventions, the *nomoi*, that create the citizen. Yet precisely in Aristotle's work we see how this insight into the socially constituted aspect of citizenship goes hand in hand with an exclusionary vision of the psychosexual attributes of citizenship. Even if it is regime types that determine who a citizen is, in Aristotle's view, only some are "by nature fit" to exercise the virtues of citizenship, others are not. Slaves, women, and non-Greeks are not only excluded from the statutory privileges of citizenship, but their exclusion is viewed as rational insofar as these individuals do not possess the virtues of mind, body, and character essential to citizenship. This tension between the social constitution of the citizen and the psychosexual "nature," said to be essential to citizenship, accompanies struggles over the meaning of citizenship down to the present day. Struggles over whether women should have the vote, whether nonwhite and colonial peoples are capable of self-rule, or whether a gay person can hold certain kinds of public office are illustrations of the tension between the social and the naturalistic dimensions of citizenship.

SOCIAL RIGHTS AND BENEFITS

The view that citizenship can be understood as a status that grants one a certain bundle of entitlements, benefits as well as obligations, derives from T. H. Marshall (1950). Marshall's catalog of civil, political, and social rights is based on the cumulative logic of struggles for the expansion of democracy in the nineteenth and early twentieth centuries. "Civil rights" arise with the birth of the absolutist state and, in their earliest and most basic form, entail the rights to the protection of life, liberty, and property; the right to freedom of conscience; and certain associational rights, such as those of contract and marriage.

"Political rights" in the narrow sense refer to the rights of self-determination, to hold and to run for office, to enjoy freedom of speech and opinion, and to establish political and nonpolitical associations, including a free press and free institutions of science and culture.

"Social rights" are last in Marshall's catalog because they have been achieved historically through the struggles of the workers', women's, and other social movements of the last two centuries. Social rights involve the right to form trade unions as well as other professional and trade associations; health-care rights, unemployment compensation, old-age pensions, child care, housing and educational subsidies, and so on. These social rights vary widely from one country to another and depend thoroughly on the social class compromises prevalent in any given welfare-state democracy.

Were we to try to apply Marshall's catalog to the condition of foreigners in the European Union, we would note an interesting reversal. In all European countries, foreigners who are third-country nationals possess full protection of their civil rights under the law as well as enjoying most social rights. Noncitizens of EU states enjoy the same protection in the eyes of the law as citizens, their earnings and property are equally protected, and they enjoy freedom of conscience and religion.

Under the provisions of the social-welfare democracies of European states, most foreign residents are entitled to health-care benefits, unemployment compensation, old-age pensions, child care, some housing and educational subsidies, as well as certain social-welfare benefits, such as minimum income compensation. These social benefits are not conferred automatically. They depend on the length of residence in the host country, the residency status of the individual involved—whether permanent or temporary—and, most commonly, the particular kind of wage or service contract. Despite variations among member states, in most EU countries foreigners benefit from some of these social rights, while the enjoyment of political membership is either blocked off or made extremely difficult.

In *Limits of Citizenship: Migrants and Postnational Membership in Europe*, Yasemin Soysal introduces the concept of an "incorporation regime" (Soysal 1994). She thereby suggests that every host country possesses certain legal, economic, and policy regulations according to which the status of being a foreigner in that country is defined. Often, however, the collective status and identity of such groups will simply be considered the consequence of cultural traditions and historical developments that these groups presumably have brought with them from their countries of origin. The interaction between the home and the host cultures and traditions is thereby ignored.

For example: the incorporation policy of the former Bundesrepublik was to integrate guest workers into the juridical system not in virtue of their membership in a particular ethnic group, but rather, in the first place, through their status as individual persons and, in the second place, as workers and employees. Claims to civil and social rights would accrue to them as individuals and as workers. It is this status identity that entitled the individual to a particular set of rights and benefits.

In the Netherlands, by contrast, the regime of incorporation has proceeded quite differently. The National Advisory Council of Ethnic Minorities, which was founded by the Dutch government in 1982, designates Turks, Moroccans, Tunisians, Surinamese, populations of the Antilles and Molucca Islands, as well as Greeks, Spanish, Portuguese, and Gypsies, as "official minorities" (van Amersfoort 1982). When an ethnic group attains the status of official minority, then the claims of such a group to housing, education, employment, and other forms of social and cultural support are also acknowledged. Such official minority groups then acquire the rights to establish and carry out education in their own languages and to form religious and cultural organizations and associations.

This sociological analysis of citizenship and incorporation regimes suggests a methodological perspective that allows us to conceptualize the collective identity of foreigners as resulting from the complex interaction between various factors: those social and cultural attributes of immigrant groups that originate in their home country, and the juridical, political, social, as well as cultural norms and practices of the host country. This, then, suggests the questions: Why are certain rights granted to foreigners and others withheld? Why are certain identity-marking characteristics privileged in certain contexts and not in others? Note the difference between Germany and Holland in their practices of defining the collective and individual status of foreigners. What is the relationship between the singling out of certain criteria as being constitutive of the foreigners' identity, and the history and self-understanding of a particular country? The treatment of the "others" reveals who we are, because in Julia Kristeva's words, "Nous sommes étrangers à nous-mêmes" (We are strangers to ourselves) (Kristeva 1991).

Political Participation Rights in Europe Today

The highest privilege of citizenship is the possession of political rights— rights to vote and to run for and hold office—in the narrow sense. It is also through the entitlement to and exercise of these rights that one's status as a "citizen," as a member of the body politic, will be established. The lines that divide members from strangers, citizens from foreigners, the "we" from the "they," are drawn most sharply around these privileges. Modern Western political thought has usually proceeded from the methodological fiction of a closed society.

Political theory on these issues lags far behind actual developments. None of the following host countries of the European Union grant foreigners the right of participation in national elections: Denmark, the Netherlands, Sweden, Belgium, France, Austria, Germany, and England.[10] Yet in Denmark, as well as Sweden, foreigners can participate in local and regional elections and be candidates for them. In Norway, Finland, and Holland these rights are granted at the local but not regional levels. In Switzerland, which is not a member of the European Union, the cantons of Neuchâtel and Jura grant foreigners these rights as well. Similar attempts in Berlin, Hamburg, and Schleswig-Holstein to grant local election rights to those foreigners who have resided in Germany for more than five years had been declared "unconstitutional" by the German Constitutional Court (Weiler 1995), but this ruling was reversed in 1997 by the German Supreme Court (Bundesverfassungsgericht) for EU citizens resident in Germany, in compliance with the terms of the Maastricht Treaty (Bundesverfassungsgericht

1997). What, though, is the link between the status of active citizenship and "national membership"?

The acquisition of citizenship rights proceeds in most countries of the world in line with three principles: of territory, origin, or naturalization. The principle of territoriality, known as *jus soli*, means that a political community has sovereign claims over a territory: persons who live in this territory are considered either as falling under the dominion or authority of this sovereign or are themselves viewed as being part of the sovereign. The first case corresponds to predemocratic understandings of sovereignty, and, as was the case with the absolutist regimes of Europe, defines citizens as subjects. Historically, the Ottoman Empire as well as the Hapsburg monarchy and the German Kaiser regime followed this pattern. These old regimes always granted certain protected groups special citizenship rights and privileges, as was the case, for example, for the *Reichsjuden*— the Jews of the Empire—during the period of the Hapsburg Double Monarchy.

The territorial principle of citizenship can also have a democratic variant. The principles of citizenship, introduced by the American and the French Revolutions, follow this variant. According to the democratic understanding of the *jus soli*, each child who is born on the territory of a democratic sovereign is potentially a member of this sovereign and therefore has claims to citizenship (Brubaker 1992, 45).

The second principle according to which citizenship is granted is that of ethnic origin or belonging, *jus sanguinis*. If one considers France and the United States as prime examples of countries in which citizenship is based on the *jus soli*, the acquisition of German citizenship, until recently, was seen as a paradigmatic example of *jus sanguinis*.[11] The principle of *jus sanguinis* means that citizenship is attained in virtue of belonging to a people or ethnic group. How is "belonging" to a people or ethnic group to be established? Biological lineage is the simplest and clearest criterion for defining this. The German citizenship law of July 23, 1913—*das Reichs- und Staatsbürgerschaftgesetz*—which formed the basis of Germany's citizenship law until January 1, 2000, stated that citizenship was inherited (Klusmeyer 1993). This law was formulated with the specific political purpose of making it impossible for the large numbers of Jews and Poles then residing in the Kaiserreich to acquire German citizenship (Wertheimer 1987). Only a century earlier, however, the Prussian Edict of Emancipation of 1812 had granted Jews in Prussia the status of citizenship without taking into account criteria of ethnic belonging (Huber 1961). During the Reichstag, the German Social Democrats, much like the present coalition government, sought to reintroduce *jus soli* into German citizenship legislation.

The third practice through which citizenship is granted is "naturalization" or "nationalization." For countries such as the United States, Canada, Australia, and New Zealand, which view themselves as immigration countries, this procedure is as important as the acquisition of citizenship rights through birthright or descent. Increasingly, European Union countries as well that had not hitherto viewed themselves as immigration societies are recognizing the significance of naturalization procedures and reexamining their old practices.

Naturalization usually involves fulfilling certain years of residency in the country whose citizenship is sought; some proof of language competence; in some cases, as with the United States, for example, a demonstration of "civic knowledge"; evidence of gainful employment and proof that one will not be a "financial burden on the system"; and some certification of good character or conduct, usually satisfied either through police records or through letters of affidavit by citizens who know the person. Most countries grant naturalization requests on the basis of family bonds—spouse, child, parents, siblings.

It is important to emphasize that naturalization procedures as well as decisions have rarely been subject to strict scrutiny by the courts and in terms of human-rights violations. This institutional aspect of citizenship has usually been shrouded in mists of bureaucratic logic, or has been subject to the vacillating will of democratic majorities. Such practices are currently coming under increased scrutiny within the context of the European Union as well.

Citizenship and Political Theory

I have examined dilemmas of citizenship in contemporary Europe from the standpoint of normative political philosophy and suggested why these political developments should lead to a rethinking of normative categories to bring them more into contact with the new sociological and institutional realities of citizenship in the contemporary world.

A central thesis of my argument is that theories of citizenship have often relied on obsolete and misleading assumptions. The first is the fiction of a "closed society." Political philosophers have often assumed a "closed society" with nonporous borders, as in Rawls's crystal-clear formulation: "... we have assumed that a democratic society, like any political society, is to be viewed as a complete and closed social system. It is complete in that it is self-sufficient and has a place for all the main purposes of human life. It is also closed, in that entry into it is only by birth and exit from it is only by death. . . . For the moment we leave aside entirely relations with other societies and postpone all questions of justice between peoples until a conception of justice for a well-ordered society is on hand. Thus, we are not seen as joining society at the age of reason, as we might join an association, but as being born into a society where we will lead a complete life" (Rawls 1993, 41).

In the light of global developments in industry, finance, communication, tourism, and armament, it is implausible today to proceed from the Rawlsian assumption, even if this is the counterfactual one that "a democratic society can be viewed as a complete and a closed social system." A theory of political justice must necessarily include a theory of international justice.[12] Not only the current level of development of a global civil society, but more significantly, the fact that in democratic societies the right of exit remains a fundamental right of the citizen, makes this fiction obsolete.

Furthermore, to be a foreigner does not mean to be beyond the reach of the law. It means to have a specific kind of legal and political identity that includes certain rights and obligations while precluding others. Many European host countries are softening those legal restrictions that have previously made it impossible for foreigners to participate in elections and running for office. The restrictions that have barred foreigners from political membership rest, in the final analysis, on assumptions of who the citizens themselves are and what the virtues of citizenship consist of. In this respect, neither the principle of *jus sanguinis* nor that of *jus soli* is consistent and plausible enough to justify the theory and practice of democratic citizenship. There is a hiatus between the self-understanding of democracies and the acquisition of citizenship. Whereas democracy is a form of life that rests on active consent and participation, citizenship is distributed according to passive criteria of belonging, such as birth on a given piece of land, and socialization in that country, or ethnic belonging to a people.

A second assumption that has been greatly misleading in these debates is that of "state-centeredness." In insisting that consent was expressed through participation in the numerous activities of civil society, Locke was right (see Locke [1690] 1980). Our contemporary societies are even more complex, fragmented, and contradictory social structures than those in Locke's time. In such societies, human conduct and interactions assume many and diverse forms. We are just as fully members of a family, of a neighborhood, of a religious community, or of a social movement as we are members of a state. Although the modern nation-state remains a possible structural expression of democratic self-determination, the complexity of our social lives integrates us into associations that lie above and below the level of the nation-state. These associations mediate the manner in which we relate to the state. If we stop viewing the state as the privileged apex of collective identity, but instead, along with Rawls, "as a union of unions," then citizenship should also be understood as a form of collective identity mediated in and through the institutions of civil society.[13] In the European context, this means that foreigners' claims to citizenship in a political entity should not be established through self-regarding nationalist considerations, but because these individuals show themselves to be capable of membership in civil society through the exercise of certain tasks and the fulfillment of certain conditions. Civil citizenship should lead to political citizenship (Janoski 1998).

What are some reasonable conditions through the fulfillment of which transitions from one status of alienage to another can be carried out?[14] Length and nature of residency in a particular country are undoubtedly top among such criteria. Minimal knowledge of the language of the host country, as well as a certain "civil knowledge" about the laws and governmental forms of that country, are others. Criteria such as these can be formulated and applied reasonably.

Currently, there are three competing models of political incorporation of immigrants into the European Union: the German, the Dutch, and the French models. The German model favors nationalization through naturalization and the extension of rights to third-country nationals as a result of their decision to forfeit the citizenship of their countries of origin. After the liberalization of German citizenship from *jus sanguinis* (blood right) to *jus soli* (territorial right), all children born to foreign parents, one of whom had been a legal resident of Germany for eight years, automatically obtain German citizenship. At age twenty-three they must forfeit either German citizenship or that of their country of origin. Dual citizenship is not permitted and remains a highly volatile political issue. Apart from some attempts on the part of the Green party to bring local and regional voting rights for foreign residents to the political table, the current political focus of the German left and liberals is on the newly passed immigration bill, which now legally recognizes and permits entry into Germany for the purposes of immigration. In addition, Germany has lowered to eight years the required residency duration for the naturalization of young immigrants between the ages of sixteen and twenty-three. For adult foreigners, the residency requirement prior to access to citizenship remains fifteen years, as compared with the usual five to eight years for most other countries, including the United States.

The Dutch model is unique in that the city of Amsterdam grants city citizenship to its foreign residents after five years and permits them to take part in citywide elections and to form political parties. The government of Amsterdam has gone farthest in dissociating the expectation of a homogeneous cultural identity from the exercise of political citizenship rights. The granting of political rights to third-country national residents of the city of Amsterdam does not alter the status of these individuals within the European Union. They would still not be able to freely move to France from the Netherlands, for example, and assume residency and employment there. However, the fact that their interests and voices are represented at the municipal level means that they will be effective participants in the national dialogue concerning their juridical status.

The French model, like the German one, accepts an equalization of the rights of third-country nationals only after they are naturalized. The French model is more liberal than the German one in that the granting of *jus soli* citizenship to immigrant children is no longer made dependent on the residency status of their parents; rather, their access to French citizenship is automatic once they have resided in France during their formative high-school years. For several years, the ruling Socialist government in France, unhappy with the automatism with which French citizenship could be acquired, requested of immigrant youth a formal demonstration of the will to be a French citizen after their eighteenth year. Many young people who had neither the information nor the resources to take advantage of this legislation fell through the cracks. The current practice substitutes socialization via the French school system for a demonstration of the will to republican citizenship. Children born in France of two foreign-born parents are French if they live in France and have done so throughout their adolescence. Immigrant children born on French soil become French citizens at thirteen through the request of their parents, at sixteen through their own request, and automatically at eighteen. Dual citizenship is granted in some cases only and is not generally encouraged.

These developments point in contradictory directions: although throughout the European Union a dissociation of cultural identity from the exercise of political citizenship can be observed for EU citizens, for third-country resident nationals these ties are reinforced between identities and institutions, between national membership and democratic citizenship rights. Nevertheless, a trend toward the liberalization of citizenship rights is visible throughout the European Union. With the exception of Austria, Luxembourg, and Greece, most EU countries permit citizenship by naturalization; and, after the reform of Germany's *jus sanguinis* citizenship law in January 1999, most EU countries practice a form of more or less liberalized *jus soli*. The city of Amsterdam is an exception to this trend toward "participation through nationalization" in that it makes not the will to nationalize but the will to live and participate in a city the basis for the acquisition of democratic participation rights.

The discrepancy that exists in the political participation rights of EU citizens and third-country nationals across the European Union and within each member country is one aspect of the two-tiered status of membership that is currently developing. Equally significant are the restrictions on the mobility and employment opportunities of third-country nationals with legal residency status. Given the totally unclear status of European citizenship as distinct from national membership, an EU-wide residency status still appears inconceivable.

Immigration and Emigration: Are They Symmetrical?

Returning to the central philosophical problem concerning the principles of liberal-democratic membership, are there any justifiable conditions under which a liberal-democratic polity can close its borders to outsiders seeking admission? My short answer is, "No, there are none." There are some justifiable restrictions on the quality and quantity of new immigration that nation-states can allow, but never a situation where borders would be completely closed. Furthermore, many of these plausibly justifiable restrictions, such as limiting the entry of individuals and groups who can be identified as posing a military, security, or immunological threat to a country, themselves often permit serious contestation. Think of how the claim that certain individuals pose a "national security threat" can and has been misused throughout history to prevent political dissidents from entering countries and has led to the creation of categories of "unwanted" aliens.[15] The virtues of liberal democracies do not consist in their capacity to close their borders but in their capacity to hear the claims of those who, for whatever reason, knock at their doors. Hearing these claims does not mean automatically granting them or recognizing them, but it does mean that the moral claim of the one who is seeking admission imposes a reciprocal duty to examine each case on its merits.

In other words, there is a fundamental human right to exit as well as to seek admission into a political community, a right that is grounded in the recognition of the individual as an autonomous person entitled to the exercise of other rights. The fundamental right to human liberty entails the right to entry and exit. This fundamental right creates a set of reciprocal obligations and duties whereby states should not prevent the exit of those who want to leave, nor completely block off those who want to enter. Any restrictions to be placed on the right of entry and exit must be made compatible with, as well as being limited by, this fundamental human right.

This right of entry and exit is a moral claim and not a legal right, which would be defended by an established authority with legal, coercive powers.[16] This right articulates a moral claim in that the recognition of the fundamental human liberty to express allegiance to the political order knowingly and willingly entails the right to exit when such allegiance is not forthcoming. Citizens are not prisoners of their respective states. Only a polity that violates other fundamental human liberties would also limit the freedom of its citizens to exit.

In one of the few contemporary discussions of these issues, Michael Walzer argues that "The fact that individuals can rightly leave their own country, however, doesn't generate a right to enter another (any other). Immigration and emigration are morally asymmetrical" (Walzer 1983, 40). This is wrong: the asymmetry of these rights cannot be maintained, for two reasons. The first is a pragmatic consideration, which is also morally relevant. In a world where the surface of the earth is already divided into nation-states, or at least into political units that exercise sovereignty over their territory, the right to exit effectively means that one lands on someone else's territory; at every stretch of the passage, one would be crossing into the sovereign territory of some other political entity. Therefore, to acknowledge a right to exit means to acknowledge a right to entry. This *right to entry* must be distinguished from the *claim to membership*, but at this stage only the right to entry is under consideration.

The second reason this asymmetry breaks down is that the fundamental right to exit is only meaningful if one can reverse moral perspectives and recognize that, for some, to be able to go means, for others, that strangers will come, but also that we are all potentially strangers in other lands. If we want to argue that we have a right to leave, then we are also saying that others have to recognize us potentially as strangers who may want to enter their country. But if we want this claim recognized for ourselves, then we also must recognize it for others. Only the mutual recognition of the reciprocal obligations generated by this right gives it meaning as a moral claim. There is a fundamental human right to exit only if there is also a fundamental human right to entry—to admittance, but not necessarily to membership.

What is the distinction between *admittance* and *membership*?[17] All organized political communities have the right to control criteria of membership and procedures of inclusion and exclusion in their polities. Criteria that must be fulfilled, qualifications that must be met, and procedures that must be followed are usually stipulated by all liberal democracies in granting access to membership and eventually citizenship. Admittance does not create an automatic entitlement to membership, but it does entail the moral right to know how and why one can or cannot be a member, whether one will or will not be granted refugee status or permanent residency. A liberal democratic polity must treat the other, the foreigner and the stranger, in accordance with internationally recognized norms of human respect and dignity, and this means according to transparent regulations for which identifiable governmental authorities can be held accountable. Furthermore, nonmembers and their advocates must have the right to litigate and contest decisions concerning immigration, asylum, and refugee status (cf. Walzer 1983, 60). The prerogative of democratic sovereigns to define criteria of political inclusion is not an unconditional right, but should be subject to legal as well as moral scrutiny. Democratic sovereignty and human-rights considerations must mutually limit and control each other.

Liberal democracies are always under a burden of proof when policing their borders, therefore, to prove that their methods do not violate fundamental human rights. A democratic state may wish to examine marriage certificates among citizens and noncitizens for their veracity, but a democratic state that subjects women to gynecological exams in order to test whether or not marriage was consummated, as Margaret Thatcher's England did, is violating fundamental human rights of equal treatment and respect of bodily integrity.

Democratic states anxious to maintain certain standards of living among their population are free to regulate their labor markets and punish employers employing illegal aliens without proper documentation, at low wages and unjust conditions, or they may choose to recruit only those workers from certain foreign countries who possess certain skills. But a democratic state that brings in such individuals must also specify under what conditions they may or may not continue to stay in the country, whether they can change their status once within the country, and what kinds of rights and benefits they are entitled to in virtue of having been granted admission. A liberal democracy cannot push entire categories of peoples away, as Germany attempted to do in the early 1990s with the argument that immigrants and asylum seekers negatively affected the domestic standard of living. Besides the dubious causal economic connections established in such assertions, there is the more fundamental problem of the violation of human rights, whether of asylum seekers under internationally recognized conventions or of foreign residents seeking political membership. Economic self-interest grounds can never alone serve as moral trumps in immigration and asylum policies, and liberal democracies must seek to balance their economic well-being—if, in fact, external immigration is affecting domestic markets as adversely as some argue—with commitment to, and respect for, fundamental human rights.[18]

Sovereignty, Human Rights, and the Nation-State

In his 1923 work *The Crisis of Parliamentary Democracy*, Carl Schmitt wrote: "Every actual democracy rests on the principle that not only are equals equal but unequals will not be treated equally. Democracy requires, therefore, first homogeneity and second—if the need arises—elimination or eradication of heterogeneity. . . . Equality is only interesting and valuable politically so long as it has substance, and for that reason the possibility and the risk of inequality . . . [that] every adult person, simply as a person, should eo ipso be politically equal to every other person, this is a liberal, not a democratic idea" (Schmitt [1923] 1985, 9–11). Schmitt drives a wedge between liberal and democratic conceptions of equality. Although he understands liberalism to advocate universal moral equality, he views democracy as only stipulating the equality of all as members of a sovereign people. This argument neglects the specificity of modern, as opposed to ancient, projects of democracy.

For the moderns, the moral equality of individuals qua human beings and their equality as citizens are imbricated in each other. The modern social contract of the nation-state bases its legitimacy on the principle that the consociates of the nation are entitled to equal treatment as right-bearing persons precisely because they are also human beings; citizenship rights rest on this more fundamental moral equality that individuals enjoy as persons. "The Rights of Man" and "The Rights of the Citizen" are coeval for the moderns.

To be sure, there are conflicts and tensions in these formulations: every national social contract circumscribes the circle of its citizens, thus creating distinctions among those who are signatories of the social contract and those to whom the contract applies but who have no standing as signatories. Modern liberal democracies, established in the wake of the American and French Revolutions, proclaim at one and the same time that the consociates of the sovereign body are to treat one another as rights-bearing individuals in virtue of their humanity. Yet these very proclamations, articulated in the name of universal truths of nature, reason, or God, also define and delimit boundaries, creating exclusions within the sovereign people as well as without. There are "mere auxiliaries to the Republic" within—as Kant called women, children, and propertyless servants within (Kant [1797] 1996, 92)—and foreigners and strangers without. This tension does not arise, as Carl Schmitt assumes, because liberalism and democracy contradict each other. Rather, there is a constitutive dilemma in the attempt of modern nation-states to justify their legitimacy through recourse to universalist moral principles of human rights, which then get particularistically circumscribed. The tension between the universalistic scope of the principles that legitimize the social contract of the modern nation and the claim of this nation to define itself as a closed community plays itself out in the history of the reforms and revolutions of the past two centuries.

When Hannah Arendt wrote that "the right to have rights" was a fundamental claim, as well as an insoluble political problem, she did not mean that aliens, foreigners, and residents did not possess any rights (Arendt [1951] 1979, 226). In certain circumstances (e.g., Jews in Germany, Greek and Armenian nationals in the period of the founding of the republic of Turkey, or German refugees in Vichy France, to select but a few cases), entire groups of peoples were "denaturalized," or "denationalized," and lost the protection of a sovereign legal body. For Arendt, neither the theoretical nor the institutional solutions to this problem were at hand. Theoretically, she needed to explore further the tension between national sovereignty and human-rights claims; institutionally, several arrangements have emerged since the end of World War II that express the learning process of nations in dealing with the horrors of the past century: the limiting and testing of parliamentarian majorities through constitutional courts, particularly in the domain of human-rights issues; the 1951 Convention relating to the Status of Refugees; the creation of the UN High Commissioner on Refugees (UNHCR); the institution of the World Court, and, more recently, of an International Criminal Court through the treaty of Rome (Robinson 1999). Although procedures of constitutional review, which are becoming more prevalent in European political practice through the development of the European Court of Justice, can help protect the fundamental human and civil rights of ethnic, religious, linguistic, sexual, and other minorities, the UN conventions remain nonenforceable humanitarian guidelines. To this day, the authority of the World Court of Justice in the Hague is contested. Even the International Court of Justice will deal first and foremost with "crimes against humanity." There are still no global courts of justice with the jurisdiction to punish sovereign states for the way they treat refugees, foreigners, and aliens, nor is there a global law-enforcement agency that would carry out such injunctions. In this domain, voluntarily self-incurred obligations on the part of nation-states through the signing of treaties remain the norm.

Yet the treatment of aliens, foreigners, and others is a crucial test for the moral conscience and political reflexivity of liberal democracies. Defining the identity of the sovereign nation is itself a process of fluid, open, and contentious public debate: the lines separating "we" and "you," "us" and "them," more often than not rest on unexamined prejudices, ancient battles, historical injustices, and sheer administrative fiat. The beginnings of every modern nation-state carry the traces of some violence and injustice. So far, Carl Schmitt is right. Nonetheless, modern liberal democracies are self-limiting collectivities that at one and the same time constitute the nation as sovereign and proclaim that the sovereignty of the nation derives its legitimacy from its adherence to fundamental human-rights principles. "We, the people" is an inherently fraught formula, containing in its very articulation the dilemmas of universal respect for human rights and particularistic sovereignty claims (Ackerman 1991). The rights of foreigners and aliens, whether they be refugees or guest workers, asylum seekers or adventurers, indicate that threshold, that boundary, at the site of which the identity of "we, the people" is defined and renegotiated, bounded and unraveled, circumscribed, or rendered fluid.

Notes

Earlier versions of this essay were read at the American Political Science Association meetings in Washington in August 1997; as a plenary address to the German Political Science Association meetings in Bamberg in October 1997; and at the "Dilemmas of European Citizenship" conference at Harvard University, also in October 1997, and at the conference on "Reimagining Belonging: Self and Community in an Era of Nationalism and Postnationality," organized by the Center for International Studies of Aalborg University, Denmark, in May 1999. I would like to thank Jürgen Habermas, Daniel Bell, Veit Bader, Richard Tuck, Carolin Emcke, Glyn Morgan, Sanford Levinson, Andrea SanGiovanni, Sayres Rudy, and Arash Abizadeh for their comments on earlier drafts. Comments and questions raised by Riva Kastoryano, Yasemin Soysal, Yael Tamir, James Tully, and Ulf Hedetoft during the Aalborg conference greatly influenced the final form of these reflections. For the printed version I alone am responsible.

Seyla Benhabib

An earlier version of this essay appeared in German as Benhabib, *Demokratische Gleichheit und kulturelle Vielfalt*, the 1997 Horkheimer Lectures (Frankfurt: Fischer Verlag, 1999), chapter 3. An expanded English version of these lectures appears as *The Claims of Culture: Equality and Diversity in the Global Era* (Princeton, N.J.: Princeton University Press, 2002).

An earlier English translation was published as Benhabib, "Citizens, Residents and Aliens in a Changing World: Political Membership in the Global Era," *Social Research* 66:3 (fall 1999): 709–44. This essay is a revised and expanded version of that article and is reprinted here with the permission of the editors of *Social Research*. In addition to updating demographic figures, this essay also incorporates developments in immigration and asylum issues occurring within the EU as a result of the Treaty of Amsterdam (1997) and the Tampere Council Resolutions (October 1999).

1 Cited by Rainer Muenz, "Migrants, Aliens, Citizens: European Migration and Its Consequences," conference paper presented for the European Forum, 1995–96 Citizenship Project, European University Institute, Florence (April 1996), 14. Recent publications do not indicate great variations in these figures. The 1999 figures for the percentage of foreigners in Germany was 8.9 percent, and their number roughly 7.3 million.

   After the passage of the new "asylum laws" in Germany, first on June 26, 1992, and then on July 27, 1993, Germany is controlling its borders and the number of foreigners allowed into the country much more effectively; however, since 1996, and largely as a result of the civil wars among the member states of the former Yugoslav federation, inflows of asylum seekers into Germany increased in numbers to 100,440 in 1996; this figure is much lower than the 438,200 who applied for asylum in 1992, but still higher than the 57,400 asylum seekers in 1987.

2 Next to foreign workers, asylum applicants, and refugees, the third significant category of "outsiders" in Germany is the "ethnic Germans." They are not native-born Germans but ethnic Germans who, since the thirteenth century, settled in various Central European, Baltic, and formerly Soviet territories. After World War II, millions from this group, referred to as the *"Vertriebene"* (expellees) and *"Aussiedler"* (outsettlers), were expelled from the Soviet Union and other Central and East European countries. A 1953 statute defines the *Aussiedler* as *"Volkszugehörige,"* belonging to the people, and article 116 (1) of the Basic Law of Germany allows them the right to resettle in Germany. Since the early 1980s, some 1,900,000 expellees from Poland, Romania, and the former Soviet Union have entered Germany. See Kanstroom 1993, 165–67). As of 2001, 3.2 million *Aussiedler* lived in Germany and made up 3.9 percent of the population (see Muenz 2001, 1). For an overview of the changing composition of immigrant groups in various European countries, see Messina 1996.

3 The persecution of the Kurdish population in the northern and southeastern regions of Turkey in particular, and the continuing conflict between the Kurdish Communist Party and the Turkish government, have given rise to a new group of asylum seekers—ethnic Kurds who are officially Turkish citizens but persecuted by a country friendly to Germany and seeking membership in the European Union. In 1995, twenty-five thousand Turkish citizens are reported to have sought asylum in Germany; they were preceded by thirty-three thousand citizens from states of the

former Yugoslavia. The capture in 1999 of the fugitive leader of the Kurdish Communist Party, Abdullah Öcalan, led to confrontations in all major European cities among Kurdish sympathizers and local and international government authorities. In Berlin, confrontations occurred when Kurdish guerrillas attacked Turkish businesses and community centers. These disturbances and the civil war–like conditions created in major German cities were important factors in the rejection by large parts of the German public of the new "dual citizenship" legislation proposed by the Social Democratic–Green coalition.

4 See article 8 of C, Part II: "1. Citizenship of the Union is hereby established. Every Person holding the Nationality of a Member State shall be a citizen of the Union." Facsimile reproduction on file with the author.

5 The institution of citizenship among individuals who do not have a common language, a common public sphere, and effective channels of participation is giving rise to a number of important and compelling contemporary debates in political theory and jurisprudence. Some see European citizenship as a fig leaf to cover the considerable divestment of the democratic powers of sovereign peoples to an anonymous "Eurocracy" sitting in Brussels and Geneva; others warn of the growing "democracy deficit" in the Union. Citizenship without participation looms on the horizon, they argue (see Preuss 1995; Balibar 1996; Lehning 1996; Lehning and Weale 1997). See also "Citizenship and Immigration" 1998.

6 See Pintasilgo 1995–96. Other members of this Committee of the Wise are Eduardo Garcia de Enterria, Hartmut Kaelble, Louka Katseli, Frederic Pascal, Bengt Westerberg, and Shirley Williams. Jytte Klausen (1995) pleads for a strong differentiation of citizenship rights from redistributive policies. Although the trend in the European Union context is toward the integration of such rights and redistributive benefits through Union-wide "social rights" for third-country nationals, the curtailment of social rights and benefits, which they have hitherto enjoyed, looms in the offing. Klausen sees an inevitable trade-off between the continuance of protective welfare communities, globalization, and the development of less exclusionary absorption and immigration politics (266). The danger in the current context, though, is that the political voicelessness of third-country nationals in the EU will make it all the more likely that their social rights will be curtailed without, however, a corresponding liberalization trade-off in naturalization and immigration policies. See also de Swaan 1997. For a helpful overview of the current state of policy and jurisprudential reasoning in the Union, see Shaw 1997.

7 See Neuman 1993. The Dublin convention and the second Schengen agreement were signed in June 1990. Schengen included initially Belgium, the Netherlands, Luxembourg, France, and Germany. Italy joined the group in December 1990, Portugal and Spain in June 1991, Sweden, Finland, and Austria subsequently. Both agreements contain rules for determining a "responsible state" that agrees to process an applicant for asylum from a non-EU country. The Schengen agreement attempts to abolish border controls along the common frontiers of the parties and to compensate for the relaxation of borders by more vigilant migration and law-enforcement policies at airports. A Schengen Information System was also established that creates an electronic database to facilitate control of criminals and terrorists (see ibid., 506–7; Kanastroom 1993, 198ff.).

8 A few notable exceptions to this widespread neglect of citizenship issues have been Barbalet 1988; Shklar 1991; Schuck and Smith 1985. Undoubtedly, conditions of globalization the world over are leading to a renewal of interest in citizenship in political theory as well (see Spinner 1994).

9 Although this essay focuses on Europe in general, and Germany in particular, with the introduction of NAFTA similar developments are taking place in the North American continent. So far, the fact that the United States and Canada define themselves as "countries of immigration" has created a situation that is normatively different from that of most European Union countries, which do not consider themselves immigrant societies. The passage of Proposition 187 in California, the ensuing battle against the curtailment of social benefits to nonlegal resident aliens, the shameful treatment of Haitian refugees, as well as administrative irregularities at the Immigration and Naturalization Service concerning adequate background checkups of prospective citizens, and so on, are all events pointing to the growing salience of these issues for the United States. Normatively, the theory and practice of acceptance into the political commonwealth through incorporation into civil society are most clearly practiced in Canada and the United States. The practices of immigration and naturalization in these countries present a clear alternative to the models prevailing on the European Continent.

10 The United Kingdom does permit national voting rights to those who hold Commonwealth citizenship (citizens of Canada, Australia, New Zealand, the West Indies, etc.). On the complexities of British nationality and naturalization laws, see Hansen 2002.

11 In "Access to Citizenship: A Comparison of Twenty-Five Nationality Laws," Patrick Weil argues that "starting with different legal traditions and different historical patterns of immigration, emigration and minorities, convergence occurs; they converge through different paths and political agendas because, in the context of stabilization of borders and incorporation of democratic values, many of these countries faced problems of immigration. The *jus soli* states became slightly more restrictive and the *jus sanguinis* ones moved towards *jus soli*" (Weil 2000, 3–4). Weil is expressing the same hopes and reaching the same conclusions as the authors of the *Asylum Acquis Handbook* (van Krieken 2000), all of whom similarly urge EU-wide convergence and harmonization. I personally see a bumpier road ahead and anticipate that there will be backlashes, coming both from the left and the right against an all-too speedy liberal harmonization of citizenship and asylum regulations. Particularly with the expansion of the EU to twenty-one countries in 2003 (when the Czech Republic, Cyprus, Poland, Hungary, Slovenia, and Estonia become members) and to twenty-seven in 2007 (with the inclusion of Romania, Bulgaria, Lithuania, Latvia, the Slovak Republic, and Malta), different historical and constitutional traditions regarding the treatment of minorities and foreigners will have to mix and mingle with one another in a very short span of time. Consider, for example, the number of issues that will arise concerning the Roma and Sinti and other Gypsy populations of Europe, whose migratory patterns of movement cut across Spain, the Czech Republic, Hungary, and Romania. The EU will be faced with the citizenship claims of one of Europe's oldest deterritorialized peoples, and thus will have to reconsider the strong linkage between nationality and citizenship that still forms the normative

basis of citizenship of the Union—only citizens of member EU states can be citizens of the EU, and others cannot.

The fact that EU expansion plans do not yet include Turkey and the former republics of Yugoslavia, and the fact that populations drawn from these countries still form the largest group of third-country nationals in the European Union, only suggests that EU expansion will exacerbate existing discrepancies rather than ameliorate them.

12 Several of Rawls's students, aware of the magnitude of this gap, have expanded the premises of political liberalism into the field of international justice (see O'Neil 1986; Pogge 1992, 42). Rawls began to address some of these issues in Rawls 1999.

13 Craig Calhoun has pointed out that, in the modern nation-state, citizenship status is an unmediated relationship between the state and the individual, in that citizenship is not normatively dependent on membership in some secondary mediating body. This is, of course, legally and constitutionally true, in that citizenship is an individual right and not a privilege of a corporate body, such as a guild, for example, as it was in the Middle Ages. However, I am stressing that the relationship of the individual to the state is sociologically, de facto even if not de jure, mediated by civil society and its institutions. In fact, through the recognition of family unification as a basic human right, international law also acknowledges this mediated relationship to membership in the state. Furthermore, almost all liberal democracies respect the principle that the economic, scientific, artistic, technological, and medical needs of civil society offer sufficient conditions for the entry as well as the granting of permission to work to many foreigners. In this respect too, the nation-state accepts the mediation of civil society institutions on the road leading to political membership. I am pleading here for a clearer recognition of this mediation process between civil society—including the family and the market—and the state.

14 From the standpoint of political philosophy, we are entering the domain of administrative detail, which might be better left to legislators and bureaucrats. As Hegel is reported to have quipped about Fichte's political theory, he did not have to be concerned about passports! Yet today the passport has become the symbolic document that represents all the perplexities and inequities of current citizenship regimes and practices. It is no less worthy of philosophical reflection than the postcard!

Also, criteria of naturalization for immigrants, such as length of residency and language requirements, can impact diverse sectors of the foreign population of a specific country very differently. These issues of differential impact can, in turn, enable or hinder the acquisition of citizenship rights by different groups. For example, a language proficiency proof of some sort seems an eminently reasonable requirement on the part of a host country in granting residency permits and citizenship to foreigners. On the other hand, this requirement will most likely disadvantage women and the elderly, who usually, though not in all cases, enter the host country under family unification clauses and who do not participate in the civil society and economy or the public sphere of the host country, or do so to a very limited extent. Under these circumstances, language proficiency requirements that are not accompanied by subsidized language instruction can be discriminatory against women and the elderly members of the foreign population.

15 In view of the terrorist attacks on the World Trade Center and the Pentagon on September 11, 2001, and the legitimate security concerns of the United States and

other countries around the world, this claim may appear extreme. In a liberal democracy, liberty can be curtailed for the sake of assuring greater liberty. Security concerns may be legitimate grounds for policing borders more effectively, instituting stiffer tests of scrutiny for those who seek entry, and the like. However, since September 11 we are also faced with some unprecedented legal developments in the United States that threaten to undermine the civil liberties of innocent people.

The USA Patriot Act, which was passed by Congress on October 25, 2001, proceeds, as Ronald Dworkin has pointed out, from a "breathtakingly vague and broad definition of terrorism and of aiding terrorism" (Dworkin 2002, 44) and relaxes rules that protect people suspected of crime from unfair investigation and prosecution. There are close to six hundred detainees in U.S. prisons of Middle Eastern origin who have been denied counsel and even visiting rights with their families. In numerous cases, their crime seems to be no more than an infraction of immigration laws such as overstaying their visas.

Furthermore, the status of the captured al Qaeda and Taliban soldiers, who have been quartered in Guantánamo Bay, Cuba, remains unclear from the standpoint of international law. Because Guantánamo Bay is a military base and not part of the territorial United States, it is constitutionally a no-man's-land. It serves as an extraterritorial and extralegal space in which the "unwanted business" of various administrations, such as the locking up of Haitian refugees under the Clinton administration, can be carried out. Furthermore, faced with the outcry of world public opinion and particularly of European allies, the treatment of the captured prisoners was subject to increased scrutiny. Without clarifying the extralegal status of Guantánamo Bay, the attorney general and President Bush introduced a distinction between "legal combatants," that is, prisoners of war who would fall under the protection of the Geneva Convention, and "illegal combatants," whose rights would not be so protected. As a precedent, President Bush appealed to the distinction introduced during the Vietnam War era between South Vietnamese army members and civilians, who were considered prisoners of war, and members of the National Liberation Front, who were not. Yet the juridical tenability of these distinctions in light of customary international law as well as the Geneva Convention remains a matter of contention.

16 This distinction was brought to my attention by Jürgen Habermas. However, although no authority exists for coercing nation-states to accept refugees and asylum seekers, citizens' groups of the concerned countries may themselves litigate against their own government and agencies on the grounds that these may have violated fundamental human rights, the constitution, or administrative procedures in their treatment of foreigners. In such cases, concerned citizens act as the advocates of the foreigner against their own governmental authority. Of course, this legal right to "sue" one's own state authorities is not equivalent to a coercive right against them, but, as recent battles over the treatment of refugees, asylum seekers, and immigrants the world over show, there is a "communicative power" that derives from such actions and that may attain coercive influence.

17 I want to thank Glyn Morgan for bringing this distinction to my attention in his comments at the "Dilemmas of European Citizenship" conference at Harvard University, October 1997.

18 Since the adoption of Proposition 187 in California through a referendum in 1994

(denying all state services, including medical care, to illegal immigrants), a number of measures have been enacted that outstrip even Proposition 187 in their severity. Although a federal district court judge in Los Angeles struck down Proposition 187 in 1996 (the case is under appeal), as part of the state's welfare-reform agenda, Congress enacted a bill that denied certain welfare benefits, including food stamps and financial support for the aged and the disabled, to all immigrants, whether legal or illegal. The law passed on August 22, 1996, was unusual in that it applied even to those admitted before that date; a year later, a law that restored certain benefits to the infirm and the aged who had been admitted prior to August 22, 1996, was passed, and in June 1998 food stamps were restored to children, the elderly, and the disabled lawfully admitted to the United States before that date. Owen Fiss (1998, 5), in a provocative piece, argues that these amendments raise, "with special urgency and clarity, the question whether enactments imposing social disabilities on immigrants can be squared with the Constitution, particularly the provision that guarantees to all persons—not all citizens, but all persons—equal protection of the laws." See also the responses to his article that follow.

Works Cited

Ackerman, Bruce. 1991. *We, the People.* Cambridge: Belknap Press at Harvard University.

Arendt, Hannah. [1951] 1979. *The Origins of Totalitarianism.* New York: Harcourt, Brace Jovanovich.

Aristotle. 1941. "Politics." In *Basic Works of Aristotle,* ed. Richard McKeon, trans. B. Jowett. New York: Random House.

Ausländerrecht. 1997. *Die Gesetzestexte des "Deutschen Bundesrechts."* Frankfurt: Suhrkamp.

Balibar, Étienne. 1996. "Is European Citizenship Possible?" *Public Culture* 8: 355–76.

Barbalet, J. M. 1988. *Citizenship: Rights, Struggle, and Class Inequality.* Minneapolis: University of Minnesota Press.

Barber, Benjamin. 1995. *Jihad vs. McWorld: How Globalism and Tribalism Are Reshaping the World.* New York: Ballantine Books.

Bauböck, Rainer. 1994. *Transnational Citizenship: Membership and Rights in International Migration.* Aldershot: Edward Elgar.

———. 1998. "The Crossing and Blurring of Boundaries in International Migration: Challenges for Social and Political Theory." In *Blurred Boundaries: Migration, Ethnicity, Citizenship,* ed. Rainer Bauböck and J. Rundell. Vienna: Ashgate Publications.

Beiner, Ronald, ed. 1995. *Theorizing Citizenship.* Albany: State University of New York Press.

Benhabib, Seyla. 1992. *Situating the Self: Gender, Community and Postmodernism in Contemporary Ethics.* New York and London: Routledge and Polity Press.

———. 1997a. "Strange Multiplicities: The Politics of Identity and Difference in a Global Context." In *The Divided Self: Identity and Globalization,* publication of Macalaster College International Program 4 (spring 1997): 27–59.

———. 1997b. "Wer Sind Wir? Probleme politischer Identitäten im ausgehenden 20. Jahrhundert." *Working Papers in Political Science* 42. Vienna: Institut für Höhere Studien.

———. 1999a. *Demokratische Gleichheit und Kulturelle Vielfalt: Die Horkheimer Vorlesungen.* Frankfurt: Fischer Verlag.

———. 1999b. "Germany Opens Up." *Nation,* June 21, 6.

————. 1999c. "Citizens, Residents and Aliens in a Changing World: Political Membership in the Global Era." *Social Research* 66:3 (fall): 709–44.

————. 2002. *The Claims of Culture: Equality and Diversity in the Global Era.* Princeton, N.J.: Princeton University Press.

Brubaker, Rogers. 1992. *Citizenship and Nationhood in France and Germany.* Cambridge: Harvard University Press.

Bundesverfassungsgericht. 1997. "Unionsbürgerwahlrecht I-," Beschluss der 3. Kammer des 2. Senats vom 8.1.1997. 2BvR 2862/95 [decision of the German Supreme Court concerning the election rights of EU citizens].

Carens, Joseph. 1995. "Aliens and Citizens: The Case for Open Borders." In *Theorizing Citizenship,* ed. Ronald Beiner. Albany: State University of New York Press. 229–55.

————. 2000. *Culture, Citizenship, and Community: A Conceptual Exploration of Justice and Evenhandedness.* Oxford: Oxford University Press.

"Citizenship and Immigration." 1998. Special section in *Constellations: An International Journal of Critical and Democratic Theory* 4:3 (January).

Cohen, Jean L. 1999. "Changing Paradigms of Citizenship and the Exclusiveness of the Demos." *International Journal of Sociology* 14:3 (September): 245–68.

Council of Europe Publishing. 1996. *Recent Demographic Developments in Europe.* Brussels: Council of Europe Publishing.

de Jong, Cornelius. 2000. "Harmonization of Asylum and Immigration Policies: The Long and Winding Road from Amsterdam via Vienna to Tampere." In *The Asylum Acquis Handbook: The Foundations for a Common European Asylum Policy,* ed. Peter J. van Krieken, 21–37. The Hague: T. M. C. Asser Press.

de Swaan, Abram. 1997. "The Receding Prospects for Transnational Social Policy." *Theory and Society: Renewal and Critique in Social Theory* 26:4 (August): 561–75.

Dworkin, Ronald. 2002. "The Threat to Patriotism." *New York Review of Books* 49:3 (February 28): 44–47.

Fiss, Owen. 1998. "The Immigrant as Pariah." *Boston Review* 23:5 (October–November): 4–6.

Friedman, Jonathan. 1995. *Cultural Identity and Global Process.* London: Sage Publications.

Galston, William. 1991. *Liberal Purposes: Goods, Virtues, and Duties in the Liberal State.* Cambridge: Cambridge University Press.

Hansen, Randall. 2002. "From Subjects to Citizens: Immigration and Nationality Law in the United Kingdom." In *Towards a European Nationality,* ed. Randall Hansen and Patrick Weil, 69–95. Wiltshire: Palgrave.

Heiberg, Marianne, ed. 1994. *Subduing Sovereignty: Sovereignty and the Right to Intervene.* London: Pinter Publishers.

Honig, Bonnie. 1998. "Immigrant America? How 'Foreignness' Solves Democracy's Problems." *Social Text* 3 (fall 1998): 1–27.

————. 2001. *Democracy and the Foreigner.* Princeton, N.J.: Princeton University Press.

Huber, Ernst R. 1961. *Dokumente zur deutschen Verfassungsgeschichte* 1. Stuttgart: Kohlhammer.

Ignatieff, Michael. 1994. *Blood and Belonging: Journeys into the New Nationalism.* New York: Farrar, Straus and Giroux.

Janoski, Thomas. 1998. *Citizenship and Civil Society.* New York: Cambridge University Press.

Judt, Tony. 1996. *A Grand Illusion? An Essay on Europe.* New York: Hill and Wang.

Kanstroom, Daniel. 1993. "Wer Sind Wir Wieder? Laws of Asylum, Immigration, and

Citizenship in the Struggle for the Soul of the New Germany." *Yale Journal of International Law* 18:155.

Kant, Immanuel. [1795] 1963. "Perpetual Peace." In *On History*, trans. Lewis White Beck, 85–137. Indianapolis and New York: Bobbs-Merrill.

———. [1797] 1996. *The Metaphysics of Morals.* Trans. Mary Gregor. Cambridge: Cambridge University Press.

Kessler, Charles R. 1998. "The Promise of American Citizenship." In *Immigration and Citizenship in the Twenty-first Century*, ed. Noah M. J. Pickus, 3–41. New York: Rowman and Littlefield.

Klausen, Jytte. 1995. "Social Rights Advocacy and State Building. T. H. Marshall in the Hands of the Reformers." *World Politics* 47 (January 1995): 244–67.

Kleger, Heinz. 1995. "Transnationale Staatsbürgerschaft oder: Lässt sich Staatsbürgerschaft entnationalisieren?" *Archiv für Rechts- und Sozialphilosophie* 62: 85–99.

Klusmeyer, Douglas B. 1993. "Aliens, Immigrants, and Citizens: The Politics of Inclusion in the Federal Republic of Germany." *Daedalus* (summer issue on the topic "Reconstructing Nations and States") 122:3: 81–114.

Kristeva, Julia. 1991. *Strangers to Ourselves.* Trans. Leon S. Roudiez. New York: Columbia University Press.

Kymlicka, Will, and Wayne Norman. 1995. "Return of the Citizen: A Survey of Recent Work on Citizenship Theory." In *Theorizing Citizenship*, ed. Ronald Beiner. Albany: State University of New York Press. 283–323.

Lehning, Percy B. 1996. "European Citizenship: A Mirage?" Paper delivered at the Tenth International Conference of Europeanists, Chicago, March 14–16.

Lehning, Percy B., and Albert Weale, eds. 1997. *Citizenship, Democracy and Justice in the New Europe.* London and New York: Routledge.

Locke, John. [1690] 1980. *Second Treatise of Civil Government.* Ed. C. B. McPherson. Indianapolis: Hackett.

Macedo, Stephen. 1990. *Liberal Virtues: Citizenship, Virtue and Community.* Oxford: Oxford University Press.

Marshall, T. H. 1950. *Citizenship and Social Class and Other Essays.* London: Cambridge University Press.

Mendes, Candido, and Luis E. Soares. 1996. *Cultural Pluralism, Identity, and Globalization.* Rio de Janeiro: UNESCO/ISSC/EDUCAM Publications.

Messina, Anthony. 1996. "The Not So Silent Revolution. Postwar Migration to Western Europe." *World Politics* 49 (October): 130–54.

Morgan, Glyn. 1997. Comments delivered at the "Dilemmas of European Citizenship" conference at Harvard University, October.

Muenz, Rainer. 1996. "Migrants, Aliens, Citizens: European Migration and Its Consequences." Conference paper presented for the European Forum, 1995–96 Citizenship Project, European University Institute, Florence. April.

———. 2001. "Ethnos or Demos? Migration and Citizenship in Germany." Lecture delivered at the Center for European Studies. On file with the author.

Neuman, Gerald L. 1993. "Buffer Zones against Refugees: Dublin, Schengen and the German Asylum Amendment." *Virginia Journal of International Law* 33: 503–26.

O'Neil, Onora. 1986. *Faces of Hunger: An Essay on Poverty, Justice and Development.* New York: George Allen and Unwin.

Pintasilgo, Maria de Lourdes. 1995–96. "Für ein Europa der politischen und sozialen

Grundrechte." Report of the "Committee of the Wise." Brussels: Publications of the European Commission (October 1995–February 1996).

Plotke, David. 1996. "Immigration and Political Incorporation in the Contemporary United States." Manuscript.

Pogge, Thomas. 1992. "Cosmopolitanism and Sovereignty." *Ethics* 103: 48–75.

Preuss, Ulrich. 1995. "Problems of a Concept of European Citizenship." *European Law Journal* 1:3 (November): 267–81.

Rawls, John. 1993. *Political Liberalism.* New York: Columbia University Press.

———. 1999. *The Law of Peoples.* Cambridge: Harvard University Press.

Robinson, Darryl. 1999. "Defining 'Crimes against Humanity' at the Rome Conference." *American Journal of International Law* (January): 43–57.

Sandel, Michael. 1996. *Democracy's Discontent: America in Search of a Public Philosophy.* Cambridge: Belknap Press at Harvard University.

Schmitt, Carl. [1923] 1985. *The Crisis of Parliamentary Democracy.* Trans. Ellen Kennedy. Cambridge: MIT Press.

Schuck, Peter H., and Rogers M. Smith. 1985. *Citizenship without Consent.* New Haven: Yale University Press.

Shaw, Joe. 1997. "The Many Pasts and Futures of European Citizenship in the European Union." *European Law Review* 22: 554–72.

Shklar, Judith. 1991. "American Citizenship. The Quest for Inclusion." *The Tanner Lectures on Human Values* 10: 386–439. Cambridge: Harvard University Press.

SOPEMI Publications. 1998 and 2000. (The OECD Continuous Reporting System for Migration.) *Trends in International Migration.* Annual Report. Paris.

Soysal, Yasemin Nuhoğlu. 1994. *Limits of Citizenship: Migrants and Postnational Membership in Europe.* Chicago: University of Chicago Press.

Spinner, Jeff. 1994. *The Boundaries of Citizenship: Race, Ethnicity, and Nationality in the Liberal State.* Baltimore and London: Johns Hopkins University Press.

van Amersfoort, Hans. 1982. *Immigrants and the Formation of Minority Groups: The Dutch Experience.* Cambridge: Cambridge University Press.

van Krieken, Peter J., ed. 2000. *The Asylum Acquis Handbook: The Foundations for a Common European Asylum Policy.* The Hague: T. M. C. Asser Press.

Walzer. Michael. 1983. *Spheres of Justice: A Defense of Pluralism and Equality.* New York: Basic Books.

Weil, Patrick. 2000. "Access to Citizenship: A Comparison of Twenty-five Nationality Laws." On file with the author.

Weiler, Joseph H. 1995. "Does Europe Need a Constitution? Demos, Telos and the German Maastricht Decision." *European Law Journal* 1:3 (November): 219–58.

Wertheimer, Jack. 1987. *Unwelcome Strangers: East European Jews in Imperial Germany.* New York: Oxford University Press.

7

Citizenship and Belonging:

Beyond Blood and Soil

Citizenship Identity

Since the early 1980s the question of citizenship has been a major theme in political debates as well as in research at the intersection of the social sciences, law, and political philosophy. In Europe, the political construction of the European Union, on the one hand, and the incorporation of immigrants into nation-states, on the other, have prompted reflection on the concept of citizenship. These two phenomena, which are a priori separate, raise the question of the relevance of the nation-state and its constitutive elements (citizenship and nationality), as well as that of the relation of nation-states and citizenship to identity.

The concepts of citizenship and nationality, which are interdependent and "interchangeable" within the nation-state framework, are defined above all by membership in a political community (Leca 1992). This membership is shaped by rights (social, political, and cultural) and duties that are embodied in the very concept of citizenship. The concept's implementation by law implies the integration or the incorporation of "foreigners" into the national community with which they are expected to share certain moral and political values. In addition, these foreigners are supposed to adopt or even to "appropriate" historical references as proof of their belonging and of their loyalty to the founding principles of the nation, the only community born of modernity, according to Max Weber (1978).

Debates on citizenship and nationhood reveal precisely these kinds of expectations. They refer to the formation of the nation-state, to its principles, its political traditions, and its identity. This perspective contrasts understandings of citizenship in France and Germany, defined as two republics with two different histories of immigration and assimilation, each representing different political traditions. France is typically represented as an instance of the ideal nation-state type on account of its commitment to egalitarian principles based on notions of "national assimilation." Germany, by contrast, is considered "exclusivist" because of the significance accorded to criteria of membership based on ancestry. Whereas French public discourse emphasizes an elective and political understanding of the nation, the German nation is defined as a cultural and ethnic unity based on common descent as a sign of belonging (Brubaker 1992; Dumont 1991).

Reality, however, is more complex. Obviously, such representations of the nation help to explain, and to some extent justify, the politics of citizenship practiced in both countries. But lately, reality seems to have affected the course of history. The experience of immigration and settlement, coupled with the demand for equality and recognition as citizens, have changed both the understanding of and the laws on citizenship, by reconfiguring the relation between ancestry and birth, that is, blood and soil, in both countries. As a result, the conception of immigration and citizenship in France and Germany has to some extent been modified. Indeed, according to recent French citizenship laws, a child born of foreign parents can become French at the age of sixteen (Weil 1997). In Germany, however, a child born in Germany after January 2000 is automatically German if one of its parents was born in Germany or has resided in the country without interruption during the previous eight years.

Politics and rights of citizenship obviously have an impact on the strategies and degree of participation of immigrants. But the practice of citizenship goes beyond its legal definition, for it finds expression in quite different terms and in a distinct domain. More specifically, the politics of citizenship pertains to agents' political engagement, to their participation in public space. Citizenship can thus be practiced within a cultural, ethnic, or religious community, and even within a "community of circumstance," to use Jean Leca's (1993) term, as well as within a national community. The multiple allegiances resulting from political participation raise the question of an individual's belonging and loyalty to the national community. These allegiances have even become a source of "suspicion" for nation-states, as every discussion of, or public debate on, citizenship and nationhood makes apparent. As a matter of fact, since the 1980s the scope of debates on citizenship related to immigration undoubtedly reflects fears on the part of the political class and the public more generally that citizenship might be depreciated or somehow "desacralized" as a result of the attachment of "immigrants" or "foreigners" to their country of origin. The threat lies in putatively "primordial ties" to a transposed cultural community instead of to the political community of the country of settlement. Immigration, then, emerges as a fundamental issue for nation-states, precisely because it potentially questions the link between citizenship and nationality. Yet, what is truly at stake is the limits of laws and their links with social reality. The key question is: To what extent can legal citizenship be a solution to exclusion and demands for equality?

The question of citizenship thus sets the stage for negotiations of identities between states and immigrants (Kastoryano 1996). The struggle for equality that citizenship entails is effectively extended to a different domain where negotiations of interest turn into negotiations of identity. For states, it is a question of negotiating the means of inclusion of immigrants into the political community on the basis of a new equilibrium between community structures and national institutions. For individuals, citizenship becomes a principle of equality and a way of struggling against "exclusion," be it political, social, or cultural. It becomes a means of claiming recognition as a "citizen," a means of expressing an attachment and loyalty to both a national and an ethnic community in what is essentially a form of liberal and republican participation (Dagger 1997). This conception of citizenship raises the question of the relevance of the triple link between citizenship, nationality, and identity, that is, the link between a political community and a cultural community, where the former functions as a source of right and legitimacy, and the latter as a source of identity.

The separation of three of the nation-state's constitutive elements— citizenship, nationality, and identity—(the fourth being territory) is reinforced by the political construction of Europe. In fact, political participation within the European Union multiplies the memberships and allegiances of individuals and groups and increases the ambiguity between citizenship and nationality, between rights and identity, and between politics and culture.

My aim in this essay is to show how various conceptions of citizenship get articulated through political participation, and my claim is that there is no contradiction, either normatively or empirically, between multilevel participation (or multiple allegiances) and political citizenship. Although citizenship may find expression in various domains (voluntary associations, cultural communities, civil society), only "legal" citizenship allows for a full participation of individuals and groups in a given political community. Similarly, at the European level, despite a transnational participation of immigrants encouraged by the very nature of the European Union and its institutions, the demand for recognition underlying the political strategies of immigrants remains within the framework of the state's legitimacy.

Participation and Engagement

The legal status of citizenship based on birth or ascription crystallizes the representation of the nation-state, its founding principles and values, the ideology on which the national project rests and in which future generations and "newcomers" are expected to believe. Despite the question of its compatibility with identity, legal citizenship remains the key to equal inclusion and full participation in the political community. The politics of citizenship and nationality revealed in the naturalization laws clearly affects political participation and the collective or even individual strategies of immigrants.

In the nineteenth century, the concept of citizenship was expanded so as to encompass diverse domains such as education, health, and welfare. After World War II, the British sociologist T. H. Marshall reconsidered citizenship in terms of social class, complementing the political and legal dimensions of the discussion of rights and equality with a social approach. According to Marshall (1964), citizenship as political rights is prior to citizenship as social rights. Yet, as far as immigrant populations in Europe are concerned, Yasemin Soysal (1994) notes, social rights precede political rights. Indeed, immigrants settle into a form of "social citizenship" on arrival and especially through their integration into the labor market. Immigrants are guaranteed equal access to social rights and equal protection by the Constitution. This kind of "passive citizenship," to use Habermas's (1995) typology, finds its legitimacy in the development of the welfare state and does not include participation in the political community. The latter requires a form of "active citizenship" that is acquired in the case of immigrants through a process of naturalization involving factors such as the duration of their stay, their contribution to society, and their ability "naturally" to identify with the national community.

The concept of citizenship embodies values and action. According to Will Kymlicka and Wayne Norman (1994), it incarnates "responsibility and civic virtues." It thus involves issues that go beyond political status and rights linked to a given national identity. Citizenship should rather be defined as a process of identity formation that emerges through direct or indirect participation and in the name of shared interests of individuals and groups, whether immigrant or not. It finds expression through an individual's commitment to the common good (Leca 1986). This kind of commitment can take the form of participation in a voluntary association recognized by public authorities or community activities of a local or broader cultural, ethnic, and religious variety. In short, it is a question of a commitment to civil society, as well as to a given political community. Citizenship is thus a form of participation in public space, defined not only as a space of communication and shared power, but also as a space of political socialization. *Citizenship identity* thus accompanies political involvement and is the result of this kind of socialization in the context of institutions and their relation to the state.

Yet, legal citizenship affects the ways in which political actors elaborate strategies for participation. In France and Germany, for example, immigrants acquire different tools and elaborate different strategies for political participation. In France, where access to citizenship is based on relatively easy naturalization and the practice of *jus solis*, direct participation is available to younger generations, who thus constitute an important part of the electorate. In Germany, on the other hand, restrictive citizenship laws have prompted activists to develop a set of "compensatory" strategies involving a search for indirect participation through integration and participation in civil society. It is a matter, then, of mobilization within voluntary associations as a way of asserting a collective presence and claim that might affect public opinion and political decisions on behalf of immigrants. In this way a collective involvement or participation in public life is shaped by the very associations that initiate the exercise of citizenship. These associations thus implement a *citizenship identity* that is actively constructed.

Civic participation implies direct participation in a political community and is derived from a "politicization of identities," as is the civil participation available to foreigners in Germany. This process emphasizes identities expressed within voluntary organizations and that constitute a resource for political action. Furthermore, encouraged by the state, such organizations have become a space for the political socialization of immigrants, a space where the rules of the game are internalized and a political culture is assimilated at the same time that solidarity is defined along the lines of various identities. This process of politicization allows immigrants to assert themselves in relation to the state. More specifically, it is a matter of negotiating an identity with the state that, once duly recognized, legitimates the relevant agents as citizens and ensures their representation within national institutions.

In France and Germany, so-called immigrant associations, which are supported by the government as long as their activities fall within the framework of the two countries' respective "integration policies," have been loci of political socialization for immigrant populations since the 1980s. Within these associations individuals of the same national, regional, ethnic, or religious origin establish a collective identity, define limits, create new bonds, and ultimately learn the political behavior that allows them to position themselves vis-à-vis the state. In these community-oriented organizations, discourse alternates with action. They appear increasingly to function as a sanctuary where culture, religion, the nation, and ethnic origins can be interpreted and consolidated, and this in turn enables agents to face the state and negotiate each of the identified elements with public authorities. This "politicization" of identities finds a legitimacy in an identity consciousness that is largely fueled by public debates and reinforced by local or national politicians and specific government practices. Consciousness-raising in connection with cultural differences quickly becomes political action when it is accompanied by demands for their recognition. Consequently, the creation of voluntary associations clearly serves a dual objective: the development of a collective consciousness of difference and the integration of immigrant populations into state structures, that is, an institutional assimilation.

Associations, it is clear, inscribe the notion of "us" and identity-based interests within the demands and political activities of immigrant populations. Political participation thus becomes an extension of community action, and *citizenship identity* is founded in the struggle for universal values—the fight against racism and exclusion and in favor of equality. The same elements that cement the reconstructed cultural community are also the values that integrate newcomers into the national community.

In France, participation also places the very concept of citizenship at the antipodes of exclusion, which highlights its social aspect while maintaining its political and legal aspects. But when legal citizenship is claimed, as it is in Germany, the concept refers to rights: the right to permanent residency, the right to be protected against expulsion, the right to be protected against racism, and the right to political equality. Citizenship thus becomes a way of guaranteeing protection rather than of ensuring cultural integration. At the same time, citizenship implies a struggle for the recognition of the rights inherent in the very concept of citizenship.

In France, the struggle against racism and exclusion has had the effect of blurring the boundaries between a collective "we" and a larger political community. In Germany, the demand for citizenship as protection has led foreigners and Germans to adopt a strategy of withdrawal and regroupment. In France, the political participation of immigrant classes vis-à-vis the national community occurs through a shift from *civil participation*, manifested in particular through association involvement, to *civic participation*, expressed through the act of voting. What is at stake here is the transition from a form of citizenship defined by participation in community institutions only to a form of citizenship manifested by rights that integrate the individual directly into the political community.

In Germany, the "compensatory strategies" developed by militants do not exclude integration. On the contrary, they lead to a search for indirect methods to achieve it. The lack of electoral influence is, for example, compensated for at the local level by a form of citizenship that depends on its social practice and that is defined by the creation of groups of foreigners whose task it is to find their place in relation to the federal government or the *Länder*. Mobilization in this case bespeaks a desire to participate in a democratic system, and the extent of foreign residents' participation in local government is evidence of immigrants' commitment to the idea of establishing a process of representation. Further evidence along these lines can be found in their participation, in the urban areas, in the debates concerning foreigners and the right to vote in local elections, in their election of spokespersons for the purposes of representation, and, clearly, in the demand for equal rights for all (Yalçin-Heckman 1995).

Thus, participation in global institutions where "civic virtue" is supposedly acquired leads to a de facto commitment to national political life. It initiates the very exercise of citizenship and generates the "pride" that individuals express when they are involved in established institutions (at the local or national level) where the interests of participants are represented. The formation of this new citizen identity is in sum the result of a process of what Habermas (1992) calls "political acculturation," that is, the result of an internalization of the national values of the host country. It is important not to forget the educational socialization of the younger generations, who are referred to by the Turkish deputy in the Bundestag, Cem Özdemir, as "new indigenous peoples" (*neue Inländer*). In his mind, they "have experienced the liberty of civil and urban society and follow their own path without yielding to parental pressure or external influences; they are fully impregnated with the local culture (and are thus culturally indigenous or shaped from within)" (personal interview with Özdemir,

Bonn, spring 1995). At that point, the acquisition of German nationality, which in this case is synonymous with citizenship, is not only a right but a moral obligation.

A citizenship that expresses itself in both community-level and national institutions runs counter to the traditional analysis of republican citizenship that combines political involvement and national sentiment by systematically attaching citizenship to its structure, the nation-state, where its identity-based and political aspects are conflated. But actually, whether citizenship be political, juridical, social, or economic and its content identity-based, cultural, or legal, this combination boils down to a sense of loyalty directed at once toward the group, the community, civil society, and the state.

Individual strategies emerge as a result of this kind of interpenetration of three spaces and modes of participation. In France, the relevant strategy can be observed at the level of voter behavior and is increasingly collectivist (Dazi and Leveau 1988). In Germany, it is a matter of a collectivist strategy, but also a compensatory one, for citizen identity does not make agents "spectators who vote," as Rousseau put it, but agents who, by influencing public opinion or government decisions, seek to make others vote.

Although a "social citizenship" that includes foreigners in existing corporate structures translates as direct participation in civil society, this participation is only indirect with regard to purely political citizenship. Only legal citizenship carries the right to equal participation in the political community in the full sense of the term. Its relation to a claimed identity does not subvert that right. On the contrary, it poses the question of recognition and representation within the framework of the legitimacy of the state.

Citizenship and Recognition

The question of citizenship is particularly important because it is intertwined with the issue of recognition (Taylor 1992). The demand for recognition allows groups that claim a specific identity to emerge from the political sidelines and to be integrated fully into the state's structures. In this regard, being recognized is linked to a struggle for emancipation. But whereas emancipation in the Enlightenment period involved separating religion from public life and individuals from their communities in order to ensure that they would identify with the national community, the demand for recognition in this case is born of a desire to be part of a community with equal rights within the framework of the state.

Recognition policies point up contradictions in the very definition of the nation-state; that is, they foreground existing contradictions between the social reality that filters through the demand for recognition, on the one hand, and the political traditions that are imagined as the founding principles of the nation-state, on the other. In France, for example, the issue of a recognition of collective identities is closely linked to Islam. Since the 1990s, local authorities have been guided by a "fear of Islam" (the religion of the North African population in France), and this fear has been used in arguments that seek to establish an essential "incompatibility" between a secular, "republican citizenship" and an attachment to a quite different religious, national, and ethnic identity. The assertion of an Islamic identity, and the emergence of an ethnicity that crystallizes around certain means of political participation, are thus construed as a challenge to the doctrine of a single nation characterized by its cultural unity and the common identity of its citizens. This principle of unity claims to mask all cultural, regional, linguistic, and other differences in the public domain.

The mobilization of the political class around the controversy over students wearing the Islamic veil to school (first in 1989 and then in 1994) focused on French secularism, construed as the very pillar of social cohesion, and had the effect of making the Islamic religion the key to the collective identification of North African immigrants and their demand for recognition. The separation between church and state grants institutional judicial statutes to the Catholic clergy, to the Protestants of the National Federation of Protestant Churches of France, and to Jews governed by the Consistory created by Napoleon. This kind of "recognition" is based on an argument in favor of respect for freedom of religion and the neutrality of the secular state. The question of Islam's status in France causes the old duality between religion and the state to resurface in public debate a century later and raises the issue of whether Islam should be recognized on the same basis as the other religions, and how. Debates about the recognition of Islam have had the effect of repositioning the different religions figuring in the public space that challenges the concept of republican secularism and its practices and at the same time the link between the state and religion in France.

The stakes involved in this kind of recognition are significant. They are measured, among other things, in terms of the size of the "Muslim electorate," even if the latter is sociologically varied and politically diverse; we are dealing here with a potentially powerful pressure group. More important, however, is the fact that the question of Islam's recognition, much like the citizenship question, raises the issue of the principle of equality. This is so on account of the cultural and political acculturation of the population in question, which aspires to combine French citizenship with Muslim beliefs. So high are the stakes that public debate over the very conditions for attributing nationality has been rekindled.

In Germany, the demand for recognition has to do with the status of an ethnic minority that is rooted at once in a Turkish national identity and a Muslim religious identity, two elements that are considered "foreign" to a German collective identity.

The national minority defines itself as foreign in terms of its legal status, while the religious minority defines itself in relation to the marginalization of Islam as compared with other religions that enjoy an official status. The claim for recognition expressed by the Turkish population has placed the issue of citizenship as a right over and against the "hatred for foreigners" and has been fueled by the spectacular racist attacks that have occurred regularly since 1990, as well as by the arrival of the *Aussiedler,* those persons of German origin who are naturalized de facto and de jure upon arrival in Germany.

The problem is that claiming this right brings us back to the issue of legal citizenship, which, conceived in this manner, gives priority to the judicial aspect of the issue, leaving aside the question of identity. The additional step of accepting a dual nationality would directly challenge the fundamental German law combining citizenship and nationality, and the relevant demand thus becomes an element of conflict open to negotiation.

The demands by Turks for dual citizenship emphasize a clear distinction between nationality, citizenship, and identity. At the same time, it is worth noting that this distinction already exists in German political vocabulary. Both citizenship (*Staatsbürgerschaft*) and nationality (*Staatsangehörigkeit*) refer to the state, the first in terms of a system, the second in terms of membership. The reference to dual citizenship lies in this duality. The minority in question manifests a willingness to integrate into the political community by demanding citizenship and expressing its attachment to the nationality of origin. The substance of the debate turns on the conditions of access to citizenship and refers to a reexamination of the concept of the state and its relationship to the definition of the nation. By demanding dual citizenship, Turkish citizens define citizenship as a judicial tool that affords them political representation and nationality as an ethnic identity. This is, in fact, similar to what Germans conceive for themselves. Minority status keeps the respective identities separate, and the debates over dual nationality end up articulating a dual reference to identity.

The acquisition of citizenship on the part of foreigners will possibly not prevent racism in everyday life or in the public sphere, but at least the ethnic minority can use its political force (the vote) to influence political decisions. In Germany, the political influence of the Turks appears to manifest itself within the framework of civil society. In addition to the effects of their associations on public opinion, it is also a matter of making their economic weight evident. As economic agents, immigrants play an important role in the relationship between Germany and Turkey, and some of them dictate the fate of German investment projects in the Turkish-speaking republics of the former Soviet Union. Statistics regularly report on the Turkish population's investments and consumer practices.

But can the security founded on economic presence compensate for the political insecurity caused by not having the right to protection? Can economic integration pave the way for political rights? History gives a partial answer to this question in the sense that during the nineteenth century Germany's economic forces were able to integrate the country into the international economic competition at the time of the great depression of 1873–96. It was because of this that the economic sector later became so important and held such sway over the country's political decisions. By virtue of the same logic, since 1990 the Organization of Turkish Doctors, and later numerous businessmen's associations in different *Länder*, have acted as pressure groups capable of negotiating collective interests ranging from social and cultural rights to measures to be taken against xenophobia. Recalling the role played by economic factors in the redefinition of German identity after the war, these associations are also banking on success in this area to transform themselves into a political force. With this view in mind, they carefully avoid posing as victims and seek, on the contrary, to call attention to their contributions to German society, which become a way of commanding the "respect" of the German authorities.

Does such an approach replace the interpretation of citizenship linked to the bourgeois status of medieval origin *(Bürger)*? In Germany, this second view of citizenship corresponds more closely to membership in civil society than to an allegiance to the political community. Civil society is in effect understood as a society of bourgeois *(die bürgerliche Gesellschaft)* that is not only separate from the state and its institutions, but in fact is in opposition to them. In this sense, any individual participating in public life dominated by economic competition can be considered a citizen. It is within this logic that one should interpret the term *ausländische Mitbürger* (foreign co-citizens), introduced into the public debate by the Greens. The expression in essence indicates an acceptance of Turkish citizens in German society through economic citizenship, in the absence of political citizenship. Becoming a bourgeois would in this case be a step toward naturalization, as the German term *Einbürgerung* suggests, even when used in reference to the state (*Staatsbürger*) rather than the city, as is the case with the bourgeois.

This very specific concept of citizenship makes politics subservient to the economy. It is accompanied by a discourse that emphasizes identification with a global society where economic success is viewed as the foundation of "ethnic pride." Identification with an ethnic community finds its place only in civil society, where citizenship is exercised. But, at the same time, economic success ensures a negotiating power and lends legitimacy to the demand for dual citizenship and for recognition within society.

The right to participate in the exercise of power through legal, political citizenship has yet to be won. The dual nationality demanded by the Turks finds a basis in a logic that would reduce nationality to an identity and citizenship to a right. And this would lead precisely to a bargaining for a moral, national-ethnic personality built on a dual reference to German civil society through residency (with the rights and duties that are linked to it) and to the nationality of the country of origin (for those who recognize themselves in this identity). The result would be the construction of a national minority, and it thus becomes clear that the success of negotiations for citizenship hinges on this ethnic identification expressed through minority status.

In France and Germany, participation and political involvement visibly fit into the historical continuity of the role of the state in France and of civil society in Germany. Having said this, records of membership and political involvement show that the practice of citizenship is detached from a concept exclusively linked to national identity. In a discourse that links citizenship to the phenomenon of exclusion, the concept of citizenship appears above all as a measure of compensation in the social sphere for failings in the political and legal spheres. A citizenship that is limited to active participation in civil society accomplishes its political function even when deprived of legal status. Thus, in Germany, participation in a so-called republican political community or a citizenship oriented toward civil society calls into question the definition and practice of citizenship. It is a matter, more specifically, of a citizenship to counter social exclusion and to foster political inclusion.

Furthermore, citizenship as civic participation does not always theoretically preclude the expression of collective identities. The principle of new ethnic identifications defined in religious or national terms becomes one of the stakes of citizenship that is open to negotiation. It essentially implies defining the limits of what differences can be recognized. The

expression of a citizen's attachment to other communities (ethnic or religious) does not contradict, either empirically or normatively, the exercise
of citizenship. On the contrary, officially recognizing these identities
would allow them to develop within the framework of representative institutions far from the influence of the country of origin. Not recognizing
them, on the other hand, poses the problem of equality between different
identities and how they are represented. What is needed is some kind of
balance between civil society and the state, a link between cultural diversity and citizenship that threatens neither civic principles nor the ultimate
identity of the political community as a whole.

Postnational or Transnational Membership?

Such an approach goes beyond the concept of citizenship within the
framework of the nation-state and consequently leads to a dissociation of
citizenship from nationality, which in turn reduces the former to political
rights and gives the latter a purely identity-based dimension that is developed and elaborated during the process of negotiating its recognition. On
the whole, the debate results in an examination of the relationship between culture and politics and the new definitions of membership that are
today qualified as "postnational"; it takes on particular significance in the
context of the construction of a political Europe.

Indeed, many social scientists have developed concepts such as that of
the postnational to underline the limits of and difficulties encountered by
nation-states when confronted with a changing political context. In developing the concept of the postnational with regard to European citizenship,
the French philosopher Jean-Marc Ferry (1991) suggests a membership beyond the nation-state. Another model is provided by Habermas, who develops the concept of "constitutional patriotism." This model implies the
separation between the very elements of nationality and citizenship that
are linked in the context of the nation-state, that is, a separation between
the feelings of membership that are nurtured by national citizenship and
the juridical practice of citizenship, which extends beyond the nation-
state. A citizenship beyond territorial boundaries led Rainer Bauböck to
elaborate the concept of "transnational citizenship," which he sees as the
liberal democratic response to the question of how citizenship can remain
equal and inclusive in a global age (Bauböck 1994). Yasemin Soysal (1994),
on the other hand, focuses her discussion of transnationality on the immigrant population of Europe, using the concept of "postnational membership" to define a citizenship that would be related to international norms

understood mainly in terms of human rights applied to individuals following residency.

Yet, as far as citizenship of the European Union is concerned, the EU seems to involve a projection of the nation-state model in which citizenship and nationality are linked (article 8 of the Maastricht Treaty). At the same time, article 8 grants citizens of the Union the right to free circulation and the freedom to reside and work on the territory of a member state. These individuals even have the right to vote in local elections on the territory of a member state of which they are not citizens, but merely residents. This article introduces de facto a new conception of citizenship that is *extraterritorial* inasmuch as it dissociates citizenship from national territory. Its application makes visible multiple references, as well as the multiple allegiances of citizens, thereby disconnecting once again citizenship and nationality, as well as identity and territoriality.

This multiplicity appears clearly in modes of political participation in Europe. In fact, citizens of the European Union as well as residents participate in the politics of the Union through transnational networks combining identity—be it national, religious, or both—and interest. These transnational networks, which may be national, religious, or monetary, are frequently in competition with one another and effectively reach across Europe. This kind of participation contributes to the formation of a *transnational European sphere*, in the sense that it is defined as a space of multiple interactions between individuals, groups, nation-states, and supranational institutions, and, above all, as a space where transnational networks can build bridges between national societies and Europe.

Obviously, transnational networks represent a form of political participation beyond the nation-state with different levels and areas of citizen rights and identifications. Their construction of these rights and identifications introduces a new mode of participation and mobilization and effectively initiates a European citizenship. The process makes possible the expression of inclusion in a new political space beyond the state but nonetheless in interaction with the state. In fact, the presence of a transnational community defined by a common fight against racism confers on the noncitizens of the Union the "right" to participate in the formation of a political Europe. The elaboration of a transnational network leads also to an identification with the European society of non-Europeans residing in a member state. Citizenship implies, in this context, an element of responsibility for the construction of a new "community of faith" that is supposed to represent the European Union and is expressed by the "will to live together" (Renan 1882), as was the case in the formation of a national political community.

In the country of residence, citizenship identity is shaped by political participation and collective action. On the European level, citizenship identity is forged in relation to supranational institutions that help to construe Europe as the public good, thereby generating a new kind of political identification for individuals and groups involved in transnational mobilization. The relevant mode of participation can be seen as a second stage of immigrants' political socialization in European space, a space where they now exercise citizenship beyond national boundaries and beyond the political territories of the state. In this regard, individuals—be they immigrants or legal citizens of a member state—act together in this new space and transform it into a common space for political socialization and the exercise of power. Participation thus becomes a way of asserting "political acculturation" on a national level as a precondition for political involvement on the European level.

Paradoxically enough, however, European citizenship—understood as a more global concept of membership than that associated with nation-states—introduces the allegiance of immigrants to their home country into the negotiation process, for it is a matter of expressing allegiance both to a state of residence and to a given transnational community. In fact, transnational practices of social relations lead immigrants settled in different national societies to interact with each other in a new global space where the cultural and political specificities of national societies (host and home) are combined with emerging multilevel and multinational activities. Transnational networks linking the country of origin to the country of residence and promoting participation in both spaces bring to light multiple membership and multiple loyalties. Furthermore, transnational participation appears as the institutional expression of multiple belonging, where the country of origin becomes a source of identity and the country of residence a source of rights, and the emerging transnational space a space of political action combining two or more countries.

It is precisely this aspect of multiple identification and allegiance that provokes passionate debates on the construction of Europe, for it disrupts the relations not only between citizenship and nationality, but also between states and nations, culture and politics, as well as between a political community and the territorial nature of participation. It signals, therefore, the nonrelevance of the nation-state and its integrative ideology in the face of identity claims being expressed within and beyond national borders.

Of course, an organization that transcends national borders, as a transnational community does, brings to the fore the principle of multiple identifications that can be derived from the logic of a political Europe.

Yet, transnational participation in Europe is a sign of the Europeanization of political action and mobilization, but not of the Europeanization of claims. Claims for recognition and equality remain attached to the state as a practical framework for mobilization and negotiation and as a legal as well as institutional framework for recognition.

Thus, the emergence of transnational communities does not lead to the erosion of the nation-state, but to a redefinition of its political structure and of the balance between nation and state, where the state is considered as the driving force behind the construction of global structures and the nation as a resource for democratic political action (Lapeyronnie 1998). In fact, transnational networks appear more and more as a crucial structure for negotiating a claimed and represented identity or interest with the state, whereas the idea of nation is reserved for mobilization. Following the same logic, by encouraging such structures, supranational institutions effectively promote a transnational space, thereby paradoxically reinforcing the role of the state in the political construction of Europe, and of the nation as a unit of identification.

Yet, the nonrelevance of the nation-state in a political Europe does not necessarily imply the erosion of the nation-state. The construction of a political Europe following the model of nation-state building raises the question of the gap between a model and its application in a given political and cultural context. On the other hand, empirical evidence shows that states remain the driving force behind the European Union. Even though they are constrained by supranational norms, states retain their autonomy at the level of internal decisions, and in international relations they remain the main negotiators. The relevance of the nation stems from the fact that it continues to be perceived as a key vehicle for identification, mobilization, and resistance. The nation is at the basis of any transnational enterprise. The persistence of the nation-state as a model political unit in the construction of Europe relies very much on its capacity to negotiate, within and beyond national borders, that is, on its capacity to adapt structurally and institutionally to new realities, and its capacity to negotiate its identities.

Works Cited

Bauböck, Rainer. 1994. *Transnational Citizenship: Membership and Rights in International Migration.* Aldershot: Edward Elgar.

Brubaker, Rogers. 1992. *Citizenship and Nationhood in France and Germany.* Cambridge: Harvard University Press.

Dagger, Richard. 1997. *Civic Virtues: Rights, Citizenship and Republican Liberalism.* New York: Oxford University Press.

Dazi, Fatiha, and Rémy Leveau. 1988. "L'intégration par le politique: le vote 'beur.'" *Études* (September): 179–88.

Dumont, Louis. 1991. *L'idéologie allemande. France-Allemagne et retour.* Paris: Gallimard.

Ferry, Jean-Marc. 1991. "Pertinence du postnational." *Esprit* 11: 80–94.

Habermas, Jürgen. 1992. "Immigration et chauvinisme du bien-être." *Revue Nouvelle* 10: 76–84.

———. 1995. "Citizenship and National Identity: Some Reflections on the Future of Europe." In *Theorizing Citizenship,* ed. Ronald Beiner, 255–83. Albany: State University of New York Press.

Kastoryano, Riva. 1996. *La France, l'Allemagne et leurs immigrés: Négocier l'identité.* Paris: Armand Colin.

———. 2002. *Negotiating Identities: States and Immigrants in France and Germany.* Princeton, N.J.: Princeton University Press.

———, ed. 1998. *Quelle identité pour l'Europe? Le multiculturalisme à l'épreuve.* Paris: Presses de Sciences-Po.

Kymlicka, Will. 1995. *Multicultural Citizenship.* Oxford: Oxford University Press.

Kymlicka, Will, and Wayne Norman. 1994. "Return of the Citizen: A Survey on Recent Work on Citizenship Theory." *Ethics* 104 (January): 352–81.

Lapeyronnie, Didier. 1998. "Nation, démocratie et identités en Europe." In *Quelle identité pour l'Europe? Le multiculturalisme à l'épreuve,* ed. Riva Kastoryano, 219–46. Paris: Presses de Sciences-Po.

Leca, Jean. 1986. "L'individualisme et citoyenneté." In *Sur l'individualisme,* ed. Pierre Birnbaum and Jean Leca, 159–213. Paris: Presses de la FNSP.

———. 1992. "Nationalité et cityonneté dans l'Europe des immigrations." In *Logiques d'État et immigration en Europe,* ed. Jacqueline Costa-Lascoux and Patrick Weil, 18–60. Paris: Kimé.

———. 1993. "Après Maastricht: Sur la prétendue résurgence du nationalisme." *Témoin* 1: 29–38.

Marshall, T. H. 1964. *Class, Citizenship and Social Development.* Chicago: University of Chicago Press.

Özdemir, Cem. 1997. *Ich bin Inländer. Ein anatolischer Schwabe im Bundestag.* Munich: Deutscher Taschenbuch Verlag.

Renan, Ernest. 1882. *Qu'est-ce qu'une nation?* New edition 1992. Paris: Presses Pocket.

Soysal, Yasemin Nuhoğlu. 1994. *Limits of Citizenship: Migrants and Postnational Membership in Europe.* Chicago: University of Chicago Press.

Taylor, Charles. 1992. "The Politics of Recognition." In *Multiculturalism and the Politics of Recognition,* ed. A. Gutmann, 25–73. Princeton, N.J.: Princeton University Press.

Weber, Max. 1978. *Economy and Society.* Berkeley: University of California Press.

Weil, Patrick. 1997. *Rapport au Premier Ministre sur la nationalité.* Paris: La Documentation Française.

Yalçin-Heckmann, Lale. 1995. "The Perils of Ethnic Associational Life in Europe: Turkish Migrants in Germany and France." Paper submitted to the Workshop titled "Culture, Communication and Discourse: Negotiating Difference in Multi-Ethnic Alliances," Universities of Manchester and Keele, December 9–12.

Yasemin Nuhoğlu Soysal

8

Citizenship and Identity:

Living in Diasporas in Postwar Europe?

Like most Palestinians who experienced dispossession and displacement
from their homes and territory, Edward Said, the Jerusalem-born, British-
educated, and American literary critic, ruminates on life in exile as a "perpetual self-invention and constant restlessness." In accounting for his life
as an émigré, he quotes from Theodor Adorno's *Minima Moralia* (1974):
"The past life of emigres is . . . annulled . . . [it is a] life that cannot be directly actualized; anything that lives on merely as thought and recollection. For this a special rubric has been invented. It is called 'background'
and appears on the questionnaire as an appendix, after sex, age and profession" (Said 1998, 6).

Diaspora is the location where this background finds meaning. Diaspora is a past invented for the present, and perpetually labored into shapes
and meanings consistent with the present. As such, it exists not as a lived
reality, but as part of a broader scheme to insert continuity and coherence
into life stories that are presumably broken under the conditions of mi-
grancy and exile. It is the reification of categorical homelands, traditions,
collective memories, and formidable longings. It is a category of awareness, in which present-tense practices lack capacity in and of themselves,
but attain significance vis-à-vis the inventiveness of the past.

Diaspora is not a new concept. In its classical usage, it provides a normative model for Jewish history and experience, lived in a state of "worldlessness."[1] Lately, however, it has found much usage as an analytic category in the vast immigration literature on the global dispersion of migrant populations. It captures much of our analytic and popular imagination, and claims explanatory fortitude in narrating the presence and condition of immigrant populations.[2]

This is something I would like to question: the deployment of diaspora as an analytic category in explaining the contemporary immigration experience. The thrust of my questioning has to do with the very assumption that underlies the concept: its insistence on privileging the nation-state model and nationally defined formations when conversing about a global process such as immigration. My argument is that this axiomatic primacy granted to nations and nation-states as units of analysis is difficult to hold in the face of contemporary changes in the geography and practice of citizenship and belonging. I shall discuss here the postwar developments that render diaspora untenable as an analytic and normative category, and direct our discussions to new formations of membership, claims-making, and belonging—which either remain invisible to the conventional conceptions of diaspora or are frequently deemed insignificant in the face of its normative weight.

The dominant conceptualizations of diaspora presumptively accept the formation of tightly bounded communities and solidarities (on the basis of common cultural and ethnic references) between places of origin and arrival (Cohen 1997; van Hear 1998). Diasporas form when populations disperse from their homeland to foreign lands, engage in movements between the country of origin and the country of destination, and carry out bidirectional transactions—economic, political, and cultural. In this formulation, the primary orientation and attachment of diasporic populations is to their homelands and cultures; and their claims and citizenship practices arise from this homebound, ethnic-based orientation. In other words, diaspora is a way of theorizing formations that are ethnocultural, and that constitute foreignness within other nations and ethnicities. As such, the category of diaspora is an extension of the nation-state model, in that it assumes a congruence between the territorial state and the national community, and by implication a congruence between territory, culture, and identity. And it is this boundedness, or closure, that necessitates the definition of diasporas—that is, those who naturally bond together on the basis of their ethnic otherness and identity. Diaspora is the extension of the place left behind, the "home"; thus, the presumed rootlessness of immigrant populations in the here and now of the diaspora, and their perpetual longing for then and there. This theoretical move, that is, designating immigrant populations as diasporas, ignores the historical contingency of the nation-state, identity, and community, and reifies them as natural.

In the postwar era, the boundaries and imperatives within which diasporas are expected to take shape have changed. Particularly in Europe, in response to transformations affecting the contemporary politics, economies, and institutions of the nation-state system, new forms of citizenship, belonging, and claims have emerged. These new forms undermine the "national order of things,"[3] thus the very premise of diaspora. Diaspora, as an analytic category, is too limiting to explicate the contemporary contours of membership and belonging. We have to move beyond the customary and static precepts of diaspora and expand our theoretical and political vocabulary.

A more challenging and productive perspective is achieved by focusing on the proliferating sites of making and enacting citizenship. In a world of incessant migrations, it is in these novel geographies of citizenship that we recognize the dynamics and distribution of rights and identities, and patterns of exclusion and inclusion. My goal is to address the new forms and sites of citizenship and the broader processes that occasion their emergence. I begin by summarizing briefly the developments that contextualize the changes in the institution and practice of citizenship in postwar Europe. Then, I elaborate the two paradoxes that I see as crucial in understanding the contemporary formations of citizenship, and exclusions and inclusions. The first paradox relates to rights and identity, the two main components of citizenship, and their increasing decoupling. The second paradox relates to the ways collective claims are made and mobilized: an increasing tendency toward particularistic and group-based claims and their legitimation through universalistic discourses of personhood and strategies. Finally, I suggest that these two paradoxes warrant a reconsideration of approaches to immigrants and membership, and categories of exclusion and inclusion.

Postwar Changes in the European State System

Contrary to the predominant understandings and conceptualizations in sociology, my work suggests that the limits of citizenship are not singularly located in a nation-state but also encompass the local and the transnational. Contemporary practice of citizenship is increasingly decoupled from belonging in the national collective. Regardless of their historical or cultural ties to the German nation, and even without a formal German nationality, Turkish immigrants in Berlin make claims on Berlin's authority structures and participate in Berlin's public institutions. When they make demands for the teaching of Islam in state schools, the Pakistani immigrants in Britain mobilize around a Muslim identity, but they appeal to a universalistic language of "human rights" to justify their claims. And they not only mobilize to affect the local school authorities, but also pressure the national government, and take their case to the European Court of Human Rights. These examples undermine the predominant models of citizenship, which are normatively predicated upon the integrity of national communities and their boundaries. To provide a meaningful understanding of contemporary formations of citizenship, and exclusion and inclusion, we need to incorporate these seeming anomalies into our analytic "tool kit."

The background to the arguments I am advancing is a series of interlocking legal, institutional, and ideological changes in the European state system in the postwar period. These changes, which I have discussed elsewhere (Soysal 1994), have complicated the national order of citizenship and introduced new dynamics for membership and participation in the public sphere. Here I cite four developments that have significant implications for the institution of citizenship and the notions of identity and rights:

1 The transformations in the existing national and ethnic composition of European countries, as a consequence of massive migratory flows not only from the immediate European periphery, but also from "distant lands."

2 The increasing intensification of transnational discourse and legal instruments that codify "human rights" or personhood as a world-level principle. This elaboration of individual rights, in international agreements and institutions, but also in scientific and popular discourses, has laid the ground on which more expansive claims and rights can be advanced, and has led to the introduction of new forms of rights—for women, children, minorities, immigrants, and even animals and plants (see Turner 1986).

3 The increasing legitimacy of the right to "one's own culture" and identity. This right has been furthered by the massive decolonizations in the postwar period, as well as through the work of international organizations such as the United Nations, UNESCO, and the Council of Europe. Collective identity has been redefined as a category of human rights. Codified as a right, identities have become important organizational and symbolic tools for creating new

group solidarities and mobilizing resources (as in the case of women, environmentalists, gay men and lesbians, regional identities and interests, indigenous groups, and immigrants).

4 The diffusion of sovereignty and the emergence of multilevel polities, as with the gradual unfolding of the European Union and the devolution of some European nation-states into culturally and administratively autonomous regions (Schmitter 1992; Marks and McAdam 1996). The diffusion and sharing of sovereignty among local, national, and transnational political institutions enable new actors, open up an array of new organizational strategies, and facilitate competition over resources and definitions.

All these developments—the transformations in the population composition of the European states, the legitimation of rights at the transnational level, the codification of collective identities as rights, and the increasing diffusion of sovereignty—have paradoxical implications for national citizenship: with regard to the ways that rights and identities are defined and allocated, and the ways in which collective claims are made and mobilized. A discussion of these paradoxes of citizenship will also clarify my objection to the uncritical reinsertion of the concept of the diaspora into our discussions and analyses.

Paradoxes of Citizenship

DECOUPLING OF RIGHTS AND IDENTITY

The first paradox is the increasing decoupling of rights and identity. In the nation-state mode of political community, national belonging constitutes the source of rights and duties of individuals; and citizenship is delimited by national collectivity. The postwar era, however, has witnessed an increasing recasting of (national) citizenship rights as human (or personhood) rights (Soysal 1994).[4] Rights that were once associated with belonging in a national community have become increasingly abstract, and legitimated at the transnational level.

The postwar reification of personhood and individual rights expands the boundaries of political community by legitimating individuals' participation and claims beyond their membership status in a particular nation-state. With the breakdown of the link between the national community and rights arise multiple forms of citizenship that are no longer anchored in national collectives, and that expand the sets of rights-bearing members within and without the nation-state. These forms are exemplified in the membership of the long-term noncitizen immigrants, who hold various rights and privileges without a formal nationality status; in the increasing instances of dual citizenship, which breaches the traditional notions of political membership and loyalty in a single state; in European Union citizenship, which represents a multitiered form of membership; and in subnational citizenships in culturally or administratively autonomous regions of Europe (for example, the Basque country, Catalonia, and Scotland).

As the source and legitimacy of rights shift to the transnational level, paradoxically, identities remain particularistic, and locally defined and organized. The same global rules and institutional frameworks that celebrate personhood and human rights at the same time naturalize collective identities around national and ethnoreligious particularisms.

As already noted, this has a lot to do with the work of international organizations (such as the United Nations, UNESCO, and the Council of Europe, as well as the discipline of anthropology), through which the universal right to "one's own culture" has gained increasing legitimacy, and collective identity has been redefined as a category of human rights. What are considered particularistic characteristics of collectivities—culture, language, and standard ethnic traits—have become variants of the universal core of humanness or selfhood. This identity represents the "unchosen," and is naturalized through the language of kinship, homeland, nation, and territory. One cannot help but have identity (see Anderson 1983; Appadurai 1996; Gupta and Ferguson 1992; Herzfeld 1992; Malkki 1995; Soysal 1996).

The seeming naturalness and inevitability of diaspora formations (and theorizing immigrant communities as diasporas) are part and parcel of this global and hegemonic discourse of identity. Once institutionalized as natural, the discourse about identities creates ever-increasing claims about cultural distinctiveness and group rights. Ethnic and national identities are enacted and improvised for mobilizing and making claims in national and world polities, authenticating diaspora as an idiom for the politics of identity. On the other hand, as exercised in individual and collective actors' narratives and strategies, identity also authorizes ethnic nationalisms and sovereignties. Thus, while rights acquire a more universalistic form and are divorced from national belonging (thus giving rise to more inclusionary forms of membership), identities become intentionally particularistic and exclusionary practices (on the basis of identity) prevail. This can be seen in the increasingly restrictive immigration policies of European countries, the vocalization of ethnic minority and religious groups for cultural closure, and the discriminatory citizenship practices of many of the former Soviet republics. Thus, more inclusionary forms of rights clash with more exclusionary practices of identity.

MAKING PARTICULARISTIC CLAIMS THROUGH UNIVERSALISTIC DISCOURSES OF PERSONHOOD AND STRATEGIES

The second paradox of citizenship regards collective claims-making and participation in public spheres—in other words, the practice of citizenship by individuals and groups. With the postwar reconfigurations in citizenship described in the preceding section, the old categories that attach individuals to nationally defined status positions and distributory mechanisms become blurred. This inevitably changes the nature and locus of struggles for social equality and rights. New forms of mobilizing and advancing claims and participation emerge beyond the frame of national citizenship.

Classical notions of citizenship assume the existence of actors whose rights and identities are grounded within the bounds of national collectives, and these collectives constitute the "authentic" sites for the realization of claims-making and civic participation. My research reveals two trends that diverge from this predominant prescription of citizenship. First, there is an increasing tendency to advance particularistic identities and demands, which at the same time are located in and legitimated by the universalistic discourses of human or personhood rights. Second, the mobilization of claims takes place independent of nationally delimited collectives and at different levels (local, national, and transnational). In other words, the social and political stages for claims-making proliferate.

I will examine these two trends by citing empirical evidence from Muslim immigrant communities and their participation and mobilization in European public spheres. Although the emerging forms can be observed among other groups, my focus is on Muslim immigrants because these communities are visibly at the center of contention.

The first trend concerns the nature of the claims and discourse. Immigrant groups in Europe mobilize around claims for particularistic provisions and emphasize their group identities. Their claims, however, are not simply grounded in the particularities of religious or ethnic narratives. On the contrary, they appeal to the universalistic principles and dominant discourses of equality, emancipation, and individual rights. In other words, the claims that immigrants advance and the identities that they mobilize, though particularistic, derive their legitimacy and authority from universalistic discourses of personhood and human rights. Diaspora theories, with their singular focus on ethnic transactions and community formation, bypass these larger scripts, which activate and energize those very claims and identities. In turn, they misread immigrant mobilization simply as an enactment of ethnicity.

When Muslim immigrant associations advocate the rights and needs of immigrant children in school, for example, they employ a discourse that appropriates the rights of the individual as its central theme and invoke international instruments and conventions on human rights to frame their position. They advance demands about native-language instruction, Islamic *foulard* (scarf), or *halal* food by asserting the "natural" right of individuals to their own cultures, rather than drawing upon religious teachings and traditions.

In 1989, for example, the issue of Islamic *foulard* erupted into a national crisis and debate in France, when three North African students were expelled from school for insisting on wearing their scarves in class. The issue became not only a topical dispute over immigrant integration and French laicism, but entered into the public arena as a matter of the rights of individuals. During the debates, the head of the Great Mosque of Paris declared the rules preventing the wearing of scarves in school to be discriminatory on the grounds of individual rights. His emphasis was on personal rights, rather than religious traditions or duties: "If a girl asks to have her hair covered, I believe it is her most basic right" (*Washington Post*, October 23, 1989). In this case, Muslim identity, while symbolized by the head scarf, was asserted and authenticated by the very categories and language of the host society, that is, through a discourse that accentuated individual rights.

Another episode occurred in Germany. On November 12, 1995—the birthday of Fatima (the daughter of the prophet Muhammad)—the Shi'ite Ehlibeyt mosque in Berlin invited "all Muslim women" to a celebration of the World Women's Day. Speakers included not only the (male) clergy of the mosque, but also Muslim women of different nationalities, including Turks, Arabs, and Germans. The focal point of the speeches was to highlight women's emancipation, including demands to end discrimination against Muslim women in workplaces and schools, especially on the basis of their wearing the Islamic head scarf. The issues raised encapsulated the very terms of contemporary gender discourse. The keynote speaker, a young imam, traced the issue of the rights of women to the Qur'an. Referring to the United Nations Fourth World Conference on Women in Beijing (1995), he claimed that the assertion "Women's rights are human rights" was an original teaching of Islam and its culture. He declared indignantly: "In the Beijing conference, when someone said, 'Women's rights are human rights,' thousands of women cheered and clapped. What were they cheering for? We already said that fourteen hundred years ago! That is our word!" The meeting was an instance of linking the Islamic moral realm to contemporary concerns and discourses about women, speaking to and through them.

A caveat is called for here: Muslim groups in European countries obviously do not speak in a uniform framework. The examples just cited by no means exhaust the range of narratives employed by Muslim groups. Islamic positions are sometimes based on religiously codified family laws that sanction status disparity between genders. Again, speaking for the Islamic veil, a Turkish imam in Nantua, France, declared the practice to be "God's law" and put pressure on Turkish families to withdraw their daughters from school. This led to serious divisions among the Turkish immigrant community and to his eventual deportation from France (Kepel 1997, 222–23). Such proclamations clearly point to alternative, and often conflicting, claims and leadership among Muslim communities. My aim is simply to delineate the prevalent universalistic forms of making claims by Muslim groups that are commonly overlooked, and to elucidate their implications.

There is significant variation in the accommodation of the claims advanced. Some claims face organizational resistance; others are more readily accepted and incorporated into formal state structures. The educational authorities in Britain, for example, are more willing to accommodate the claims for Islamic dress codes, or even the teaching of immigrant languages in schools. On the other hand, religiously codified family laws (e.g., polygamy, female circumcision) that create status disparity between genders are not viewed as legitimate demands. Here, the principle of gender equality contests the principle of religious equality, both of which are clearly embedded in European citizenships and transnational frameworks. In Europe, the treatment of women is codified in secular laws and institutions; thus, the attempt to subject it to a religious, private domain generates conflict. In my research, I attempt to untangle the contradictory dynamics among different legitimating discourses and principles, and explain how these dynamics lead to conflicting claims and empowerments in the public sphere.[5]

The Muslim organizations I study do not justify their demands by simply invoking religious teachings or traditions, but rather through a language of rights—thus, citizenship. By using the language of rights, they exercise civic projects and link themselves to the broader public spheres. The projects of citizenship in which they engage, however, are not necessarily nationally bounded. They are both spatially and symbolically multireferential.

When Muslim associations make demands about veiling in schools, their claim is not one of belonging to an existing "French collectivity," but to the educational system itself, which they see as their most natural right. This is not necessarily a disengagement from the collective life, but the collective is no longer bounded by a preordained national community. Indeed, they try to redefine the very nature of national community.

The second trend with regard to claims-making is that the organizational strategies employed by immigrant groups increasingly acquire a transnational and subnational character. The terms of their participation extend beyond the limits of the national, span multiple localities, transnationally connect public spheres, and thus diversify the "spaces for and of politics."[6] For example, political parties, mosque organizations, and community associations operate at local levels but do not confine their claims only to their localities. During the local elections in Berlin in 1995, Turkish immigrant organizations demanded local voting rights and to vote in European elections, while at the same time they put pressure on the Turkish government to facilitate their rights to vote in Turkish national elections, thereby envisaging their participation in multiple civic spaces—in Berlin, in Europe, and in Turkey. Similar claims are being made by Mexican and Central American immigrant groups in the United States, who demand dual citizenship and dual voting rights in their countries of origin and residence. Indeed, the governments of Mexico, Colombia, and the Dominican Republic have passed legislation allowing dual nationality.

The mobilization of immigrant groups to pursue their claims entails multiple states and political agencies and targets transnational and subnational institutions. The Islamic *foulard* issue, for example, was not simply a matter confined to the discretion of a local school board, but traversed local, national, and transnational jurisdictions—from local educational authorities to the European Court of Human Rights. And, in the early 1990s, when the local authorities in London refused to permit the opening of another Islamic primary school, the Islamic Foundation decided to take the issue to the European Court of Human Rights. More and more Muslim associations are operating on a European level, establishing umbrella organizations and forums to coordinate their activities and pursue a Europe-wide agenda (Kastoryano 1996).

Therefore, while the claims and mobilization of Muslim groups aim to further particularistic identities and solidarities, paradoxically, they appeal to the universalistic principles of human rights and connect themselves to a diverse set of public spheres. Their civic projects and mobilization are not simply a reinvention of ethnic or religious particularisms. They are not ethnically self-referential, but reflect larger scripts of rights and person-hood. Drawing on universalistic repertoires of claims-making, they participate in and contribute to the reification of host society and global discourses.

These solidarities and participatory forms cannot be captured by the concept of diaspora. By focusing on the ethnic axis of homelands and abroad, the theories of diaspora overlook the transgressions of national boundaries and collectives and forget the new ways in which immigrants experience and enact their membership. In this new topography of membership, what constitutes the grounds for civic projects is no longer the "horizontal connectedness" among members of an ethnic community (that is, mutual trust and solidarity on the basis of ethnic belonging), but rather participation in and by "vertical connection" to common, universalistic discourses that transcend the very ethnic idiom of community.

Second-generation immigrants, who are seen as enigmatic producers of diasporic cultures and identities, help to complete the picture. Far from being simple extensions of their "homelands," second-generation immigrants—Maghrebins, Pakistanis, Turks, Caribbeans, Bengalis living in the capitals of Europe—negotiate and map collective identities that are dissociated from ethnocultural citizenships (Baumann 1996; Soysal 1999). They appropriate their identity symbols as much from global cultural flows as from host or home country cultural practices. As "youth subcultures," they are increasingly part of the global (Gilroy 1993; Amit-Talai and Wulff 1995; Hannerz 1996), in many ways bypassing the national or traditional. Thus, it should come as no surprise that Turkish youth in Germany listen to rap music as much as, if not more than, they listen to Turkish Şarkı or German lieder; or that immigrant "youth gangs" adopt names in English: Two Nation Force, Turkish Power Boys, Cobras, and Bulldogs; or that they form rap groups with names like Cartel, Microphone Mafia, and Islamic Force, and that their graffiti on Berlin walls replicates the styles of New York.

This profusion of immigrant experience illustrates the fact that public spaces within which immigrants act, mobilize, advance claims, and produce cultures are broader than the ethnic dominion of diaspora. Their connections to multilevel discourses and their access to diverse citizenship practices are invisible in most diasporic theorizing. And the expanse and multireferentiality of their mobilizing cannot be contained by bi-directional ethnic transactions and arrangements.

Conclusion

The experience of postwar immigrants in Europe indicates a diversion from the classical forms of participating in the public sphere, mobilizing identities, and making claims. The decolonization and civil-rights movements and the early women's movement of the 1960s were largely attempts to redefine individuals as part of the national collectivity. Similarly, labor movements were historically linked to the shaping of a national citizenry. It is no coincidence that the welfare state developed as part of the national project, attaching labor movements to nations (as in Bismarck's Germany). However, the emerging formations of collective participation and claims-making in Europe today are less and less nationally delimited citizenship projects. Individuals and collective groups set their agenda for the realization of rights through particularistic identities, which are embedded in, and driven by, universalistic and homogenizing discourses of personhood and human rights. This shift in focus from national collectivity to particularistic identities does not necessarily imply disengagement from participating in common public spheres or creating disaggregated civic arenas. On the contrary, it is evidence of the emerging participatory forms and multiple arenas whereby individuals enact their citizenship.

Citizenship has come to the fore as a trying issue, both theoretically and politically. Theories and policy prescriptions, however, have yet to respond to the changes in citizenship, rights, and identity. Three correctives to current sociological thinking on citizenship and identity might be suggested:

First, the much taken-for-granted dichotomy of particular versus universal no longer holds. The mechanisms by which the universalistic rights discourse not only reinforces particularistic identities and claims, but also concurrently normalizes these same identities, must be considered. The particularistic identities and claims encountered today are inevitable outcomes of universalistic principles. Thus, the question is not one of positive or negative recognition (or even accommodation) of these claims and identities, but the very process of negotiation, contestation, and dialogue in which these claims and identities are mobilized. After all, confrontation and dialogue are at the basis of democratic public spheres.

Second, absolute, clear-cut patterns of exclusions and inclusions no longer exist, nor do they coincide with the bounds of the national. Access to a formal nationality status is not the main indicator for inclusion or exclusion in Europe today. Rights, membership, and participation are increasingly matters beyond the vocabulary of national citizenship. Thus, on the one hand, we need to identify contexts and processes that are beyond the nation-state, and lead to simultaneous inclusions and exclusions. On the other hand, we need to bring back onto the political agenda one of the main premises of sociology: inclusion and exclusion are also issues of distribution.

Third, debates about membership and identities can no longer be framed in terms of the dichotomy between national and transnational, or a linear transition from one to the other. Rather than treating national and transnational as stages in progress, they need to be incorporated into theoretical frameworks as variables, and treated as concurrent levels within which the current practices of citizenship and identity can be understood.

Postscript

Theories are stubborn. Nation and ethnicity, the "invented traditions" of the nineteenth century, in the words of Eric Hobsbawm, may be with us for some time. They may even be reinvented, and given new life, as in the renewal of old concepts such as diaspora. The concept of diaspora effortlessly casts contemporary population movements as perpetual ethnic arrangements, transactions, and belongings. In so doing, it suspends immigrant experience between host and home countries, native and foreign lands, homebound desires and losses—thereby obscuring the new topography and practices of citizenship, which are multiconnected, multireferential, and postnational.

Diaspora finds a strong placement in political and intellectual discourse through its naturalizing metaphors of roots, soil, and kinship. Lacking analytic rigor, however, it is destined to be a trope for nostalgia. Diaspora indexes timeless recollection and animates what has come to be known as identity politics. On this, Edward Said gets the last word: "Identity as such is about as boring a subject as one can imagine. Nothing seems less interesting than the narcissistic self-study that today passes in many places for identity politics, or ethnic studies, or affirmations of roots, cultural pride, drum-beating nationalism and so on. We have to defend peoples and identities threatened with extinction or subordinated because they are considered inferior, but that is very different from aggrandising a past invented for present reasons" (1998, 7).

Notes

Ideas presented here have been debated at various times and places, cyber and real, with Miriam Feldblum, Levent Soysal, Mette Hjort, Jane Jenson, Doug McAdam,

Deborah Yashar, Gershon Shafir, Maria Baganha, Damian Tambini, and Hans van der Veen. My thanks to them.

1 From Ron H. Feldman's introduction to Hannah Arendt's *The Jew as Pariah* (1978, 22).
2 To get a feel for how expansive the diaspora literature has become, one simply needs to check the list of recent conference titles, funded research programs, and forthcoming books. The University of Washington Press alone promises several volumes on the topic—a disapora for all major immigrant groups.
3 The phrase is from Liisa H. Malkki (1995).
4 I use the term *human rights* in its broad, abstract sense, not necessarily referring to specific international conventions or instruments and their categorical contents.
5 By emphasizing the universality of discourses and strategies employed by immigrant groups, I am not taking a naive position and assuming that individuals or groups will bond together and arrive at agreeable positions. Here I diverge from the Habermasian project, according to which the discursive process, when rational, serves to bring reason and will together and create consensus without coercion (Habermas 1962). The public sphere necessarily involves conflict, contestation, and incoherent outcomes, however rational. In that sense, the role of the discursive participatory process is to focus on agendas of contestation and to provide space for strategic action, rather than consensus building (Eder 1995).
6 I borrow the phrase from Jane Jenson (1993, 138).

Works Cited

Adorno, Theodor W. 1974. *Minima Moralia: Reflections from Damaged Life.* London: Verso.
Amit-Talai, Vered, and Helena Wulff, eds. 1995. *Youth Cultures: A Cross-Cultural Perspective.* London: Routledge.
Anderson, Benedict. 1983. *Imagined Communities.* London: Verso.
Appadurai, Arjun. 1996. *Modernity at Large: Cultural Dimensions of Globalization.* Minneapolis: University of Minnesota Press.
Arendt, Hannah. 1978. *The Jew as Pariah: Jewish Identity and Politics in the Modern Age.* Ed. and Introd. Ron H. Feldman. New York: Grove Press.
Baumann, Gerd. 1996. *Contesting Culture: Discourses of Identity in Multi-Ethnic London.* Cambridge: Cambridge University Press.
Cohen, Robin. 1997. *Global Diasporas: An Introduction.* Seattle: University of Washington Press.
Eder, Klaus. 1995. "The Institutionalization of Environmentalism: Ecological Discourse and the Second Transformation of the Public Sphere." Unpublished manuscript. Florence: European University Institute.
Gilroy, Paul. 1993. *The Black Atlantic: Modernity and Double Consciousness.* Cambridge: Harvard University Press.
Gupta, Akil, and James Ferguson. 1992. "Beyond 'Culture': Space, Identity, and the Politics of Difference." *Cultural Anthropology* 7: 6–23.
Habermas, Jürgen. 1962 [1989]. *The Structural Transformation of the Public Sphere.* Cambridge: MIT Press.
Hannerz, Ulf. 1996. *Transnational Connections: Culture, People, Places.* New York: Routledge.

Herzfeld, Michael. 1992. *The Social Production of Indifference: Exploring the Symbolic Roots of Western Bureaucracy.* New York: Berg.

Jenson, Jane. 1993. "De-constructing Dualities: Making Rights Claims in Political Institutions." In *New Approaches to Welfare Theory*, ed. Glenn Drover and Patrick Kerans, 127–43. Aldershot: Edward Elgar.

Kastoryano, Riva. 1996. *La France, l'Allemagne et leurs immigrés: Négocier l'identité.* Paris: Armand Colin.

Kepel, Gilles. 1997. *Allah in the West: Islamic Movements in America and Europe.* Stanford, Calif.: Stanford University Press.

Malkki, Liisa H. 1995. *Purity and Exile: Violence, Memory, and National Cosmology among Hutu Refugees in Tanzania.* Chicago: University of Chicago Press.

Marks, Gary, and Doug McAdam. 1996. "Social Movements and the Changing Structure of Political Opportunity in the European Union." *West European Politics* 19:2: 249–87.

Said, Edward. 1998. "Between Worlds." *London Review of Books* 20:9: 3–7.

Schmitter, Philippe C. 1992. "Interests, Powers, and Functions: Emergent Properties and Unintended Consequences in the European Polity." Unpublished manuscript. Stanford University, Department of Political Science.

Soysal, Levent. 1999. "Projects of Culture: An Ethnographic Episode in the Life of Migrant Youth in Berlin." Ph.D. thesis, Harvard University.

Soysal, Yasemin Nuhoğlu. 1994. *Limits of Citizenship: Migrants and Postnational Membership in Europe.* Chicago: University of Chicago Press.

———. 1996. "Boundaries and Identity: Immigrants in Europe." European Forum. Working Paper Series. Florence: European University Institute.

Turner, Bryan S. 1986. "Personhood and Citizenship." *Theory and Society* 3: 1–16.

van Hear, Nicholas. 1998. *New Diasporas: The Mass Exodus, Dispersal and Regrouping of Migrant Communities.* Oxford: Oxford University Press.

9

Reimagining Belonging in Circumstances of Cultural Diversity: A Citizen Approach

One of the most difficult problems facing culturally diverse political societies is to develop a sense of belonging to the association as a whole. These
societies tend toward fragmentation and disintegration because the members often develop a stronger sense of belonging to their overlapping linguistic, religious, ethnic, indigenous, regional, and national associations
than to their larger political society. If a difference-blind liberal identity or
a uniform nationalist identity is promoted to overcome the fragmentation,
the effect is more often than not to incite resistance to the degree of
assimilation these policies impose, and so to exacerbate fragmentation
rather than create a sense of belonging. In response to the failure of these
two traditional approaches, some constitutional democracies have turned
to policies of group rights for cultural minorities. Yet, although these juridical solutions sometimes protect minorities from assimilation by the
dominant majority, they do little if anything by themselves to generate a
sense of belonging to the larger association and often impede it, for they
strengthen the sense of belonging to the protected minority and often
heighten the tensions with the members of the larger society and with the
other minorities.[1]

I would like to present another approach to the problem of reimagining
belonging in conditions of cultural diversity. This is the democratic ap-

proach of enabling citizens themselves to reimagine and create the appropriate sense of belonging to their culturally diverse association by means, and as a result, of their participation in the struggles over the political, legal, and constitutional recognition and accommodation of their identity-related differences and similarities over time. Such a citizen-centered proposal draws critically on the democratic and republican traditions, which have always been concerned to create bonds of belonging by means of citizen participation. Citizens come to imagine themselves as free and equal members of the *demos* or *civitas* by means, and as a result, of the freedom to participate in public life, either directly, by participating themselves, or indirectly, by identification with their trusted representatives.

In the first section, I discuss the role this traditional freedom of citizen participation plays in engendering a sense (or "imaginary") of belonging. In the following sections, I discuss the deeply modified and complex forms that the freedom of participation would have to take in culturally diverse societies to engender the appropriate form of citizen awareness of, and identification with, an association of free, equal, and diverse citizens. This is not only the freedom to participate in accord with one's cultural differences, once a struggle for recognition has been won. It is also the freedom to participate in the ongoing contests over if and how identity-related differences are to be publicly discussed, recognized, and accommodated in the first place, as well as in the ineliminable struggles to review and renegotiate established forms of recognition. For, as strange as it sounds, it is through participation in negotiations over conflicting demands for and against forms of recognition of cultural diversity, in which citizens win some campaigns and lose others, that citizens become aware of the limitations of imagining belonging along the lines of difference-blind liberalism or uniform nationalism and begin to reimagine belonging in line with their dawning awareness of the burdens of mutual respect and fair cooperation in circumstances of cultural diversity.[2]

Democratic Freedom and Belonging

A CLASSIC ACCOUNT OF THE FREEDOM OF CITIZENS AND BELONGING

Let us recall the main features of the democratic freedom of citizens before employing it as a form of critical reflection on the contemporary problem of belonging in culturally diverse societies. Citizenship can be defined in terms of two concepts: "free peoples" and "free citizens." A collection of humans becomes, or takes on the identity of, a "free people" by virtue of governing themselves by their own laws over time. This activity of self-rule is described by Quentin Skinner as

> a system in which the sole power of making laws remains with the people or their accredited representatives, and in which all individual members of the body politic—rulers and citizens alike—remain equally subject to whatever laws they choose to impose on themselves. (Skinner 1998, 74)

There are two, coequal principles involved in being a "free people": the rule of law (rulers and citizens alike remain equally subject to the law) and self-rule (rulers and citizens impose the laws on themselves). These two coequal or equiprimordial democratic and republican principles of "constitutionalism" and "popular sovereignty" have been endorsed by liberals such as John Rawls and Jürgen Habermas as the basic principles of "democratic legitimacy" in the contemporary age (Rawls 1996, 396–408; Habermas 1998).

This characterization of a "free people" is internally related to the second concept, that of "free citizens." A "free people" subject themselves to the law through their own participation; that is, they are "free citizens" just insofar as they have a voice in their form of self-government. In Skinner's phrase, they "impose [the laws] on themselves." To be a "free citizen" it is not sufficient simply to be a member of a free people. It is necessary to participate in some direct or indirect way in the exercise of political power: to be an "active" citizen. If members do not have a voice in the way in which political power is exercised, and thus power is exercised over them without their say, "behind their backs," then they are by definition "unfree"—"subjects" rather than "free citizens."

The ideal of "free citizens" is, in its most utopian formulation, "that all acts of legislation duly reflect the explicit consent of every member of the body politic as a whole" (Skinner 1998, 30). For well-known reasons, this ideal is unrealizable in practice, especially in the complex and multilayered political arrangements of today, where participation is sometimes direct, sometimes represented and mediated. Nevertheless, the underlying thesis remains valid. Members of a free people only become "free citizens" insofar as they not only have the opportunity to participate in some way or another, but actually participate. This thesis does not *equate* "individual freedom" with the activity of political participation, as Skinner cautions (ibid., 74 n. 38). Rather, it is to say that there is another *aspect* of political freedom that consists precisely in the activity of participation itself. This is, as Hannah Arendt put it, "civic freedom" or the "freedom of citizens" (Arendt 1977, 148–56).

The freedom of citizen participation is the means of "maintaining" and "protecting" our "individual liberty," as Skinner argues, but it is also, and just as importantly, the way we become, or take on the identity of, citizens (Skinner 1998, 74 n. 38; 1984); that is, just as a "free people" is a collective achievement (the bringing into being and sustaining of a self-governing people over time), so too is citizenship an achievement, something that is brought into being through its exercise. For republicans and democrats, citizenship is not equated with a set of rights and duties (as is often the case for liberals), nor is it sharing in a national identity (as is often the case for nationalists). It is an achievement acquired through engaging in the multitude of activities of imposing the laws on ourselves. Citizenship, therefore, is an identity that we come to acquire by being "free citizens," by direct or mediated engagement in the institutions of self-rule of a free people.

Three features of our identity as free citizens are relevant to the problem of belonging. First, it is a form of self-awareness and self-formation that one comes to acquire through engagement with others in the civic, political, and legal spheres where the exercise of political power is discussed, negotiated, and adjudicated. Second, a specific form of self-consciousness is acquired through participation: the awareness of oneself as a member of, and as belonging to, the political association. Now, this sense of belonging to the political association is, as Habermas puts it, not only the awareness of ourselves as equal subjects of the constitutional rule of law. This alone, he stresses, is insufficient to generate solidarity and loyalty among the members of modern political associations. It is necessary also to foster the awareness of ourselves as, in some sense, involved—as agents, authors, or contributors—in the making and amending of the laws.

This is what is meant by self-rule or popular sovereignty. But, this condition of "democratic legitimacy" can be made good only if the members of the association have some sort of say in the way political power is exercised over them through the laws, because it is precisely this activity of civic freedom that, in fact, creates, or makes good, the awareness of the laws as "self-imposed," rather than as imposed nondemocratically, behind our backs (Habermas 1996).

Third, the form of participation that is necessary for the constitution of a citizen identity is not the ideal of formulating, passing, and enacting the laws. Rather, the necessary threshold of participation involves "having a say" or being "in on" the public dialogues over how and by whom political power is exercised. Citizenship is intersubjective and dialogical (a form of identity we achieve in public dialogues with others).

Finally, public dialogues over the public good in which we become free citizens and free peoples exhibit three features. First, public dialogues are the exercise of practical, not theoretical, reason. They involve a range of communicative and strategic activities of argumentation: persuasion, inquiry, negotiation, information seeking, deliberation, rhetoric, and eristic (Walton 1998). Second, they are "agonistic" in character: citizens and representatives compete for, and endlessly dispute over, forms of mutual recognition and rule in accordance with shared (yet variously interpreted and ordered) principles of freedom, equality, and respect for difference. Third, political dialogues are always "negotiations," not "consensus." Any agreement is partial or conditional to some extent, open to reasonable redescription and challenge. An element of reasonable disagreement, of nonconsensus, and so of dissent, contestation, renegotiation, and compromise, attends any (provisional) agreement as a kind of permanent provocation. An openness to always listen to the other side, *audi alteram partem*, and to negotiate a revisable accommodation, rather than to aim at an unconditional consensus, is at the heart of the exercise of public reason in the republican and democratic traditions.[3]

In sum, free citizenship is an identity that members acquire through exchanging reasons in public dialogues over how and by whom political power is exercised. "Having a voice" in these activities of discussion and negotiation generates bonds of solidarity and a sense of belonging to the political association. The self-governing association one identifies with by virtue of becoming a citizen through such participation is what we call a "free people," or "free peoples" in the case of multinational associations. Because the public discussions are marked by contestation and disagreement, it cannot be anything they agree on that gives citizens an identity and holds them together. Rather, it is nothing more, or less, than participation in the activities of public dialogue and negotiation themselves.

It follows that citizen identity and belonging are not acquired by the possession of constitutional rights and duties, or by agreements on comprehensive goods or values, a shared national identity or identities, and fundamental principles of justice, or by agreements on universal procedures of negotiation. Of course, liberals and nationalists are right that some of these conditions of constitutional democracy are necessary and important. Nevertheless, there are two reasons why these principles, procedures, shared goods, and shared identities cannot adequately account for legitimate citizenship and belonging. First, as Arendt famously argued, they are the background conditions of citizenship, not the activity of citizenship (Arendt 1977, 148–51). These conditions all derive from one of the two principles of a "free people" mentioned earlier—the principle of the "rule of law." They need to be complemented by the second principle of popular sovereignty (free citizens are subject only to those conditions that "they choose to impose on themselves" through participation).

The second reason these conditions are insufficient is that citizens, rulers, and theorists disagree over them. They are always open to question, reasonable disagreement, contestation, deliberation, negotiation, and amendment over time, in the course of a free people imposing them on themselves. They are not only the conditions of free political dialogue and negotiation, but also what those negotiations are often *about*. This is what classical republicans mean when they say that politics is in the realm of *negotium* not *otium*. As a result, the conditions of citizenship are not fixed, but open to discussion and debate by free citizens in the course of imposing them on themselves. This is the only way that the two principles of legitimacy of a "free people"—constitutionalism and popular sovereignty— can be treated as equiprimordial.

THE CONTEMPORARY PROBLEM OF BELONGING IN LIGHT OF A CLASSIC ACCOUNT

On this account, the contemporary problem of belonging can be interpreted as follows. Engaging in agonistic and interminable public negotiations, both *within* and *over* the conditions of citizenship, constitutes and sustains our identities as "free citizens" and generates the sense of belonging to a free people or federation of free peoples. In the public discussions, citizens disclose the identities they wish to see recognized and others acknowledge these and respond, either by agreeing or disagreeing, or by advancing demands for recognition of their own. Conversely, when these activities of *citizenization* are unavailable or arbitrarily restricted, the members of a political association remain "subjects" rather than "citizens" because the laws are imposed on them without their say. The association is then experienced as alien and imposed, as a structure of domination that is by definition "unfree and illegitimate." Subjects turn to other communities of dialogue available to them, centered on their language, culture, ethnicity, region, nationality, gender, sexual orientation, and the like. As a result of being in on *these* discussions, they identify with and belong to these communities rather than to their political community. In these forums, they debate how they can reform the political association so they can get in or, if this path is blocked, how they can secede. The political association tends toward fragmentation, instability, and disintegration. It is held together, if at all, by force, fraud, and conflict management rather than by sentiments and imaginings of belonging created by the free activities of citizens.

In a well-ordered constitutional democracy, many avenues of participation are readily available to block this kind of alienation. Citizens are always able to participate both directly and indirectly in political discussions that bear on the exercise of political power. They can participate directly in a variety of public spheres, local initiatives, referenda, consultative meetings, political parties, elections to local, regional, federal, national, and supranational representative bodies, public service, interest groups, dissent, protest, civil disobedience, and local and global struggles for the establishment of public norms across the private sector. They can also participate indirectly through relations of critical trust with their elected representatives, public servants, courts, intermediary organizations, and especially in public discussions facilitated by radio, television, print media, and the Internet.

Nevertheless, in seeking to engage in the public dialogues and negotiations in these ways, many of the identity-diverse members of contemporary societies claim to experience arbitrary constraints that block their free participation, and thereby disable them from becoming free citizens. These constraints are the prevailing overt and covert "norms of public recognition" they must follow in order to participate and be recognized *as* citizens. The prevailing norms of public recognition define the identity of citizens. Citizens who express themselves through different languages, cultures, and national identities claim that the prevailing norms unjustly constrain participation in two different ways. First, they misrecognize or exclude these identity-related differences through which diverse citizens speak, act, and express themselves politically; second, they impose and assimilate citizens to an alien identity (the identity of the dominant culture, under the guise of being a difference-blind liberal identity or a shared uninational identity). They are thus treated as subjects rather than as citizens, unfree to question and seek to amend the norms of the very activities in which they are supposed to constitute themselves as free citizens and free peoples. These members experience the norms of citizenship as imposed and alien, rather than as self-imposed and their own. Such challenges to dominant norms of citizen identity in the name of cultural diversity are called "the politics of identity" and "struggles for recognition" (Taylor 1994).

Having interpreted the problem of belonging in culturally diverse polities as a problem of the democratic freedom to participate, I will now describe three characteristics of cultural identities and three types of recognition struggle in the following section. We will then be in a position to see how these demands for recognition can be approached from our perspective of citizen participation in order to engender the appropriate sense and imaginary of belonging in the final two sections.

Three Characteristics of Identity Politics and Three Types of Struggle

First, what makes struggles over recognition so volatile and intractable is their diverse character. Identity politics is not a politics of many separate, bounded, and internally uniform nations, cultures, or other forms of identity, each seeking separate and compatible recognition and political associations, even though leaders often portray them in this manner and employ powerful processes of assimilation to eliminate internal differences. Rather, demands are articulated around crisscrossing and overlapping allegiances: indigenousness, nationality, culture, region, religion, ethnicity, language, sexual orientation, gender, immigration, and individual expression. A minority nation or language group demanding recognition from a larger political association often finds minorities, indigenous peoples, multicultural citizens, or immigrants within who also demand recognition and protection. Cultural feminists find that their identity-related demands are crossed by national, linguistic, cultural, religious, immigrant, and sexual-orientation differences among women, and nationalist and culturalist movements find, in turn, that women do not always agree with men. Members of a minority seeking recognition against an intransigent majority along one identity-related difference will have crosscutting allegiances because of other aspects of their identity that they share with members of the other side (Habermas 1994b).

It does not follow from the absence of separate, bounded, and internally uniform identities that identity politics is dissolving through its own fragmentation, or that, as a result, humans can now relegate identity to a "subpolitical" realm and agree on principles, rights, and institutions, unmediated by identity-related differences. Quite the contrary. The increasing diversity and insecurity of identity-related differences in an era of globalization fuel the demands for their political recognition and protection. What does follow is the now commonplace observation that no identity is ever quite identical to itself: it always contains an irreducible element of alterity. Identity is multiplex or aspectival. Accordingly, "diversity" or the multiplicity of overlapping identities and their corresponding allegiances is the first characteristic of identity politics (Tully 1999b, 5–14).

Second, this "hybridization" should not be treated as if it were *the* fundamental characteristic, even though it is the fundamental *experience* for some people, especially those living in exile or multicultural cities (Bhabha 1994). It is certainly possible to bring a group of people together to agree to defend and promote one aspect of their identity, such as language, nationality, or indigenousness, across their other identity-related differences, and this identification can be sustained for generations (as, for example, ranking one's Scottish identity prior to British or Catalonian prior to Spanish). What the multiplicity of overlapping identities entails is the second characteristic of identity politics: the public priority granted to one identity at any time, the way and by whom it is articulated, and the form of public recognition and accommodation demanded must always be open to democratic processes of questioning, reinterpretation, deliberation, and negotiation by the bearers of that identity (Tully 2001, 13–23).

An identity negotiated in these human—all too human—circumstances will not be fixed or authentic, but it can still be plausible rather than implausible, well supported rather than imposed, reasonable rather than unreasonable, empowering rather than disabling, liberating rather than oppressive; that is, it will be a mutable and ongoing construct of practical and intersubjective dialogue, not of theoretical reason on one side or unmediated ascription on the other. Consequently, identity politics consists of three processes of negotiation that interact in complex ways: (1) among the diverse members of a group struggling for recognition, (2) between them and the other group(s) within a polity to whom their demand for recognition is made, and (3) among the members of the latter group(s) (whose identity comes into question as a result of the struggle, whether they like it or not—as, for example, men, heterosexuals, and members of dominant cultures and language groups discover).

The third and most elusive characteristic of identity politics is the concept of "identity" itself. It is not one's theoretical identity, what one is as a matter of scientific fact or theoretical reason. It is one's practical identity, a mode of being in the world with others. A practical identity is a form of both self-awareness and self-formation. It is a structure of strong evaluations in accord with which humans value themselves, find their lives worth living and their actions worth undertaking, and the description under which they require, as a condition of self-worth, that others recognize and respect them. A practical identity is thus relational and intersubjective in a double sense. It is acquired and sustained in conversational relations with those who share it and those who do not (Tully 2000b). Any practical identity projects onto those who do not share it another identity, the non-X, who, in reciprocity, seek mutual recognition and respect for their identity, which is seldom the one others project onto them. This is why negotiation and agonistic contestation are so basic to identity politics (Connolly 1995).

The injustice distinctive of identity politics follows from these three characteristics. Individuals and groups are thwarted in their attempts to negotiate and gain reciprocal public recognition and accommodation of their practical identities as an aspect of their citizen identity. Their identities are misrecognized or not recognized at all in the dominant norms of public recognition. Instead, an alien identity is imposed on them, without their say, through processes of subjectification, either assimilating them to the dominant identity or constructing them as marginal and expendable others. Given the three characteristics of identities, there is a corresponding multiplicity of types of misrecognition and injury, and so of apt forms of recognition (Emcke 2000). Participation in practices of negotiation of identity, the security of these processes of identity discussion and formation, and gaining the acknowledgment and respect of these by others are the prerequisites of the liberal sense of self-worth of individuals and groups that empowers them to become free, equal, and autonomous agents in both private and public life (Tully 1999b, 189–91). As a result, the demeaning and disrespect of their identities through sexism, heterosexism, racism, nationalist, linguistic, and culturalist chauvinism, and the imposition of dominant cultures through processes that destroy identities and assimilate or marginalize individuals and groups are not only unjust. They also undermine the self-respect, and hence the very abilities, of the people concerned not only to resist these injustices, but also to act effectively even if they opt to assimilate. This causes the well-known pathologies of oppression, marginalization, and assimilation: lack of self-respect and self-esteem, alienation, transgenerational poverty, substance abuse, unemployment, the destruction of communities, high levels of suicide, and the like (Young 1990).

Legitimate struggles to overcome an imposed identity and to gain public recognition of a nonimposed identity through the three processes of negotiation mentioned earlier are not direct challenges to the principles of constitutional democracy: freedom, equality, respect for diversity, due process, the rule of law, federalism, mutual respect, consent, self-determination, and political, civic, social, and minority rights. These principles are appealed to by both sides in identity politics: to condemn the imposed identity and to justify the recognition of an identity-related difference, on one side, and to defend the established norms of citizen identity on the other. Of course, these principles are interpreted and applied in different ways, but it is seldom the principles themselves that are in dispute. Rather, the objection is that these principles are not interpreted, applied, and acted on either in a difference-blind manner, as liberals often claim, or in accordance with a national identity that all citizens share equally, as nationalists often claim. Rather, they are employed in a manner that is partial to the identity-related differences of the able, heterosexuals, males, and members of the dominant linguistic, cultural, ethnic, national, and religious groups; and, conversely, the principles are handled in a manner that is biased against the practical identities of others. The solution is not to try to apply the principles in an impartial manner or in accordance with a common national identity *in all cases*, for in many cases this is not possible. Politics and public life have to be conducted in some language or other, in accord with some mode of overt and covert conduct or other; statutory holidays, elections, and the like will fall on some religious holidays; some versions of history will be taught in the educational systems and embodied in the public narratives and iconography; powers of self-government have to be distributed according to some principle of subsidiarity or another; and so on. The suggestion is, rather, to interpret and apply these principles in an "evenhanded" or "difference-aware" manner: one that is not partial to any particular identity at the expense of others but is based on mutual respect for the diversity of identities of the sovereign citizens of the association, so there is a genuine parity of participation.[4]

Schematically, three types of struggles over recognition involve demands to negotiate the norms of public recognition to achieve parity of participation. The first is for the mutual recognition and respect for identity-related differences in the broad cultural sphere of contemporary societies. All types of identity politics involve demands to negotiate the ways some members of a political association are disrespected and misrecognized in the sphere of cultures and values where members first learn and internalize their attitudes toward others. The aim is first to expose and overcome racism, sexism, ableism, ethnocentrism, Eurocentrism, sexual harassment, linguistic, cultural, and national stereotypes, and other forms of overt and covert diversity-blind and diversity-partial speech and behavior. Second, the objective is to foster awareness of and respect for diversity in all areas of society so all members can participate on the basis of *mutual respect*. This type of demand usually calls for curriculum reform, training in cultural diversity at work, and the democratic negotiation of diversity-sensitive equity policies and standards in the public, private, and voluntary sectors (Benhabib 1996; Tully 1999a).

The second type of demand is for multicultural and multiethnic citizenship. These are demands to participate in the public institutions and practices of contemporary societies in ways that recognize and affirm, rather than misrecognize and exclude, the diverse identities of citizens. Linguistic, cultural, ethnic, and religious minorities wish to participate in the same institutions as the dominant groups, but in ways that protect and respect their identity-related differences: for example, to have some schooling in their minority languages and cultures, access to media, to be able to use their languages and cultural ways in legal and political institutions and at work (whether one is Muslim in France or Surinamese in the Netherlands), to reform representative institutions so they fairly represent the identity diversity of the population, to have day-care facilities so women and single parents can participate on a par with heterosexual males, to speak, deliberate, and act in public in a different voice, same-sex benefits, to observe a religious or cultural practice in public without discrimination, for constitutional charters of rights to be interpreted and applied in a diversity-sensitive manner, to establish minority and group rights where necessary, and so on—so all citizens and minorities can participate equally, but not identically, with others (Kymlicka 1995a, 1995b; Kymlicka and Norman 2000).

The third type of demand is for multinational or multipeoples polities—constitutional associations of more than one "free people." These are demands to establish political and legal institutions autonomous in varying degrees from the larger political association. Here, suppressed nations within multinational societies and indigenous peoples argue that the proper recognition of their identity *as* nations and *as* peoples entails that they have a right of self-determination: a right to govern themselves by their own laws. They may exercise this right either by determining a new subsidiary, federal, or confederal relation within the existing constitutional association of which they are a part or, if this meaningful exercise of the right of self-determination is blocked, by secession and the establishment of an independent nation-state. It is only by these means of self-government, they argue, that they are able to protect and live in accordance with their identity—their nationality and their indigenousness—and be "free peoples." If they are constrained to participate in the institutions of the dominant society, then they are misrecognized (as minorities within the dominant society rather than as nations or peoples) and their identity-related differences will be overwhelmed and assimilated by the majority.

Multinational demands have become increasingly prominent in recent years. The response is often to suppress the demand and assimilate the minority or to engage in armed conflict that smoulders for generations or ends in secession. However, the struggles have also given rise to experiments in the "federalization" of multinational political associations: that is, regional autonomy, subsidiarity, dispersed and shared sovereignty, and flexible federal and confederal arrangements. Spain, Belgium, the United Kingdom, Canada-Quebec, and the European Union are all examples of this kind of experimentation (Gagnon and Tully 2001). And, in Norway, Canada, the United States, Australia, New Zealand, and South America, the struggles of indigenous peoples to overcome internal colonization and gain recognition as "free peoples" are giving rise to experiments in new forms of indigenous self-determination and treaty-federalism with the larger, surrounding nonindigenous governments (Havemann 1999).

The third type is the most revealing of the difficulties of identity politics. It brings into play the full diversity of overlapping identities and three processes of negotiation characteristic of identity politics. Those making the demand must try to convince a majority of their own internally diverse members through public dialogue and consultation that they are not a province, region, or minority of some kind, as the current form of recognition has it, but a distinct nation or people, and that this is worth fighting for. They must also persuade the larger society of which they are a part, with all its internal diversity, and then persuade it to enter into negotiations to change the current constitutional relation to some form of greater autonomy and lesser association. As these contentious negotiations take place, they almost always provoke the other two types of demand (for the recognition of cultural diversity and multicultural citizenship) within and often across the nation or people demanding recognition. The diverse citizens within, such as linguistic minorities and multicultural immigrants, wish to ensure that their identity-related differences will not be effaced in the new institutions of self-government by a policy of either impartial liberalism or uniform nationalism. Yet, cultural diversity and multicultural citizenship have to be recognized and accommodated in a form that does not infringe too deeply on, or undermine, the identity of the nation or people, for this is the reason self-governing institutions of nationhood are demanded in the first place.[5]

Disputation and Belonging

Bearing in mind these complex conditions and burdens of participation in culturally diverse societies, how can the classical account of free citizens and free peoples be reconceived so members can participate equally and equitably, become citizens, and, in so doing, create a sense of belonging to and identification with their constitutional democracy without unreasonable requirements of integration? As we have seen, the diverse and dialogical character of the aspectival identities that citizens struggle to overcome (if they are imposed and intolerable) or to have recognized (if they are the product of discussion and negotiation among the citizens who bear them), as well as the impossibility of either screening out identity-related differences or reaching consensus on a uniform national identity in every case, already suggest that processes of democratic negotiation might be the best mode of working out disputes over norms of public recognition. This suggestion can be substantiated and the features of such practices of participation and disputation can be specified, step by step, by addressing the central questions that bear on their composition in the light of our classical account as an object of comparison and contrast. These practices must serve two purposes: to provide procedures for the conciliation of disputes over recognition and, as a by-product of direct and indirect participation, to generate ties of belonging among the disputants.

The first central question is, who decides which identities of the members of a political association are unjustly imposed and which are worthy of recognition and accommodation? The answer marks a democratic revolution in political thought in the late-twentieth and early-twenty-first centuries. It is no longer assumed that the identities worthy of recognition, and so constitutive of citizen identity, can be determined outside of the political process itself, by theoretical reason. It is now widely assumed that the identities worthy of recognition must be worked out by the citizens and their representatives, through participation in the exchange of public reasons in processes of negotiation. In John Rawls's famous phrase, the question is "political not metaphysical" (Rawls 1999).

There are several reasons for this. The first is that there is a significant emphasis on democracy or popular sovereignty in both theory and practice today: that is, on our first classical principle of self-rule. In theory, *Quod omnes tangit* (what touches all must be agreed to by all), one of the classical principles of Western constitutionalism, has been revived and given dialogical reformulation as the principle of democratic legitimacy: "only those norms can claim to be valid that meet (or could meet) with the approval of all affected in their capacity as participants in a practical discourse" (Habermas 1994a, 66). As we saw in the first section, the sovereignty of the people to reach agreements among themselves on the basic norms of citizenship of their political association through deliberation is now said to be a principle equal in status to the constitutional rule of law.

In practice, there has been a corresponding proliferation of practices of democratic negotiation of the conditions of membership of a vast and increasing range of associations, from private- and public-sector bargaining to democratic constitutional change, international agreements, and evolving institutions of cosmopolitan democracy (Hirst 1994; Held, Archibugi, and Kohler 1998). In virtually every organization of human interaction and coordination, disputes over the prevailing rules of mutual recognition are referred to democratic practices of polling, listening, consultation, negotiation, mediation, ratification, referenda, and dispute resolution. Moreover, new disciplines of negotiation, mediation, and dispute resolution have been developed to train experts in "getting to yes" and to reflect critically on the burgeoning practices of democratic participation and negotiation (Ury 1998).

The second reason stems from the negotiated character of identity politics. It is the people themselves who must experience an identity as imposed and unjust; they must come to support a demand for the recognition of another identity from a first-person perspective; and they must gain the mutual recognition, respect, and support of others who do not share the identity. All this requires discussion and negotiation by the people involved in the three processes of negotiation (discussed in the second section), not by elites and representatives alone. On this modified classical account, a proposed identity only counts *as an identity* if it has come to be embraced in this democratic and dialogical manner, and it is recognized only if it has come to be affirmed by others in the same fashion. If an identity is advanced by a political elite without popular deliberation and support, and if it is recognized by another elite or an unelected court without passing through democratic will formation in the broader society, then it is not likely to be supported on either side; that is, it is not likely to be seen as an identity, on one side, or as worthy of respect in practice, on the other. It will tend to be experienced as imposed, the struggle for recognition will be intensified rather than resolved, and fragmentation will increase rather than decrease.

The third reason follows from the diversity of overlapping identities. When a demand for the recognition of an identity-related difference is advanced, it is necessary to ensure that this demand has the support of those for whom it is presented and that it does not silence or suppress another identity-related difference equally worthy of recognition. The only way this can be ensured is if the people affected have a voice in the proceedings. People must be able to advance alternative formulations of the demand that take into account the diversity of the people demanding recognition; others must be able to raise their objections to it and defend the status quo or respond with counterproposals; and others must be able to advance demands of their own that would otherwise be overridden. Accordingly, another principle of the classical account of public dialogues has been reintroduced: *audi alteram partem* (always listen to the other side[s]) (Bellamy 1999, 121). The democratic negotiations of identity politics, accordingly, are not the dyadic dialogues of modern theories of recognition, but "multilogues" (Tully 1999b, 99–116).

The fourth reason is that such popular-based negotiations can provide a stabilizing sense of belonging. A struggle for recognition signals that a norm of public recognition by which citizens coordinate their interaction has been disrupted somewhere in the system of social cooperation comprising the society as a whole. If the dispute is not resolved, it can lead to anything from disaffection to secession. Negotiations open to citizens and trusted representatives aim to provide a new (or renewed) norm of recognition that is acceptable because the people who must bear it have had a say in its formulation and have come to see that it is well supported (even when they do not all agree with it). They identify with it. This is the classical sense of belonging appropriate to a democracy.

There is one important limitation to the maxim that struggles over recognition must be worked out through negotiations among the people affected. In many cases of identity politics, those demanding the recognition of their identity-related differences are minorities. If their demands are put not only to the discussion of all but also to the decision making of all, their fate is placed in the hands of the majority. Yet this is precisely the injustice they are trying to overcome with their demand. Democratic discussion and negotiation are necessary for the four reasons just given. However, it is not necessary for the final decision on a question concerning a minority to be made by a majority or by a consensus of all affected. The former is unfair to the minority and the latter is utopian.

Democratic discussions need to be placed in the broader reflective equilibrium of the institutions of the rule of law: representative governments, courts, and the legal, constitutional, and international law protection of human rights. If a demand for recognition is fully and openly discussed, supported, and agreed to by the majority of the minority making the demand (applying *audi alteram partem* within); if it is well discussed and well supported by the other people affected and to whom it is addressed; if it accords with or can be shown plausibly to be an improvement on existing legislation, minority rights, and international covenants; if it finds support in representative institutions and their committees of inquiry; or if the courts rule in its favor, then any of these institutions of the rule of law, depending on the particular case, can and should make the decision, even if there is an organized and vocal opposition to it by a segment of the majority affected. However, they should make the decision only on the condition that it is open to review and reconsideration in the future. Prejudices against different identities run deep within the dominant identities of contemporary individuals and groups and they are supported by sedimented structures of political and economic domination. Discussion and deliberation can bring people around to see their own prejudices to some extent, but in the real time and context of politics, the force of argument needs to be supplemented by the force of law in cases where the majority has a political or economic interest in upholding the biased form of recognition in dispute.

The second central question is, what are the procedures by which the people, in conjunction with their legal and political institutions, negotiate and reach agreements over disputed identities? The widely proposed answer is again classically democratic—the correct procedures are the exchange of reasons pro and contra in public negotiations. The basic idea is that an identity will be worthy of recognition and respect just insofar as it can be made good to, or find widespread support among, those affected through the fair exchange of reasons. A fair exchange of reasons will determine which identities are reasonable, and so worthy of recognition, and which are unreasonable, and so either prohibited, or at least not publicly supportable.

The conditions for the fair exchange of reasons are themselves contested by theorists and negotiators (as should be expected), but the following are commonly included. A member (individual or group) of a political association has the right to present demands to modify the forms of public recognition, and the others have a duty to acknowledge the demand and enter into negotiations pro and con, if the demand is well supported by those for whom it is presented, the reasons for it seem plausible, and the demand takes into account the concerns of others affected by the norm in question; the interlocutors in the negotiations treat each other as free and equal and accept that they are bearers of other practical identities that deserve to be treated with respect; and any resolution should rest as much as possible on the agreement of those affected and should be open to periodic review. If the dominant members refuse to enter into negotiations, or drag their feet endlessly in the negotiations and implementation, then those making the demand have the right to engage in civil disobedience to bring them to negotiate in good faith. These are roughly the minimal conditions of mutual recognition and reciprocity that ensure that a discussion is not biased toward any particular cultural identity from the outset. Muslim, atheist, indigenous, male and female interlocutors will interpret "free and equal" in dissimilar yet reasonable ways (ways that the others will see initially as unfreedom and inequality), but, because this sort of disagreement is precisely what identity politics is about, it is not possible to filter out these differences at the outset without prejudging which identities are worthy of recognition (Weinstock 2000). Of course, in the actual context of particular cases, further conditions are usually accepted by the interlocutors.[6]

The reasons exchanged involve the full gambit of reasonable and rhetorical devices discovered by the classical theorists and reworked by contemporary theorists of rhetoric and informal argument (Young 1997, 38–74; Walton 1998). The exchanges are of two types: those that aim at mutual understanding of the identities in dispute and those that aim at mutual agreement on the recognition-worthiness of the identities in dispute. In the first type of exchange, the interlocutors aim to understand the identities in question from the point of view of those who bear them and seek recognition. To gain mutual understanding it is necessary to listen to the reasons why a particular identity is important to the group advancing it, even if these are not reasons for others. An ethnic, religious, cultural, or linguistic minority, a nation, or an indigenous people will have reasons for embracing their identity that derive from that identity. These *internal* reasons will not be reasons for supporting their demand as far as the other members of society are concerned. However, they will be important to the other members in understanding why the identity is so important to them and why the members of the minority can agree to pledge allegiance to the political association only if this identity is secure. Misunderstanding, stereotyping, and deep cleavages will prevail in multicultural and multinational societies as long as these internal reasons are not exchanged in public as a basis for mutual understanding among identity-diverse citizens. Citizens need not only to know that there are culturally different others in the association, or wanting to get in, but also to gain some understanding of those different cultural identities and the narratives and histories in terms of which they have meaning and worth for their bearers.

In the second type of exchange of reasons, the aim is to reach agreement on which identities are worthy of recognition and how they are to be accommodated, as well as which should be prohibited. These reasons cannot appeal to particular identities, for they need to convince other interlocutors who do not share that identity and its internal reasons, even if they understand and respect it. Exchanges aimed at reaching agreement, therefore, search for reasons that identity-diverse citizens can share. These shared reasons are various. Mutual respect for individuals and minorities, toleration, freedom, equality of peoples, autonomy, community, international human rights, various kinds of historical arguments, and so on are reasons shared by most. The basic conditions of the discussions themselves rule out certain identities: first and foremost, those unilateral demands that fail reciprocally to listen and respond to the demands of others. Reaching agreement, then, is a process that involves searching for these sorts of shared reasons, interpreting and applying them for and against the identities in dispute, and working toward an agreeable form of mutual recognition and institutional accommodation of the identities, or aspects of identities, that are shown to be justifiable and supportable. Through these exchanges citizens are able to move around and see to some extent their shared political association from the perspectives of other cultures, nations, sexual orientations, and so on. In the course of this movement, they become aware on reflection of their own perspective as partial and limited, like the others. The interplay of internal and shared reasons tends also to expose and unsettle the sedimented and unreflective prejudices and stereotypes internal to their own practical identities (Laden 2001).

The forms of recognition and accommodation of identities they negotiate and renegotiate through the exchange of these two types of reasons constitute their shared culturally diverse identity *as* citizens of the same association. This is an identity they will all have reasons for supporting, not despite their identity-related differences, but rather because it gives some acknowledgment of their diverse identities; it is a form of public recognition that they have a say in fighting for and establishing, and its imperfections are always open to challenge and renegotiation in turn. As a result, the practices of participation in which this culturally diverse citizen identity is negotiated, accommodated, and renegotiated engender a sense of identification with and belonging to the political association as a whole (Tully 1999b, 198–208). It is not only the freedom to participate in accord with norms that recognize respectworthy aspects of one's practical identity that engenders a sense of belonging and overcomes fragmentation. The freedom to participate directly or vicariously in contests over recognition is just as important in creating a sense of belonging.

Conclusion: Freedom and Belonging

Citizens will be able to imagine and develop a strong sense of belonging when their demands for recognition of cultural differences pass through the democratic procedures of negotiation outlined in this essay and gain recognition and affirmation in the institutions and practices of their diverse political association. In this type of case, they are free to participate in the shared identity space of a modern society in accordance with the recognition-worthy cultural differences that matter to them. They also will be able to develop a sense of belonging when the demands they put forward fail to pass these democratic tests of internal and shared public reasons; that is, when their demands are exposed as inconsistent with the (contested) family of principles of freedom, equality, mutual respect, federalism, the protection of individual and minority rights, and so on. In this type of case, they come to see on reflection (induced by participation in the discussions) that their demands are unreasonable (usually because their demands fail to reciprocally recognize the legitimate demands of others). If they continue to complain, there is no further obligation to listen to them and their disaffection is unavoidable.

The main argument, however, is that citizens also can reimagine and develop a strong sense of belonging in a third type of case. This is when their demand is well supported by good internal and shared reasons, yet it fails to gain public recognition after long and difficult negotiations because good reasons on the other side carried the day. These disputants, who strongly disagree with the outcome because they have good reasons for believing it is imperfect and unjust, will nevertheless have reasons to identify with the political association as long as the democratic procedures of negotiation are fair and the outcome is always open to review and challenge in the future. Direct or representative participation in the intersubjective and agonistic activity of putting forward a demand to amend the norms of public recognition, of seeing it acknowledged and responded to by other citizens and representatives, of modifying the demand and responding in turn, of losing some contests and winning others, and of knowing that one can always fight again generates a sense of respect for one's fellow adversaries and a sense of attachment to the form of political association that allows this kind of democratic game to be played freely, with a minimum of domination. In the course of the struggles, the disputants reimagine themselves as citizens of an association that allows them to exercise their popular sovereignty by engaging in activities of having a say over the norms of public recognition in a manner appropriate to the equiprimordial rule of law and the circumstances of cultural diversity. Because this is the most common type of case in culturally diverse constitutional democracies today, it is important to conclude by clarifying how belonging rather than fragmentation is created in these circumstances.

First, agreements on contested norms of recognition are "overlapping" rather than transcendent (Rawls 1996, 133–72). The interlocutors do not transcend their practical identities and reach agreement from an impartial perspective, they exchange internal and shared reasons from within their practical identities, moving around to some extent to the perspectives of others, and reach agreements on an identity-sensitive norm of recognition. One of the most important discoveries of the past four decades of dispute resolution is that people with very different ethnic, religious, national, cultural, and linguistic identities can nevertheless reach overlapping and imperfect agreements on norms of public recognition, such as charters of individual and group rights and duties, as long as these are formulated, interpreted, and applied in an identity-sensitive manner.[7]

Second, overlapping agreements do not conform to the ideal of a consensus. They are negotiated, provisional, and contextual settlements that involve compromise, an element of nonconsensus, and hence require review and revision after implementation. The reasons for this derive from the three characteristics of identity politics. Recall that in a struggle for recognition there are three simultaneous processes of negotiation and they influence one another. As the interlocutors proceed, the rule of *audi alteram partem* is applied again and again by diverse individuals and groups whose identities are affected by the proposed form of recognition, demanding that their identities in turn are given due recognition and accommodation in the agreement. It is unreasonable to assume that each could receive the recognition they believe they deserve on the basis of their internal reasons alone. Such a recognition would become possible in principle only if identities were separate, bounded, and homogeneous. Because they are multiple, overlapping, and contested, their due recognition involves a complex back-and-forth accommodation and mutual compromise. Therefore, the agreement will be an attempt to give each legitimate claim its due recognition and this will always involve compromise. It will be a complex "accommodation," like the Northern Ireland Accord (Bellamy 1999, 91–140).

Third, negotiations always take place in "real time" and under real constraints (Hoy and McCarthy 1994, 203–69). Not all voices will be heard (including future generations) and not all compromises will be acceptable to all affected. The habitual identities of the participants in the discussions will be shaped by the unjust relations of power and wealth that are held in place and legitimated by the prevailing norm of public recognition that is in dispute. Therefore, contestants will exchange reasons in unequal and asymmetrical ways in the negotiations. As we have seen, in some cases a court or representative body will not unreasonably bring the negotiations to a (provisional) close, and its judgment too will be shaped by the prevailing and sedimented norms of recognition in question. Yet, the dissenters may turn out in the longer run to have been right after all. Any agreement can be interpreted in different ways, and this gives rise to disagreements over the institutions that are supposed to implement the agreement and over the way those institutions operate. As citizens experiment with the implementation of the agreement over time, conflicts will develop in practice that they did not foresee in the negotiations. Moreover, the change in identities brought about by interacting in the institutions and practices that implement the new norm of recognition will itself alter the retrospective view the participants have of the agreement. By this time, a new generation will enter and bring generational differences with it.

Fourth, even with the best will and circumstances there can be "reasonable disagreement" over any practical norm of action coordination. There can be good shared reasons on all sides. This has nothing to do with bias or interest but simply with the intrinsic features of practical reasoning at this level of generality and complexity (Rawls 1996, 54–58).

For these four reasons, citizens in culturally diverse societies come to accept the inevitability of reasonable dissent from any norm of public recognition and the right to challenge, discuss, and seek to amend it, and thus to reimagine membership accordingly.

Moreover, struggles over recognition are not only the instrumental means to achieve the goal of recognition, but also the public display of the intolerability of the present form of misrecognition of a well-supported cultural identity and the public display of an alternative mode of recognition of an esteem-worthy cultural identity. The other members of the society acknowledge this public disclosure and respond in kind. This initiates the back-and-forth activity of disclosure and acknowledgment. Although these agonistic games of disclosure and acknowledgment, which may continue for generations, often fall short of gaining full and well-supported public recognition of the identities in dispute, they are far from trivial.

These games of disclosure and acknowledgment are the democratic means of discharging ressentiment at the present, often sedimented, structure of recognition. If these democratic means are unavailable, then dissenters turn to other, nondemocratic and violent, means to discharge. The public displays of how a minority would like to be seen and recognized by the other members also serve to generate a level of both self-respect and self-esteem among the members of the minority (in contrast to the standard view that recognition alone generates self-respect and self-esteem). Even when the others respond by denying recognition and putting forward counterarguments for the status quo, this contestatory degree of acknowledgment makes the minority feel at least part of the larger society, by virtue of being in on a dialogue that it may be able to win in the longer run. Participation in these difficult and often heated exchanges enables the members of a misrecognized minority to acquire the skills and self-assurance to present, defend, and gain support for their demand. Also, they learn to appreciate the legitimate concerns of others, to develop a degree of respect for them, and to interact democratically with them. Although these games are serious, they also involve, as in any competitive game, an important play element that is often overlooked in cost-benefit analysis of citizen participation and that builds a camaraderie across differences; that is, they become citizens (Tully 2001).

The final reason why the source of belonging must be found in the citizen participation in struggles over recognition, rather than in the utopian dream of a just and definitive resolution, is that the identities of the participants change in the course of the discussions and negotiations. The self-understandings of those presenting the demand and those responding change in dialogue-dependent ways. Nothing has changed more over the past four decades of identity politics than the identities of men and women, immigrants and old-timers, indigenous and nonindigenous persons, Muslims and Christians, Europeans and non-Europeans, and the members of cultural minorities and majorities. The ground of belonging cannot be this or that ordering of the norms of public recognition, for these are at best appropriate to a specific time in the ongoing dialogue. Fortunately for free and open democracies, engaged citizens also develop a second-order understanding of themselves as interrelated members of a shared larger polity that enables them to change the norms of cooperation as they change themselves, thereby reimagining belonging.

A culturally diverse society will not overcome fragmentation and generate a sense of belonging by trying to impose difference-blind policies in all cases, by attempting to forge a homogeneous national identity, or by distributing group rights. Rather, the key to belonging and legitimacy is always to ensure that citizens and their trusted representatives are free to engage in democratic practices of testing the prevailing norms of recognition, negotiating their amendment, and experimenting with institutions of implementation and review. Fragmentation is the by-product of the false premise that there is some definitive ordering of the norms of public recognition that ends the struggles once and for all. Belonging is the by-product of the democratic freedom that follows from abandoning this false and dangerous premise.

Notes

1 For a defense of these three approaches of difference-blind liberalism, a more or less uniform nationalism, and group rights, see, respectively, Barry 2000; Poole 1999; and Kymlicka 1995a, 1995b.

2 This essay is a considerably revised version of Tully 2000a for the purposes of this volume. It is a presentation of a citizen-centered approach, which I have developed and defended in more detail elsewhere. More specifically, the first type of freedom of participation (in accordance with one's publicly recognized respectworthy identity-related differences) is investigated in Tully 1999b, whereas the second type of freedom (to participate in public contests involving the exchange of reasons over the recognition of identity-related differences) is investigated in Tully 1999a, 2000c, 2000b, and 2001.

3 These three features of public dialogues are discussed later in this essay. For the classical account, see Skinner 1994; 1996, 66–214.

4 For the argument that struggles over recognition can be accommodated within the prevailing principles and values of constitutional democracy suitably understood, see especially Carens 2000 and Laden 2001. Denninger 2000 is correct to say that diversity is a "new" type of demand requiring new processes of democratic negotiation, yet Habermas (2000) is also correct to reply that diversity can be treated fairly within the principles of freedom, equality, and respect for difference, as long as these are open to different yet defensible interpretations.

5 This essay is based on my collaborative research on struggles involving all three types of demand (see Gagnon and Tully 2001).

6 I have adapted these minimal conditions from the Supreme Court of Canada in *Reference re the Secession of Quebec* 1998. I have discussed this important exercise in "reconciling diversity with unity" in Tully 2000c and 2001. For its application to the European Union, see Shaw 1999.

7 The Supreme Court of Canada argues that the Canadian constitution, including its democratic processes of discussion and amendment, is an example (Tully 2000c).

Works Cited

Arendt, Hannah. 1977. "What Is Freedom?" In *Between Past and Future*, 143–72. Harmondsworth, England: Penguin.

Barry, Brian. 2000. *Culture and Equality*. Cambridge: Polity Press.

Bellamy, Richard. 1999. *Liberalism and Pluralism: Towards a Politics of Compromise*. London: Routledge.

Benhabib, Seyla, ed. 1996. *Democracy and Difference: Contesting the Boundaries of the Political.* Princeton, N.J.: Princeton University Press.

Bhabha, Homi K. 1994. *The Location of Culture.* London: Routledge.

Carens, Joseph H. 2000. *Culture, Citizenship, and Community: A Contextual Exploration of Justice as Evenhandedness.* Oxford: Oxford University Press.

Connolly, William. 1995. *The Ethos of Pluralization.* Minneapolis: University of Minnesota Press.

Denninger, Erhard. 2000. "'Security, Diversity, Solidarity' instead of 'Freedom, Equality, Fraternity.'" *Constellations* 7:4 (December): 507–21.

Emcke, Carolin. 2000. "Between Choice and Coercion: Identities, Injuries, and Different Forms of Recognition." *Constellations* 7:4 (December): 483–95.

Gagnon, Alain-G., and James Tully, eds. 2001. *Multinational Democracies.* Cambridge: Cambridge University Press.

Habermas, Jürgen. 1994a. "Discourse Ethics: Notes on a Program of Philosophical Justification." In *Moral Consciousness and Communicative Action,* trans. Christian Lenhardt and Shierry Weber Nicholsen, 43–115. Cambridge: MIT Press.

———. 1994b. "Struggles for Recognition in the Constitutional State." In *Multiculturalism,* ed. A. Gutmann, 107–49. Princeton, N.J.: Princeton University Press.

———. 1996. "Popular Sovereignty as Procedure." In *Between Facts and Norms: Contributions to a Discourse Theory of Law and Democracy,* trans. William Rehg, 463–90. Cambridge: MIT Press.

———. 1998. "Reconciliation through the Public Use of Reason." In *The Inclusion of the Other,* ed. Ciaran Cronin and Paul De Greiff, 49–74. Cambridge: MIT Press.

———. 2000. "Remarks on Erhard Denninger's Triad of Diversity, Security, and Solidarity." *Constellations* 7:4 (December): 522–28.

Havemann, Paul, ed. 1999. *Indigenous Peoples' Rights in Australia, Canada, and New Zealand.* Oxford: Oxford University Press.

Held, David, Daniele Archibugi, and Martin Kohler, eds. 1998. *Re-imagining Political Community: Studies in Cosmopolitan Democracy.* Cambridge: Polity Press.

Hirst, Paul. 1994. *Associative Democracy: New Forms of Economic and Social Governance.* Cambridge: Polity Press.

Hoy, David, and Thomas McCarthy. 1994. *Critical Theory.* Oxford: Basil Blackwell.

Kymlicka, Will. 1995a. *Multicultural Citizenship.* Oxford: Oxford University Press.

———, ed. 1995b. *The Rights of Minority Cultures.* Oxford: Oxford University Press.

Kymlicka, Will, and Wayne Norman, eds. 2000. *Citizenship in Diverse Societies.* Oxford: Oxford University Press.

Laden, Anthony. 2001. *Reasonably Radical: Deliberative Liberalism and the Politics of Identity.* Ithaca, N.Y.: Cornell University Press.

Poole, Ross. 1999. *Nation and Identity.* London: Routledge.

Rawls, John. 1996. *Political Liberalism.* New York: Columbia University Press.

———. 1999. "Justice as Fairness: Political not Metaphysical." In *Collected Papers,* ed. Samuel Freeman, 388–414. Cambridge: Harvard University Press.

Shaw, Jo. 1999. "Relating Constitutionalism and Flexibility in the European Union." In *Constitutional Change in the European Union: From Uniformity to Flexibility,* ed. J. Scott and G. de Burca, 337–58. London: Hart Publishing.

Skinner, Quentin. 1984. "The Idea of Negative Liberty: Philosophical and Historical

James Tully

Perspectives." In *Philosophy in History,* ed. Richard Rorty, J. B. Schneewind, and Quentin Skinner, 193–224. Cambridge: Cambridge University Press.

———. 1994. "Moral Ambiguity and the Renaissance Art of Eloquence." *Essays in Criticism* 44:4: 267–92.

———. 1996. *Reason and Rhetoric in the Philosophy of Hobbes.* Cambridge: Cambridge University Press.

———. 1998. *Liberty before Liberalism.* Cambridge: Cambridge University Press.

Taylor, Charles. 1994. "The Politics of Recognition." In *Multiculturalism,* ed. Amy Gutmann, 25–74. Princeton, N.J.: Princeton University Press.

Tully, James. 1999a. "The Agonic Freedom of Citizens." *Economy and Society* 28:2 (May): 161–82.

———. 1999b [1995]. *Strange Multiplicity: Constitutionalism in an Age of Diversity.* Cambridge: Cambridge University Press.

———. 2000a. "The Challenge of Reimagining Citizenship and Belonging in Multicultural and Multinational Societies." In *The Demands of Citizenship,* ed. Catriona McKinnon and Iain Hampsher-Monk, 212–34. London and New York: Continuum.

———. 2000b. "Struggles over Recognition and Distribution." *Constellations* 7:4 (December): 469–82.

———. 2000c. *The Unattained Yet Attainable Democracy: Canada and Quebec Face the New Century.* Montreal: McGill University and Programme d'études sur le Québec.

———. 2001. "Introduction." In *Multinational Democracies,* ed. Alain-G. Gagnon and James Tully, 1–34. Cambridge: Cambridge University Press.

Ury, John. 1998. *Promoting Deliberative Democracy: Listening within Limits.* Cambridge: Cambridge University Press.

Walton, David. 1998. *The New Dialectic: Conversational Contexts of Arguments.* Toronto: University of Toronto Press.

Weinstock, Daniel. 2000. "Saving Democracy from Deliberation." In *Canadian Political Philosophy,* ed. Ronald Beiner and W. Norman, 78–91. Oxford and Toronto: Oxford University Press.

Young, Iris Marion. 1990. *The Politics of Difference.* Princeton, N.J.: Princeton University Press.

———. 1997. *Intersecting Voices: Dilemmas of Gender, Political Philosophy and Policy.* Princeton, N.J.: Princeton University Press.

Michèle Lamont

10

Working Men's Imagined Communities:

The Boundaries of Race, Immigration, and Poverty

in France and the United States

This essay concerns definitions of cultural memberships used by working-class men in France and the United States. It identifies alternative logics of social segmentation that are at work in French and American societies, focusing on categories through which members view one another as significant others who share fundamental moral worldviews and/or cultural traits. I draw on 150 in-depth interviews conducted with low-status white-collar workers and blue-collar workers residing in the suburbs of New York and Paris to explore in an inductive manner the symbolic boundaries through which they define "people like us." More specifically, I analyze the symbolic boundaries that workers trace when they are asked to describe the kinds of people they like and dislike, whom they feel inferior and superior to, and whom they are similar to and different from. In the process, I identify the differences that are at the center of individual maps of perception as well as the differences that are not salient in the way people discuss worth, status, and, indirectly, community membership. The result is a comparative sociology of models of inclusion and exclusion that operate on the basis of different status cues, such as color, class, and immigrant status.

This research reveals two institutionalized national "models" of social segmentation:[1] One could argue that the French model is more Durkheimian in that it combines strong external boundaries and weak internal boundaries. For French workers, "us" includes all the French, but with increasing frequency, "les français de souche" only, while a large portion of the men I talked to view immigrants—reduced here to Muslim immigrants—as unable to assimilate to a universalistic French culture. The poor and blacks are still included in the definition of the French "us," as understandings of the social bond structuring French society continue to downplay internal divisions and to emphasize humanitarianism, collective responsibility toward indigent fellow citizens, and a certain universalism qua republicanism. In contrast, American workers draw moral boundaries against the poor and African-Americans in the name of work ethic and responsibility; immigrants who partake in the American dream are more easily made part of "us" than African-Americans, although anti-immigrant boundaries are present in the interviews.

Analyzing these models is particularly urgent in a context of mounting neoliberalism and racism, which both entail a narrowing of bonds of solidarity. Both models involve exclusion, but boundaries are structured differently across cases. In particular, the relative decoupling of racism and blackness in the French case sheds light on the American case by putting it in perspective.

We will see that the "imagined communities" I document are not primarily framed in political terms: in France as in the United States, workers use moral and cultural arguments about differences and similarities to define "people like us."[2] They refer to the struggles of their own daily lives, which are central to their own concept of self, and judge negatively others whom they perceive as not meeting basic moral standards (in terms of work ethic, sense of responsibility, perseverance, etc.). In the worldview of many of these workers, moral, racial, and class boundaries work hand in hand to provide them with a space for self-worth and dignity.

For the purpose of this essay, I am concerned with national differences, and neglect intranational variations. In fact, I am more concerned with national differences in the repertoires of arguments about worth and boundaries than with the individuals who are articulating them. Without entering into a detailed discussion of the connections between mental maps and the cultural and institutional environment in which they are found (I will occasionally use the undertheorized notions of "fit" and "resonance" [Schudson 1992] to discuss these connections), in the context of this discussion, I will simply offer a snapshot of the boundary patterns privileged by French and American workers. The full picture is provided in Lamont (2000a).

Before encountering the data, I should add a few words on my method and approach (for more details, see the Methodological Appendix). Too often, scholars interested in identity predefine one of its aspects as particularly important and discuss it on the basis of anecdotal evidence. In contrast, my approach is resolutely inductive: I draw on in-depth interviews to reconstruct the symbolic boundaries or mental maps through which individuals define *us* and *them*. From there, I identify the most salient principles of classification and identification that are operating behind these definitions. I asked people I interviewed to describe their friends and foes, role models and heroes, and likes and dislikes. I also asked them to describe the types of people, abstract and concrete, toward whom they felt superior and inferior and similar and different. Hence, I tap criteria of categorization and evaluation, and, by extension, criteria used to define self-identity. Thereby, I can reveal the natural order through which workers rank others when, for example, they declare that, of course, it is more important to be honest than refined or that money is not a good indicator of a person's value.

Again, the interviews on which this analysis is based were conducted with individuals living in the New York and Paris suburbs. These men were randomly selected from phone books of the working-class community. Each interview lasted approximately two hours and was conducted by me at a time and place of the respondent's choosing.[3] I interviewed native black and white workers in the New York suburbs and North African workers and native white workers in the Paris suburbs. I view as comparable blacks in the United States and North African immigrants in France, because these groups are at the bottom of their national labor market. They are also the prime victims of racism in the two countries I studied. I focus on stable working-class men, rather than on the underclass or the middle class, because this is a largely understudied group, yet a crucial one from a political standpoint (it includes the bulk of American swing voters, for instance).

I interviewed men only because the research described here extends my book *Money, Morals, and Manners* (1992), an earlier study of professionals and managers that focused on men only, that is, on the category of individuals who have most power in the workplace. In this essay and in my more recent book (Lamont 2000a), I compare workers without a college degree with college-educated professionals to understand the cultural importance of a crucial but also largely understudied boundary, the college degree, that separates the top 25 percent of the population from the rest.

I compare France and the United States because these two countries have defined themselves as redeemers of the world, as the privileged carriers of the universal ideals of freedom, equality, and liberty, although their respective histories have, until recently, included segregation and colonialism. Today, 28 percent of the French population has voted for the openly racist and anti-Semitic Front National at least once, whereas in the United States, symbolic racism has replaced blatant racism within large segments of the population.

French Cultures of Solidarity

In a Durkheimian vein, Jeffrey Alexander (1992, 291) argues that "members of national communities often believe that 'the world,' and this notably includes their own nation, is filled with people who either do not deserve freedom and communal support or are not capable of sustaining them (in part because they are immoral egoists). Members of the national community do not want to 'save' such persons. They do not wish to include them, protect them, or offer them rights because they conceive them as being unworthy, amoral, and in some sense 'uncivilized.'" In contemporary France, these unworthy people are primarily the growing number of Muslim immigrants originating from North Africa, as "Islam marks the frontier of what is foreign" (Kastoryano 1996, 63).

Between 1960 and 1974, the majority of immigrants to France came from North Africa (Morocco, Algeria, Tunisia), and they often arrived under temporary permits directing them into the worst-paid, least-desirable jobs in manufacturing, mining, and public work. These immigrants were a visible minority who, after 1974, could establish their families on French soil. Their numbers grew rapidly and by 1990 they represented 34 percent of the immigrant population, and 5 percent of the population living on French territory.[4] They concentrated on the outskirts of major cities, where they encountered a variety of problems—crime, drug and alcohol abuse, alienation—associated with poverty and poor housing. Many French citizens came to blame social problems and unemployment on foreigners, by which they generally mean North Africans. A sense of competition and the breakdown of traditional working-class culture eventually translated into xenophobia and calls for repatriation of non-Europeans (Wieviorka 1992). This trend increased and resulted in a major breakthrough when, in the 1984 European parliamentary election, the Front National, whose main program was to oppose immigration, received more than 11 percent of the vote. This party, which regularly garners 15 percent of the French electorate (Perrineau 1991), laments the disappearance of the old white and culturally homogeneous France, one in which neighborhoods were safe and truly French, and popular culture and collective identity coexisted in an organic way, undisturbed by the mores, smells, and bizarre clothing of non-European immigrants (Mayer and Perrineau 1989).

In the interviews I conducted, a sizable portion of native French workers draw strong boundaries toward North Africans, and in doing so, they use three primary types of arguments.[5]

First, North Africans are viewed as lacking in work ethic and sense of responsibility, and as having access to a larger share of the collective wealth than they are entitled to. This is particularly unbearable to workers because it violates their sense of group positioning (Blumer 1958). Interestingly, whereas American workers condemn blacks for their lack of self-reliance, French workers are angry because immigrants are favored by a disloyal paternalist state, at a time when the quality of life and education in working-class neighborhoods is perceived as being in steady decline.

Second, French workers draw boundaries against North Africans on the basis of their lack of civility: they spit in front of people, never apologize, are rude, and lack respect for others. They also have barbarous mores (e.g., they kill goats on their balconies during Ramadan). They destroy French quality of life and should go back home.

The third and most fatal failing of North African immigrants is their inability or refusal to assimilate, which violates republican ideals, and is perceived by workers as a major threat to their personal and national identity. Republican ideals include the Jacobean notions of equality, universalism, and national unity. These ideals negate particularism based on religion, locality, race, corporate membership, and birth. They also presume a voluntaristic or contractual approach to political participation: anyone can join in the polity as long as he or she assimilates and comes to share a political culture. That North Africans are perceived as refusing this contract (by resisting assimilation) invalidates their right to reside in France. In contrast, throughout French history, other immigrant groups have not been as intensely stigmatized, because they were perceived as assimilating quickly (through the army, unions, schools, or left-wing political parties), or as being there only temporarily (Noiriel 1988). This refusal to assimilate is particularly resented because being French is one of the most high-status aspects of workers' identity, and because French political culture defines this republicanism as quintessentially French, and even as one of the most sacred contributions of the French nation to the world.

Whereas French intellectuals and social scientists often stress the role played by republicanism in limiting racism in France (e.g., Régis Debray,

Alain Finkielkraut, Pierre-André Taguieff, Dominique Schnapper), in fact, this sacred culture draws a clear line between in-group and out-group, that is, between those who share it and those who do not. It simultaneously creates strong external boundaries and downplays internal stratification bases within the population that could act as alternative identity bases (including race and class) by making assimilation a sine qua non for social membership.

It is largely because they are Muslims that North African immigrants are construed by native French workers as either particularly resistant to assimilation or as unable to assimilate. Indeed, as Muslims they are described as fundamentally other, and in some cases, as culturally incompatible with the French (in contrast, American racists do not use culturalist arguments as exclusively, resorting also to historical, biological, and psychological arguments [see Lamont 2000b]). In the words of a railway technician:

> We have to be honest; the problem is that they don't have the same education, the same values as we do. We have a general Christian education, most of the French do not believe in God but they all have a Christian education that regulates our relationship. But in the Muslim world, the Koran doesn't have the same values at all. They send children to get killed in the minefields of Iraq. But in France, if you kill children, it is really a scandal. But in those countries, social things are not as important. The mother is happy to send her child to go get killed in the minefields. She will cry, it is true, she will have the same pain as a European mother, but it is not the same thing. . . . And there is also the respect of the value of life itself. Women in the Muslim world have no place. Whereas here in France, I have washed dishes . . . at some point, my wife had a depression, and I stayed with my children. Their education is different.

Undoubtedly, this rejection is linked to the defense of a "true French culture" that is threatened not only from the inside by foreigners but also from the outside by Americanization. Moreover, colonial notions of France's *"mission civilisatrice"* and of French superiority remain present in the mind of many workers, especially when it comes to barbaric former African colonies. Elements of these available cultural repertoires are appropriated by French workers to reinforce boundaries against Muslims: differences in the degree of their religious involvement are downplayed, and even *"beurs"* (second-generation children of immigrants) who have French citizenship are widely perceived to be immigrants.

The importance of immigrants in the boundaries that the French interviewees draw is particularly remarkable when compared with the place that these men give to alternative bases of community segmentation in their discourse on "the other," and particularly the place they give to racial others (mostly blacks) and to the poor.

Interviews strongly suggest that race is not an important basis of exclusion among French workers. Indeed, very few workers mention race when drawing boundaries, suggesting a decoupling between racism and blackness that is surprising from an American perspective. Two interviewees pointed to the laziness of blacks, and one brought to my attention the absence of racism, offering as a piece of evidence the fact that as French citizens, black *Martiniquais* and *Guadeloupains* are by right and de facto fully and equally included in the national collectivity, again on the basis of republican ideals. One survey showed that when asked which category of immigrants poses the greatest difficulty for integration, 50 percent of the French respondents identified North Africans, far more than the 19 percent who pointed to black Africans or the 15 percent who named Asians (Horowitz 1992, 19). Less recent survey data consistently provide evidence that negative feelings toward North African immigrants are much stronger than negative feelings toward blacks, toward European immigrants, or toward other racial minorities.[6]

A number of factors combine with the culture of republicanism to create weak boundaries against blacks, as compared to North Africans:

1 Most North Africans are first- or second-generation immigrants. Blacks are more heterogeneous: although some are recent immigrants from sub-Saharan Africa, those from the *Dom-Toms* (overseas departments and territories) have been French for several generations. This works against defining "us" in opposition to "blacks," and partly trumps the low status of blacks as formerly colonized people.

2 Blacks living in France are more heterogeneous religiously than North Africans—for instance, Senegalese are predominantly Muslims, whereas Congolese are Catholic[7]—which also works against institutionalizing a clear distinction between "us" and "blacks." Although North Africans include a small Jewish population, they are often presumed to be homogeneously Muslims.

3 Muslims are more salient to French workers because they constitute a larger group than blacks (again, they make up almost 5 percent of the French population as compared to less than 2 percent for blacks).[8]

4 The process of decolonization was much more peaceful in French sub-Saharan Africa than in North Africa, which sustained less negative stereotypes of blacks than of North Africans.

5 Historically, a sizable proportion of black African immigrants came to France to be educated.[9] This population was of a more elite background and was more readily assimilated than many North African low-skilled workers. Their presence worked against negative views of blacks, at a time when low-skill black Africans had less easy access to French shores than their North African counterpart owing to geographical distance.[10]

The arrival of a rapidly increasing number of West African immigrants might be undoing this relative dissociation between blackness and racism.[11] In particular, the policy of family reunification that was put in place after 1974 brought in large numbers of African families, which made Muslim African migration more visible in part by focusing public attention on polygamy and traditional female genital mutilation (Barou 1996). Nevertheless, overall, the combined characteristics of blacks living in France work against a clear polarization between "Frenchness" and "blackness" in a manner unparalleled for North Africans. Racial "others," such as Asians, have assimilated successfully. They contribute to the playing down of racial differences as a basis for internal differentiation within French society.[12]

French workers also downplay the internal segmentation of their society by integrating among "people like us" individuals located in the lower echelons of society. Indeed, they rarely express feelings of superiority toward the poor. These categories of individuals are often simply relatively absent from their descriptions of boundaries. A detailed analysis of the interviews suggests that the majority of the French respondents are indifferent toward or silent about the poor, whereas this is the case for only a quarter of the American workers (a majority of them draw boundaries against the poor). Also, a number of French workers explicitly express solidarity toward people below them in the social structure, drawing on a vocabulary of class struggle and class solidarity to point out that "we are all wage earners, we are all exploited." References to welfare recipients and the unemployed are often accompanied by a critique of the capitalist system. For instance, a bank clerk says, "I think it is unacceptable that some people are unemployed while others can work as much as they want." A wood salesman concurs when he says that market mechanisms should not determine salaries, and he concludes, "all workers should be reasonably well paid." Like many others, this salesman opposes classical liberalism and its invisible hand because it is inhuman and penalizes the weakest. Social welfare is not in question, but the undue protection of foreigners who are not truly part of the collective "us" is.

Republicanism, Christianity, and socialism all provide elements of cultural repertoires that favor such weak internal boundaries by stressing the importance of social solidarity among citizens (independent of race), among the poor, and among workers, respectively.[13] Along these lines, when asked to choose, from a list of traits, five qualities that they find particularly important in others, a third of the French workers chose *solidaire* or *égalitaire*, in contrast to fewer than a fifth of their American counterparts; also, none of the French chose "successful," but again, a fifth of their American counterparts did. French workers often reject social climbing in the name of personal integrity; to it are opposed notions of togetherness, *"partage,"* and egalitarianism. They frequently have negative attitudes toward money and power, which they most often experience as something that is coercive, repressive, and disempowering. They often describe the upper half as exploitative and dehumanizing, suggesting that class, and the discourse of class struggle, remains very salient in their worldview (contra Beck [1994] and others).[14]

Collectivity American-Style

In the mind of many American workers, social and cultural membership remains largely equated with being white and being at least lower-middle or working-class. Indeed, whereas the French workers I talked to did not draw strong boundaries against the poor, the opposite is true in the United States. Although a number of American interviewees are critical of the upper half for their moral failings (Lamont 1999), they more often evaluate people on the basis of their "success" and more readily draw boundaries against individuals below themselves on the socioeconomic ladder, as compared to the French. In doing so, they often resort to arguments having to do with work ethic and ambition. For instance, Frank Thompson from Hempstead, Long Island, says that if he had to draw a line to distinguish superior and inferior people, he would draw it against "some people out there I think that could do better and don't try. There's nothing wrong if you don't want to become something, but don't blame somebody else for it." Also, a worker from Linden, New Jersey, who does not have a college degree says that he feels superior to "people who have no control over their lives. If a person just does nothing to help themselves, I'm very hard on these people."

The interviews suggest a close association between moral and class boundaries in the United States. The literature has clearly documented the association between poverty and irresponsibility, laziness, and lack of self-sufficiency (e.g., Katz 1989), and my interviews reveal similar constructs.[15] For instance, after declaring proudly that he is a diehard Republican, one of the men I talked to explained that being Republican means "Don't give anything for nothing. Incentive . . . Go get a job . . . [We should not] make it so easy to stay on unemployment, on welfare." Another explained that he is a conservative Republican because he does not "like people who try to take advantage of things and take, take, and give nothing back." These men are angry that they have to pay so much in taxes to support the poor who "don't work at all and get everything for free." They more often stress traditional aspects of morality (e.g., the Ten Commandments and the defense of a traditional work ethic) than the French.[16] When asked to choose from a list traits that they disliked most, half chose "lazy" in contrast to a fifth of their French counterparts. Moreover, when asked to choose five traits that they appreciate, nine out of ten respondents chose "responsible," and half chose "hardworking" in contrast to, respectively, half and a fifth of the French.[17]

Let's turn now to American racism. When asked to whom they feel superior and inferior, the majority of American interviewees constantly and subtly shift from moral to racial boundaries, drawing both at once, and justify racist attitudes via moral arguments. The rhetoric they use to draw boundaries against blacks resembles the one they use to reject the poor: they stress their alleged lack of work ethic and sense of responsibility. They also point to their inability to educate their children properly, particularly in moral matters. Again, they accuse blacks of "getting away with murder . . . with things that I wouldn't even think of doing" (civil servant). They view African-Americans as "having a tendency to . . . try to get off doing less, the least . . . possible as long as they still maintain being able to keep the job, where whites will put in that extra oomph" (electronics technician). Another electronics technician summarizes the way many perceive the situation:

> I work side by side constantly with blacks, and I have no problem with
> it . . . I am prejudiced to a point . . . What is a nice way to say it? . . . I know
> this is a generality and it does not go for all, it goes for a portion. It's this
> whole unemployment and welfare gig. What you see mostly on there is

blacks. I see it from working with some of them and the conversations I hear. . . . A lot of the blacks on welfare have no desire to get off it. Why should they? It's free money. I can't stand to see my hard-earned money going to pay for someone who wants to sit on his or her ass all day long and get free money. That's bullshit, and it may be white thinking, but, hey, I feel it is true to a point. . . . You hear it on TV all the time: "We don't have to do this because we were slaves four hundred years ago. You owe it to us." I don't owe you shit, period. I had nothing to do with that and I'm not going to pay for it. . . . Also, I don't like the deal where a black person can say anything about a white, and that's not considered prejudice. But let a white person say even the tiniest little thing about a black person, and bang, get up in front of Reverend Al Sharpton and all the other schmucks. That's bullshit. That's double standard all the way along the line.

This passage illustrates how, for some American workers, class, racial, and moral boundaries work hand in hand in such a way that the community of "people like us" is defined very narrowly and certainly excludes blacks, who are largely constructed as living off working people.[18] That boundaries against the poor and blacks in the United States are so strong is undoubtedly related to the fact that these two groups are associated with one another (in contrast, in the French context, the long-term unemployed are mostly white French workers who are victims of economic restructuring). Hence, in the United States, blackness and poverty trace the limits of social membership, and this trend is likely to become more accentuated in the context of a growing opposition between all nonblacks and blacks (Gans 1999), and this, despite the centrality of egalitarianism in American political culture (Lipset 1979; Tocqueville 1945).[19]

In this context, immigrants, and particularly Caucasian immigrants, who attempt to achieve the American dream are easily made part of "us" (Lieberson 1980). These immigrants still hold a privileged place in the country's collective self-image in part because this country is mainly a country of immigrants. Indeed, my interviews suggest that, in the words of Michael Walzer (1992), the United States remains a "nation of nations" where external boundaries remain relatively weak. When describing their mental maps, few workers point to immigrants, and when they do, it is rarely to single out their moral failures. Some point to failure to assimilate, and are slighted by what they perceive to be a lack of desire to learn English among immigrants. However, they tend to be more concerned with the dangers this represents for the decline of the relative status of the nation, than for immigrants' moral character. National surveys also show that in the early 1980s, the percentage of Americans who did not perceive immigrants as "basically good, honest people" was only around 20 percent, and the percentage who did not consider them as hardworking was only 18 percent (Lapniski et al. 1997, 367). Moreover, Espenshade and Belanger's (1998) survey analyses reveal that if Americans have negative feelings toward immigrants, these are ambivalent and not strongly held.[20]

Stronger boundaries toward immigrants might be found in states with larger immigrant populations (although New Jersey and New York are among the states with the most immigrants) and in regions where the black–white polarization is mitigated by a multiracial demographic composition. Also, recent debates about Latino immigration may suggest that we have entered a new phase of xenophobia (which is confirmed by increases in the percentage of the population that expresses negative attitudes toward immigrants—see Espenshade and Belanger [1998] and Lapniski et al. [1997]). Although I do not want to downplay the importance of this recurring feature of American society, I would contend that because of its history, by definition, the United States cannot adopt strong external boundaries, whereas in France, such strong external boundaries are facilitated by a social contract articulated around the clearly demarcated and shared political culture of republicanism.

Conclusion

This brief sketch of the boundary patterns that prevail in France and the United States still begs qualification and raises a number of questions. However, in a nutshell, it does suggest the presence of somewhat contrasted models in which moral boundaries play a key role. In France, strong boundaries are erected toward Muslim immigrants whose culture is viewed as fundamentally incompatible with a universalistic French culture, while immigrants who can become French (e.g., Italians, Hispanics, and Portuguese) are taken in as members of the collectivity (Noiriel 1988). Simultaneously, boundaries against blacks and the poor are downplayed in the name of French universalism and a view of morality that stresses solidarity, egalitarianism, and humanism and is influenced by Christianity, socialism, and republicanism. In contrast, in the United States, strong moral boundaries are drawn against the poor and African-Americans on the basis of responsibility and work ethics, while immigrants who partake in the American dream are made part of the collective "us." In general, immigrants are much less salient in the boundary work of American workers than they are in that of French workers. Furthermore, when they are critical of immigrants, American workers condemn less their moral character than the fact that they bring down the status of the United States when they refuse to assimilate.

Analyzing how workers define worth and cultural membership is particularly pressing in the present era of neoliberalism. We know that national welfare systems reveal implicit rules about conceptions of merit and social citizenship that vary across societies.[21] Yet, conceptions of moral communities and cultural membership that underlie policy choices remain underexamined.[22] Using the tools of cultural sociology, I attempted to get at moral communities by focusing on the schemata of evaluation used by ordinary citizens. National social policies are more likely to be adopted if they resonate with conceptions of the boundaries of the community that citizens uphold (Ellwood 1988).[23] Moreover, boundary ideologies also have a powerful impact on the agenda of political parties and the electoral strategies they use. We must study these conceptions if we are to make sense of some of the most important social and political changes that we are facing today, at a time when community boundaries appear to be narrowing and when principles of solidarity seem to apply to an increasingly small number of "people like us."[24] That French and American workers adopt contrasting models for defining their imagined community suggests that national differences remain strong despite growing trends toward globalization and the celebration of postnationalism.

Methodological Appendix

In the United States, I talked with sixty stable blue-collar workers who have a high-school degree but not a college degree.[25] This includes thirty self-identified African-Americans and thirty self-identified Euro-Americans, who were, when possible, matched in terms of occupation and age.[26] I also talked with fifteen Euro-American low-status white-collar workers. They were randomly selected from phone books of working-class towns located in the New York suburbs, such as Elizabeth and Linden, in New Jersey, and Hempstead on Long Island.

In France, I talked with thirty white native-born blue-collar workers and fifteen white-collar workers. I also talked with thirty North African immigrants. The criteria of selection for the French workers were parallel to those used for American workers. As for North African workers, the criterion of level of education was not applied because most members of this group have attended school only a few years. Both groups of interviewees were found in the working-class suburbs of Paris such as Aubervilliers, Stains, and Ivry-sur-Seine.

This random selection and the relatively large number of respondents aimed not at building a representative sample, but at tapping a wide range of perspectives within a community of workers. Although produced in specifically structured interactional contexts, interviews can get at relatively stable aspects of identity by focusing on the respondents' assumptions.

Although the growing presence of women and immigrants has dramatically altered the character of the French and the American working class,[27] this class remains a highly gendered—masculine—cultural construct. In both countries, I talked to men only in order to minimize cultural variations unrelated to occupation and race or ethnicity; this choice is justified in part because the larger study within which this particular project takes place is concerned with cultural differentiation between college- and noncollege-educated men, and not with the character of the American working class.

Notes

The research in this essay has been supported by the National Science Foundation, the Russell Sage Foundation, the John Simon Guggenheim Foundation, the Marshall Funds of the United States, and the Institute for Advanced Study. It has also benefited from grants from the Center for International Studies, Princeton University.

1   I use the notion of model circumspectly in light of the criticism addressed to this notion in the recent literature on national identity and immigration (e.g., Favell 1997).
2   The concept of "imagined community" is borrowed from Benedict Anderson (1991, 6–7), who argued that most communities are imagined because community members never know most of their fellow members. He also characterizes communities as limited—meaning that they have external boundaries and are not coterminous with humankind. Finally, Anderson conceives of communities as involving deep, horizontal comradeship.
3   These interviews were long enough for me to develop a complex view of the ways in which these men understood the similarities and differences between themselves and others. Respondents were asked to describe concretely and abstractly people with whom they prefer not to associate, those in relation to whom they feel superior and inferior, and those who evoke hostility, indifference, and sympathy. They were also asked to describe negative and positive traits in their coworkers and acquaintances, as well as their child-rearing values. The criteria of evaluation behind their responses were systematically compared to create a template of their mental map of their grammar of evaluation.
4   In 1990, European immigrants made up 40 percent of the 3,607,590 foreigners living in France, while Africans made up 46 percent of foreigners, and 6.4 percent of

the French population. Of these Africans, 34 percent originated in Algeria, Tunisia, and Morocco, with only 5 percent coming from the sub-Saharan francophone countries (Institut National de la Statistique et des Études Économiques 1993, 16). This last figure is increasing very rapidly: in 1975, sub-Saharan Africans made up only 2 percent of foreigners residing in France (ibid.).

5 Twenty percent of the French white-collar workers and 50 percent of the French blue-collar workers (respectively, three and fifteen interviewees) made statements that create a hierarchy between the French and North Africans. In contrast, in the United States, respectively, 60 percent and 63 percent of the Euro-American white- and blue-collar workers (i.e., eight and eighteen individuals) made such statements. Conversely, the antiracist rhetoric is less widely spread in the United States than in France: while respectively 20 percent and 13 percent of Euro-American white- and blue-collar respondents make antiracist statements of the types described later in this essay (respectively six and five respondents), it is the case for 73 percent and 23 percent of French white- and blue-collar workers (respectively, ten and seven individuals). More Americans have neutral positions or do not discuss racial inequality. It is the case for 20 percent of the American white-collar workers and 30 percent of the American blue-collar workers, compared to 6 percent and 26 percent of their French counterparts, respectively. For the purpose of this essay, I borrow from Aptheker (1992) in defining antiracism as a rhetoric aimed at disproving racial inferiority. Drawing on Goldberg (1993, 98), I define racism as a rhetoric aimed at promoting exclusion based on racial membership and produced by a dominant group against a dominated group.

6 Already in 1966, a survey showed that ten negative attributes were viewed as applying primarily to Algerians by 129 respondents, while only thirty-nine believed that these attributes applied primarily to black Africans and thirteen to Portuguese (Hannoun 1987). A national survey conducted in 1973–74 also found that 34 percent and 21 percent had a rather bad or a bad opinion of North Africans compared to only 15 percent and 8 percent for black Africans—the figures for European immigrants hover around 5 percent (Girard, Charbit, and Lamy 1974, 1028).

7 Tribalat (1995) finds that 40 percent of the black Africans she surveyed were from Muslim countries, and 14 percent are from exclusively Christian or animist areas (21). Nearly half of the black African immigrants are from religiously heterogeneous regions.

8 See note 4.

9 Delerm (1964) estimated that the black African population in France in 1964 was composed of 10,000 to 12,000 students; 4,000 to 5,000 former students who stayed; 5,000 interns ("stagiaires au titre de la coopération"); and 40,000 to 50,000 workers, of which 28,000 inhabited the Parisian metropolitan area (522–23).

10 Bergues (1973) discusses a 1965 survey that revealed favorable views held by the French about black Africans. She wrote: "they are considered pleasant, polite, hard-working, quite childish, but of good disposition"; "the general opinion is that the coming of African workers is a good thing, if we need workers and they take on jobs that the French do not want" (73). Bergues also remarked that "Good relations are generally established between black Africans and French workers or other Europeans. Only the relations with the North African groups appear difficult" (74).

11 If many respondents made anti-immigrant statements during the interview, many

also opposed racism. When presented with a list of qualities and traits and asked which of these they view most negatively, half of the French white-collar workers I talked to chose "racist" in contrast to a quarter of their American counterparts. This was also the case for two-thirds of the French blue-collar workers and a little more than a third of the American blue-collar workers.

12 I describe the boundaries drawn against immigrants as the external boundaries of the national imagined community because the majority of immigrants are not French citizens. Those who are, mostly the *beurs* (second-generation children of immigrants), continue to be described as "foreigners." Because citizenship is so central in the construction of boundaries in France, I take black French citizens to be inside the imagined national community.

13 The inclusion of the poor within the collective definitions of community produced by French workers resonates with France's institutional policy toward the poor. The Socialist Party gave priority to unemployment (i.e., to "solidarity" and "fighting exclusion" from the early 1980s on [Kouchner 1989]). It created the "revenu minimum d' insertion" (RMI) to facilitate the inclusion of the unemployed and of part-time workers. This is part of a well-established national tradition of solidaristic social insurance policy that favors the poor and the self-employed (for a history, see Paugam [1993] and Baldwin [1990]; for a comparison of pension, private health care, poor relief, and other social-benefits programs in France, Canada, and the United States, see Esping-Anderson [1990, 70–71]. For a broader discussion of issues of exclusion in France, see Castel [1995]).

14 Sociologists suggest that the boundary between the working class and the bourgeoisie was more salient in public debates prior to 1980 than it is now. Its importance has diminished with the weakening of the French Communist Party and the decline in the rate of unionization in the late 1970s (Mouriaux 1991). This boundary and the boundary drawn against immigrants were not very salient in the interviews that I conducted with professionals and managers. For an explanation for these trends, see Lamont (1992, chapter 3).

15 As many have argued, Americans take poverty to reflect personal deficiency, and they often blame the victim for structural inequality. To illustrate this argument, Cook (1979) has found that American adults are less likely to want to help poor adults than any other segment of the needy population, including children and the handicapped, blaming them for their own fate.

16 For an excellent comparison of French and American policies and approaches to poverty, see Silver (1993).

17 Note, however, that black workers, in contrast to French workers, are much more likely to value the "caring self" over the "disciplined self" in their definitions of worthy persons. This translates into weaker boundaries toward the poor, although workers often state the necessity of keeping this group at bay to protect their own resources, and because the boundary between the black mainstream society and the underclass often remains tenuous. The black–white gap in support of helping the poor and supporting welfare is 24 percent, with only 31 percent of the whites supporting policies that help the poor compared to 55 percent of African-Americans (Bobo and Smith 1994, 388). Furthermore, "The black–white gap in support for more spending on Social Security [which benefits all classes and blacks and whites alike] is only 13 percentage points [highest for blacks], whereas the gap is

48 percentage points when questions refer explicitly to [policies that benefit] blacks" (ibid.).

18 The racist views of the men I talked to are not exceptional. In their extensive study of change in racial attitudes in the United States, Schuman, Steeh, and Bobo (1985) found that although more educated respondents show higher levels of support for integration, they also tend to oppose placing whites in settings in which they are no longer in the majority (199). More generally, these authors find that, for both blacks and whites, questions that pertain to the implementation of policies "always reveal a much lower level of support than for the principles themselves" (197). They also observe that "by 1983, the approval of integrated marriage had reached only the same level that approval of integrated transportation had reached in the early 1940s [i.e., 40 percent]" (195).

19 My interviews bring support to authors who have suggested that, for Americans, moral obligations apply to an increasingly limited number of people defined by common blood, ethnicity, and religion, or by physical proximity that translates into a similar income level (Perin 1988; Sleeper 1991; Varenne 1977; Wolfe 1989).

20 For instance, immigration ranks lower than "don't know" in surveys asking respondents what the "most important problems" facing the nation are.

21 See Skocpol (1995) and Quadagno (1994). Skrentny (1996, 237–38) notes that these books point to, but do not elaborate on, the importance of moral communities in policy making. Sociologists have contrasted the French and American welfare systems: whereas the American system provides programs that are often means-tested and offer comparatively few benefits to narrow sectors of the population, French welfare programs are generally universal. For a historical discussion of French welfare benefits, see Chapman (1995).

22 In contrast, recent studies of welfare retrenchment policies tend to focus almost exclusively on institutional factors (see Pierson 1994). For a more synthetic approach, see Noble (1997).

23 For an analysis of the place of resonance in the institutionalization of meaning, see Schudson (1989).

24 As pointed out by Offe (1987, 528), advanced industrial societies face increasing skepticism concerning the notion that social policies and welfare provisions are "public goods," as individuals come to evaluate them in terms of gains, losses, and free riding: "The disorganization of broad, relatively stable, and encompassing commonalties of economic interests, associational affiliation, or culture values and life-styles is in my view the key to an adequate understanding of the general weakening of solidaristic commitments" (527).

25 These workers have been working full-time and steadily for at least five years. They do not supervise more than ten workers. I explicitly do not use income as a criterion of selection of respondents in order to include workers of various economic statuses in the sample. I consider the fact of not having a college degree as most determinant of workers' life chances and privilege this criterion in creating the sample. Respectively, 30 percent and 50 percent of white and black respondents have completed some college courses, while the remaining individuals have a high-school degree or GED.

26 Hundreds of letters were sent to potential respondents living in working-class suburbs in the New York area. In a follow-up phone interview, these men were asked to

self-identify themselves racially and I chose interviewees who categorized themselves as blacks and whites and who met other criteria of selection pertaining to occupation, age, nationality, and level of education. I take the terms *black* and *white* to be moving categories that are the object of intersubjective negotiation within determined parameters.

27 Space limitations prevent me from dealing with the complexity of the changing social, occupational, and economic characteristics of the working class.

Works Cited

Alexander, Jeffrey. 1992. "Citizen and Enemy as Symbolic Classification: On the Polarizing Discourse of Civil Society." In *Cultivating Differences: Symbolic Boundaries and the Making of Inequality*, ed. Michèle Lamont and Marcel Fournier. 289–308. Chicago: University of Chicago Press.

Anderson, Benedict. 1991. *Imagined Communities: Reflections on the Origin and Spread of Nationalism.* 2d ed. London: Verso.

Aptheker, Herbert. 1992. *Anti-Racism in U.S. History.* New York: Greenwood.

Baldwin, Peter. 1990. *The Politics of Social Solidarity: Class Bases of the European Welfare State.* New York: Cambridge University Press.

Barou, Jacques. 1996. "Les immigrations africaines." In *Un siècle d'immigration en France: 1945 à nos jours. Du chantier à la citoyenneté?,* ed. David Assouline and M. Lallaoui, 31–46. Paris: Diffusion Syros.

Beck, Ulrich. 1994. "The Reinvention of Politics: Toward a Theory of Reflexive Modernization." In *Reflective Modernization: Politics, Traditions and Aesthetics in the Modern Social Order,* ed. Ulrich Beck, Anthony Giddens, and Scott Lash, 1–55. Stanford, Calif.: Stanford University Press.

Bergues, Hélène. 1973. "L'immigration de travailleurs noirs en France et particulièrement dans la région parisienne." *Population* 28:1: 59–79.

Blumer, Herbert. 1958. "Race Prejudice as a Sense of Group Position." *Pacific Sociological Review* 1: 3–7.

Bobo, Lawrence, and Ryan A. Smith. 1994. "Antipoverty Policy, Affirmative Action, and Racial Attitudes." In *Confronting Poverty: Prescriptions for Change,* ed. Sheldon H. Danziger, Gary D. Sandefur, and Daniel H. Weinberg, 365–95. New York: Russell Sage Foundation.

Castel, Robert. 1995. *Les métamorphoses de la question sociale.* Paris: Fayard.

Chapman, Herrick. 1995. "French Democracy and the Welfare State." In *The Social Construction of Democracy, 1870–1990,* ed. George R. Andrews and Herrick Chapman, 291–314. New York: New York University Press.

Delerm, Robert. 1964. "La population noire en France." *Population* 19:3: 515–28.

Ellwood, David T. 1988. *Poor Support: Poverty in the American Family.* New York: Basic Books.

Espenshade, Thomas J., and Maryann Belanger. 1998. "Immigration and Public Opinion." In *Crossings: Mexican Immigration in Interdisciplinary Perspectives,* ed. Marcelo Suárez-Orozco, 363–403. Cambridge: Harvard University Press.

Esping-Anderson, Gosta. 1990. *The Three Worlds of Welfare Capitalism.* Cambridge: Polity Press.

Favell, Adrian. 1997. *Philosophies of Integration: Immigration and the Idea of Citizenship in France and Britain.* London: Macmillan.

Gans, Herbert. 1999. "The Possibility of a New Racial Hierarchy in the Twenty-first Century United States." In *The Cultural Territories of Race: Black and White Boundaries,* ed. Michèle Lamont, 371–90. Chicago: University of Chicago Press, and New York: Russell Sage Foundation.

Girard, Alain, Yves Charbit, Marie-Laurence Lamy. 1974. "Attitudes des français à l'égard de l'immigration étrangère: Nouvelle enquête d'opinion." *Population* 6: 1015–69.

Goldberg, David. 1993. *Racist Culture: Philosophy and the Politics of Meaning.* New York: Blackwell.

Hannoun, Michel. 1987. *L'homme est l'espérance de l'homme: Rapport sur le racisme et les discriminations en France.* Paris: La Documentation Française, Collection des rapports officiels.

Horowitz, Donald L. 1992. "Immigration and Group Relations in France and the United States." In *Immigrants in Two Democracies: French and American Experience,* ed. Donald L. Horowitz and Gérard Noiriel, 3–35. New York: New York University Press.

Institut National de la Statistique et des Études Économiques. 1993. *Recensement de la population de 1990. Les populations des DOM-TOM, nées et originaires, résidant en France.* Paris: La Documentation Française.

Kastoryano, Riva. 1996. *La France, L'Allemagne et leurs immigrés: Négocier l'identité.* Paris: Armand Colin.

Katz, Michael. 1989. *The Undeserving Poor: From the War on Poverty to the War on Welfare.* New York: Pantheon Books.

Kouchner, Bernard. 1989. *Les nouvelles solidarités: Actes des assises internationales de janvier 1989.* Paris: Presses Universitaires de France.

Lamont, Michèle. 1992. *Money, Morals, and Manners: The Culture of the French and the American Upper-Middle Class.* Chicago: University of Chicago Press.

———. 1999. "Above 'People Above': Status and Worth among White and Black Workers." In *The Cultural Territories of Race: Black and White Boundaries,* ed. Michèle Lamont, 127–50. Chicago: University of Chicago Press, and New York: Russell Sage Foundation.

———. 2000a. *The Dignity of Working Men: Morality and the Boundaries of Race, Class, and Immigration.* Cambridge: Harvard University Press, and New York: Russell Sage Foundation.

———. 2000b. "The Rhetoric of Racism and Anti-Racism in France and the United States." In *Rethinking Comparative Cultural Sociology: Repertoires of Evaluation in France and the United States,* ed. Michèle Lamont and Laurent Thévenot, 22–55. Cambridge: Cambridge University Press, and Paris: Presses de la Maison des Sciences de l'Homme.

Lapniski, John S., Pia Peltola, Greg Shaw, and Alan Yang. 1997. "The Pools-Trends: Immigrants and Immigration." *Public Opinion Quarterly* 61: 356–83.

Lieberson, Stanley. 1980. *A Piece of the Pie: Black and White Immigrants since 1880.* Berkeley: University of California Press.

Lipset, Seymour Martin. 1979. *The First New Nation: The United States in Historical and Comparative Perspective.* New York: Norton.

Lomax Cook, Fay. 1979. *Who Should Be Helped? Public Support for Social Services.* Beverly Hills, Calif.: Sage.

Mayer, Nonna, and Pascal Perrineau. 1989. *Le Front National à découvert*. Paris: Presses de la Fondation Nationale de Science Politique.

Mouriaux, René. 1991. "Stratégies syndicales face au chômage et à l'intervention industrielle de l'État dans la période 1962–87." In *Searching for the New France*, ed. James F. Hollifield and George Ross, 173–92. New York and London: Routledge.

Noble, David. 1997. *Welfare as We Knew It: A Political History of the American Welfare State*. New York: Oxford University Press.

Noiriel, Gérard. 1988. *Le creuset français: Histoire de l'immigration, XIXe–XXe siècle*. Paris: Seuil.

Offe, Claus. 1987. "Democracy against the Welfare State? Structural Foundations of Neoconservative Political Opportunities." *Political Theory* 15:4: 501–37.

Paugam, Serge. 1993. *La société française et ses pauvres*. Paris: Presses Universitaires de France.

Perin, Constance. 1988. *Belonging in America*. Madison: University of Wisconsin Press.

Perrineau, Pascal. 1991. "Le Front National: du désert à l'enracinement." In *Face au racisme*, vol 2, *Analyses, hypothèses, perspectives*, ed. Pierre-André Taguieff. Paris: La Découverte.

Pierson, Paul. 1994. *Dismantling the Welfare State? Reagan, Thatcher, and the Politics of Retrenchment*. Cambridge: Cambridge University Press.

Quadagno, Jill. 1994. *The Color of Welfare: How Racism Undermined the War on Poverty*. New York: Oxford University Press.

Schudson, Michael. 1989. "How Culture Works: Perspectives from Media Studies on the Efficacy of Symbols." *Theory and Society* 18: 153–80.

———. 1992. *Watergate in American Memory: How We Remember, Forget, and Reconstruct the Past*. New York: Basic Books.

Schuman, Howard, Charlotte Steeh, and Lawrence Bobo. 1985. *Racial Attitudes in America: Trends and Interpretation*. Cambridge: Harvard University Press.

Silver, Hilary. 1993. "National Conceptions of the New Urban Poverty: Social Structural Change in Britain, France, and the United States." *International Journal of Urban and Regional Research* 17:3: 336–54.

Skocpol, Theda. 1995. *Protecting Soldiers and Mothers: The Political Origins of Social Policy in the United States*. Cambridge: Harvard University Press.

Skrentny, John David. 1996. *The Ironies of Affirmative Action: Politics, Culture, and Justice in America*. Chicago: University of Chicago Press.

Sleeper, Jim. 1991. *The Closest of Strangers: Liberalism and the Politics of Race in New York*. New York: Norton.

Tocqueville, Alexis de. 1945. *Democracy in America*. New York: Vintage.

Tribalat, Michèle. 1995. *Faire France: Une enquête sur les immigrés et leurs enfants*. Paris: La Découverte.

Varenne, Herve. 1977. *Americans Together: Structured Diversity in a Midwestern Town*. New York: Teachers College Press.

Walzer, Michael. 1992. *What It Means to Be an American*. New York: Marsilio.

Wieviorka, Michel. 1991. *L'espace du racisme*. Paris: Seuil.

———. 1992. *La France raciste*. Paris: Points.

Wolfe, Alan. 1989. *Whose Keeper? Social Science and Moral Obligation*. Berkeley and Los Angeles: University of California Press.

Michael Herzfeld

11

Cultural Fundamentalism

and the Regimentation of Identity:

The Embodiment of Orthodox Values

in a Modernist Setting

At the edge of the conflict between NATO and Serbia, predominantly Orthodox Greece—a country cast in the role of the pagan ancestor of Western civilization as the price of its so-called independence—has had a complex and rarely easy relationship with various Western powers as well as with both Islam and Catholicism. The Greek experience both reproduces and complicates prevalent ideas about national identity, ethnicity, and community—the institutional frameworks of belonging. It also, and concomitantly, challenges currently regnant images of modernity, and suggests that the kind of belonging some Greeks envision rests on very different premises from those underlying all the dominant models.

Nationalism neither grows out of a conceptual vacuum nor, despite the view of Anderson (1983) and Gellner (1983), is it patterned in fundamentally the same way everywhere. Greek nationalism does share some common sources and features with the nationalisms of neighboring countries: romantic Herderian underpinnings, socially organized *ressentiment* (cf. Greenfeld 1992) in relation to both Turkey and the West, religious—and specifically Orthodox—reinforcements of the secular state. But Greece was created specifically as a *Western* presence, while the Slavic nations have been largely excluded from the West. What Western commentators have rarely noted is that it is the *imposed* character of Greece's specific idiosyncrasy in this regard that now, in fact, bids fair to unite it with erstwhile foes in common opposition to "the West."

Most currently fashionable views of Balkan national identities belong to the category of what Stolcke (1995) has called "cultural fundamentalism." They represent a view that anthropologists today distrust profoundly. Not since Barth's edited volume *Ethnic Groups and Boundaries* in 1969, a scant decade after the *most recent* anthropological disquisition on culture acknowledged by Samuel Huntington (1996; see Kroeber and Kluckhohn 1952; Herzfeld 1997a), have anthropologists seriously entertained the idea that cultures have fixed, essential, unchanging "characters" or "mentalities," even while nationalists have sought to embrace that very idea (e.g., Handler 1985, 1988; Jackson 1995). Yet major international powers and political commentators alike (and often in concert) seem bent on forcing smaller nations to reproduce the logic of discrete identities and cultural immutability.

Such convergence (see Connor 1993; but cf. Tambiah 1989) signals reckless irresponsibility—especially when perpetrated by those, usually not anthropologists, whose counsel is sought and valued by the wielders of significant global or national power (see Razsa and Lindstrom 1998). In this framework, the persistent evolutionist view of the Balkans as a site of "age-old hatreds" and "atavistic" sentiments is egregiously misleading as well as disingenuous. Instructively, moreover, that notion is also remarkably similar to the idea of genetically inherited nature that underlies many of the charges flung back and forth between enemies in Balkan societies. For there is no doubt that violence, as in so many other parts of the world, appears frequently and tragically in Balkan societies: the particular social organization of the feud has been much studied in this area (Boehm 1984; Hasluck 1954; Hammel 1968; Herzfeld 1985; Seremetakis 1991). But to say that Balkan people are *more* violent than others is either demonstrably untrue—nothing like the decimation of Corsica by clan warfare in the nineteenth century (Wilson 1988) has ever been reported for a Balkan society—or, simply, undemonstrable. Western commentators who justify intervention in the Balkans on such grounds are invoking a *shared* rhetoric while representing it as alien and "other." The idea of an essential "Balkan mentality" ironically shows how much the ethnonationalist leaders and policymakers and political scientists share; what they hold in common appears, for example, in the constitutions of the post-Titoist successor states (Hayden 1996).

Such a supralocal "natural" solidarity entails several premises. First and foremost is the idea that members are somehow "the same." As Anderson

(1983) argues, you do not have to have daily contact with your conationals in order to "know" what you share with them. The appeal of this relationship rests on the naturalizing properties of resemblance (Herzfeld 1997b): it is grounded in the same logic that leads parents to dispute which of them a newborn baby resembles more. That is not a trivial comparison. Ethnogenesis is usually conceptualized as the phylogenetic extension of the ontogenetic fact of birth—a link, moreover, nicely captured in the etymological derivation of the word *nation* (from Latin *natio*) itself.

Herein lies part, at least, of the explanation of the Balkans' seemingly endemic ethnonationalism. That there is a discernible pattern cannot be denied. It is especially evident in the successor states to the former Yugoslavia, in the increasingly homogeneous and also increasingly exclusivist language of their respective constitutions (Hayden 1996). It may be reinforced by the sense of greater external threat, most obviously in the case of Greece as it uneasily tries to second-guess Turkey's longer-term intentions. Yet another explanation may lie in the fact that these countries share an Ottoman past—although here one might as easily argue that coexistence rather than violence was the inherited norm—that multiethnic Sarajevo's refusal to disintegrate altogether, rather than the killings of Mostar and Srebrenica, represents the residue of Ottoman administrative philosophy and practice in the region.

Above all, the role of the Eastern Orthodox churches seems crucial, although not in the sense that Huntington (1996) implies—that is, of a Balkan region beset by the "medieval" intransigence of a decidedly "un-Western" religious tradition. Stereotypes by their very definition cannot be judged true or false (although they may approximate to experience). But they do possess *performative force*—in other words, their production, use, and aggressive deployment have material consequences and a direct impact on people's lives (Herzfeld 1997b, 156–64). To the extent that stereotypes acquire through repetition the "feel" of nature and truth, they are demonstrably effective in providing excuses and rationalization of violence of many kinds and in protecting the perpetrators from criticism or punishment. This is why cultural fundamentalism, whether academic or political, flourishes under conditions of instability: it is a seeking for categorical security, and often arises in response to external interference.

This does not mean that stereotypes are an imported, Western monopoly. The Balkan lands are rife with local variants. Indeed, my argument depends on recognizing that they are part of the discourse that Balkans *share* with their Western critics and self-appointed judges and protectors—

that the difference posited by the latter is itself an example of such a stereotypical construction.

Greece occupies a special place in the Western imagination, for which the "oriental" church of Greece constituted an irrational irritant in the imagined historic core of the Enlightenment project of "Western civilization." Instructed by local exponents of that project, Greeks were for their part forced to view as "foreign" whatever was most familiar to them in their everyday lives, including many of their religious practices (see Stewart 1989). Where foreigners saw in the Greeks' enthusiasm for collecting and reinterpreting folklore and antiquities a form of compliance with this imperative, Greeks saw their efforts as establishing a claim on that emergent property known as "modernity." The tragic paradox is thus that they acted as though their only means of achieving European modernity was by recourse to the externally constructed ancient past. In reaction, especially after the collapse of Greek power in Asia Minor in 1922, and again as Greece gradually and partially threw off Western political controls after the collapse of the colonels' irredentist regime in 1974, there emerged an alternative, nativist perspective that culminated in Neo-Orthodox dreams of Byzantium reborn.

So-called Western rationality, which manifests itself today as a technology capable of operating quite literally disembodied acts of bellicose destruction against Greece's religious and political allies, is historically associated with the Cartesian and Enlightenment traditions to which some Orthodox theologians explicitly oppose a mystical and nondualistic vision of the world. These theologians bitterly criticize some elements of their own national culture as imitations of Western "Protestantism." Indeed, theirs is a call for reenchantment. And it leads to a very different understanding of the relationship among personhood, religion, and national identity.

Above all, it recasts some of the regnant international wisdom to the Greeks' advantage. So the West, say its adherents, calls Greeks irrational for their refusal to let the name "Macedonia" serve for a neighboring country, having first created the conditions under which Greece had no logical recourse but to insist on the Greekness of the name. Could Macedonia be reconceptualized, not as the usurper of a Greek name, but as part of an extended Orthodox realm freed from the divisive neo-Classicism of the West? Such a move would also render the logic of Western rationalism irrelevant to the region, suggest new and sentimentally satisfying alliances that would nevertheless avoid recognizing Turkish and Arab cultural influences, and work against the *Western* vicarious fatalism that predestines the

Balkans to hopeless, violent division. The fact that this ideology is well represented in both of the main political parties in Greece suggests an emergent recasting of belonging in the Balkans.

We should not be surprised if the movement spreads outward from Greece, moreover, not only because Mount Athos hosts Serbian, Russian, and Bulgarian monasteries and is the incubator of Neo-Orthodoxy for Greece itself, but also because the very success of technological consumerism creates the conditions for an especially strong motivational force for a supranationalistic surge of rage expressed as ressentiment (see Greenfeld 1992). Neo-Orthodoxy clearly feeds on the West's own explicitly *cultural* fundamentalism, couched in the quasi-religious language of Enlightenment rationalism. In reaction, the religious fervor that increasingly leads Greeks and Russians to identify with Serbia—and to discount Western accounts of Serbian atrocities as vindictive misrepresentation—offers a locally cogent response, one that many may feel is the only distinctive way of resisting co-optation by the West.

Terms such as *tradition* and *modernity* tempt us to think that there are universal standards or fixed points in time against which these responses can be assessed. But this is clearly nonsense. The terms have a lively *rhetorical* existence, to be sure, but we would be ill served if we used them as analytic categories today. Although it is usual to see Weber's vision of modernity as definitive, and perhaps as realizable through a variety of different cultural trajectories (see Faubion 1993; Panourgiá 1995; and Sutton 1994, for analyses of the Greek situation, and Argyrou 1996 on Cyprus), even this familiar device seems to restore the integrity of modernity as a project. It seems much more useful, as both Argyrou and Sutton suggest, to view the terms as rhetorical markers for a series of ideological arguments created by hugely accelerated processes of globalization and transnational contact.

Thus, *tradition* indicates a hegemonic relationship (see also Collier 1997). There is a pervasive notion that the traditional is "out of our time." In that context, the label *traditional* is both glorifying and marginalizing for—to name some classic examples—peasants, "tribals" in countries such as India or Thailand, "nomads" in Jordan and Israel, "localists" in Scotland (Nadel-Klein 1991), and "picturesque" artisans producing charmingly rough goods for tourists and condescending urbanites everywhere.

Modernity is a correspondingly ambivalent property, and nowhere more so than in the *Altneuland* of Greece—to apply a Zionist metaphor to the strikingly parallel case of Hellenism (Herzfeld 1982, 13, 158). National identity is officially grounded in the idea of an ancient nation resurrected in its old territory (cartographic essentialism). But Greece must also contend with several layers of local cultural accretion—for example, Turkish elements—that are deemed, thanks to the imposed wisdom of the Western powers, to be vastly inferior to the invented past, and to constitute barriers to the achievement of "true" modernity. Hence the curious paradox that for Greeks the achievement of modernity must rest on claims to antiquity. It also, concomitantly, depends on a rejection of everything that threatens the purity of the Greeks' Classical heritage, yet that seemingly obsessive addiction to all things Classical—"ancestor obsession" (*proghonopliksía*), as the Greeks themselves have wryly labeled it—is surely the most serious barrier to Greece's recognition by others as a serious claimant to modernity.

In other words, signs of a glorious antiquity were also sources of marginalization, indications that Greece was still hostage to a past the burden of which the West had always insisted that Greece should assume. Even today major policy decisions often seem to respond above all to this intrusive imperative: Greek insistence on the Greeks' sole right to the name "Macedonia," for example, while often rationalized in terms of Realpolitik and the risk of territorial claims by an expansionist neighbor claiming that name for itself, always end up in protestations of national "history" and appeals to etymology (Bulgarian and Macedonian claims to the historical figure of Alexander the Great do not ease the situation, it is true). The glorious classical past may provide some solace in the face of national humiliation, but it is easily recognized as a tool of that same humiliation, and many Greeks have long been bitterly aware—if reluctant to admit—that this is a Greekness not of their own making.

A central theme in modern Greek historiography, exemplified in the writings of Constantine Paparrhregopoulos and Spyridon Zambelios in the nineteenth century, has held that the true spirit of the Greeks was not that of the Roman conquerors who imposed the corrupt Byzantine court on a hapless populace (and whose alien role reappears in the Bavarian monarchy that graced the early years of Greek independence), nor yet that of the Byzantine higher clergy whose successors in the Patriarchate had unsuccessfully tried to appease the Ottoman authorities when the War of Independence broke out in 1821. These writers claimed instead that ordinary folks, the lower clergy among them, were the true repositories of the ancient values—which, far from being pagan and therefore evil, were the precursors of the True Faith. They found the "evidence" for this other continuity in the folklore of the Greek countryside, as did the classicizers, but they sought in it the evidence of an essential Christianity that they claimed for the Greek people rather than simply a connection with the antiquity so assiduously sought by the pro-Western elite (see Herzfeld 1982).

Their arguments fed a deep resentment against the West that had origins predating the foundation of the state. Greek verse laments for the fall of cities to the Turks, some of them dating from the first appearance of Turkish ships in the Aegean, speak bitterly of the unwisdom of putting one's faith in the "blond lineages that came from the West"—the Catholic powers that, some thought, were more than willing to see their old adversaries, the Orthodox, become the subjects of a rapacious Muslim power instead. Popular Orthodoxy became the repository of a deep-rooted suspicion of the entire notion of a Western tradition, while some clergy feared that even an emasculated knowledge of the Classical language might presage a return to pagan beliefs and practices.

Orthodoxy is thus a model of purity; danger lurks in every aberration from its tenets. The Old Calendrists, who reject the change from the Julian to the Gregorian calendar as used in the West, probably represent this perspective in its most extreme form. Many members of the established Greek Orthodox Church regard the Old Calendrists as "more religious" than themselves. Even allowing for exaggeration or irony, there is some evidence that this is in fact not quite the compliment it seems. Religiosity is precisely what makes the members of the mainstream nervous: they associate it with "fanaticism," an evil that they associate with Islam, and with everything that is opposed to a Western notion of modernity. On the other hand, one Cretan man married to an Old Calendrist expressed this sentiment as, ostensibly at least, a form of respect, leading me to suspect that it might be easier, in a society where women are usually more visibly engaged in religious acts than are men, for a male supporter of the Greek Orthodox Church to take an Old Calendrist wife than it would be for an Orthodox woman to take an Old Calendrist husband: she would be upstaged by the latter in precisely the one sphere of her undisputed authority, and he would have to suffer the indignity—in Greek terms—of seeing his wife uphold modernity in contrast to his own traditionalism. It is also germane that the Old Calendrists still suffer a measure of persecution at the hands of both the secular and the ecclesiastical authorities; if they are indeed to be considered "purer" than the established church, their persecution lends weight to the charge that the latter has strayed too far from the true tenets of Orthodoxy.

Indeed, the official church is today a target for Neo-Orthodox thinkers, who view it as itself excessively "Protestant." This coincides with the popular view of the established church as hopelessly corrupt, collaborationist, and authoritarian, in contrast with the heroism and dedication of local priests. Indeed, for most of the laity Christ remains the emblem of their own suffering at the hands of rapacious authorities. There is an obvious parallel here with the Andalusian Anarchists who burned sacred figures in the churches because they identified these with their high-class donors rather than with the divine figures they supposedly represented (Maddox 1995). In a sense, the Spanish Anarchists were repeating the logic of the Iconoclasts of Byzantine times—crusaders against material hedonism and the fetishization of power, challenging the claims of the institutional church to represent the truths of religious faith. Such ideas are part of the common ground of political discourse in Greece, and nowhere more so than in the limiting case offered by the revolutionary guerrillas of 1821 and today by the animal thieves of highland Crete—people whose opposition to the rule of law becomes, in their own estimation, their strongest claim on a Greek spirit imbued with pride, independence, and a refusal to surrender autonomy to anyone.

The history of the 1821 revolution, with its wild mountain guerrillas at odds with the clergy in Constantinople and the consequent grounding of the new state's authority in a history of rebellion, offers a model and a reason for Greeks to see less of a contradiction between religiosity and left-wing populism than might be expected: Jesus, for many Greeks, is the archetypical victim of repression by a venal and bureaucratic priesthood. There are two more sources of this compatibility. The first is that even the most left-leaning Greeks inhabit domestic spaces that are palpably organized on Orthodox principles (see Hirschon 1989, 136–40). The second reason is probably the one that has also perpetuated such practices in left-wing communities: a long-standing realization that the ordinary clergy—noncelibate tillers of the soil and heads of households—stood for a religion very far removed from the arcane ritualism and wealth accumulation of the higher clergy and the monasteries. Thus, while the official view was that the church had served to preserve the language and faith of the people, along with its essential Greekness, this was a Greekness always in tension with the realities of a secular nation-state conceived on the Western European model.

Probably the crucial challenge to the uneasy symbiosis of European Enlightenment models with the values of a popular Orthodoxy came with the military regime of 1967–74. The collapse of the junta in 1974, in the aftermath of the Turkish invasion of Cyprus, an event for which it bore a large measure of responsibility, threw a harsh light on its cultural programs. Prominent among these was the imposition of a strict use of *katharévousa*, the neo-Classical language that the highly rationalist prophet of nationhood Adamantios Koraes had developed (and to which the clergy were at times opposed). As Chrestou (1983, 43) points out, Koraes was obsessed with what he saw as the cultural inferiority and backwardness of the Greeks, and his attempt to reclaim high antiquity through the reconstruction of language was the nationalist complement to the Calvinism that oriented his theology and was to affect religious thought in Greece immediately after the achievement of independence. This was the fatal combination that, according to Yannaras (1972, 1978, 1996), characterized the Greek bourgeois elite and came to a head in the oddly protestantizing Orthodoxy of the colonels nearly two centuries later. Their theology was crude, but their language was worse. As a result, when the regime fell, while its theology became vulnerable, its aggressive linguistic neo-Classicism simply collapsed.

In religion, the colonels—notably Papadopoulos—were activists, but very much in a nationalist mode that displeased such theological scholars as the young Yannaras, who saw in the Masonic form of the ultra-Orthodox organizations that had supported the regime a bureaucratic and materialist ethic contrary to both his left-wing values and his religious sensibility. In the view of such thinkers, the specious neo-Classicism of the colonels became the mark of their alienation from the True Faith—a nationwide dramatization of a tension already widely felt to exist.

After the colonels' fall, acknowledging this split was a necessary move if the damage to the reputation of the Orthodox religion wrought by the colonels' extremely public acts of devotion was to be undone. The protracted struggle to remove from the Holy Synod those bishops who had been appointed by the junta's archbishop of Athens, Serafim, was one important illustration of this persistent difficulty. The popular reaction, moreover, harmonized with another article of popular political faith: that all the nation's ills were of foreign origin. If the neo-Classicism of the official state could be represented as foreign to Greece—which, in a literal historical sense, it was—then Orthodoxy could come to the rescue with no damage to the nation's claims on an ancient heritage. Instead of glorying in that heritage as a pagan era wholly different from the present, Greeks could now enjoy it as a precursor to the Christian faith of today.

The theodicy to which it appealed, moreover, could represent the source of today's ills as not only the Turks but also the West—a return, played out far more viciously in neighboring Bosnia, to the demonization of Islam and Rome alike (it is no coincidence that during the worst phases of that conflict the church in Greece campaigned actively on behalf of the

Serbian cause, with notable effects in foreign policy, and managed to elicit the active sympathy of some of the most committed members of the pro-ex-USSR communist party). It was now acceptable to berate the West for its fickleness and for its corruption, as the source of those weaknesses that laid the world of true believers open to the violence of the East. This was fertile ground for a rapprochement of Orthodoxy and socialism.

The political disaffection on which Neo-Orthodoxy feeds is closely linked to a widespread antirationalism. This does not mean that Neo-Orthodoxy is "irrational"; it does mean that it rejected "rationalism" (*ortholoyismós*) as a Western-imposed ideology. Its exponents have identified the Western model of rationality as intrusive to their culture and values, elevating to the level of political doctrine and practice a moralistic model of causation that is no less culture-bound—but which, these people say, at least represents *their* culture.

What is that model of causation? It is, in effect, one that preserves the individual autonomy so central to Greek notions of selfhood by rejecting the very possibility of accountability *except in the privacy of the home and before God*. It is, in other words, a social and ethical concept of accountability rather than an abstract and legal one. The logic runs more or less like this: if I accept the blame for some disaster, I will place my own dependents at risk (at least of ridicule, if not of material sanctions). Moreover, we "know," as an article of faith, that "they" are responsible for our ills. Those who claim to be on our side "do not let us" seek justice—whether they are the men in a coffeehouse who are restraining me from stabbing someone who has just called me names, a commonly experienced reality, or "the Americans" who "won't let" Greece give Turkey what it deserves. This view of how the world works is grounded in everyday social experience— the coffeehouse scene is a case in point—and Greece's repeated diplomatic humiliations, which do sometimes acquire the character of a self-fulfilling prophecy, appear to bear the conventional wisdom out in full measure. The entire model of events, moreover, is couched in the language of a symbolism of chance and fate that, by its very familiarity, gives it the character of a self-evident truth (Herzfeld 1992). Images of the writing hand—Churchill, Roosevelt, and Stalin drawing maps at Yalta, for example, much like bureaucrats signing documents—draw on the imagery of fate's inscription, linking "factual history" to "symbolic truth" and fusing them in an amalgam that has proven to be quite irresistible for significant segments of the Greek electorate.

P. Nikiforos Diamandouros (1994) suggests that the split that runs across the political parties can be characterized as dividing the "underdogs" from the "reformers." The underdogs, he argues, are those who would prefer to seek political safety in the game of accusing the West of all the nation's ills; the reformers are those who want to do something about it. Diamandouros makes no secret of his preference for the latter. But his terminology, although perhaps a little overdrawn (it might be more realistic to acknowledge that these are two *rhetorics* and that politicians can sometimes draw selectively and strategically on both), is especially useful in that it emphasizes that in the Greek political arena individuals are usually essentialized as representing one trend or the other—another illustration of the pervasive binarism of Greek public discourse.

But this terminology also creates a potential difficulty: it suggests the incompatibility of modernity and the particular political theodicy I have been describing. I would argue, to the contrary, that once one disposes of the (symbolic) opposition between rational/modern and symbolic/traditional modes, such a view would mean nothing. Even among the theologically Neo-Orthodox, there are some—admittedly a minority—who argue passionately that technological modernization is not necessarily antithetical to restoring traditional religious and other values (notably Ramfos 2000). Faubion (1993) has argued in the Greek context that it must be possible to imagine multiple modernities, moreover, and in that light a modernity of religious character is entirely conceivable. The alternative is to revert to the orientalist and intolerant language of ayatollah bashing—an approach that, as we have seen, reproduces and thereby reinforces the problem it is ostensibly intended to resolve.

Recognizing the possibility of a religious modernity is nevertheless no simple step. The dominant trend in Greek Neo-Orthodoxy has set itself against the "protestantization" that a Weberian reading—such as Faubion's, for example—would require us to see as a sign of at least emergent modernity. Indeed, Yannaras's claim that the nineteenth-century development of Greek state ideology led to a Cartesian separation of everyday life from the presence of the divine and ultimately to a rejection of transcendence and of pure authority (*afthendía*) in the midst of real life is precisely the Orthodox theological corollary of Weber's account of disenchantment, which in the West was a bureaucratization *of* religious practice as much as it was a bureaucratic reaction *against* bureaucracy (e.g., Holmes 1989; see Yannaras 1972, 18–21). For Yannaras, moreover, the loss of transcendence means the end of a world in which the divine suffused all existence, making the rule of a separate body of law itself unnecessary—a philosophical elaboration of the popular idea that the modern world is a fragmentary relic of a once perfectly ethical human condition. Such "structural nostalgia"

(Herzfeld 1997b) is not a far cry from Cretan sheep-thieves' claim that their predecessors never swore false oaths of innocence or even needed to take an oath at all, whereas today their conflicts always end up in court. It is hardly irrelevant that these shepherds represent an extreme instantiation of a Greek self-image imbued with the pride of autonomy and total insubordination toward the state.

The sense of alienation from the rationalization of religion has grown much stronger in the last two decades or so. Recent developments in the Protestant churches worldwide, notably the ordination of women and an increased willingness in some areas to tolerate homosexuality, are anathema to the Orthodox clergy at all levels, leading not only to a closing of the ranks internally, but perhaps, if the outcome of a recent theological conference in Thessaloniki is any guide (see *Boston Globe*, May 17, 1997, A16), to a sudden inversion whereby the Orthodox churches may find themselves in a hitherto improbable alliance with Rome against what both see as modernist corruptions. Even allowing for the fact that they would find plenty of sympathizers among some of the more fundamentalist Protestant groups, they are exhibiting a *view* of Protestantism that is radically Weberian in equating it with a rationalistic modernity. In other words, it is *their* taxonomy that classifies "modernity" as separate from (acceptable forms of) "religion." It is, I suggest, an inversion of the hegemony identified by Charles Stewart (1989), who argues that the distinction between folk and official religion is a convenient invention of the ecclesiastical institution to legitimize its own practices as the only acceptable model. In this case, a grassroots religious movement—many of the Athonite monks come from humble backgrounds—explicitly rejects all forms of authority not grounded in local society and seeks to stem the tide of a cultural process that it sees as threatening the authority of the church itself. The Neo-Orthodox critique thus reiterates concerns that have been quietly building ever since the establishment of the secular state (again, we can see in this process parallels in the confrontation between the *Haredim* and self-styled secular Jews in Israel). Nor, in spite of its leftist orientation, is it an Eastern Orthodox version of liberation theology, for it is profoundly nationalistic and extends the hand of charity only to its own sympathizers—as, for example, in the selectivity of its charitable work with refugees from Bosnia.

The claims of Neo-Orthodox commentators regarding the alleged stifling of Orthodox theology following the establishment of the Greek nation-state (e.g., Chrestou 1983) also parallel the antiacademicism of the Greek left. In both cases, the dead hand of the Bavarian court of King

Otho symbolizes Western repression. For the artists and writers of the left, indeed, the rise of that court on the backs of the guerrilla chieftains symbolized and prefigured their own brutal mistreatment in cold-war Greece (see Herzfeld 1997c)—and it is worth remembering in this connection that these leftists were also much given to invoking christological metaphors in their rhetoric, taking upon themselves the lineaments of a Christ-like figure suffering at the hands of fascist Pharisees who would eventually be "resurrected" at the day of revolutionary judgment. More tamely, Neo-Orthodox writers accuse the German-inspired School of Theology in the University of Athens of having encouraged the development of "handbook theology" (Chrestou 1983, 48), substituting rote learning and bureaucratic organization for the passions of the truly devoted adept and becoming by degrees the channel for Protestant proselytization as well as a center of opposition to the authority of the Patriarchate in Constantinople. Both the traditional leftists and the Neo-Orthodox thus see in the foreign-imposed Bavarian court the original flowering of the bureaucratic pettiness and soulless bourgeois materialism that, in their view, blight the present age. Yannaras's diatribes against the scholasticism of the West finds fertile ground in Greece because it elaborates both popular discontent (and stereotypes) and the intense demoticism of the intellectuals of the left. It represents a revolt against "foreign" modernity.

Modernist Greeks do not necessarily reject religion. They may embrace it in a rationalistic fashion, alleging scientific justifications for its claims, as they do for such concepts as the evil eye. But this rationalism, Neo-Orthodox thinkers argue, is itself unfaithful to the ideals of Orthodoxy, because it entails making the human mind the measure of all things, rather than permitting the mystery of the divine to permeate every lived moment. Yannaras, whose active and religiously based opposition to the junta won him many admirers, accused the colonels' ultrareligious organizations of being little more than Protestant fifth columns, noting that at the same time that they were luring ordinary people away from the *churches* (to their inspirational gatherings), they were exiling Christ from *the church*—that immanent and all-embracing symbol and substance of the Christian ecumene. This is not far from the injunction, often heard in the Greek countryside, to attend to the Builder rather than to the building.

Yannaras leaves one in no doubt where he stands: the traditional, he argues, is virtuous and eternal, the modern tawdry and ephemeral. This is a version of structural nostalgia that he attempts to translate into a program for the future, rendering modernity reversible inasmuch as humanity can be rescued from the temptations offered by a diabolical West.

Michael Herzfeld

Where will this all lead? Is Greece about to turn to spiritual values that will clash with its present attempts to claim a technological and ethical modernity? The answer is not a simple one, and will in part depend on what happens in other Orthodox lands. Neo-Orthodoxy represents a revolt against the bureaucratic determinism of a state imbued with German models of efficiency, legal precision, and bureaucratic rationality; but it must also fight with the benefits—which it represents as evils—of a consumerism explicitly associated with Western bourgeois values through its entailment in the European Union bureaucracy.

It also, and this may perhaps be its undoing, calls for a new discipline of the body. Jane Cowan (1990) has pointed to the ways in which the human body serves as a site for the interplay of normative and transgressive values, and especially for the performance of gendered identities. One can certainly also argue, as, for example, Brownell (1995) has for China, that some forms of bodily discipline provide sites for the inculcation of official values, although my own experience with Greek craft apprentices suggests that among the latter these embodiments also include practices of insubordination—practices that nevertheless ultimately have the effect of confirming the unruliness of these young workers and thereby implicitly justifying their ongoing subordination to those who exercise power over them. The problem for Neo-Orthodoxy is that there exists no evidence to suggest any enthusiasm for a return to the formal bodily discipline of the monastic or artisanal life of yore; most Greeks cynically associate the monasteries with sexual depravity, if they think about monks' bodies at all.

Such tensions between regimentation and a stereotypical proclivity for resistance permeate the Greek national self-imagination. They certainly came to a head during the time of the colonels' regime, with its notorious use of metaphors of surgical intervention and diseased and undisciplined bodies. But theirs was the "Protestant" model rather than the monastic idiom of such church fathers as Saint John Chrysostom: it demanded mental regimentation for temporal purposes rather than for achieving communion with the divine.

In the resurgent Neo-Orthodox model, however, mental and physical being are unified in a single ontology. People belong, not to a consumerist or to a rigidly disciplined society, but to a universal fellowship in which the material and the symbolic are mutually indistinguishable, and in which the submission of the body becomes the fulfillment of the soul. Will this model achieve a large following? Or is it simply another rhetorical device allowing politicians to exploit the disaffection of the masses with a consumerist and rationalist society that seems to have betrayed them?

Acknowledgments

The ideas on Neo-Orthodoxy developed in this paper received their initial airing and stimulation at the University of Washington at the kind invitation of Charles Keyes and Reşat Kasaba. I am extremely grateful to Maria Couroucli, Ryan Preston, and Vassiliki Yiakoumaki for their helpful and generous advice in the final stages of writing this article.

Works Cited

Anderson, Benedict R. 1983. *Imagined Communities: Reflections on the Origin and Spread of Nationalism.* London: Verso.

Argyrou, Vassos. 1996. *Tradition and Modernity in the Mediterranean: The Wedding as Symbolic Struggle.* Cambridge: Cambridge University Press.

Barth, Fredrik, ed. 1969. *Ethnic Groups and Boundaries: The Social Organization of Culture Difference.* London: Allen & Unwin.

Boehm, Christopher. 1984. *Blood Revenge: The Anthropology of Feuding in Montenegro and Other Tribal Societies.* Lawrence: University Press of Kansas.

Brownell, Susan. 1995. *Training the Body for China: Sports in the Moral Order of the People's Republic.* Chicago: University of Chicago Press.

Chrestou, Panagiotes K. 1983. "Neohellenic Theology at the Crossroads." *Greek Orthodox Theological Review* 28: 39–54.

Collier, Jane Fishburne. 1997. *From Duty to Desire: Remaking Families in a Spanish Village.* Princeton, N.J.: Princeton University Press.

Connor, Walker. 1993. "Beyond Reason: The Nature of the Ethnonational Bond." *Ethnic and Racial Studies* 16: 373–89.

Cowan, Jane K. 1990. *Dance and the Body Politic in Northern Greece.* Princeton, N.J.: Princeton University Press.

Diamandouros, P. Nikiforos. 1994. *Cultural Dualism and Political Change in Postauthoritarian Greece.* Madrid: Centro Juan March de Estudios Avanzados en Ciencias Sociales, Estudio no. 50.

Faubion, James D. 1993. *Modern Greek Lessons: A Primer in Historical Constructivism.* Princeton, N.J.: Princeton University Press.

Gellner, Ernest. 1983. *Nations and Nationalism: New Perspectives on the Past.* Oxford: Basil Blackwell.

Greenfeld, Liah. 1992. *Nationalism: Five Roads to Modernity.* Cambridge: Harvard University Press.

Hammel, Eugene A. 1968. *Alternative Social Structures and Ritual Relations in the Balkans.* Englewood Cliffs, N.J.: Prentice Hall.

Hasluck, Margaret M. H. 1954. *The Unwritten Law in Albania.* Cambridge: Cambridge University Press.

Hayden, Robert M. 1996. "Imagined Communities and Real Victims: Self-Determination and Ethnic Cleansing in Yugoslavia." *American Ethnologist* 23: 783–801.

Herzfeld, Michael. 1982. *Ours Once More: Folklore, Ideology, and the Making of Modern Greece.* Austin: University of Texas Press.

———. 1985. *The Poetics of Manhood: Contest and Identity in a Cretan Mountain Village.* Princeton, N.J.: Princeton University Press.

———. 1987. *Anthropology through the Looking-Glass: Critical Ethnography in the Margins of Europe.* Cambridge: Cambridge University Press.

———. 1992. *The Social Production of Indifference: Exploring the Symbolic Roots of Western Bureaucracy.* Oxford: Berg.

———. 1997a. "Anthropology and the Politics of Significance." *Social Analysis* 41: 107–38.

———. 1997b. *Cultural Intimacy: Social Poetics in the Nation-State.* New York: Routledge.

———. 1997c. *Portrait of a Greek Imagination: An Ethnographic Biography of Andreas Nenedakis.* Chicago: University of Chicago Press.

Hirschon, Renée. 1989. *Heirs of the Greek Catastrophe: The Social Life of Asia Minor Refugees in Piraeus.* Oxford: Clarendon Press.

Holmes, Douglas R. 1989. *Cultural Disenchantments: Worker Peasantries in Northeast Italy.* Princeton, N.J.: Princeton University Press.

Huntington, Samuel P. 1996. *The Clash of Civilizations and the Remaking of World Order.* New York: Simon and Schuster.

Kroeber, A. L., and Clyde Kluckhohn. 1952. *Culture: A Critical Review of Concepts and Definitions. Papers of the Peabody Museum of American Archaeology and Ethnology.* Cambridge: The Museum (Harvard University).

Lloyd, G. E. R. 1966. *Polarity and Analogy: Two Types of Argumentation in Early Greek Thought.* Cambridge: Cambridge University Press.

Maddox, Richard. 1995. "Revolutionary Anticlericalism and Hegemonic Processes in an Andalusian Town." *American Ethnologist* 22: 125–43.

Nadel-Klein, Jane. 1991. "Reweaving the Fringe: Localism, Tradition, and Representation in British Ethnography." *American Ethnologist* 18: 500–517.

Panourgiá, E. Neni K. 1995. *Fragments of Death, Fables of Identity: An Athenian Anthropography.* Madison: University of Wisconsin Press.

Ramfos, Stelios. 2000. "I Ekklisía ke o eksingkhronismós tis." *Kathimerini* 6 (February): 16.

Razsa, Maple, and Nicole Lindstrom. 1998. "Desnicu mije ili prepravijanje svetskog-poretka" [The right hand washes the other or the reconstruction of the world order], *Arkzin* (Zagreb, Croatia) 4 (January): 40–43 (translation kindly supplied by the authors).

Seremetakis, C. Nadia. 1991. *The Last Word: Women, Death, and Divination in Inner Mani.* Chicago: University of Chicago Press.

Stewart, Charles. 1989. "Hegemony or Rationality? The Position of the Supernatural in Modern Greece." *Yearbook of Modern Greek Studies* 7: 77–104.

Stolcke, Verena. 1995. "Talking Culture: New Boundaries, New Rhetorics of Exclusion in Europe." *Current Anthropology* 6: 1–24.

Sutton, David E. 1994. "Tradition and Modernity: Kalymnian Constructions of Identity and Otherness." *Journal of Modern Greek Studies* 12: 239–60.

Tambiah, Stanley J. 1989. "Ethnic Conflict in the World Today." *American Ethnologist* 16: 335–49.

Wilson, Stephen. 1988. *Feuding, Conflict, and Banditry in Nineteenth-Century Corsica.* Cambridge: Cambridge University Press.

Yannaras, Khristos. 1972. *Orthodhokísa ke Dhísi: I Theoloya stin Elládha smera.* Athens: Athena.

————. 1978. *H neoellinikí taftótita.* Athens: Grigori.

————. 1996. *Ellinótropos politikí.* Athens: Ikaros.

PART III

Images of Home,

Belonging,

and Exile

Ulf Hannerz

12

Where We Are and Who We Want to Be

In his autobiography *Long Walk to Freedom* (1995, 649–56, 728), Nelson Mandela describes life in the house that was his home for a little more than a year, in the Victor Verster prison compound at the outskirts of Paarl, in the Cape wine district; a halfway house before his final release. It was a comfortable whitewashed cottage with a swimming pool in the backyard. Mandela was provided with a cook, who, although he was Warrant Officer Swart, was certainly white. Swart prepared breakfast, lunch, and dinner for Mandela, gourmet meals when there were visitors, and in between would bake bread, brew ginger beer, and make dishes that Mandela asked for because he remembered them from his childhood. Although Swart protested to begin with, Mandela insisted on doing the dishes and making his own bed. "I could go to sleep and wake up as I pleased," Mandela recalls, "swim whenever I wanted, eat when I was hungry—all were delicious sensations." It turned out that Swart had once been one of Mandela's prison guards during those long, harsh years on Robben Island, but now, Mandela says, "he was a decent, sweet-tempered fellow without any prejudice and he became like a younger brother to me." Yet there was other company as well. Comrades in the political struggle came to visit and confer, and on his seventy-first birthday, for the first time ever in his life, Mandela could have his wife and children and grand-children all in one place.

Then, a few years after his release from prison, when he had a chance to build a house of his own in his childhood village, Mandela built it according to the floor plan of the cottage in the Victor Verster prison camp. "People often commented on this," he notes; but that prison camp house had been the first comfortable home he ever had, and he had liked it very much. Moreover, because he was familiar with its dimensions, he "would not have to wander at night looking for the kitchen." So, for one of the twentieth century's best-known freedom fighters, "home" was modeled on a prison—one can only guess at what some of the comments might have been. There seemed to be a clash between who Mandela was, or ought to be, and his sense of where he felt at home.

Spaces and identities intertwine or clash in many ways, not least in times of great forced or voluntary mobility. It is such connections and dis-connections that I will explore here—between, on the one hand, the sites where contemporary human beings find themselves or which they seek out in their imagination, and on the other hand, who they want to be or do not want to be. And, by extension, this also often turns out to be a mat-ter of how they want to be, or who they want to be with.

At Home

"Home" is a complicated concept. It may be foolhardy to try and define it, for notions of home involve meanings, practices, and symbols distinctive to particular human groups. They may even in some ways be quite person-al and private. Probably people also think about home most acutely when they are away, or are thinking about going away, or when they have been away. And thus what it is depends on what "away" is—it is a contrastive concept, a contrastive feeling. And in our times there is a lot of such con-trasting going on. "Away" is travel, tourism, migration, pilgrimage, escape, exile, diaspora.

Let me nevertheless try to offer a generalized version of "home." For an increasing number of people, it may not resemble the real thing, so per-haps it is a somewhat antiquated imagery—I admit to sensing a certain affinity with classic concepts of gemeinschaft, of folk society, or of genu-ine as opposed to spurious culture.[1] Yet I believe that many of us recognize its characteristic features, and have some such place at least in a corner of our memories.

First of all, we probably think about home as something not extending very far in space—if not just a house, then perhaps a neighborhood or a local community. It is familiar space because we crisscross through it again and again, perhaps even on foot. We are likely to have seen it day and night, in all seasons. It is certainly a physical environment, but in no small part a social environment. Its core social relationships tend to be long-term, face-to-face, broadly inclusive in terms of content—relationships with "significant others," involving a strong emotional load. Even if we have a somewhat more expanded sense of what is home so that not all relationships are like that, it is familiar social space because we have it quite well mapped—even the people we do not know personally act in more or less expected ways. You may actually have accumulated layers upon layers of precedents and assumptions that would be rather inaccessible to a stranger; but to you, there is a sense of relative transparency in social traffic.

This is "everyday" territory. Much of what goes on is repetitive, redundant, seemingly infinite. It also tends to be practical. People participate actively here, acquiring and maintaining skills, applying what they take to be common sense, and, if conditions permit, probably feeling at ease. And "home" is also a special kind of bodily and sensual experience, of immersion in an immediately accessible environment. It is a matter of being there, in touch, with all one's senses, of being able to see, hear, feel, taste, and smell all more or less at once.

In its fullest sense, "home" may also come early. It is the first environment we ever become aware of, and thereafter we may remain at least sufficiently long to develop a sense of belonging there. The figure of thought combining home with childhood continues to be a strong one. But although we may like the "roots" metaphor, what human beings actually have are feet, and so that certainty of staying in a place is false. Over time, not least nowadays, we may be more or less accomplished home makers in a series of locations.

Strikingly, I think we can recognize most of these characteristics of home, if not quite all, in Nelson Mandela's account of life in the cottage at the Victor Verster prison camp. Finally, after all those years in confinement, Mandela could return to his most important social relationships, to family members and political allies. Even Warrant Officer Swart turned into something like a younger brother. Mandela could make his own small practical decisions, and exercise everyday skills. He could be there with all his senses, admiring the trees shading his house, enjoying the taste of the food, experiencing the movements of his body and limbs when he took a swim. This was not home, of course, in the sense of childhood and first experiences. Yet there was even a kind of simulation of these, as Mandela asked Swart to prepare for him his simple childhood dishes. Perhaps when later he returned to his actual childhood village and had something like his prison camp cottage re-created there, it was not just a practical matter of making sure that he would find the kitchen at night, but also of finally merging those memories of two cherished homes.

The Superior Elsewhere

But then there is "away," the many varieties of "away." In the current vocabulary of globalization, one often comes across the term *deterritorialization*. Sometimes it is employed entirely appropriately, but frequently it is really not the case that people, things, or relationships are everywhere and nowhere in particular. It may be, rather, that their total attachment to a single place has loosened, but that deterritorialization is relative—there is, rather, something like a more or less fixed "biterritorialization," or "multiterritorialization." Many people now divide their attention, and even their presence, between at least two places, and it may or may not be clear, even to them, which is more "home" than the other. One is reminded here of Agnes Heller's (1995, 1) anecdote, in an intriguing discussion of spatial and temporal conceptions of home, about a woman sitting next to her in an airplane, obviously almost constantly on the move, speaking five languages, having three apartments in three cities. After some thought, she responded to Heller's question "Where are you at home?" with "Perhaps where my cat lives."

But home sometimes becomes a bit too much of itself. Most often among young people, who cannot stand so much continuity, so much repetitiveness, so much transparency, there may just be a crushing sense of boredom. Home is a bit of a prison. So impatiently they dream of "the world," a larger city perhaps, and in the end some will take off for it.

Nelson Mandela, much as he enjoyed his final prison camp cottage, was still aware that it was a place of confinement. And even in his childhood he had known that there was an exciting elsewhere. Again, from *Long Walk to Freedom*, here is his recollection of the evening when, as a young man, he first arrived in Johannesburg:

> we saw before us, glinting in the distance, a maze of lights that seemed to stretch in all directions. Electricity, to me, had always been a novelty and a luxury, and here was a vast landscape of electricity, a city of light. I was terribly excited to see the city I had been hearing about since I was a child.

Johannesburg had always been depicted as a city of dreams, a place where one could transform oneself from a poor peasant into a wealthy sophisticate, a city of danger and of opportunity. I remembered the stories that Banabakhe [a friend] had told us at circumcision school, of buildings so tall you could not see the tops, of crowds of people speaking languages you had never heard of, of sleek motor cars and beautiful women and dashing gangsters. It was eGoli, the city of gold, where I would soon be making my home. (Mandela 1995, 69)

What the young Mandela's Johannesburg, the city of light and dreams and gold, exemplifies is the role of center–periphery relationships in our symbolic geography. Some commentators now claim that the world has moved beyond center–periphery structures, but I find it hard to believe them—perhaps especially because so many of them are located at what would be centers; for it is in the nature of things that the privileged vantage points for an understanding of center–periphery relationships are at the peripheries. If there has been a change, it is one in which the symbolic geography has become more complex. The world may have become more multicentric, transnational center–periphery relationships more subculturally segmented, the rise and fall of centers more rapid. We now have not only the Romes and Jerusalems, but also the Wall Streets, the Bourbon Streets, and the Castro Streets.

Center–periphery linkages make up one class of biterritorializations (if not multiterritorializations). Yet "the center" in this world of imagination is not necessarily, as some earlier social theorists (e.g., Shils ([1961] 1975) have had it, a site of deference. Going there may be a kind of pilgrimage, but that should not be taken too literally. At least as much, centers may be "where the action is," promising arenas for ludic as well as instrumental action. In large part, perhaps one goes there, as the young Mandela sensed, because this kind of center has what "home" lacks: risk, excitement, anonymity, opportunity. He had learned from those village tales that going to the big city could be the way of becoming someone else, accomplishing a personal transformation. A more desirable identity, a more fully realized you, would come about only through escape—permanent or temporary.

But if "home" is found to be imperfect, there could be the alternative, in principle at least, of trying to remodel it, to resemble more some "elsewhere." Arjun Appadurai (1991, 198ff.) has drawn attention to the way in which especially the electronic media have changed the balance between imagination and lived experience. Imagination becomes a major social practice, as more people are more aware of alternative possible lives. Sometimes the practice of fantasy is not so clearly linked to particular places. Frequently, however, media involvement as well as travel allow us now to find our utopias materialized, whether we fully understand them or not, in identifiable, actually existing sites. Thus, the reformers and revolutionaries of the twentieth century were able to look to the Soviet Union for a future that would work, to the kibbutzim of Israel for a collective way of life, to the rain forests of the Fourth World for ways of staying in tune with the environment. Often, obviously, those hopes of making a more perfect home fail, and not so seldom they were based on faulty visions anyway; at times they may succeed. And mostly, they are not attempts to change those general qualities of homeness sketched earlier, but rather other features of some particular home.

Too Little "Home," at Home and Abroad

On the other hand, people may experience some kind of homeness deficit, when they feel that they do not get an adequate offering of one or more of those qualities described earlier. It may be that they no longer "recognize the neighborhood." Others have moved in who do not seek the qualities of homeness there, but perhaps even its opposite. Or these newcomers' homeness simply has another content, with other routines, other enduring relationships, other preferred sensibilities.

So some human contacts become opaque rather than transparent, built on uncertainty and even suspicion rather than trust. There appear to be no subtle, informal, but effective ways of resolving small conflicts. And there may be strange noises, sights, tastes, and smells. If you come in only at this stage and have your own early experiences in this situation, there is some chance that this is what you will take to be "home." You build your map of everyday life as now constituted, acquire expectations and a common sense to go with it, feel comfortably or even appreciatively familiar with those sounds and those fragrances. But that is not certain, in particular, perhaps, if your seniors feed you their interpretation of the situation: they have not left home, but home has left them.

With time, another modus vivendi may be worked out. Or those old-timers may pull out of the place they have given up on as a home. Or then again, a more acute conflict develops, a turf war with or without generals. They can only be fully themselves and at ease, some feel, if they do not have to be with others. On a large or small scale, nativism and xenophobia may emerge out of a sense of endangered homeness, along lines that are perhaps gradually becoming better understood, but not necessarily therefore more easily prevented or remedied.

The migrant, or refugee, or exile, also experiences a deficit of homeness, but here we are dealing again with a category of biterritorialization. He or she may leave behind many of those long-term relationships, and the well-understood, competent handling of everydayness is exchanged for the unease of never quite being sure of one's grasp of things, of whether in a moment one will be making a fool of oneself. Perhaps one has to seek the help and advice of one's children, quicker to find their feet again, on matters of street wisdom and on handling the front desks of alien bureaucracies, and that may well be a humiliating experience. This migrant may struggle to substitute new alternatives for as many of the old relationships and capacities as possible. But in large part, particularly when the departure from home was not entirely a freely chosen act, this displacement is also often accompanied by attempts at replacement, a reconstruction of as much as possible of home—if not relationships with the same people, relationships with the same kind of people, migrants from the same home, with the same sense of transparency and trust; whenever possible, a frequently self-conscious celebration of an array of home-related experiences.

The American anthropologist Debbora Battaglia (1995) has described the First Annual Trobriand Yam Festival, held in Port Moresby, the capital of Papua New Guinea, in 1985. The Trobrianders, of course, are famous in anthropology—it was among them that Bronislaw Malinowski invented ethnographic fieldwork. But the people who organized the First Annual Trobriand Yam Festival were not in the Trobriand Islands, they were migrants to a metropolis. The choice of a yam festival as a way of bringing members of the Trobriand diaspora together, and to raise their profile nationally, appears telling in terms of what has already been said. Battaglia quotes Malinowski to the effect that Trobriand aesthetics, as he understood it early in the twentieth century, had its roots in the garden, and in "things which promise safety, prosperity, abundance and sensual pleasure." One of her own 1980s Port Moresby informants says much the same thing:

> Sometimes a man works in a store. He gets paid but his paycheck is already spent, and he is hungry. Then he can go to the garden. He looks out over the yams growing and he feels full. Just watching the garden he feels satisfied. (Battaglia 1995, 80)

Again, then, being at home entails a fullness of sensual experience, and at the same time a sense of being able to practice one's know-how. The Trobrianders at home might know this without necessarily reflecting on it, but the Trobrianders in the city found in the yam garden a quite tangible expression of their nostalgia. One might assume that the migrant voice one just heard was the down-to-earth opinion of someone fresh from the islands, still a cultivator at heart; but it belongs to someone with a higher degree from Harvard, and his own international consulting business.

One might indeed suggest that nostalgia is something that migrants away from home share with the people who sense their home vanishing while they are still in it. Both look backward to a past that is wholly, or at least in part, more desirable than the present. Yet these are different nostalgias. Moving from a Trobriand to a New York intellectual, a comment by Edward Said, in his Reith lectures, throws light on the matter:

> There is a popular but wholly mistaken assumption that being exiled is to be totally cut off, isolated, hopelessly separated from your place of origin. Would that surgically clean separation were true, because then at least you could have the consolation of knowing that what you have left behind is, in a sense, unthinkable and completely irrecoverable. The fact is that for most exiles the difficulty consists not simply in being forced to live away from home, but rather, given today's world, in living with the many reminders that you are in exile, that your home is not in fact so far away, and that the normal traffic of everyday contemporary life keeps you in constant but tantalizing and unfulfilled touch with the old place. The exile therefore exists in a median state, neither completely at one with the new setting nor fully disencumbered of the old, beset with half-involvements and half-detachments, nostalgic and sentimental on one level, an adept mimic or a secret outcast on another. (Said 1994, 48–49)

There is a nostalgia purely in time, then, where the loss of a home cannot be reversed. And there is a nostalgia in time and space, where a migrant can reclaim the home, and in a manner and to a degree perhaps return to the past, by going back. The exile in a strict sense may be constrained from doing so, despite being tantalizingly in touch. For many others who have been mobile in space the possibility may be more real, and continuously present. In fact, a complicating, divisive truth about the First Annual Trobriand Yam Festival in Port Moresby was that its sponsor was a self-proclaimed "urban cowboy," who was rumored to be thinking of launching a campaign for elected office in the homeland. He was where he was, but not everybody there liked the idea of who he wanted to be.

Ulf Hannerz

We can be at home in a local habitat, then, and find life's satisfactions there. Or we want to shift into someone else by going somewhere else, and thus, until we realize those daydreams at least, we engage in a mostly prospective biterritoriality. Some of those satisfactions may be lost, and we may feel that we are in some way diminished, as we stay put, but our habitat itself changes. Or they are lost because for some pressing reason we move, and the biterritoriality of our perspective becomes rather more retrospective.

But in these instances our basic concept of what constitutes "home" may still be rather stable. We should look at that concept again. Can the qualities taken to be characteristic of "home" be organized in space in other ways? It certainly seems as if particularly the technological changes in transportation and communication over the past century have had their implications for the ways in which relationships and experiences come together in a round of life.

A generation ago, Marshall McLuhan (e.g., 1964) claimed that "the medium is the message," and the world was turning into a "global village." McLuhan's facts, arguments, and prophecies were debated and often rejected, but his concerns are still in large part with us. The notion of a global village is in some ways very irritating, and clearly mistaken. World social structure is not now much like that of a village. Yet the idea that media forms and capacities in themselves may have implications for our use of our senses, our accumulated understandings, and our views of ourselves and others, seems to have become more central. We should remind ourselves, too, that McLuhan was writing in an era of television and radio, not yet one of cyberspace.

About halfway between McLuhan and us already, Benedict Anderson (1983) returned to what McLuhan had referred to as "the Gutenberg Galaxy," and to considering the influence of print, in combination with capitalism, in the growth of nations as imagined communities. A sense of "we-ness," it seemed, had grown around, not face-to-face relationships, but shoulder-to-shoulder relationships, as people turning toward the same media realized more fully that they were in something together. A little later, radio mostly contributed to a similar nation-building effect; Orvar Löfgren (1990) has shown persuasively how for a long time a single-channel Swedish radio instructed his and my compatriots in another imagined geography and provided us with topics that we shared, and knew that we all shared.

Television became something else again. Writing and print are mostly language-based media, turning sound into sight, but remaining in a single symbolic modality. With radio, sound came back into communication beyond the immediate, face-to-face environment, but still only one of the senses was fully engaged. Television still did not allow us to taste, smell, and touch, but the combination of more natural-seeming sight and sound entailed more of a sensual immersion, of a feeling of "being there."

We continue to argue over the implications of this broader appeal to, or assault on, the senses. Does the view of starving African children or of victims of a grenade attack thrown into a Balkan market provoke some kind of electronic empathy, leading even to some kind of action? This would seem more likely the response of a global village. Or do views of disaster, war, and suffering, broadcast on a daily basis as "infotainment," turn into another commodity, as Arthur and Joan Kleinman (1996) suspect? Or will people become more wary of the great "elsewhere"? Perhaps the increasing capacity of the media to represent the world to our senses makes "away" experientially a little more like home. Yet if reporting on it habitually shows it as a dangerous place, it may make home even more special, a territory whose borders must be policed against intrusions from the outside. A foreign news editor in Stockholm told me she was aware of the possible bias toward trouble and danger. Her paper tried to avoid supporting such a view of the outside world, as it could foster isolationism and xenophobia among the public. Yet all media organizations may not be so concerned with the issue, and in any case it may be a tendency not so easily countered.

But if technologies now somewhat blur the boundary between home and away, this is certainly not so much owing to the impact of mass media, but rather to the diversity of small-scale, personal media, in combination with travel. Letter writing, telephone, fax, home videos, and E-mail allow relationships to be extended with some of the intimacy of home, even as at least one of the parties is elsewhere. It has become part of the popular imagination that encounters that take place in the anonymity of cyberspace can develop into the close, enduring relationships of "home." The film *You've Got Mail* is built entirely around the transformation of a relationship from media anonymity to face-to-face surrender, against the background of the vibrant all-senses richness of New York's Upper West Side. Yet surely things more often go in the opposite direction: we maintain relationships that have already had a period, often an initial period, of face-to-face closeness, and that can continue in their new technological form to draw on established understandings, expectations, and trust. It is these media technologies that increasingly allow biterritorialization or multi-territorialization, and homes away from home. They do so together with technologies of travel that allow people to move, not only one way and only once, but continuously and frequently back and forth, so that spatial distances may really seem to be to a degree rendered powerless. And, of course, cable television and video rentals of movies from one's own home country, in one's own language, also now allow migrants to reach back rather than out. In a way, all other things being equal, we may increasingly be who we are and want to be, wherever we are.

At Home in Cosmopolis

These present-day tendencies toward a spatial reconfiguration of relationships and experiences are relevant to a consideration of a notion that has again come to draw an increasing interest—that of cosmopolitanism. The term is often used loosely, but *Webster's Third International Dictionary of the English Language* (1981 edition) defines *cosmopolitan* as "marked by interest in, familiarity with, or knowledge and appreciation of many parts of the world" and *cosmopolitanism* as "the theory or advocacy of the formation of a world society or cosmopolis" and as "a climate of opinion distinguished by the absence of narrow national loyalties or parochial prejudices and by a readiness to borrow from other lands or regions in the formation of cultural or artistic patterns."

It seems, then, that there are two major facets of cosmopolitanism. One is aesthetic and experiential, involving an appreciation of cultural diversity. The other is political and programmatic and is concerned, in a rather activist way, with the construction of cosmopolis, the world society. Much of the time, these two facets seem to be considered separately from one another. At the same time, there have been mixed feelings about cosmopolitans. Now and then, *cosmopolitans* has simply become a term of disapproval, used xenophobically to refer to minorities who are suspected of divided loyalties: Russian Jews, for example, under Stalinism and in other periods. In other contexts, the more political variety of cosmopolitanism may be depicted as elitist, in either of two ways, or both at the same time. On the one hand, the cosmopolitan is seen as escaping from local or particularly national contexts, avoiding responsibility, not sharing in a common burden. On the other hand, cosmopolitanism may be engaged precisely in creating another burden for ordinary people, a mode of domination yet further removed from control from below than anything previously encountered. The more experiential tendency in cosmopolitanism, meanwhile, may be viewed as a somewhat self-indulgent way of identity building through selective personal appropriation from the world's inventory of cultural forms.

In an earlier article (Hannerz 1990), I portrayed the cosmopolitan as a type in the current period of global interconnectedness, when an increasing number of people are geographically mobile under fairly comfortable circumstances and can enjoy taking in cultural diversity along the way. It was a formulation that dwelled on the more experiential and aesthetic tendency in cosmopolitanism. It seemed to me that there were two main components to such cosmopolitanism: an appreciation of initially alien cultural forms, and an attempt to build up skills in handling them that would be a matter of mastery and surrender at the same time. I argued that among some categories of the mobile in this world, such active reaching out for cultural diversity in experience as a value for its own sake might not come so easily: for exiles, refugees, or labor migrants, the condition of being "away" may be involuntary, forced, even traumatic. Rather than finding pleasure in the alien, they may try hard to hold on to whatever homeness they have got left. The more likely cosmopolitan would be someone who all the time "knows where the exit is." Which is to say that there is a more or less uncomplicated, or at least safe, sense of "home" to return to. I suggested, too, that the cosmopolitan stance might have some kind of affinity with the expansive management of meaning of intellectuals, accustomed to what Gouldner (1979) had described as "cultures of critical discourse."

To some, this inquiry into the bases of cosmopolitanism might seem elitist, but that is not the point.[2] It is, rather, a matter of realizing that the cosmopolitan stance toward new experience may result more easily in some life situations than others. At any rate, it now appears that the emphasis has shifted toward the more political aspect of cosmopolitanism, and my interest here is in seeing if in that context, one might usefully try to bring the two cosmopolitanisms together. The new politically oriented cosmopolitanism, engaging with ideas of global citizenship and civil society, is no doubt a reaction to the tendency of contemporary globalization to be driven by market forces—indeed, to the extent of being taken, frequently, to be practically isomorphic with them. Even if the politics of globalization may have its components of top-down elite activity, the efforts to which the cosmopolitan label is now more likely to be attached tend to be more bottom-up oriented, a matter of organizing across borders for some variety of purposes: human rights, environmental issues, and others. One might look at this in terms of those familiar contrasts between thinking and acting locally or globally. In some situations, both thinking and acting locally continue to be entirely sufficient. Thinking locally and acting globally can be irresponsible and even disastrous—exporting toxic waste is an example. There has been some inclination to believe that thinking globally and acting locally is the superior stance, and there may be a certain clear-eyed realism about it, insofar as things on the local arena are simply more manageable. Yet, for certain purposes, this stance may be insufficient—there are global problems that need to be attacked globally. The emergent debate over a cosmopolitan politics fits well here. The "cosmopolitan manifesto" published by Ulrich Beck, the German sociologist, in newspapers and periodicals in several countries is a notable example (Beck 1998).[3]

What, if any, is the relationship between a political cosmopolitanism of this kind and the more aesthetic and experiential cosmopolitanism referred to earlier? Perhaps each can exist separately. I am inclined to believe that there are now more experiential than political cosmopolitans in the world, more people who are enjoying cultural diversity for its own sake than who are actively engaged with any kind of transnational political organizing. Even so, the two may not be entirely independent of each other.

Let us take a step back to recent debates over nationalism.[4] We often distinguish between two basic types of nationalism, one sometimes referred to as "ethnic" and the other as "civic"; the labels vary. The "ethnic" variety is indeed based on ethnicity, or something very much like it. Belonging to the nation tends to be based on an ascriptive criterion, and an assumption of cultural homogeneity and considerable historical depth. Consequently, this is a nationalism based on great symbolic density, a major resource in contexts where solidarity has to be mobilized. The other side of the coin is that this kind of nationalism is often rigid and exclusivist when it comes to membership. Civic nationalism is more clearly political. What is needed for membership is a commitment to an overarching political order: a constitution, a republic. In principle, regardless of culture and history, you too can join. But admirable as such openness and flexibility may be, some would argue that there is in civic nationalism a certain cultural deficit. It may be too symbolically narrow and thin to gain full commitments.

Switch this line of argument to the political vision of cosmopolis. It is a criticism not so seldom heard of transnational culture in general that it is thin. To quote one prominent scholar of ethnonationalism, Anthony D. Smith (1991, 157–58), what is transnational is "shallow," "fundamentally artificial," "indifferent to place and time," and so forth. I have attempted elsewhere to argue that this is not necessarily so. For a growing number of people, of several kinds, personal border-crossing involvements with different places, cultures, and nations can be central, deeply affecting experiences (cf. Hannerz 1996, 81ff.).

The question we confront now is whether a more strictly political cosmopolitanism, however worthy, might not be characterized by some of the same cultural thinness as civic nationalism; and if, on the other hand, a variety of experiential cosmopolitanisms, rather than being merely individual self-indulgences, could not become so intertwined with political cosmopolitanism as to provide it with an important resource base of affect and a sense of competence. In the recent United States–based debate over cosmopolitanism versus patriotism, Martha Nussbaum (1996, 15), for one, while strongly cosmopolitan in her own preferences (yet at the same time seeing no necessary conflict between the two), has recognized that kind of weakness in a philosophical or programmatic cosmopolitanism. "Becoming a citizen of the world is often a lonely business," she writes. "It is . . . a kind of exile—from the comfort of local truths, from the warm, nestling feeling of patriotism, from the absorbing drama of pride in oneself and one's own." And, she continues, cosmopolitanism "offers only reason and the love of humanity, which may seem at times less colorful than other sources of belonging."

Nussbaum's (1997) own recipe for filling out the contours of cosmopolitanism has primarily been one of making organized education more oriented toward other cultures, other philosophies, other religions. Yet perhaps the more haphazard and disorderly growth of experiential cosmopolitanism is what could parallel more directly the warmth, the drama, and the color of ethnonationalism, and thus offer a greater cultural density to political cosmopolitanism—while at the same time pointing in another direction; for as a cosmopolitanism, it is expansive, although not in a confrontational mode. It is inclusive rather than exclusive; it emphasizes the achievement rather than the ascription of understandings and social relationships.

Veteran British foreign correspondent James Cameron (1969, 312) wrote the following lines as he began to contemplate the end of his career, lines that present a perhaps extreme instance of an immersion with the senses in the world, and an anticipatory nostalgia with regard to a future loss of a very large home:

> I would not wish to contemplate a future in which I should not again see the surf-boats go out in Ghana, nor drink at the Cockpit in Singapore nor

the Crillon in Paris, nor see the lotus-lakes in Cashmir or the Tung Tan market in Peking or the Staten Island Ferry in New York, or the windmills in Mykonos or the Baie d'Along in Tonking.

Perhaps this is where multiterritorialization comes close to deterritorialization. Cameron wrote these lines in a house on the coast of Ireland, but that was not really a place where he had long-standing roots either. His childhood had involved following in the footsteps of a peripatetic father, and he professes to have no sharp recollections of any one place from this period. Yet again, there is no necessary conflict between identifications with a larger and a more restrictively understood home. As noted earlier, cosmopolitans may feel most at ease when they know where the exit is; Kwame Anthony Appiah (1996), American academic philosopher, son of a West African lawyer-politician, and grandson of a British cabinet minister, says something similar when he argues for what he calls "rooted cosmopolitanism."

Experiential cosmopolitanism need not be as self-consciously expansive as the kind sketched here. It might rather involve a kind of piecemeal buildup of a sense of being at home in cosmopolis—a growth of trust and of mastery as one overcomes an early sense of embattledness in coming to terms with a changing life situation. It does not both begin and end with a love of all humanity, but starts with a modest, small-scale, undeliberate personal networking, which, as all of it comes together, reminds one more of Georg Simmel ([1922] 1955), with his understandings of overlapping and intersecting group affiliations, than of Samuel Huntington (1996), with his insistence on the clash of tectonic-plate civilizational blocs. Quite simply, it may grow out of a confirmation that one can grow good-looking and -tasting yams in one's garden in the diaspora as well; out of the extension of a kind of fictive brotherhood even to someone as initially distant as Warrant Officer Swart; and out of the satisfaction that in a new domicile, one has learned to find the kitchen at night.

Notes

1 There is also a close parallel with my own formulation of "the local," within the context of "global–local" contrasts (Hannerz 1996, 25ff.).
2 In one reaction, Robbins (1993) claimed to find that the cosmopolitan's privileges were "most grossly accepted" in my article; to me this indicates a remarkable insensitivity to a tone of irony in my portrayal of that privilege that I had thought was obvious.
3 See also David Held's (1995, 267ff.) analysis of cosmopolitan democracy.
4 See, for example, several contributions to Goldmann, Hannerz, and Westin (2000).

Works Cited

Anderson, Benedict. 1983. *Imagined Communities*. London: Verso.

Appadurai, Arjun. 1991. "Global Ethnoscapes: Notes and Queries for a Transnational Anthropology." In *Recapturing Anthropology*, ed. Richard G. Fox, 191–210. Santa Fe, N.Mex.: School of American Research Press.

Appiah, Kwame Anthony. 1996. "Cosmopolitan Patriots." In *For Love of Country*, ed. Joshua Cohen, 21–29. Boston: Beacon Press.

Battaglia, Debbora. 1995. "On Practical Nostalgia: Self-Prospecting among Urban Trobrianders." In *Rhetorics of Self-Making*, ed. Debbora Battaglia, 77–96. Berkeley: University of California Press.

Beck, Ulrich. 1998. "The Cosmopolitan Manifesto." *New Statesman*. March 20, 28–30.

Cameron, James. 1969. *Point of Departure*. London: Panther.

Goldmann, Kjell, Ulf Hannerz, and Charles Westin, eds. 2000. *Nationalism and Internationalism in the Post–Cold War Era*. London: Routledge.

Gouldner, Alvin W. 1979. *The Future of the Intellectuals and the Rise of the New Class*. London: Macmillan.

Hannerz, Ulf. 1990. "Cosmopolitans and Locals in World Culture." In *Global Culture*, ed. Mike Featherstone, 237–51. London: Sage.

———. 1996. *Transnational Connections*. London: Routledge.

Held, David. 1995. *Democracy and the Global Order*. Cambridge: Polity Press.

Heller, Agnes. 1995. "Where Are We at Home?" *Thesis Eleven* 41: 1–18.

Huntington, Samuel P. 1996. *The Clash of Civilizations and the Remaking of World Order*. New York: Simon and Schuster.

Kleinman, Arthur, and Joan Kleinman. 1996. "The Appeal of Experience; The Dismay of Images: Cultural Appropriations of Suffering in Our Times." *Daedalus* 125:1: 1–23.

Löfgren, Orvar. 1990. "Medierna i nationsbygget: hur press, radio och TV gjort Sverige svenskt." In *Medier och kulturer*, ed. Ulf Hannerz, 85–120. Stockholm: Carlssons.

Mandela, Nelson. 1995. *Long Walk to Freedom*. London: Abacus.

McLuhan, Marshall. 1964. *Understanding Media*. New York: McGraw-Hill.

Nussbaum, Martha C. 1996. "Patriotism and Cosmopolitanism." In *For Love of Country*, ed. Joshua Cohen, 2–17. Boston: Beacon Press.

———. 1997. *Cultivating Humanity*. Cambridge: Harvard University Press.

Robbins, Bruce. 1993. *Secular Vocations*. London: Verso.

Said, Edward W. 1994. *Representations of the Intellectual*. New York: Pantheon Books.

Shils, Edward. [1961] 1975. *Center and Periphery*. Chicago: University of Chicago Press.

Simmel, Georg. [1922] 1955. *Conflict and the Web of Group Affiliations*. New York: Free Press.

Smith, Anthony D. 1991. *National Identity*. London: Penguin.

Benjamin Lee

13

The Subjects of Circulation

The cataclysmic events of the late 1980s and early 1990s—the downfall of the Soviet Union, the liberation of Eastern Europe, democracy movements in Asia—brought to more jaded observers in the United States the spectacle of people who desperately wanted Western-style democracy and were prepared to die for it. As Slavoj Žižek (1994) has so nicely put it, what fascinated the West was the "reinvention of democracy," perhaps in a better more global way—an "international civil society" that would transcend the parochialism of nation-states and bring about a more equitable world. Yet scarcely a decade later, we face the prospects of a new millennium dominated by the rise of destructive nationalisms and the growing social inequalities brought about by a predatory economic globalization.

The revival and circulation of the notions of civil society and its political complement, the public sphere, lay in its promise to be able to link national politics with a more democratic world order. At the national level, civil society referred to a set of autonomous civil associations and institutions that would act as a buffer between the market and the state. The classic public sphere consisted of specific institutions such as coffeehouses, salons, publishing houses, journals, and newspapers that could nurture public discussions on issues of common concern that would ideally have an effect on public policy. The international version of civil society would grow out of transnational institutions such as the United Nations, the World Bank, nongovernmental organizations, and the International Monetary Fund and transnational social movements such as those focused on the environment, human rights, and women's issues. It would similarly nurture international discussions of issues of global common concern, in ways that could determine international and national policies, and also act as a buffer between the inequitable dimensions of economic globalization and the narrower concerns of individual nations. The result would be a transnational public sphere that would expand democratic values and human rights through a potential "dialogue of cultures."

The events of the last decade have shown that these early hopes are being undercut by the realities of globalization. Conceptions of civil society and the public sphere seem quaintly out of touch with the "fractal" nature of contemporary global flows and processes. If, as Benedict Anderson (1991) has argued, print capitalism provided the tools for imagining the nation, a mass-mediated global economy is producing transnational imaginations of the social that seem to run counter to the political ideologies of nations and states. The very transnational processes invoked for the possible creation of an international civil society are already undermining the power and sovereignty of nation-states so that they cannot be the building blocks of such an order.

One of the problems of earlier approaches to civil society and the public sphere is their reliance on fixed national forms of the market and political subjectivity. The recent work of scholars such as Arjun Appadurai, Craig Calhoun, Charles Taylor, and Michael Warner can be seen as developing alternative approaches that link the development of modern forms of subjectivity to cultural processes of circulation. By treating civil society and the public sphere as sociohistorically specific phenomena that are "in motion" rather than abstract idealizations, they expand Jürgen Habermas's original insights into a framework for analyzing the creation of new forms of subjectivity that are crucial to the development of modernity and contemporary globalization.

Habermas's crucial insight is that the public sphere was a specific set of civil society institutions that formed a "holding environment" for the development of new forms of collective subjectivity such as public opinion and popular sovereignty that provide the basis for the notion of "the people" at the heart of nationalist consciousness. The public sphere was a new way of imagining the social, how people make up a society and are supposed to act in it—what Charles Taylor has called a new "social imaginary" that radically broke with earlier social imaginaries based on notions of religious hierarchy and the divine right of kings. As the organizing social imaginary of civil society, it also interacted with the two other social imaginaries that it "buffered": the market and the state.

The public sphere, citizen-state, and the market organized complex flows of people, commodities, and ideas into what might be called new "cultures of circulation" that would transform the global cultural economy of colonialism into a system of nation-states. Cultures of circulation are created by the forms that circulate through them; these forms also provide the building blocks for the creation of new social imaginaries that are at the heart of the development of modernity. For example, Benedict Anderson (1991) has argued that the development of nationalism can be seen as the product of the interactions between specific cultural forms such as novels and newspapers and their circulation through a globalized print capitalism; the result is a new social imaginary and cultural formation that crystallizes around the idea of a constitutionalized peoplehood.

Placing civil society and the public sphere in the context of global circulations provides a crucial cultural dimension to our understanding of contemporary globalization. Concepts of peoplehood and collective agency interact with cultures of circulation produced by the mass media and information technologies to create the social imaginaries at the heart of new nationalisms, social movements, and transnational formations. Even research itself can be seen as a special type of social imaginary created by an increasingly internationalized "imagined community" of scholars whose work circulates through exchanges, conferences, and publications. Coordinating the "double circulation" of communities of research and what they study is increasingly the central challenge for contemporary research and scholarship.

Imagining the Social

The public sphere, citizen-state, and market are what Charles Taylor (unpublished paper) has called "social imaginaries"—ways of imagining the social that themselves mediate collective life. Although social imaginaries may have explicit theoretical formulations, they also consist of implicit understandings that underlie and make possible common practices. They are embedded in the habitus of a population, or carried in modes of address, stories, symbols, and the like. According to Taylor, these imaginaries are social in a double sense: they are commonly shared, social ways through which people imagine their society. And they are imaginary in a double sense: they exist by virtue of representations or implicit understandings and they are the means by which individuals construct and understand their identities and places in the world.

The three social imaginaries of the public sphere, citizen-state, and market contain new forms of subjectivity and identity that are linked to specific social practices such as reading and rational calculation that require the development of the requisite supportive social institutions, whether they be coffeehouses and publishing firms or clearinghouses and banks. Each of them presupposes a new sense of belonging based on a growing sense of equality and individualism in which all individuals stand in the same fundamental unmediated relationship to the social body they are part of—what Taylor, drawing on the work of Craig Calhoun, has called "direct access." In the public sphere, for example, all the participants should have an equal opportunity to speak and be heard in shaping public opinion. In the modern citizen-state, each citizen stands in direct relationship to the object of common allegiance, the state, via the notion of "we, the people" that legitimates it. In a market economy, people enter contractual relations on an equal footing; whatever particular reasons they have for entering into economic relations with others is irrelevant to the functioning of the market.

Another way in which these modern social imaginaries differ from previous ones is that they are primarily relations among strangers who nevertheless see themselves as sharing direct access to a larger social totality, whether it be the nation or a market; the sense of belonging must include people who in principle may never know or meet one another. Although these new imaginaries are made possible through various forms of mass mediation, they also create and organize spaces of circulation for the media and embed face-to-face communication in open-ended audiences and publics. In this respect, the bourgeois public sphere has left its imprint on contemporary social imaginaries in its legacy of individual rights that transcend face-to-face relations and apply equally to all citizens.

Finally, modern social imaginaries see societies as brought about by self-reflexive collective action in purely secular time, rather than as grounded in the cosmos or hierarchies of temporal orders tied to notions such as the Great Chain of Being. Secular time is all-inclusive, with a crosscutting notion of simultaneity, and infinitely divisible into measurable discrete units; it is the time in which all events occur and which has no higher or lower points, as was the case in religious chronologies. The demise of notions of higher times linked to higher orders of being also made it possible to conceive of societies as self-created and self-regulating. At one extreme, these collective entities became self-reflexively created agents, such as "the people," the "market," or the "nation," all of which are seen as created through their own collective social action rather than as the product of some external agency or as existing since time immemorial.

Imagining people as members and creators of a moral order of equal cooperating individuals, united in their acceptance and understanding of such an order, was a remarkable historical creation. It required breaking loose from older understandings of the unity of society as linked to hierarchical kingdoms, divinely founded churches, or legal-tribal orders existing since time out of mind. The overturning of external hierarchies of value was not limited to the revolutionary traditions of the public sphere or the citizen-state. In the early days of the development of the market, the spread of double-entry bookkeeping relied on the idea that "God balances the books," and only gradually did people come to see the market as run by its own rules of economic calculation.

Modern Social Imaginaries

In his book *Modernity at Large*, Arjun Appadurai makes a crucial connection between the creation of modern social imaginaries and global circulations. Circulation is more than the movement of people, ideas, and commodities from one society to another; it is also a cultural process with its own types of abstraction and constraint that are produced by the nature of the circulating forms and the "imagined communities" that interpret and use them. In addition to the circulation of financial instruments and technologies (what he calls financescapes and technoscapes), global cultural flows consist of circulations of people (ethnoscapes), images (mediascapes), and ideas (especially politically based—ideoscapes), a classification that is not meant to be either exclusive or exhaustive. Each of these flows is subject to its own constraints and incentives, placing them in "disjunctive" relationships with one another that are increasingly the subject and object of contemporary social imaginations. They are the "building blocks" of what Appadurai, extending Benedict Anderson's work on nationalism, has termed "imagined worlds"—"the multiple worlds that are constituted by the historically situated imaginations of persons and groups spread around the globe" (Appadurai 1996, 33).

The key insight is linking imagination with circulation and circulation with semiotic form. The circulating objects are the tools for the construction of new social imaginaries, whether it be the "imagined communities" of nationalism or transnational diasporas. The circulation of specific cultural forms creates new forms of community with their hierarchies of evaluation, contrast, and difference. If we expand Appadurai's notion of global flows and scapes with Anderson's insight into what might be called the "semiotic mediation" of circulation, what appear to be complex circulations among different cultures are the product of interactions among different "cultures of circulation."

Although a culture of circulation can be identified by the objects circulating through it, it is not reducible to them. Instead, circulation interacts with the semiotic form of the circulating objects to create the cultural dimensions of the circulatory process itself. A particularly interesting and important example of the cultural "performativity" of circulation is the creation of a new form of "we" identity, that of "the people" that is at the heart of many modern social imaginaries.

Anderson suggests that one of the reasons for the poverty of philosophical thought about nationalism has been the tendency to think of it as an "ideology" and to place it alongside concepts such as liberalism and fascism. Instead, he suggests that it should be treated anthropologically, as a category closer to kinship or religion. Yet the performative dimensions of "we, the people" also link nationalism to philosophical and linguistic issues of citation, quotation, metalanguage, self-reference, and self-reflexivity that are among the most complex in philosophical and linguistic analysis. Indeed, much of the German idealist tradition that plays a crucial role in the development of modern nationalism could be considered a protracted reflection on how to analyze the performative qualities of the first-person pronoun, whether it be Kant's transcendental subject, Fichte's "I = I" self-positing subject, Hegel's *Geist* (spirit) and *Begriff* (concept), or even Marx's analysis of capital as the self-valorizing subject of capitalism. Perhaps the difficulties in giving an adequate theoretical account of nationalism lie in the complexity of its structuring ideas rather than a misplaced emphasis on ideology.

One of the discoveries of the so-called linguistic turn is that many of these issues, such as performativity, metalanguage, and narration, are not unrelated; all of them play an important role in the creation of the nationalist subject. Instead, the grammatical structures of languages systematically encode the relations between the ongoing speech event and whatever is being talked about or referred to. For example, among the pronouns (a linguistically universal category), the third-person forms are never indexical and can refer to any kind of object (*he, she, it, they* can replace or substitute for all other referential forms). The first person, on the other hand, is not only indexical, but explicitly self-referential: *I* refers to "the individual who utters the present instance of discourse containing the linguistic instance *I*" (Benveniste 1971, 218). The same structure also applies to narration, where we can distinguish between the indexical event of narration and the narrated-about events. Forms such as quotation, direct and indirect discourse, and free indirect style also distinguish between the so-called reporting event, and the source or reported speech event, and it is these very forms that make up the repertoire of narrative devices and are also at the heart of Mikhail Bakhtin's "metalinguistics."

From this perspective, both the first-person pronouns and the classic performative constructions such as "I hereby promise . . ." are examples of indexical self-reference in that they seem to create the individual or event they refer to; twisting Bakhtin a bit, speech about speech creates the speech event it speaks about. In both cases, they contrast with their third-person counterparts that are neither indexical nor self-referential. Thus "he promises . . ." is simply a report and not the making of a promise. These issues intersect with narration not only because performatives are examples of linguistic self-reference, but also because the performative verbs of speaking (and their mental act and state counterparts) are used in direct and indirect discourse to create the narrative strategies of voicing characteristic of novelistic fiction and historiography. Looked at from a logical perspective, these verbs raise a host of logical issues, such as sense and reference, referential opacity, and transparency. From a narrative perspective, they raise issues of voicing, focalization, and the generic representation of subjectivity. These two lines intersect in the performative first-person *we* and the constative nominalization "the people" and give "we, the people" epistemological and narrative implications.

The difficulties in giving an adequate analysis of nationalism lie with the semiotic complexity of its structuring tropes. The voice of the people is a rhetorical figure derived from the voices of narration. Narration is itself structured by the interplay between narrating event and narrated-about event in which the performatives and other verbs of speaking, thinking, and feeling play a crucial role; they are the vehicles par excellence through which the audience depicts the speech, thoughts, and feelings of her characters, what Jürgen Habermas called a "privateness oriented to an audience" (1989, 43).

At the same time, the circulation of different kinds of narrated texts creates the "public" that those texts address. "We, the people" names a new kind of print-mediated community produced by the semiotic nature of the texts that circulate through it. Each reading of a "nationalist" text creates a token instance of a *we* that subsumes the narrator/character/reader in a collective agency that creates itself in every act of reading. These token *we*'s,

when aggregated across acts of reading, become the basis for the imagined community of we-ness at the heart of nationalism; nationalism is a
particular example of the semiotic constitution of community, a social
imaginary created out of the semiotic mediation of circulation.

We can now see how the issues of performativity and circulation interact to create a new social imaginary, that of the citizen-state. The dual
structure of narration as narrating and narrated-about event creates two
levels of collective identification: at the level of narrating event, between
narrator/sender/author and reader/receiver/addressee, and in the narrated-
about event, between the reader and the characters who are themselves
speakers and addressees.[1] Anderson's imagined community of nationalism
is created through narratives that embrace the narrated-about characters
as referents, the author/narrator as the sender of the narrating event, and
the readers as the narrated-to addressees. Through different narrative devices such as quotation, psychonarration, and free indirect style, different
degrees of identification can be created between the narrator and the
reader and the reader and the characters. Such identifications create a feeling of interchangeability between different participant roles in the event
of narrating/reading and the narrated-about events and a feeling of continuity between the communities constituted by the narrating events and
those described in the narrated-about events. The narrating/reading event
is also felt to be shared among a community of like-minded readers; thus
every act of reading is potentially a micronational token act that instanti-
ates a macronational ideology of community.

Narrators, readers, characters are all potentially interchangeable in this
new form of self-creating collective agency in which direct access is created via narration. What we have is an expansion of performativity beyond
that of the first person and utterances, to a full-fledged model of the performative construction of interpretative communities, including the "we,
the people" of both nationalism and identity politics. "We, the people"
emerges as the performative refiguring of the large circulatory processes
of which it is a constitutive element; at the same time, it creates and names
the semiotic space through which these new forms of collective identity
will circulate, in effect creating the conditions necessary for their own circulation, not unlike the way sentential performatives create some of the
conditions necessary for their own fulfillment or uptake.

The narrated mediation of nationalist subjectivity was accompanied by
a change in how communication was viewed. Earlier ideologies of printing
saw print as extending face-to-face communication, simply increasing the
circulation of information without any qualitative transformation of it. In

the bourgeois public sphere, people began to see print as foregrounding writing's potential for unlimited dissemination, thereby creating a print-mediated difference between public discourse and the world of letters that characterized private correspondence. In his case study of the early American republican period, Michael Warner (1990) shows that a crucial transformation occurs when communication is seen not just as a face-to-face relation among people, but as a potentially limitless print-mediated discourse. Narrated texts enter this space and become the semiotic basis for new forms of subjectivity. A new vision of community is formed in which a reading public is held together in a potentially infinitely open-ended process of reading and criticism with its own norms of publicity and interpretation.

The notion of the American people would face two directions: it would be a transcendent source of legitimacy yet accessible to every citizen. This required the construction of a new ideology of the political implications of print: the printed textuality of the U.S. Constitution allows it to be seen as emanating from no individual, collectivity, or state legislature in particular, and thus from the people in general. Its circulation among "the people" militated against the particularism of local interests, and thereby solved one of the continuing problems of that period: how to balance local interests and public good. By building on the translocal nature of print mediation, it created the ground for the notion of disinterested public virtue.

Warner's analysis demonstrates the importance of seeing social imaginaries as multiplex phenomena that draw on and reorganize different cultures of circulation. Although the idea of a constitutionalized peoplehood will become one of the founding conceptions of the international system of nation-states, the U.S. variant rested on a particular ideology of communication not necessarily shared by other societies. Issues of popular sovereignty were also at the heart of the French revolutionary debates, but the underlying ideology of communication was much more of a face-to-face model. This was partially a result of Rousseau's influence, but also of the lack of any tradition of democratically elected state legislatures as in the United States. Germany would make a romanticized conception of language and race the core of an explicitly ethnicized peoplehood, whereas the Soviet Union and mainland China would develop the idea that the party was the vanguard of the people.

Warner's work suggests that the public sphere and citizen-state are social imaginaries built around specific ideologies of language and communication. As Silverstein (2000) has pointed out, Anderson's unisonance account of nationalism is really that of an ideologically driven conception of a standardized language community; from all the diversity of linguistic practices, a hegemonic standard is created, a unity in diversity that occludes its revolutionary origins and the need for perpetual vigilance against outsiders. Not surprisingly, it is Habermas who makes explicit the ideological nature of the public sphere and, by extension, nationalism. In a passage that clearly shows the influence of Frankfurt School Marxism, he writes:

> If ideologies are not only manifestations of the socially necessary consciousness in its essential falsity, if there is an aspect to them that can lay a claim to truth inasmuch as it transcends the status quo in utopian fashion, even if only for purposes of justification, then ideology exists at all only from this period on. Its origin would be the identification of "property owner" with "human being as such" in the role accruing to private people as members in the political public sphere of the bourgeois constitutional state, that is, in the identification of the public sphere in the political realm with that in the world of letters; and also in public opinion itself, in which the interest of the class, via critical public debate, could assume the appearance of the general interest, that is, in the identification of domination with its dissolution into pure reason. (Habermas 1989, 88)

The identifications of property owner with human being in general, and the interests of a specific class with that of the general interest, are at the heart of modern ideology. These equations create the space for the expression of the social contradictions they mediate; the resulting disjunction between social reality and ideology is a constitutive part of bourgeois society. The ideological construction of "we, the people" links the private expressions of subjectivity ("human being as such") with their public counterparts (the imputed potential rationality of public opinion) and gives the resulting social totality an agentive subject. It is in the interstices of the crossing of public spheres (England and colonial America; Spain and its colonies) that the modern notion of peoplehood emerges; it is a trope that transfers to an ideological level the crisis developing between the global cultural economy of colonialism and traditional forms of political legitimation; the resulting ideology of the equality of nations and peoples becomes a necessary component of an emerging *international* colonial economy.

The ideological bases of the public sphere and nationalism raise questions of their relationship to the third social imaginary, that of the market. Although it is not often thought of as an interpretative community, the market is a special type of social imaginary; the circulation of financial instruments depends on an "interpretative community" of institutions (exchanges, banks, clearinghouses, etc.) that understands and uses these forms, just as the public sphere was created out of the circulation and interpretation of books and letters. From a semiotic perspective, the system of nation-states creates the abstract forms of collective agency that provide the statistical categories and forms of calculation necessary for economic planning and the expansion of capital. For example, contemporary global capital flows presuppose the intertranslatability of financial instruments and information technologies while at the same time demanding that "local" economic activities be translated into cross-culturally comparable economic categories. These "interfaces" of translation transcend national borders and languages (of which the battle over international accounting standards and the multilingual versions of Windows 98 are just two examples) and are reminiscent of the more nationally based projects such as censuses that also required regimenting individuals and social groups into statistically denumerable categories.

Habermas's comments about the ideological dimensions of the public sphere suggest an even deeper connection between the performative subjectivities of the public sphere and nationalism and capitalism. The reference to forms of false consciousness necessary for the reproduction of society clearly refers to Marx's discussion of the role that objectification and reification play in the social reproduction of capital. For Marx, capital was not simply the financial and other resources used to produce goods and services, but rather a historically specific organization of time that produces a social totality with an internal dynamic of self-expansion in which objectification plays a key role. Objectification occurs when the social features of the totality created by the commodity and abstract labor time become seen as quasi-natural properties of the commodity itself. The price of a commodity seems to be the direct expression of the value of the commodity and also a natural property of it, like its size or shape, thereby effacing the social mediation of exchange value by abstract labor time. At the same time, the objectification of social relationships, that is, the conflation of the value of a commodity with its price, is necessary for the reproduction of capital

In the section on capital in volume 1 of *Capital*, Postone (1993) points out that Marx uses distinctly Hegelian terminology to describe value as an "automatic subject," a "self-moving substance" that is "the subject of a process, in which, while constantly assuming the form of money and of commodities, it changes its own magnitude, . . . and thus valorizes itself" (Marx, translated in Postone 1993, 75). This quasiperformativity of capital as self-positing subject connects it directly to the issues of performativity and self-reflexivity that lie at the heart of Marx's famous inversion of Hegel. Hegel's analysis of *Geist* and *Begriff* (spirit and concept) as self-reflexive and self-positing explicitly derives from the first-person pronoun *I*. Expanding on Kant's insight that "*I* accompanies all my conceptions," Hegel points out that *I* is both universal and particular, or, in more contemporary linguistic terminology, it is both metaindexical and indexical:

> All other men have it in common with me to be "I"; just as it is common to all my sensations and conceptions to be mine. But "I," in the abstract, as such, is the mere act of self-concentration or self-relation, in which we make abstraction from all conception and feeling, from every state of mind and every peculiarity of nature, talent, and experience. To this extent, "I" is the existence of a wholly *abstract* universality, a principle of abstract freedom. Hence thought, viewed as a subject, is what is expressed by the word "I." (Hegel 1975, 31)

Labor replaces thought as the self-reflexively created subject; capital is *Geist* without self-consciousness.

The development of capital as the "engine of modernity" presupposes the sociohistorically specific conjuncture of at least three factors: the development of a money form in which some commodity (in modern times usually gold or silver) is the universal equivalent, the use of money as both medium of exchange and the measure of value, and the commodification of labor itself. These conditions make it possible for the infinitely divisible continuum of price (money as a measure of value) to mediate exchange (money as the medium of exchange) and be projected onto productive labor (labor as commodity), thus allowing labor time to be measured and given a price, that is, making possible the calculation of the value of labor power. Abstract labor time is a metatemporal construction that interacts with concrete labor time to create a social totality that is constantly in motion, that destroys itself in creating and expanding itself, a dialectical dynamic that Postone (1993) describes as a "treadmill effect" peculiar to capitalism.

In his *Time, Labor, and Social Domination*, Postone argues that capital has an intrinsic dynamic of self-expansion. Each commodity represents the average amount of labor time necessary to produce it, that is, its socially necessary labor time, in the form of a generalized temporal norm of production. Increases in productivity result in more commodities being produced per unit of abstract labor time. When a productive innovation is introduced, there is a temporary increase in the value of the commodities produced by the innovation because the norm of socially necessary labor time is still set at the pre-innovation level. When the innovation generalizes, the norm is reset at the new level of socially necessary labor time; because more commodities are now being produced, the value represented by each commodity actually decreases.

The "treadmill" effect imposes a direction on the secularized time in which modern collective subjects move. Increases in productivity produce short-term gains in the amount of value produced per unit of time; competition leads to the expanded use of the innovation, and once this generalizes, the amount of value yielded per unit time returns to its previous level. This produces a society that is "directionally dynamic," driven by competition for ever-increasing levels of productivity, but resting on a contradiction: as commodities are more efficiently produced, each commodity represents less value.

Marx's account of capital could be described as a production-centered analysis of a culture of circulation that contains a sociohistorically specific organization of temporality and performativity. Capital is a self-reflexively created collective agency whose "substance" and subject is labor time, both in its abstract (the analogue to Hegel's I as universal subject) and concrete (the analogue to I as indexical particular) realizations. As both Postone (1993) and Žižek (1994) have pointed out, fetishism is not an inaccurate perception of the nature of capitalism, but rather a necessary and accurate understanding of capitalism as it appears or "manifests" itself to people:

> what we have here are relations between 'free' people, each following his or her proper egoistic interest. The predominant and determining form of their interrelations is not domination and servitude but a contract between free people who are equal in the eyes of the law. Its model is the market exchange: . . . they meet as two persons whose activity is thoroughly determined by their egoistic interest; every one of them proceeds as a good utilitarian; the other person is for him wholly delivered of all mystical aura; all he sees in his partner is another subject who follows his interest and interests him only in so far as he possesses something—a commodity—that could satisfy some of his needs. (Žižek 1994, 309–10)

The Frankfurt School would expand Marx's analysis of fetishism into a theory of ideology. They saw that the contractual presuppositions of the market model are also at the basis of social-contract models of society and the state and therefore bourgeois ideology; the Habermas quote earlier makes explicit the rhetorical transformations needed to convert class-specific interests into universal ones. To the extent that these presuppositions are also at the heart of modern notions of the citizen-state, then the public sphere, citizen-state, and market are also fetishized self-reflexive collective agencies embedded within the larger self-reflexive structure of capital itself.

One of the more interesting questions that contemporary processes of globalization raise is whether the links between subjectivity and capital suggested by Marx still hold. Although it is possible to argue that in the age of industrial capitalism analyzed by Marx value formed the leading edge of capitalism, contemporary global transformations suggest that the leading edge is no longer the mediation of production by labor, but the expansion of circulation by finance capital. In Marx's account, finance capital is valueless ("fictitious capital") because it does not involve productive labor. Instead, much of volume 3 of *Capital* is devoted to showing how such valueless forms contribute to the functioning of capitalism by redistributing value. In the final instance, value determines finance capital.

The recent exponential growth in "valueless" forms of finance capital produces a problem for traditional Marxist analysts; the very tension that Marx saw between value and material wealth seems to undermine the utility of abstract labor time as a category for analyzing contemporary globalization. Instead of labor and production determining the expansion of finance capital, finance capital seems to be increasingly independent of value, or even determining its role within the expansion of capitalism. The data seem overwhelming that some sort of major transformation is occurring. Foreign currency transactions now average more than one and a half trillion dollars a day. From the founding of the Chicago Options Exchange in 1973 when nine hundred options were traded on sixteen companies, daily volume now totals well over 1 million. In 1995, the notional value of derivatives held by just six banks (Chemical, Citibank, Morgan, Bankers Trust, Bank of America, and Chase) totaled $14 trillion; in the same year, the value of outstanding derivative contracts in twenty-six countries was estimated to be twice the amount of the world's economic output, almost $50 trillion. By the time of the Asian economic crises of 1997, the annual value of traded derivatives was more than ten times the value of global production. Although the first option transaction is credited to the Greek philosopher Thales, their explosive growth over the past two decades is the most intense expansion of any financial instrument in history; as Alfred Steinherr, the general manager of the European Investment Bank in Luxembourg, put it:

> Indeed, the advances since the mid-1970s in the ability to identify and isolate the key financial risks found in modern economies, together with the development of financial institutions and markets that can efficiently commoditise, trade and price such risk, are the crowning achievement of the evolution of modern market economies. (Steinherr 2000, xvi)

Although it is clear that the development of these new financial instruments is creating a new culture of circulation with its own interpretative communities of banks, clearinghouses, and exchanges, there has been little analysis of the semiotic properties of the forms themselves. Yet, upon closer examination, financial instruments such as derivatives contain forms of temporality that contribute to their "self-expansion." Derivatives have no value of their own but derive their value from some other asset—stocks, bonds, commodities, or currencies.

There are two basic types of derivatives: futures, which are contracts for future delivery at specified prices; and options, which allow one side the opportunity to buy from or sell to the other at a prearranged time and price. Originally used to hedge risk, futures and options are also sources of speculation because of the leverage they create: for a small amount of money one can control a correspondingly larger amount of the underlying asset. Options and futures expire at fixed dates, and the value of these instruments derives from a combination of the value of the underlying asset, the time to their expiration, the risk-free interest rate, and their volatility. Volatility is a measure of risk, and derivatives can be used to control risk through hedging, or to speculate on risk through the leverage created by the fact that they expire. The key connection with abstract labor time is that derivatives are time-governed, but their derivative status breaks any direct connection to whatever abstract labor time is involved in producing the underlying asset. In this respect, they differ from stocks in that companies may be distinguished as involving productive labor or not, that is, whether they produce surplus value or not. The creation of a meta-temporal level with respect to stocks, currencies, and commodities "floats" derivatives free from productive labor, creating truly "fictitious capital."

The end of the Bretton Woods agreement led to a huge expansion of derivatives because the floating of national currencies against one another greatly increased currency risks at the same time that the Gulf oil crisis was producing uncertainty in commodity prices. Using derivatives to hedge commodities and currencies distributes risk around a larger population and allows the fixing of price fluctuations within acceptable ranges. Hedging enhances the intertranslatability of currencies and capitals; the speculative uses increase both the quantity and velocity of capital produced and the concomitant demands for the mobility of capitals. Increasing the mobility of capitals requires their interconvertibilty, increasing the need for hedging. A treadmill-like dynamic is set up around risk (volatility); risk replaces labor in a dynamic of the ever-expanding character of finance capital. The structure of derivatives creates a break with the relationship between finance capital and value proposed by Marx; it allows circulation to have a self-reflexive dynamic that parallels that of value but is distinct from it.

Derivatives are instruments that objectify and redistribute risk. If the dynamics of labor produced forms of subjectivity characteristic of an age of the global expansion of industrial capitalism, perhaps the dynamics of risk is producing new forms of (fetishized?) subjectivity that are necessary components in the transnational expansion of capitalism in its latest phase. In *The Cultural Turn* (1998), Fredric Jameson makes some interesting speculations about the relations between finance capital and contemporary cultural phenomena such as movie previews, real-estate booms, and global stock markets; Beck's work on "risk society" (1992) suggests that new social imaginaries based on risk and "metareflexivity" may already be emerging.

At present, however, there is no comparable account that links forms of subjectivity to forms of capital the way that Marx's account specified for an earlier era. In those times the public sphere produced new forms of subjectivity shaped by its role in civil society institutions that mediated between two other nationally based social imaginaries, those of the market and the citizen-state. Contemporary processes of globalization may be producing new financial instruments that are shifting the leading edge of capitalism from the dynamics of productive labor to the dynamics of objectifying, circulating, and redistributing risk across the world. The rapidity of this global transformation, its intensity and scope, are unmatched in the history of financial instruments and may be producing the "flexible" transnational subjects and subjectivities that seem to be developing in global cities such as New York, London, or Hong Kong, all of which, as Jameson (1998) ironically points out, are characterized by stock markets and real-estate booms. Understanding how the globalization of finance capital organizes and produces these new cultures of circulation may require analyzing how their semiotic structures create new forms of temporal objectification whose quasi-performative status will be reflected in the new social imaginaries created by them.

Notes

1 See Silverstein (2000) for a more detailed and linguistically precise account.

Works Cited

Anderson, Benedict. 1991. *Imagined Communities*. London: Verso.

Appadurai, Arjun. 1996. *Modernity at Large: Cultural Dimensions of Globalization*. Minneapolis: University of Minnesota Press.

Beck, Ulrich. 1992. *Risk Society: Towards a New Modernity*. London: Sage.

Benveniste, Emile. 1971. *Problems in General Linguistics*. Trans. Mary Elizabeth Meek. Reprint, Coral Gables, Fla.: University of Miami Press.

Habermas, Jürgen. 1989. *The Structural Transformation of the Public Sphere*. Trans. Thomas Burger. Cambridge: MIT Press.

Hegel, Georg Wilhelm Friedrich. 1975. *Hegel's Logic*. Trans. William Wallace. Oxford: Clarendon Press.

Jameson, Fredric. 1998. *The Cultural Turn*. New York: Verso.

Postone, Moishe. 1993. *Time, Labor, and Social Domination*. Cambridge: Cambridge University Press.

Silverstein, Michael. 2000. "Whorfianism and the Linguistic Imagination of Nationality." In *Regimes of Language*, ed. Paul Kroskrity, 85–138. Santa Fe, N.Mex.: School of American Research Press.

Steinherr, Alfred. 2000. *Derivatives: The Wild Beast of Finance*. New York: John Wiley and Sons.

Taylor, Charles. "New Social Imaginaries." Unpublished paper.

Warner, Michael. 1990. *Letters of the Republic*. Cambridge: Harvard University Press.

Žižek, Slavoj. 1994. "How Did Marx Invent the Symptom?" In *Mapping Ideology*, ed. Slavoj Žižek, 296–331. New York: Verso.

14

The Nationalization of Anxiety:

A History of Border Crossings

Points of Entry

> The question of boundaries is the first to be encountered; from it all others flow. To draw a boundary around anything is to define, analyse and reconstruct it, in this case select, indeed adapt, a philosophy of history. (Braudel 1975, 18)

In his work on the Mediterranean in the age of Philip II, Fernand Braudel analyzes the power of boundaries. Every social setting or epoch produces its own world of borders, based on the need to signal differences or changes, but it is interesting to note that not all differences are circumscribed by boundaries. Which borders take up place, come into focus, stand out as very noticeable at different periods and in different settings? Borders are made to draw attention; they constitute a cultural signal system. The line drawn in the sand, the pause in the conversation, the door that must be opened, the ritual that has to be carried out—they all signal "Look out! Something is happening here," something starts, ends, or is radically transformed (see Fink 1993). Some cultural boundaries are so thoroughly internalized from early on that they need no warning signs, border stones, or alarm clocks.

Borders are a central theme in discussions of the making and unmaking of the power of nation-states. Through a historical anthropology of the rituals and practices of border crossings, I will explore how the dramaturgy, scenography, and choreography of such movements work to make the nation-state visible and tangible, as well as producing patterns of national belonging and displacement.

In preindustrial Europe, one of the most developed border systems kept town and countryside apart. Here the system of walls and gates not only controlled the material flow of people or goods; it also marked the differences in privileges and status and the differences in the symbolic worlds of the two territories. It was—for a long time—a very successful way of territorializing cultural difference.

In the industrial state, national borders came to play a similar, central role and the immense success of the national project during the past two centuries owes much to the skillful deployment of the pedagogy of space and the ritualization of borders. Technologies of transport and communication have often been seen as a part of a history making the world of the nineteenth and twentieth centuries more global. Goods, people, and ideas moved more freely across borders, but the same period also saw a closing or sharpening of national borders: the nation starts or ends here! In many ways, national borders became the archetypal border of the twentieth century, the model for materializing boundaries with props such as red striped bars, an abundance of warning signs, officials in uniforms. This pedagogy of space has also been very seductive in the ways in which we envisage cultural differentiation in terms of bounded space, physically or metaphorically. In cultural terms, spatial boundaries are "good to think with."

Some borderlands, however, have become better to think with than others. The image of the Rio Grande has come to symbolize the clash between north and south, the First and Third Worlds, just as Checkpoint Charlie became the icon of the confrontation between East and West. Scholars have tended to flock to such "hot borders." The Mexican border town of Tijuana was once named "one of the major laboratories of the postmodern" (Saldívar 1997, 34). It was analyzed in terms of hybridity, fluidity, and ambiguity, sometimes romanticized. But borderlands are also territories of sharp divisions and distinctions where the nation-state is made visible in changing ways and for different reasons (see the discussion in Wilson and Donnan 1998).

Early states focused on the importance of strong centers and rather porous borders, but modern (and centralizing) nation making shifted the energy to the periphery where the state, its power, its cultural capital, its routines, rules, and ideas were materialized and challenged. (For two case studies of such changes, see Sahlins 1989 and Linde-Laursen 1995.)

Borderlands are often described as no-man's-land, as *terrain vague*, unchartered margins "in the middle of nowhere," but at the same time they are black holes, attracting a lot of energy and anxiety. Traveling through them, crossing national boundaries represents a multifaceted pedagogy, which changes from setting to setting and from time to time. In this experience, a number of polarities and tensions emerge or are challenged. People not only experience a transgression of "the national," but also of intensely personal boundaries, as their bodies are searched, their personal belongings are rifled through, and intimate questions are asked. In this compressed spatial and temporal event, basic issues of identity, of belonging and nonbelonging, are raised in the construction of a universe of "homeyness" and "abroadness."

In exploring such experiences, I will take most of my examples from a less dramatic borderland—the straits of Øresund, where southern Sweden faces Denmark. In a carefully staged millennium event, the gigantic bridge connecting the two countries was opened in the summer of 2000, carrying a heavy rhetoric of dismantling old national borders and barriers, creating a twenty-first-century model for a truly transnational region—as an economic and cultural laboratory of the future (see Berg, Linde-Laursen, and Löfgren 2000).

Anything to Declare?

In 1658, the province of Scania was conquered from Denmark by the Swedes and the Øresund straits changed from a waterway uniting the center of the Danish kingdom to a border zone. The transit ports of Malmö and Helsingborg now became national outposts on the margins of Sweden.

Today the traditional borderscape of Malmö still reads like a powerful statement of terminus: Sweden ends here! By the waterfront there is a cluster of buildings, communicating state power. The mighty railway station, with a tower from which the Swedish flag used to fly, is flanked by towers of the Royal Post Office Terminal and the Customs House. Further down along the quay are the old buildings of the steamship terminal and the train ferry, where people changed from train to boat, when embarking for Copenhagen, the Continent, and the World. Together these structures made up a "Fortress Sweden," guarding the exits and entries of people, goods, and mail. Remnants of a similar border landscape exist in Helsingborg.

During all the years I have been crossing this border—in all kinds of transport, in buses or cars on ferries, on board railway cars shipped across the waters, or seated in hydrofoils, hovercrafts, or catamarans—this borderscape has lost much of its drama. There is, however, still one diffuse feeling that always surfaces. Maybe it is based on a sedimentation of decades of border-control incidents: trained dogs sniffing their way inside the bus, the drug squad methodically taking a train toilet apart (acting on a tip-off), a family of immigrants having twelve liters of homemade plum brandy confiscated, teenagers trying to hide packs of cigarettes or a bag full of export beer, customs officials reaching for their rubber gloves, passport police scanning the crowd for aliens. As the border approaches and I watch the guards make their way along the train corridors or line up at the customs counter, I feel a vague sensation of guilt and find myself trying to act normal. It is years since I tried to smuggle a bottle of duty-free alcohol across the border, I have nothing whatsoever to declare, I am an extremely legal transient, but still the choice of red and green passages gives me a jolt. Why do border crossings instill these feelings of guilt?

In the 1877 travel journal *A Summer Holiday in Scandinavia*, the reader is taken across a number of borders as the author travels through Scandinavia. He enters Sweden by train from Norway, arriving at the imposing but deserted border station:

> Our two portmanteaus were seized upon and carried into the custom-house, where the station master, in a very magnificent dress of light blue, with silver facings, a three-cornered hat on his head, and a sword by his side, was walking about with a piece of official chalk in his hand. We feared all our well-packed effects were to be tumbled about by the rude hands of the custom-house people; but we were spared that trial. Either the station master was in an amiable mood, or (very probable) our train was behind time, for after gazing benignly upon us, he asked P. if we were tourists, and being told that we bore that character, he mildly begged to know if we had anything contraband. On being informed that we possessed nothing illicit, he smiled a gracious smile, affixed a mark upon our things, and motioned to a porter to take them back to the luggage-van. (Arnold 1877, 246)

Arriving later at Helsingborg, the luggage of these British tourists was enthusiastically carried aboard the small steam ferry by a host "of industrious Swedelings" or "little Scandinavians." The ferry bound for Denmark had to be shared with peasants, cattle, and pigs, but on the other side of the Sound the Danish customs official waved them through as "friends of the ground and liegemen of the Danes." The only real trouble occurred with the German customs officials south of the Danish border, where the travelers were "insultingly inspected by an arrogant gentleman in blue and silver uniform and spectacles." After a thorough search for contraband, he found their sporting guns and triumphantly "proceeded to fine us two dollars to the vigilant majesty of the German Zollverein."

Arnold was searched for contraband but not for his identity. In 1877, passports were still a scarce phenomenon. During most of the nineteenth century, British passports were so difficult to obtain, and so expensive, that many British travelers acquired French or Italian ones when doing the Grand Tour of southern Europe, if needed (Pemble 1987, 33ff.). There were no general rules about passports or visas in nineteenth-century Europe.

States could—at times—enforce such rules for political reasons. They were often absolutist states not only with a nervous attitude to the influx of certain goods, but also with fears of spies, troublemakers, and subversive ideas and literature. Over-controlled borders were seen as a sign of underdevelopment.

The latter part of the nineteenth century brought a general easing of paperwork at border crossings. This was a period when one could travel very freely from nation to nation. In Sweden, the absolutist state had previously tried to control population movements by demanding that all Swedes carry special travel permits for both internal and international travel, but such regulations were removed in 1860 as a part of a general liberalization. The old passport system was mainly directed toward interior movements, keeping the king's subjects localized to make sure they had work and did not roam the country as vagrants, thus making demands on the poor-relief system outside their own community.

But the new freedom of movement did not apply to all travelers. Arnold was a tourist—a traveling gentleman—but for those crossing the border from Sweden to Denmark in search of work the situation was different. The nineteenth century saw a growing migration of laborers from southern Sweden to Denmark, where job opportunities were better. Poverty-stricken Swedes gathered both in Copenhagen and in the agricultural districts, but at first their national status was not a great concern of local authorities. In 1875, however, the Danish government introduced laws that made it possible to expel aliens who had not secured work. The police had the right to march them directly to the boat, but soon it became evident that these laws worked very differently for different nationalities. A special rule was made, for example, for British subjects, who were not to be exposed to harsh measures such as these. Henrik Zip Sane

(1998a, 1998b) has analyzed this period of labor migration and points out that the tightening of the laws toward the end of the nineteenth century can be seen as part of a process of turning Swedish workers into *aliens*, a separate entity that during this period also came under increasing stereotyping, with a reputation for uncivilized and criminal behavior. Swedes were troublemakers and had to be kept under extra close scrutiny by the authorities. This was a period in which the Danes in some senses focused inwards and built a new, domestic identity, after the traumatic loss of Jutland territories in the German war of 1864.

For the Swedish authorities, the main problem with Swedish–Danish border movements was not immigration but illegal emigration. The last decades of the nineteenth century saw a sharp increase in emigration, mainly to the United States, and the authorities wanted to make sure that this option was not used to escape duties such as military service, unpaid taxes, or family support. A screening of ports of embarkation was planned and there was a critique of the ways many emigrants escaped such controls by finding transatlantic passages via Denmark instead of Sweden.

In 1907, new discussions of the need for monitoring transnational movements began, but the authorities were not enthusiastic. Such a system would create an enormous administrative burden and, after all, the argument ran, wasn't the passport system something of the past, abolished half a century ago? (Samuelsson 1993, 67ff.).

Even traveling gentlemen would, however, see their freedom of movement change, as the First World War put an end to a life without passports. In Britain they were introduced in 1915, in Sweden in 1917. The new rules were a wartime emergency measure, which became institutionalized into a permanent system for monitoring not only transnational movements, but also personal identity. For cosmopolitan elites and intellectuals, this was seen as a new nuisance, as state intervention in private life. As Paul Fussell (1980, 24ff.) has noted, the new passport routines called for standardized ways of defining identity and personal characteristics. The irritation among the traveling elites had to do with their exposure to procedures that hitherto had been used for the down-and-out. The techniques of "describable individuality" (Tagg 1988, 90) had been developed for the criminals, the insane, the outcasts of late-nineteenth-century society (see the discussion in Svensson 1999). Now one was ordered to produce what looked like a mug shot and have oneself categorized in passport terms in order to travel abroad!

The passport produced new forms of modern self-reflection and identity construction. How does one describe oneself, how do the authorities squeeze a unique personality into their preprepared boxes? Does that passport photo really show a likeness of oneself? Or the more basic question: what is a likeness? (The genre of passport photos rapidly became examples of terrible unlikeness: "This awful photo is certainly not me!") The trendsetting British passport demanded not only a photo, but a list of characteristics, in terms of small, medium, and large. People now became blue-eyed or brown-eyed, blond or black-haired, of normal build, with straight or crooked noses, and fresh or ruddy complexions. A letter to the *Times* in 1915 voiced the resentment:

> Sir,
> A little light might be shed, with advantage, upon the highhanded methods of the Passport Department at the Foreign Office. On the form provided for the purpose I described my face as "intelligent." Instead of finding this characterization entered, I have received a passport on which some official utterly unknown to me has taken upon himself to call my face "oval."
> Yours very truly,
> Bassett Digby. (Quoted in Fussell 1980, 29)

People now acquired a passport identity, which later was to be reproduced in other forms—*cartes d'identité,* driving licenses, and so on. Not only could one be troubled by discrepancies of self-definition and passport images, but as a traveler one now had to live up to one's passport identity, to be able to *prove* one's identity.

This was the period when crossings became linked to new forms of anxiety: the suspicious scrutiny of passports and visas. People cross the border like a criminal under surveillance: Who are you? Is this passport photo really you? Are you quite sure you have nothing to declare?

Once people left the security of their home territory, they became *aliens* at the mercy of others. In travel narratives, a genre of border-crossing stories developed. Even as a citizen of a major power, one was now subjected to scrutiny and humiliating treatment by ridiculous officials of very minor powers, representing operetta states and banana republics!

The passport regime was part of a strong nationalization of borders. In Europe, it was heightened by the redrawing of frontiers in the Treaty of Versailles and the discussions about "natural" borders. National exits and entries became more elaborated, borders were supposed to be very visible, their passages monumental.

This production of anxiety also became a machine for focusing on national differences, which is still with us. Looking into the eyes of the customs official, we may start searching for traits of national character: "You know those rigid French officials hardly looked at our kids, but on the Italian side the customs man immediately tickled them under the chin and started joking!"

The history of border crossings illustrates the making of the nationalizing gaze, which increases with the growing emphasis on nations representing not only territories, but also national cultures and mentalities (see Löfgren 1993). People start to interpret cultural differences on both sides of the border as national, not local, regional, or class differences.

There is, of course, no unilinear development in the crafting and staging of border crossings during the twentieth century. Their forms depend on what different nations are trying to protect their borders from. What alien elements have to be kept out or what (or who) has to be kept in? In the new totalitarian regimes, borders were militarized and novel technologies of surveillance and monitoring produced. On the other side of the border, narratives of freedom often took the shape of heroic tales of escapes across the border—the genre of the Scarlet Pimpernel, people *breaking out* of their national prisons. Totally different narratives concerned those who tried to *get in*. The first half of the twentieth century saw a general sharpening of immigration laws and an increased sorting out of desirable and undesirable immigrants.

After the Second World War, border controls had to adjust to new conditions. The emergence of international mass tourism from the 1950s onwards created new categories of travel and also "the problem of the duty-free." Great energy had to be devoted to the control of petty smuggling, the search for that extra bottle of Scotch or carton of cigarettes. Smuggling duty-free became a popular game of "beating the state and its tax system," and much more energy and anxiety was channeled into this project than the actual economic gains could justify. Earning a couple of dollars could be seen as a major moral victory, but at the same time also strengthened the ties between state and citizen.

During the 1970s, increased drug traffic emerged as a more serious problem, which again resulted in new forms of policing borders and monitoring movements. Any traveler walking through the "nothing to declare" passage was a potential suspect, but some were more suspect than others. (As a student, I was often searched when commuting weekly to Copenhagen during the 1970s, until the day I decided to cut my hair and stop wearing a backpack.)

At the same time, population migrations rearranged the European social landscape. Growing numbers of migrants in search of a better life or refugees in search of security crossed, or attempted to cross, borders. New international divisions of countries with or without visa demands complicated exits and entries in the 1980s and 1990s. Drugs and what was now called "illegal immigrants" became the two main elements in the policing of borders, together with fears of international terrorism. There was often a conflation of these fears in the criminalization of border crossings. Alien substances and alien subjects became intertwined, and new control techniques, from drug-sniffing dogs to thorough body searches, changed the routines of passage.

Border controls and security surveillance are subject to sudden changes. During the 1970s, the first hijackings led to a total restructuring of airports and their security systems. In the same manner, the terrorist attacks of September 11, 2001, led to a radical redefinition of national security. It was no longer enough to monitor national borders; any domestic airport became a possible danger zone. Everyday objects such as a pair of scissors, a glass bottle, or a penknife became potential weapons as airport security guards all over the world were alerted to the new dangers.

Homecomings

"Welcome home again" was the first message that used to greet me in the arrival hall when returning by hydrofoil to Malmö and Sweden in the early 1990s. To make sure the message got across, it was stated in both Swedish and English. Some of the people lining up for the passport control, however, soon realized that this message was not to be taken literally. During these years the policing of borders was heavily increased in Sweden, as immigration laws were tightened there as well as in other European countries. A new alternative of choice (besides the red and green corridors) stated Scandinavians and non-Scandinavians. (Since 1954 there has been passport-free movement for Scandinavians inside Scandinavia.) The passport police scanned travelers for "non-Scandinavian traits." If one did not look blue-eyed and white, one was asked to step aside. Many of those Scandinavians who did not conform to such a "Scandinavian habitus" felt themselves harassed and had to carry their Scandinavian passports even for a shopping trip across the border. A black Swede realized that he or she was not Swedish enough. Since the 1990s, this selective treatment of travelers has increased; visitors from "less desired countries" may find themselves interrogated in very personal ways: What is the purpose of your visit? How long are you staying? Can you show me a return ticket? How much money are you carrying with you? Who are you going to stay with? Can you prove you have relatives here?

When illegal immigration was defined as a major problem in many Western nations, new sets of metaphors were developed to describe this development:

> a flow, a tide, a wave, an influx, a stream, a tsunami, or, after restrictions, a trickle. Immigrants are drained from their homelands. They wash up like "wretched refuse" on the shores. The country is inundated, swamped, submerged, engulfed, awash. (Christenfeld 1995, E4)

Another common metaphor is the nation as a house and the immigrant as a visitor knocking on the door or the window, standing at the threshold or in the backyard.

Welcome home again! This greeting tells us about changing conceptions of belonging and not belonging to the nation. During the twentieth century the concepts of home and homelessness became very powerful metaphors (see the discussion in Löfgren 2000; Malkki 1992; Smith 1993). As the metaphor of home is transferred to the nation, we need to ask how nations are made to look or be experienced as more homelike. How have people learned to feel at home in the nation and how has this process made others homeless? This is not only a question of a change in identity politics, but also of a slow homogenization of shared routines, habits, and frames of reference. We still lack ethnographies of this thickening of the nation into a lived everyday experience, a nationalization of trivialities (see Linde-Laursen 1993), which sometimes produces a feeling of homeyness. As a middle-aged Swedish woman put it:

> My husband and I love to go to Norway on vacation, but all the same, there is a special feeling coming back. Every time we cross the border we look at each other and sigh: Great to be back home again! We long even for the prohibitory signs.

To a non-Scandinavian, life on the Swedish or Norwegian side may look pretty much the same, but the nationalizing eye is scanning the terrain for the small differences.

Crossing the border between two very similar countries, such as Sweden and Norway, or Canada and the United States, one can still observe how differently the national (and the international) is framed on both sides of the border, although often in rather muted and unobtrusive forms. There are many tiny details, for example, that make a Swedish supermarket or post office different from a Norwegian one. Some nations have carried this homogenization of the everyday further than others, but it is not mainly a question of what and how much is shared on a national level.

Rather, the idea of the nation as homelike places it in a specific semantic universe. A home is characterized by fitting in, knowing the unwritten rules, belonging and not belonging. Who is part of the family? There are guests and hosts, and guests should learn not to outstay their welcome. Those immigrants do not really belong here, they should go home!

The crossing of borders in terms of homecomings also signals important changes in the perception of citizenship: an ethnification of national identity is involved (see Frykman 1997; Löfgren 2000). It is as a true Swede that one is welcomed home. At the same time, the construction of a national home also creates a more distinct abroad.

South of the Border

"Asia begins in Malmö!" "Keep Copenhagen clean, escort a Swede to the ferry!" These two popular pieces of Danish graffiti remind us that borderlands often are part of a national moral geography. There is a striking metaphor of north and south in many national self-representations. One's own identity is contrasted with that of others who are more southern, flamboyant, and easygoing (but less dependable) and those who are northerners, both grayer and less easygoing than one's fellow countrymen. Ideas about emotional control or lack of it seem central to these kinds of stereotypes, where north and south often stand for the cultural opposition of cold and warm (see Löfgren 1989).

During the twentieth century, Denmark took on the stereotype of the warm and bohemian south in Swedish self-representations (see Linde-Laursen 1995), whereas Danish self-representation is based on the lucky fact that the country is totally surrounded by "cultural norths," with Swedes as the Prussians of the north and the real Prussians down south. This joking relationship has also been developed by the Danish tourist industry, which once ran a campaign with the theme: "It's more fun to be a Swede in Denmark."

Seen from Malmö, Copenhagen and Denmark are "south of the border" in many respects. This cultural construction of southernness feeds on a specific characteristic of borderlands. They are often extremely productive of desire, as John Borneman has pointed out in his studies of East and West Berlin (1998, 179ff.).

Over there, across Øresund, waits a land of tempting Otherness, easygoing and fun-loving. Such fantasies are furthered by Copenhagen's position just beyond the horizon, reachable only by boat. The horizon is a great space for daydreams and desires, as Gaston Bachelard ([1958] 1994, 203ff.) has stressed.

Europe has relatively few marine borderlands like Øresund. The closest parallel is the English Channel, which has produced similar dream spaces of going south. At the gray and drab Victoria Station, the boat train for the Continent already held a promise of romance and adventure (see Fussell 1980, 15ff.). As with the Channel crossing, the short ferry trips across Øresund quite early acquired a hedonist aura. Some of the romance and rituals of the grand ocean liners (see Levenstein 1998, 125ff.) rubbed off on these more modest kinds of sea passages. The actual mode of transportation, casting away from land, sailing out into the blue, helped to produce a feeling of excitement and liberation. Even if the crossing only took one and a half hours by steamer (since the 1960s only forty-five minutes by hydrofoil), a space and time of liminality was created. From early on, this liminality was strengthened by the fact that on board one could actually *taste* the freedom. Swedes bound for Copenhagen still treat themselves to the classic ritual intake of a luxurious Danish open sandwich with shrimp and at least one bottle of Carlsberg duty-free export beer. "Go on, spoil yourself, getting there is half the fun!"

Before the bridge, the Øresund ferries provided a strange mix of passengers. Here very different rhythms and needs were confronted: Commuters on their way back from a hard day's work sat next to partying daytrippers; stressed executives worried about making their Copenhagen flight connections to New York and Tokyo, their ears glued to their cellular phones. Next to them were passengers who had refined the art of what was called *tura* (touring) in the local dialect. Most of them were senior citizens or unemployed people who went back and forth on the ferries, using them as a living room with inexpensive bar facilities. They had all the time in the world, they were not going anywhere, except back on the next returning ferry. With increased duty-free allowances between EU countries, some of them developed a profitable sideline. They bought low-priced beer and spirits in Denmark and returned with several loads every day to be sold at a profit back home.

Alcohol has long been part of the Swedish perception of the southernness of Denmark. Since the development of cheap steam connections in the latter half of the nineteenth century, Copenhagen has been a pleasure destination. This is where the Continent begins and the bright city lights are and here licensing laws are more relaxed. For thirsty or fun-loving Swedes, Copenhagen has represented a wealth of bars, entertainment, and shopping. The ferries still land in the old harbor district, which used to carry an aura of sin and sailor's fun, with bars open all night and a neighborhood that coined the phrase "roll a Swede," which meant relieving a drunk visitor of his wallet.

The experience of going "south of the border" contains other elements too. Any border crossing may provide what Jean-Didier Urbain (1998) has called "the secrets of travel," the opportunity to hide oneself or parts of one's behavior from those at home or those one encounters abroad. This "partial invisibility" and the game of make-believe are an important part of the desire for abroad. Yes, Swedes may have more fun in Denmark, trying out different behaviors—being more Swedish or less Swedish. They can disappear into the anonymity of mass travel and roam the streets of Copenhagen, sheltered by their identity as foreigners.

From a Danish point of view, Swedes too often live up to the traditional stereotypes. They drink too much and are too visible in the urban landscape. That border towns such as Copenhagen and Helsingör have been a haven for Swedish day-trippers has not improved relations between the two nations. Part of the tension about "south of the border" discourse is, of course, that my point of departure becomes someone else's north.

Even if life (or licensing laws) in Copenhagen and Malmö were (at some level) identical, the border crossing by boat would still work as a ritual of transformation, producing a readiness for Otherness, a journey into Elsewhereland. There have been laments about the bridge doing away with this romance of the sea, but other transit spaces and experiences are available. Even long before the bridge, Kastrup International Airport in Copenhagen was the hub of southern Scandinavia, where Swedes go to fly abroad.

Gateway to the World

"Someone you love will love lobster tonight." The tank with live but tired lobsters is next to the perfume area at Kastrup airport, where a young blonde woman is playing the harp, her music interrupted by loudspeaker messages: "This is a security announcement, all unattended luggage will be removed by the authorities." A flood of travelers pass between the lobsters and the harp; some of them stop for a moment, caught by the music, touched enough to get out of step. Moments earlier, they had been touched in a more robust manner, as uniformed guards let their metal detectors glide across their bodies, after X-raying their hand baggage. People step out through the passport and luggage control with a sigh of relief and feel they have been let free on international terrain. Many celebrate their vacation mood with a tax-free drink and then head off for some shopping. The world of duty-free paints a paradise outside the nation-state and the tax inspectors, but this is a very heavily policed paradise—there are more state officials and uniforms here than in any other public spaces.

People are in Kastrup for the same purpose: they are on their way to catch a flight, but their body movements show many variations. Some stroll leisurely along the shops, or have a drink or two in the business-class lounge. Others are running for their life, desperately trying to locate the departure gate. Still others are constantly checking to see if their ticket and passport are still there, nervously maneuvering in the sea of people surrounding them. The smell of perfume is mixed with that of anxiety; there is a lot of hectic travel fever in the air—an intensity that some find exhilarating and others very stressful.

What kind of place is this, a paradise of hedonistic shopping, reeking of perfume, malt whiskey, rich chocolate, and pure silk? A stress laboratory, a no-man's-land between the nation-state and the world, a surveillance machine for automated bodies, shepherded from control station to control station? As a point of entry and exit to the nation, an airport such as Kastrup has been shaped by contradictory forces over nearly a century of flying history.

"Blériot has crossed the Channel! Wars are finished: no more wars are possible! There are no longer any frontiers!" This was the message Le Corbusier heard from a colleague who stormed into his studio on July 25, 1909. The flying pioneers began to cross borders, to bridge waters. A year later, a Danish flyer was the first to cross Øresund—it took him thirty-one minutes.

Then came the Great War, which laid the foundation for the rapid development of civilian air traffic after 1918: abandoned military airfields, a surplus of planes, and out-of-work pilots. In Europe, this new traffic turned out to be transnational. On both sides of Øresund, *international* airports were built outside Copenhagen and Malmö.

Air traffic reorganized transnational travel and the rituals and practices of border crossings. A new dramaturgy, scenography, and choreography of exits and entries had to be developed, and the question was which earlier systems of transportation would provide the inspiration: transnational railways or ocean liners. The newfangled word *airport* suggests that it was the iconography of sailing that flights were modeled on. One *boarded* in the mode of the ocean liners, which in the 1920s and 1930s represented both luxury and high modernity. The flight crew took its titles and uniforms from the shipping world, and the actual rituals and aesthetics of the journey were a scaled-down emulation of the ocean crossing, with champagne and pampering by stewards (and, as of 1930, also stewardesses—the first ones trained as nurses).

Like many passenger docks and railway stations, the new airports became national monuments. The first modern one was built in 1922 in the East Prussian city of Königsberg, not in Berlin. Königsberg was the German outpost on the other side of the Polish Corridor created by the Treaty of Versailles, and for Germany this monumental airport had a logical position as a marker of national presence. From the 1930s on, airports became the focus of avant-garde architecture, ways in which nations advertised their modernity to the world. In the 1950s, airports were still sheltered gathering places for a cosmopolitan elite, but the advent of mass travel, above all through the establishment of charter flights in the late 1960s and 1970s, changed the social landscape. Airports became large-scale machines for handling great numbers of bodies. "The passenger, a mobile unit, must be controlled and guided for safety and operating efficiency, in his own interest," the official language put it (Zukowsky 1996, 51). Now the airport experience began to become very different from other borderscapes and transit spaces. In the 1970s, the new fears of hijacking and international terrorism led to an even more radical restructuring of the airport into a defense system. Airports became "the perfect field for intense control and high surveillance experimentation" (Virilio 1986, 16).

The marriage of modernist functionalism, large-scale traffic, and drastically changed security conditions created a new kind of space. For some, these new machinelike qualities and this nondescript atmosphere were a blessing. In his praise of Heathrow, J. G. Ballard writes:

> Airports, thankfully, are designed around the needs of their collaborating technologies, and seem to be almost the only form of public architecture free from the pressures of kitsch and nostalgia. . . . I welcome its transience, alienation and discontinuities, and unashamed response to the pressures of speed, disposability and the instant impulse. Here, under the flight paths of Heathrow, everything is designed for the next five minutes. (Ballard 1997, 11)

As Thomas Hylland Eriksen (1993) has pointed out, this emphasis on standardization and efficiency has turned airports into training grounds for transnational mobility. There is a lingua franca not only in signs and directions, but also in the orchestrating of movements, which makes them easy to use even for a very diverse crowd—a temporary democracy of the transit hall.

In the social sciences of the 1980s these "anyports" often became the archetypal example of a new phenomenon called "placelessness," creating a new and often one-dimensional discourse of "pseudo-places" or "non-places," nondescript, anonymous, barren territories. But this was yesterday. In the 1990s, airports started to compete as pleasure zones and sites of national welcoming. For an avant-garde architect such as Rem Koolhaas, the airport should be a concentrate of both the hyperlocal and the hyper-global (Koolhaas and Mau 1995, 1251). Airports were now being planned as "event-cities," copying the mall and even the theme park—high tech now had to be combined with high touch. The shopping galleries became longer and longer, with local attractions added, a casino in Amsterdam, Doktor Miller's World of Erotic Fantasy in Frankfurt, the Karen Blixen café in Kastrup. In these new settings, it is almost as if traveling disappears, the rush for closing gates exchanged for idling flaneurs moving through a Sensorama.

Kastrup mirrors the same historical transformations with upgraded shopping galleries, a Hans Christian Andersen theme, a wealth of local specialties and souvenirs. As the slogan in the promotional leaflet says: "Every day is national day in Denmark—celebrate with a great gift."

But the question remains to be answered: what is an airport such as Kastrup, Heathrow, Kansai? The answer still depends on what kind of traveler one is:

> I hate airports and their false cleanliness, their nostalgias, the misty eyed farewells. . . . But more especially I detest the slumped shoulders, the frightened eyes and undisguiseable sadness of the masses who congregate in its waiting rooms, its long queues; the teeming numbers who walk the plank of the slow moving conveyor track ferrying them to god-knows-what humiliation. I hate being one of these people: the men and the women with their bundles, their world and dreams contained in bags and boxes long out of fashion. Even more, I loathe the pawing fingers of the coarse young French officer at Charles De Gaulle, his rudeness and sullen manner, his angry inferiority complex.

This is the Nigerian author Okwui Enwezor (1996, 56) describing Western airports, suggesting them as a suitable parallel to the Foucauldian analysis of the prison, with the minute control and disciplining of unwanted bodies. Here one may learn what it feels like to be classified as an unwanted person, under constant scrutiny, trying to pass through the gates of fortress Europe. For millions of non-Western travelers, "the airport is a source of deep anxiety and trepidation," Enwezor concludes.

What is an airport? A very special kind of border crossing, combining the characteristics of the intimidating national fortress, a welcome wagon, a duty-free spree with an eternal cocktail hour, a gauntlet, the nonplace one never remembers or the place one never forgets. As on ferries, there is a mix of rhythms, but a different mix. This fast lane of travel produces hectic running as well as endless waiting. People may feel caged in by the claustrophobia of the waiting lounge, eyes tied to the screen messages of new delays or cancellations. There is a containment and control of movement in airports that would never be tolerated in other modes of transport. In the same way, the rational and effective smoothness of mass transportation is constantly transformed into chaos and disorder, with eating, drinking, sleeping, or waiting bodies everywhere. The transit machine may be turned into a temporary home, private life intrudes on this extremely public scene. As a passenger, one passes a Muslim couple rolling out their prayer mat right next to a basketball arcade game in Heathrow, or a group of soundly sleeping backpackers, grouped around an alarm clock in Schiphol, or one might witness the carpet traders in the transit hall of Karachi snuggling up inside their carpets as night approaches.

Millennium Mo(ve)ments: Bridging the Gap

> Welcome to Denmark. Perhaps it does not say it outright on the sign when you land at Copenhagen airport, but that's not necessary. The whole airport says it.

This is a Danish journalist at the inauguration of the new transit hall of Kastrup airport in 1998. He points out that this new welcoming scene signals the ways "we Danes see ourselves," a light and friendly country with nice inhabitants, good taste, and functional architecture. "Old welfare Denmark—a good place to be." From the airport he can see the construction of the bridge in full swing: "Beautifully designed, it will give us a land link with Asia, and in purely psychological terms we are reconquering most of southern Sweden. . . . When will Skåne become Danish again? In 2000" (Hergel 1999, 4).

The rebuilding and expansion of Kastrup as part of the millennium plans for the Øresund region aimed to turn it into what is called "a Gateway experience." The bridge spanning the Sound ends right at the airport. No more ferries and reloadings, just a smooth transnational flow from coast to coast, served by a vast new system of motorways and railroads.

In his *Travels in Portugal*, José Saramago begins his journey by stopping the car right in the middle of the border bridge, with the radiator in Portugal and the trunk in Spain. He steps out of the car and calls out to the fish swimming in the River Douro:

> What kind of language do you speak down there as you swim through your watery customs stations, and do you have to show passports and visa stamps in order to get back and forth? (Saramago 1981, 1)

He wants the fish to remind him of the dangers of just looking for differences on both sides of the river. Like the bridge spanning the Douro, the new Øresund link has had a tendency to underline the national differences rather than pointing to the similarities. Some two centuries of the nationalizing gaze have provided a useful instrument for making proper distinctions: Danish plaice and Swedish herring swim the Sound, which is lined by typically Danish beech trees and very Swedish birches; the customs officials on both sides carry distinct national mentalities under their uniforms. This kind of national optic has given flora, fauna, behaviors, people, ideas, and things specific national qualities.

As the bridge was nearing its grand millennium opening in the summer of 2000, the nationalizing discourse increased in the media, and this in a project that is really about bridging differences and creating a transnational region. There was much talk about national mentalities and character traits, examples of genuine Swedishness or Danishness. The nationalizing gaze is both an economic and a persuasive model for explaining differences, which otherwise would stand out as more complex, diffuse, or ambiguous.

The bridge, planned and discussed for more than a century, is finally there, and its future has been invested with utopian and dystopian visions. The building of this structure has been characterized as a "social experiment in transnationalism," a test surface for EU integration, a cultural laboratory. In what was called a joint "declaration of allegiance," the Danish and Swedish ministers of transport declared in 1998:

> In two years it will stand there—the Øresund Bridge. Perhaps it will symbolize the dawn of a new century, when boundaries staked out by history lose part of their significance and are replaced by coexistence, cooperation, and consensus. . . . A great deal can change when an hour on the water becomes ten minutes over the water. . . . Looking for work in another country will not be exotic but perfectly normal when we are linked together by the bridge. When an hour becomes ten minutes. . . . For us the new millennium is about building bridges and tearing down barriers. Let Øresund be an example. (Quoted in Nilsson 1999, 18)

Fifty years earlier, an American tourist had exclaimed:

> We take a train from Stockholm to Malmo. From Malmo, an aeroplane. 10
> minutes of flying over ORESUND and we are in Copenhagen. TEN MINUTES!
> (Reynolds 1928, 268)

Some have argued that such a bridge is an outdated project in the era of
cyberspace. Why is it important to invest enormous sums in order to be
able to cross in ten minutes rather than an hour—still much slower than a
phone call, an E-mail message, or a fax? Is ground transport really important in a telematic society? The magic aura of ten minutes has to do with a
long tradition of dreams about time–space compressions, but the minutes
gained on the bridge have quite another symbolic power than air travel.

While waiting for the actual bridge opening, there was a lot of cultural
bridging going on: reaching out, connecting, spanning, uniting, joining.
"Mental bridges" were being constructed in the semantics of the outreach-
ing open hand of friendship and contact. In the business community, the
region was also marketed within the other more military semantic universe of bridges: constructing bridgeheads, establishing bases for conquer-
ing new markets on the other side of the water. A tunnel cannot do the
same symbolic work, as the English Channel tunnel has already shown
(see Darian-Smith 1999).

The mental bridge building is driven by a succession of events: proclamations, meetings, conferences, get-to-know gatherings, crash courses in
intercultural understanding across the border, where local politicians,
members of the business community, university people, and administra-
tors mingle. Like most recent attempts to construct new transnational regions, the interest of most of its potential inhabitants is still lukewarm.
Here the asymmetry of the project is striking. It is the metropolitan center
of Denmark, the Copenhagen area, that is united with the more marginal
and less economically powerful southern Sweden. Although many Swedes
are enthusiastic about crossing the bridge in search of new jobs, great
shopping, culture, and the bright city lights of Copenhagen, many Danes
are less sure about taking the trip across the Sound.

The bridge makes the two nation-states visible in different ways. First,
there is a lot of bewilderment, as a project like this cuts across two national systems of politics and administration, creating openings for new kinds
of actors and combinations of interests. Second, the work to facilitate the
movement of people, goods, services, and capital across the Sound has resulted in a new awareness of the thousands of minor national differences,

which are embedded in administrative routines and public life, state regulations and legislation. This thickening of the nation-state in everyday practices has a long history, but above all it is a result of the strong homogenizing effects of the period of "welfare-state nationalism" in Denmark and Sweden after the Second World War.

Paul Virilio (1986) has asked whether the modern metropolis still has a facade, a center, a boundary. Can we still pass into it, or are we in some sense always inside? His question could be rephrased: does the nation still have a facade or are the old buildings at the Malmö harbor just relics, a set of backdrops giving a false idea of the controlled border?

New border controls have been built to guard exits and entries through the bridge, although it can be argued that the nation-state faces a much more complex landscape of boundaries today. National borders have long been seen as threatened not so much by close neighbors as by distant global and transnational forces. During most of the past century, it is American culture that lurks outside the Scandinavian borders, that must be contained, controlled, checked (O'Dell 1997). As the nature of transnational flows changes, the border landscape changes. Borders have been transgressed in new ways, throughout the history of modern nationalism, from telegraph cables to communication satellites. At different stages, new national defense technologies of policing or of screening out transnational influences have been tried, as, for example, in the media field.

Today, immigration police and custom officials on both sides of Øresund increasingly operate inside (and outside) the nation, rather than just waiting at the borders. The frontiers are mobile.

The Pedagogics of Movement

Place and space are constituted by movement, but the experience of movement can be very different (see Clifford 1997; Hannerz 1996; Urbain 1998; Van den Abbeele 1991). Moving on can be a way of staying the same. Some people move all the time, but are safely anchored in their local identities; others travel business class throughout the world and have created their own safe and secure transit spaces. The trend guru and founder of the British lifestyle magazine *Wallpaper* was asked to present his view of the future in a Swedish newspaper interview from 1999. He says:

> In communicative and cultural terms we are very mobile now. As individuals we identify more with corporations than with national borders. I am myself a citizen of both British Airways and SAS.

His view of the future is a life of two suitcases with a global booking that assures him of a bed close to any airport in the world—that is all he needs. In the next breath, he says that he has just rented a small cottage in the Swedish archipelago, which makes him wonder if this local setting is not what life is really about. This is not cultural schizophrenia, this is the way in which global elites are good at both eating and having their cultural cake. To be intensely cosmopolitan and intensely local is not a polarity, it is a great combination. Everybody should have a little red cottage in the countryside as well as standing hotel reservations all over the world.

In different periods, the notion exists that new forms of mass travel, mass migration, or mass tourism will change the world, turn locals into cosmopolitans, and break down artificial boundaries between nations, localities, classes, or generations: nineteenth-century emigration, modern-day tourism, or contemporary globe-trotting college youths will produce a more international world. But this is not always the case: today most of the young globe-trotting pioneers of the 1980s sit in their houses taking care of their families. The restlessness and mobility of youth may be just a "Sturm und Drang" stage in the life cycle, and before one accepts the idea that mobility equals cultural and social change or new identities, one has to look much closer at what people learn or experience or do not learn and experience by leaving their homes, their localities, their nations—by crossing borders.

In this essay, I have looked at the pedagogics of one specific movement, that across national borders. I have tried to show that there is a constant interrelation between the microphysics of movement, the technologies for crossing—walking or driving across, waiting in lines, taking a boat, boarding a plane—and the metaphysics of interpreting such movements in symbolic and existential terms. This fusing of motion and emotion has produced very different kinds of reactions.

The ways in which border crossings are staged today are the result of a long historical sedimentation of practices and rules, and some of them have been naturalized into givens. Once the passport, the X-ray camera, and the computerized visa system have been invented, or such problems as international terrorism, illegal entry, or smuggling have been defined, matrices and procedures might be established that are difficult "to unthink." Controls are easily frozen into necessities for the protection of the state. There is also, as I have noted, a process of conflation or slippage in which the illegalities of bodies, commodities, diseases, or ideas are merged, or, as an old Swede commented on the arrival of the bridge: "I am afraid it will bring all sorts of vermin."

The changing production and reproduction of the nation-state can be read in the transformations of the scenography, dramaturgy, and choreography of border crossings: the ways in which the borderscape is arranged against a backdrop of monumental buildings or nondescript barracks with endless corridors, warning signs, and surveillance techniques; the ways in which movements across borders are dramatized into rituals of passage, stages, and stops; and the actual choreographing of bodies and their modes of moving. In border crossings there is often a great focus on the staging of departures and arrivals, as well as on the liminalities of being betwixt and between, in transit. It is this process of intensification through various cultural techniques that gives border crossings their powerful charge.

When the state was defined as a coconut, a strong shell with a soft interior, rather than an avocado, the physicality of the border became important. A clear pedagogy of space was at work, which made the homogenization of all the stuff inside the shell easier. To this era belongs the whole dramatization of frontier crossings.

The fascination or strength of border crossings, which still exists in a world of deterritorialization and deregulation, has to do with the fact that in a world where fewer and fewer identities are based on the clear-cut pedagogy of space, the nation-state still tries to provide an absolute space: Sweden or the United States starts here! A powerful territorialization of culture and history is involved here. Few other identity projects have managed to stage this kind of representation and ritualization.

The pedagogy of space also works as a purifying process. All that is alien must be placed (and thus controlled) outside the home territory, which means that a constant process of cultural projection is at work. Border crossings help to develop certain interconnected kinds of polarities, such as familiar/alien, home/abroad, safe/dangerous, pure/impure.

At the border, the selective nationalizing gaze is scanning the terrain for alien elements, fluids, objects, individuals, influences. What must the nation be protected from—in a given situation and at a given time in history? Even more important, the actual crossing is a critical movement of identity fixation, the conflation of the national and the personal. In many ways, this is a vivid example of what Michael Taussig (1992, 111ff.; 1997) has termed "state fetishism": the magic fascination and sacred aura the state has managed to hold for its citizens.

Who am I? I am reduced to a passport carrier: I am a citizen, a *Swedish* citizen. I do belong here or I do not seem to belong and am defined as an undesired arrival. Border experiences are shaped by class and gender (see

Buijs 1993), as well as by one's position in the hierarchy of nations or eth-nicities. For immigrants and refugees, border situations may become a very strong organizing life experience. Here their position and future in the na-tion they are trying to enter are defined and their personalities judged: are they wanted or unwanted, seen as needy, trustworthy applicants or devi-ous swindlers? The same feeling strikes visitors coming from "low-ranking nations." Slavenka Draculić has described this feeling of constant humilia-tion from an Eastern European perspective. Is this person just a tourist or a visitor or is she trying to get in under false pretexts? "If you ever have been subjected to these suspicious glances, you never forget them, you can spot them at a long distance" (Draculić 1996, 21).

In psychological terms, anxiety is held-back energy. Border crossings mold and channel such anticipations, which can turn into both uneasiness and excitement, dread and desire. Through its ritual staging of such pas-sages, the nation-state gives this energy cultural form and focus.

Works Cited

Arnold, E. Lester Linden. 1877. *A Summer Holiday in Scandinavia*. London: n.p.

Bachelard, Gaston. [1958] 1994. *The Poetics of Space*. Trans. Maria Jolas. Boston: Beacon Press.

Ballard, J. G. 1997. "Going Somewhere?" *Observer Review*, September 14.

Berg, Per Olof, Anders Linde-Laursen, and Orvar Löfgren, eds. 2000. *Invoking a Trans-national Metropolis: The Making of the Øresund Region*. Lund: Studentlitteratur.

Borneman, John. 1998. "Grenzregime (Border Regime): The Wall and Its Aftermath." In *Border Identities: Nation and State at International Frontiers*, ed. Thomas M. Wilson and Hastings Donnan, 162–92. Cambridge: Cambridge University Press.

Braudel, Fernand. 1975. *The Mediterranean and the Mediterranean World in the Age of Philip II*. London: Fontana.

Buijs, Gina, ed. 1993. *Migrant Women: Crossing Boundaries and Changing Identities*. Oxford: Berg.

Christenfeld, Timothy. 1995. "Alien Expressions: Wretched Refuse Is Just the Start." *New York Times*, March 10, E4.

Clifford, James. 1997. *Routes: Travel and Translation in the Late Twentieth Century*. Cambridge: Harvard University Press.

Darian-Smith, Eve. 1999. *Bridging: The Channel Tunnel and English Legal Identity in the New Europe*. Berkeley: University of California Press.

Draculić, Slavenka. 1996. *Café Europa*. Stockholm: Pan.

Enwezor, Okwui. 1996. "In Transit." In *Interzones: A Work in Progress*, ed. Octavio Zaya and Anders Michelsen, 56–60. Copenhagen: Kunstforeningen.

Fink, Hans. 1993. "Om grænsers måder at være grænser på." *Kulturstudier* 15: 9–30.

Frykman, Jonas. 1997. "The Informalization of National Identity." *Ethnologia Europaea* 25:1: 5–16.

Fussel, Paul. 1980. *Abroad: British Literary Traveling between the Wars*. New York: New York University Press.

Hannerz, Ulf. 1996. *Transnational Connections: Culture, People, Places.* London: Routledge.

Hergel, Ole. 1999. "På det jævne." *Berlingske Tidende,* January 31, "Magasinet," 4.

Hylland Eriksen, Thomas. 1993. "Flyplassens kultur." *Samtiden* 4: 23–30.

Koolhaas, Rem, and Bruce Mau. 1995. *Small, Medium, Large, Extra-Large.* Cologne: Taschen Verlag.

Levenstein, Harvey. 1998. *Seductive Journey: American Tourists in France from Jefferson to the Jazz Age.* Chicago: University of Chicago Press.

Linde-Laursen, Anders. 1993. "The Nationalization of Trivialities: How Cleaning Becomes an Identity Marker in the Encounter of Swedes and Danes." *Ethnos* 3–4: 275–93.

———. 1995. "Det nationales natur. Studier i dansk-svenske relationer." Copenhagen: Nordisk ministerråd.

Löfgren, Orvar. 1989. "The Nationalization of Culture." *Ethnologia Europaea* 14: 1–24.

———. 2000. "The Disappearance and Return of the National: The Swedish Experience 1950–2000." In *Folklore, Heritage Politics and Ethnic Diversity: A Festschrift for Barbro Klein,* ed. Pertti J. Altonen. Botkyrka: Multicultural Centre.

Malkki, Liisa. 1992. "National Geographic: The Rooting of Peoples and the Territorialization of National Identity among Scholars and Refugees." *Cultural Anthropology* 7: 24–44.

Nilsson, Fredrik. 1999. *När en timme blir tio minuter.* Lund: Historiska media.

O'Dell, Thomas. 1997. *Culture Unbound: Americanization and the Swedish Experience.* Lund: Nordic Academic Press.

Pemble, John. 1987. *The Mediterranean Passion: Victorians and Edwardians in the South.* Oxford: Oxford University Press.

Reynolds, Bruce. 1928. *The Sweeties in Sweden.* New York: George Sully and Company.

Sahlins, Peter. 1989. *Boundaries: The Making of France and Spain in the Pyrenees.* Berkeley: University of California Press.

Saldívar, José David. 1997. *Border Matters: Remapping American Cultural Studies.* Berkeley: University of California Press.

Samuelsson, Wiwi. 1993. *Det finns gränser.* Stockholm: Utbildningsradion.

Sane, Henrik Zip. 1998a. "Da svenske invandrere blev fremmede i Danmark—nationsopbygning og lukkedhed." In *Hur en region nybildas: Öresundssymposium 1998,* ed. Erik Skärbäck, 166–70. Lund: Öresundsuniversitet.

———. 1998b. "Invandringen til Nordsjælland—Brudstykker." In *Kulturhistorisk samarbejde omkring Øresund,* ed. B. Birkbak, 21–42. Farum: Farums Arkiver og Museer.

Saramago, José. 1981. *Resa i Portugal* (translated from *Viagem a Portugal* [Lisbon: Editorial Caminho, 1981]). *Dagens Nyheter,* October 11, 1998.

Smith, Neil. 1993. "Homeless/Global: Scaling Places." In *Mapping the Futures: Local Cultures, Global Change,* ed. Jon Bird, Barry Curtis, Tim Putnam, George Robertson, and Lisa Tickner, 87–119. New York: Routledge.

Svensson, Birgitta. 1999. "Konsten att individualisera. Särskiljande metoder i fängelsets personkaraktäristik." In *Samhällets linnéaner,* ed. Bengt-Erik Eriksson and Roger Qvarsell, 46–73. Stockholm: Carlsson.

Tagg, John. 1988. *The Burden of Representation: Essays on Photographies and Histories.* London: Macmillan.

Taussig, Michael. 1992. *The Nervous System.* London: Routledge.

———. 1997. *The Magic of the State.* London: Routledge.

Urbain, Jean-Didier. 1998. *Secrets de voyage: Menteurs, imposteurs et autres voyageurs invisibles.* Paris: Essais Payot.

Van den Abbeele, Georges. 1991. *Travel as Metaphor: From Montaigne to Rousseau.* Minneapolis: University of Minnesota Press.

Virilio, Paul. 1986. "The Overexposed City." In *Zone: Fragments of a History of the Human Body,* ed. Michael Feher, Ramona Naddoff, and Nadia Tazi, 15–31. Cambridge: MIT Press.

Wilson, Thomas M., and Hastings Donnan, eds. 1998. *Border Identities: Nation and State at International Frontiers.* Cambridge: Cambridge University Press.

Zukowsky, John, ed. 1996. *Building for Air Travel: Architecture and Design for Commercial Aviation.* Chicago: Art Institute of Chicago.

Jeffrey Herf

15

Traditions of Memory and Belonging:

The Holocaust and the Germans since 1945

In the past half century, an often embattled and unpopular component of public memory in post-Nazi Germany has included the idea that belonging to a democratic Germany required facing the truth about the crimes of the Nazi past. The public interpretation of the Nazi past and its selective and divided memory played a central role in the way leaders of the two German states during the cold war thought about the issue of the nation and nationalism. Since 1989–90, the collapse of the East German government and along with it forty years of officially prescribed antifascism, followed by German unification, constitute the fundamental change affecting the way Germans in the public realm now discuss the link between memory of the Nazi past and the meaning of the nation today. As a result, the way memory connects to conceptions of the nation in postunification Germany draws on basic contours first established in the minority traditions of memory that first emerged in the early years of the Federal Republic (West Germany), and became more widespread from the 1960s to the 1980s (Herf 1997, 1999). Perhaps nowhere else have issues of memory and forgetting played such a key role in the delineation of the national self-image as in the two Germanys after 1945 and in Germany since 1989–90.

I have written a moderate revision of the conventional picture of the history of balance of memory and avoidance in the two Germanys since the war. My work on divided memory revises but does not overturn the view of the postwar period. On the whole, the most common public attitude toward the crimes of the Nazi past was silence, avoidance, premature amnesty, and delayed and denied justice. But in the midst of this familiar pattern, a distinctive, albeit minority, tradition of memory did emerge in West Germany at the same time that an official memory of the Nazi era played a key role in the politically dominant idea of the nation in East Germany. I pose two questions regarding this period. First, why, given the extent of support for Nazism within German society followed by postwar revelations of the scale of Nazi atrocities, would there be any public memory of the Holocaust in postwar Germany at all? Second, why did the memory of the Holocaust, against many initial expectations, emerge more in West Germany than it did in the self-described antifascist German Democratic Republic (GDR)?

The two necessary preconditions for the emergence of a tradition of public memory of the Holocaust after 1945 in the two Germanys were established by other nations, that is, by the unconditional and unambiguous military victory over Nazi Germany on the battlefield, the subsequent destruction of the German government, and then the postwar occupation, including the full revelations of Nazi criminality at the Nuremberg and successor trials. Allied victory and postwar occupation prevented a revival of Nazism as a major political factor. It also made possible what I have called "multiple restorations" of anti-Nazi German traditions that had been defeated and repressed in 1933, namely Communism, Social Democracy, a chastened liberalism and moderate conservatism. In the founding generation of postwar German politicians, postwar memory emerged from those who had come of age in pre-Hitler Germany.[1] In part, the West German tradition of memory and national identity would appear to be an example of "postnationality" to the extent that it represented an effort to define the nation by integrating it into broader, supranational structures. Yet the founding generation of political leaders also drew on previously defeated traditions of the German past to evoke a different, or, as the famous phrase went, "other Germany."

Konrad Adenauer (1876–1967), the leader of the postwar Christian Democracy and chancellor of the Federal Republic of Germany from 1949 to 1963, had been mayor of Cologne from 1917 to 1933. Kurt Schumacher (1895–1952), the leader of the postwar Social Democracy, served as a member of the Reichstag in the Weimar Republic. Theodor Heuss (1884–1963), the first president of the Federal Republic, worked as a journalist, was a professor of politics, and was active in liberal politics in the Weimar years as well. Ernst Reuter (1889–1953), the mayor of West Berlin during the crucial early years of the cold war, had been a Social Democratic politician in Weimar; after being held prisoner in a Nazi concentration camp, he went into political exile in Ankara, Turkey. The Communist leadership in East Germany also came of political age before 1933 and drew on an intact German political tradition. Walter Ulbricht (1893–1973), the effective head of the East German government, was born in 1893. Otto Grotewohl (1894–1964), cochair of the Socialist Unity Party (SED), and Wilhelm Pieck (1876–1960), a comrade and friend of Rosa Luxemburg and first president of the German Democratic Republic, were born in 1894 and 1876, respectively. Paul Merker (1894–1969), a leading figure of the German Communist Party since 1920, whose unsuccessful efforts to raise the Jewish question in East Berlin led to his political downfall in 1950, was also born in 1894.

More than any other figure, founding Chancellor Konrad Adenauer shaped West German policy toward the Nazi past. Although not a member of the anti-Nazi resistance, he opposed the Nazis and had been briefly imprisoned by the Gestapo. His wife's early death after the war at the age of fifty-seven stemmed from her two suicide attempts as a result of her despair over having divulged information about his whereabouts in a Gestapo interrogation. Adenauer believed that Nazism was the result of deep ills in German history and society: above all, Prussian authoritarianism; the weakness of individualism; the "materialist worldview of Marxism," which eroded religious faith and fostered nihilism; and an ideology of racial superiority that filled the vacuum left by the erosion of the dignity of all human beings grounded in Christian natural right. For Adenauer, a political leader of the Catholic Zentrum party of the Weimar era, the antidote to these ills was democracy resting on the basis of Christian natural right, and the belief in the dignity and value of every individual that flowed from it. However, Adenauer did not examine the role of Christianity in the history of European anti-Semitism.

Adenauer's pessimism about the breadth and depth of Nazism within German history and society did not lead him to adopt the pose of the avenging angel. Rather, his view of the depth of Nazi support led him to pursue a strategy of democratization by integrating former, and hopefully disillusioned, followers of Nazism, or of pursuing power by de-emphasizing memory of the crimes of the Nazi era. As early as spring and summer 1946, when the main Nuremberg Trial was still going on and thousands of suspects had yet to be charged, Adenauer repeatedly told audiences in his election speeches in the British zone of occupation that "we finally [*endlich*] should leave in peace the followers, those who did not oppress others, who did not enrich themselves, and who broke no laws" (Adenauer 1975, 92). For Adenauer, liberal democracy in post-Nazi Germany could not be established against the will of the majority. More accurately, he did not want to risk offending the will of crucial minorities who could make the difference between electoral victory and defeat. Equating the fortunes of the Christian Democratic Union (CDU) with the fate of democracy per se, Adenauer's strategy gave a de facto veto against aggressive postwar judicial procedures to the West German "amnesty lobby" of the 1950s. As a result, the more sovereign the young Federal Republic became, the more justice was delayed and denied.[2] The converse of premature amnesty and public forgetting was that those who stood under a cloud of suspicion for their beliefs and actions during the Nazi era could attain membership or a sense of belonging in the emerging Federal Republic.

Within these limits, Adenauer supported restitution payments to Jewish survivors and to the state of Israel. He publicly declared his willingness to do so in the Bundestag in September 1951, and pushed the restitution agreement through in the face of considerable opposition within his own party. On the other hand, he also restored pension rights to former members of the Wehrmacht and the Nazi regime and spoke of the honor of soldiers who had served in the German army in World War II. In his contact with American High Commissioner John J. McCloy, he pleaded for amnesty and leniency toward those who had already been convicted of crimes by the Allies in the occupation period (Schwartz 1991). He gave much higher priority to integrating ex-Nazi Germans and giving them a sense of belonging in the new Federal Republic than to supporting trials for crimes committed during the Nazi era. When Theodor Adorno, in 1959, said that repression of the Nazi past was far less the product of unconscious processes or deficient memory than it was "the product of an all too wide awake consciousness," he captured the actual practice of the Adenauer years. "In the house of the hangman," he continued, "it is best not to talk about the rope" (Adorno 1977, 558). In the Adenauer era, those who won national elections in the Federal Republic and had a democratic mandate opposed a vigorous program of justice for past crimes and supported a program of premature and undeserved amnesty. This tension between justice and early democratization is a major theme of postwar West German history, as it is of the transition from dictatorship to democracy in general. Although a different path to democratization, one that included a sharp confrontation with the past, was conceivable, implementing greater democracy with an electorate that included crucial voting blocs opposed to putting the past on trial and with the backing of Western allies who reduced pressure to bring ex-Nazis to trial meant attaining less justice.[3]

Along with these deficits regarding memory and justice, Adenauer— ironically for a conservative politician—brought about a fundamental break with past German nationalism. Adenauer, the Westernizer, argued that Germany's future must lie in a break with the disgraced traditions of anti-Western German conservatism. While the more tradition-laden Social Democrats toyed with notions of neutrality in the 1950s, Adenauer argued that the community to which the West Germans must belong was that of "the West" rather than the Prussian path of statism and authoritarianism. The West, for Adenauer, meant the traditions of individual rights, democratic government and the rule of law, NATO, the Common Market, and the integration of the Federal Republic into supranational, Atlanticist, and pan-West European institutions. The preeminence of this pro-Western conservatism, a product both of the delegitimation of its anti-Western and illiberal predecessors and of the division of the country, was a novelty in modern German history. As the political landscape shifted and Adenauer moved from the periphery to the center of German conservatism, remaining true to his Rhineland, Francophile convictions of the 1920s, he created the only truly new political tradition of the first postwar era: a conservatism that focused on individual rights rather than the glory of the state and that abandoned the anticapitalist and antibourgeois ethos of his conservative predecessors.

Within this larger context of forgetting, a minority tradition emerged rooted in Social Democratic and chastened liberal traditions. The inaugurators of the distinctive West German tradition of public memory of the Holocaust included the first Bundespräsident, the liberal Theodor Heuss; the leader of the Social Democratic Party (SPD), Kurt Schumacher; and two Social Democratic leaders, Ernst Reuter, the mayor of West Berlin in the early postwar years, and Carlo Schmid, a parliamentary leader of the SPD in Bonn.

From May 6, 1945, two days before the Nazi surrender, until his death at the age of fifty-seven on August 20, 1952, Kurt Schumacher urged his fellow Germans to confront the Nazi past, including the mass murder of European Jewry. Among postwar German political leaders, he was the first to emphatically support restitution to the Jewish survivors of the Holocaust, and to urge close and warm relations with the new state of Israel. A democratic socialist, Schumacher believed that overcoming the Nazi past meant breaking with German capitalism. Yet, his Marxism notwithstanding,

Schumacher stressed that Nazism had been more than a plot by a small group of capitalists and Nazi leaders, that it had had a mass base of support, that the Germans had fought for Hitler to the bitter end, and that the Nazi regime had been destroyed only as a result of Allied weapons. He believed that as a result of the Social Democrats' consistent opposition to the Nazis, they had earned the right to lead the nation. He spoke in the name of a still intact German tradition of Social Democracy and thus of a Germany whose own indigenous national cultural and political traditions formed a foundation for a new and different Germany.

In speaking in the name of "the other Germany," he rejected the idea of collective guilt. He did so because such accusations neglected the anti-Nazi resistance and the history of the democratic left, while also helping those who had committed crimes to escape justice, for if all were guilty, no one was responsible or could be held accountable. Yet Schumacher was blunt in his criticism of German passivity in the face of Nazi criminality. In 1945, he said that the Germans knew what was taking place in their midst. They "saw with their own eyes with what common bestiality the Nazis tortured, robbed, and hunted the Jews. Not only did they remain silent, but they would have preferred that Germany had won the Second World War, thus guaranteeing them peace and quiet and also a small profit." They had believed in dictatorship and violence, and thus were occupied by others after 1945. "This political insight," he said was "the precondition for a spiritual-intellectual and moral repentance and change" (Schumacher 1985, 217). In his postwar speeches, Schumacher supported removal of former Nazis from positions of power and influence, continuation of war-crimes trials, payment of financial restitution to Jews, and honesty about the Nazi past. In the election of 1949, the West Germans opted instead for Adenauer's very different view of the relationship between democratization and the Nazi past.

The distinctive West German governmental tradition of remembering the crimes of the Nazi past began as an elite tradition that sounded a soft dissonant note in the larger West German silence. It was inaugurated by Theodor Heuss, the first occupant of the honorific position of Bundespräsident of the Federal Republic. He used the office of president, and its insulation from the electoral struggle for political power, to publicly remember the crimes of the Nazi era, and to define the office as a repository of the nation's conscience and memory. To his critics, he was the cultured veneer of the Adenauer restoration, and an advocate of eloquent memory separated from politically consequential justice. Yet, in speeches about German history, extensive private correspondence with Jewish survivors, resistance veterans, and West German and foreign intellectuals, Heuss began an elite tradition of political recollection that would eventually contribute to broader public discussion and action. He could have done much more. Others in his position would have done much less.

Heuss delivered his most important speech regarding the Nazi past at memorial ceremonies held at the former Nazi concentration camp at Bergen-Belsen on November 29–30, 1952. Officials of the Federal Republic, many governments, and representatives of Jewish organizations gathered to dedicate a memorial to those persecuted at Bergen-Belsen. The ceremonies were a decidedly Western event that reflected the realities of the cold war and divided memory. Attending were government representatives from Britain, the United States, Denmark, Belgium, the Netherlands, Switzerland, Sweden, France, Yugoslavia, Israel, and the Jewish communities in Germany, Europe, and the United States. None of the Communist states were represented.

Nahum Goldmann spoke on behalf of the World Jewish Congress (Heuss 1952, 1655–56; 1965, 224–30). He described the destruction of European Jewry in detail and recalled "the millions who found their tragic end in Auschwitz, Treblinka, Dachau, and in Warsaw, and Vilna and Bialistock and in countless other places" (Goldmann 1952, 1–2). In this very Western ceremony at the height of the cold war, Goldmann drew attention to the *Eastern geography* of the Holocaust's killing fields and death camps. In so doing, he implicitly pointed out that the geography of memory did not coincide with the fault lines or the political priorities of the cold war in the West. The Holocaust had largely taken place in a part of Europe that, during the cold war, was "behind the Iron Curtain." Goldmann's recounting of the Holocaust inevitably called to mind German aggression on the eastern front during World War II, an invasion that eventually led to the presence of the Red Army in the center of Europe in May 1945. This was an uncomfortable and inconvenient recollection of causality when Western memory of World War II often gave short shrift to the attack on "Jewish Bolshevism" on the eastern front. To be sure, there were efforts to separate the memory of the Holocaust from memory of the attack on the Soviet Union, but on the whole it did not fit well into the discourse of the cold war.

Heuss's speech at Bergen-Belsen, "No one will lift this shame from us" ("Diese Scham nimmt uns niemand ab!"), was the most extensive statement to date of national West German reflection on the mass murder of European Jewry. It was broadcast on radio, and was the subject of reports in the West German press, especially the liberal press (Heuss 1952;

Frankfurter Rundschau 1952). Heuss took issue with those who sought to avoid the crimes of the Nazi past by pointing to alleged misdeeds of others:

> It seems to me that the tariffs of virtue [*Tugendtarif*] with which the peoples rig themselves out is a corrupting and banal affair. . . . Violence and injustice are not things for which one should or may resort to reciprocal compensation. . . . Every people has in reserve its poets of revenge or, when they get tired, its calculated publicists. (Ibid.)

"No one will lift this shame from us" is a key document of the liberal redefinition of the link between the memory and the meaning of postwar patriotism. Heuss evoked a patriotism self-confident enough to honestly face an evil past rather than seek to balance the past crimes by pointing to Communist misdeeds. He placed the language of patriotism, honor, and courage in the service of memory rather than of avoidance and resentment. For Heuss, the moral imperative to remember the past was not a burden imposed by the occupiers and victors but a legacy passed on by German history. Thus, by 1953, public memory of the Holocaust had become a part of official West German political culture. In the Heussian tradition, most importantly continued in Richard von Weizsacker's speech of May 8, 1985, in the Bundestag on the fortieth anniversary of the end of World War II, those who belonged to the nation's previously defeated but morally and politically superior traditions carried a moral obligation to speak the truth publicly about the Nazi past. Far from paralyzing the nation, as some conservative critics were later to argue, Heuss believed that clear and truthful public memory was indispensable for the emergence of a different and better Germany.[4]

Between 1950 and 1953, Ernst Reuter delivered several addresses commemorating in turn the July 20, 1944, conspiracy, the Jewish pogrom of November 1938, and the Warsaw ghetto revolt. On April 19, 1953, at a memorial on the tenth anniversary of the destruction of the Warsaw ghetto, he delivered his most impassioned statement regarding the genocide of European Jewry. It remains one of the most moving and powerful statements of its kind in postwar German political culture:

> Ten years ago today, on April 19, 1943, following Hitler's orders, the attack on the Warsaw ghetto began. Its goal was, as totalitarian discourse put it, liquidation of the ghetto. And then something began in the history of these awful years that indeed are behind us, but still today burden our souls as a nightmare. It was something that the world had not seen before: Hitler's victims rebelled. They stood together. They fought to their last breath.

They defended their lives. But by sacrificing their lives to the last person, they defended more than a short span of their lives. They defended their honor. They defended their rights. They defended everything that is sacred to every one of us in this room: the right of every human being to be free, free to live and free to raise his head to the heavens. . . .

We live in a time that is inclined to forget all too quickly. But in this hour we want to say that there are things that we are not permitted to forget, and that we do not want to forget: as Germans—I speak to you here as well as to my Jewish fellow countrymen as a German—we must not and we cannot forget the disgrace and shame that took place in our German name. (Reuter 1973–75, 714)

In the same speech, Reuter dramatically underscored his solidarity with Hitler's Jewish victims. That solidarity, as the following statements make clear, came from both moral and political convictions and from his personal experience of imprisonment in 1933–34:

Until the end of my life, I will never forget the scream in the night, the scream of my comrade who had been beaten to death. And because I will never forget it, I, along with all of the others who experienced these things, swore the following: we must dedicate our whole life to the task of making this impossible for all time. We cannot again allow individuals and peoples, races and religious confessions to attack one another. (Ibid., 716)

Proximity to events and personal memories drove him to future political action. This personal sense of loss is evident in much of the minority tradition of postwar memory. Its advocates, such as Heuss and Reuter, recall a Germany, the Germany of their youth, which the Nazis destroyed, which could not be replaced, and whose loss had impoverished their own lives. Reuter, recalling his former teacher, the German Jewish professor of philosophy Hermann Cohen, said he knew "what the Jewish component in our people meant" and that Jewish and German traditions had been more intensely intertwined "than in any other country" (ibid., 718–19). German youth after the war knew nothing of this past. They had to be taught German history, not only its music and literature, but also about the role the Jews played in the "whole intellectual structure of our people" and the intersection of the German and Jewish people and traditions (ibid., 719–21). Like Schumacher and Heuss, Reuter recalled the wound and loss that Germany had suffered as a result of the mass murder of the Jews. Faced with these crimes and tragedies, his political engagement drew far less on the confident Marxism of his radical youth than on the memory of past injustice and cruelty. He criticized the self-pity and sense of victimization that he found widespread among postwar Germans. Instead, he argued that memory of what the Germans had done to others was essential for construction of a postwar democracy. In this sense, he and his like-minded colleagues were postnationalist figures who refused, in contrast to the Nazi and nationalist ideologues of the German and European past, to foster a sense of national belonging based on embittered memory of past suffering, real and imagined.

From the earliest moments, postwar political memory included efforts to balance and weigh the relative suffering and victimization of different groups, including the Germans themselves, and even to blur the distinctions between perpetrators and victims (see Herf 2000; Moeller 2001; Reichel 1995). Carlo Schmid, the leader of the Social Democratic parliamentary faction in Bonn, made a number of critical responses to such endeavors. He was a leading voice in favor of restitution payments to Jewish survivors (Schmid 1973). In the Federal Republic, no less than in the GDR, the issue of restitution required making determinations about who was, and who was not a victim of National Socialism, who among these victims had suffered most, and who had a moral claim to restitution. The restitution (*Wiedergutmachung*) debates entailed making distinctions among the kinds and extent of suffering during the Nazi era. In the February 1951 Bundestag restitution debates, Schmid argued against an undifferentiated view of past suffering:

> Certainly, there are many victims of the Third Reich. One could say that almost all of those who survived the period are victims. But one shouldn't make this all too easy and forget that there are distinctions among them. People are beginning to forget. Indeed, things are getting to the point where even former SS and SD [Sicherheitsdienst or Security Service] men are beginning to regard themselves as victims of National Socialism . . . (rumbling among the SPD) . . . and those who were given a negative classification by the de-Nazification counsels are already beginning to consider themselves to be victims of National Socialism! (Schmid 1951, 4592; 1966, 52)

He warned against forgetting who had been "the really special victims of National Socialism" (Schmid 1966, 52). Generalizing the victim category went hand in hand with obscuring the special features of the extermination of the Jewish people:

> Among all that the Nazi regime brought about, the crimes committed against Jewish fellow human beings were the most awful, not only because

of the extent of the murder, not only because it was a matter of millions of victims, not only because of the methodical mercilessness of the gassing in Auschwitz and Maidanek, not only because these acts of butchery also fell on women and children, but also because the whole Third Reich at its base, at its core, was set up to exterminate the Jews! (vigorous applause) The Third Reich was integrated very much more around anti-Semitism than around, one is ashamed to use the term, "pro-German" sentiment. (Ibid., 53)

In other words, Nazi Germany established a sense of belonging to the nation in part through a radical differentiation against the Jewish other.[5] Schmid rejected an apolitical remorse for past victims that made no distinctions between perpetrators and victims. Such a stance was not a sign of higher morality. Rather, it represented an enduring failure to think clearly about politics and morality, or about the nature of the Nazi regime. In contrast to those who wished to place the Holocaust on the fringes of the Nazi era, Schmid insisted that it was at the core of what the Nazi regime was about, and that Germans understood this to be so at the time. Hence, to equate all victims was both morally unacceptable and historically inaccurate. It rested on a distorted and apologetic understanding of the Nazi regime.

Heuss, Reuter, and Schmid spoke for an articulate liberal and left-of-center minority. The period of the 1950s in the Federal Republic remained, on the whole, one of public silence, judicial delay, avoidance, and an unseemly reintegration of those who had compromised Nazi pasts. Yet the public assertions of this minority were the beginnings of a tradition of public memory amid this broader silence, one that has received too little recognition. Public memory of the crimes of the Nazi past expanded with the political and generational conflicts of the 1960s, but it did not begin then. The liberals and Social Democrats in the founding generation of the 1940s and 1950s merit more attention than they have received until recently. While proximity to events for millions of their fellow citizens evoked silence and avoidance, in their case that same proximity and their memories of a German-Jewish Germany that the Nazis destroyed spurred them on to defining a new West Germany as one in which memory of past crime found a public forum. The recognition of these contributions constitutes a necessary, if moderate, revision of the view of postwar memory. Their implicit, and at times explicit, message was that *all* Germans, no matter what they did during the Nazi era, stood in the continuities of German history, the good and the evil ones. Thus, although not all Germans should be accused of collective guilt, all belonged in the nation and had a responsibility to face the truth about its history. In this view, which was to assume greater importance over time, citizenship in the Federal Republic of Germany included the responsibility to speak truthfully about the crimes of the Nazi era committed against the Jews and others.

Contrary to initial expectations, the meaning of belonging in anti-fascist East Germany entailed a much lighter burden regarding memory of the Nazi Holocaust than it did in West Germany. Antifascism did encompass the burden of discussing the fascist past but official "antifascism" developed a large blind spot concerning public memory of the mass murder of European Jewry. During the Weimar period and the Nazi era, the "Jewish question" remained on the margins of German Communist public discourse. This was not surprising in light of elements of anti-Semitism in the Marxist tradition, Stalin's denial of Jewish nationality in his canonical text on the national question, and the Communist view of Nazism primarily as a dictatorial form of capitalism directed mainly against the working classes. However, the Nazi attack on "Jewish Bolshevism" and the Holocaust itself led some German Communists, and European Communists in general, to argue that this previous marginalization should be ended and that Communist sympathy for the oppressed should be extended to persecuted Jewry. Moreover, and very importantly, during World War II, many Communists—both in the Soviet Union and in Western emigration—nurtured hopes that shared experience of persecution and struggle on the eastern front in World War II would lead to a turn away from Communist orthodoxy regarding Jewish matters. Yet, after 1945, and especially after 1948, the power of the dominant traditions of German and European Communist orthodoxy were reinforced by the shifting power and political interests of the Soviet Union. The result was the repression of the memory of the Holocaust for the entire postwar period and the end of those hopes for a Communist–Jewish rapprochement that had flickered during the war and the Holocaust.[6]

The dominant German Communist views found a home in Moscow during the war and were expressed immediately after the war, in Walter Ulbricht's canonical *Die Legende vom Deutschen Sozialismus* (The legend of German socialism) (Ulbricht 1945). Ulbricht stressed the memory of Soviet suffering, heroism, redemption, and victory but marginalized the memory of the Jewish catastrophe. The wartime radio addresses and propaganda efforts of the German Communist exiles in wartime Moscow also shed important and intriguing insights into the connection between memory and dictatorship. Spokesmen of the National Committee for a Free Germany such as Wilhelm Pieck (along with Ulbricht the leading figure of the German Communist exile in Moscow) and the writer Erich Weinert, urged German soldiers and citizens to turn against the Nazi political leaders and generals. As these repeated and increasingly desperate pleas failed to result in a German revolution against Nazism, a tone of bitterness and rage against the German people became unmistakable in the exiles' statements (Herf 1997, 13–39).

For these returning exiles, memory of the Nazi past and its crimes, and of the absence of an anti-Nazi German revolt, reinforced their already powerful Communist suspicions of liberal democracy. As one can see from their "Appeal to the German People" in June of 1945, their memory of the past included memory of their past rejection by the "millions and millions" of Germans who voted for Hitler, cheered his diplomatic successes, supported his war, and failed to offer notable resistance to the regime. Despite public declarations of support for a democratic, antifascist government in the early postwar months and years, their texts contain abundant evidence of fear and distrust of their fellow Germans. The more these Communists remembered their own past persecution by the Nazi regime, its popular support in German society, and its attack on the homeland of revolution, the more they were inclined to impose another dictatorship on this dangerous people. The texts of the returning refugees suggested that they were in, but not fully of, the German nation, sentiments that make their subsequent nationalism appear all the more bizarre.

It is important to keep in mind that in the postwar years, or what I call the Nuremberg interregnum between World War II and the cold war, the issue of how to interpret the Nazi era and where the Jewish catastrophe would fit into Communist memory and policy was a subject of debate in East Berlin. In this period, a minority of German Communists led by Paul Merker and Leo Zuckermann, both of whom had fled to Mexican exile during the Nazi era, sought to place the Holocaust at the center of Communist memory. In the course of what was called "the anticosmopolitan campaign" of 1949–53, which reached its high point in the winter of 1952–53, these Communists who advocated positions favorable to Holocaust survivors and to the emerging state of Israel were driven out of their political positions, arrested, and convicted in secret trials.

The central accusation hurled at Merker and others was that they were part of an international conspiracy of American imperialists, Zionists, and Jewish monopoly capitalists working to subvert Communism from within. The anticosmopolitan campaign ended hopes for continuation of wartime solidarity between Communists and Jews. Instead, the East German, Soviet, and other East European governments placed the Jewish catastrophe on the margins of Communist antifascist memory and of the antifascist East German nation. Remarkably, less than a decade after the Holocaust, a post-Nazi German government, using Marxist-Leninist terminology, repeated anti-Semitic accusations about a rootless, international, capitalist, and hence antinational conspiracy of Jews, thus reviving what had been a staple of European anti-Semitism. Astonishingly, the antifascist government made it clear, in the winter of 1952–53, that the great "other" of modern German history, the Jews, again did not belong in the nation's memory or politics. The East Germans defined themselves as the only true antifascists and as the representatives of the nation now struggling fiercely against the antinational, subversive forces of Western imperialism. The Jews, as Jews, did not belong in this public memory and its discourse (Herf 1997, 13–39).

From its earliest days, the East German government organized annual days of remembrance for "victims of fascism." The aura surrounding these ceremonies was less one of tragic mourning than of militant memory of Communist heroism. The memory of Jewish persecution found at first little—and, over time, no—place. Center stage was devoted to celebration of a glorious and victorious history of "antifascist resistance fighters" and then to placing the legacy of this past struggle in the service of the cold war. Two speeches delivered at the dedication ceremonies of national memorials at the former Nazi concentration camps in Buchenwald and Sachsenhausen expressed the essence of the links between the idea of the nation and East German antifascism, and in so doing articulated an idea of who belonged within the heroic community of antifascist recollection.

In planning documents for the memorial in Buchenwald, Otto Grotewohl, the East German president, wrote that the memorials' most important goal was "to place the shame and disgrace of the past before the young generation so that they can draw lessons from it" (Grotewohl 1958b). Yet they must also "indicate the path toward the future . . . give expression to the will for life and struggle which developed among the prisoners" in their "resistance to Nazi barbarism." They should combine remembrance of the past and warning for the present and the future, while demonstrating that the resistance legacy was alive in the policies of East German antifascism (ibid.). Although the memorials would show the suffering of the victims, "above all, they bear witness to the indefatigable strength of the antifascist resistance fighter" and should be "towering signs of victory over fascism" (ibid., 96). In other words, the memorials were Hegelian moments set in stone, intended to encourage optimism about the future based on memory of past heroism, rather than a reflection of unredeemable past tragedy and catastrophe.

The pictures of the dedication ceremony on September 14, 1958, as well as a committee planning statement for the ceremony, convey Grotewohl's intended meaning. For the "honor of the dead" and for the "sake of the living," memory admonished "all of us" to action. "German militarism" was "again a major danger for peace in Europe," threatening the "security and independence of peoples. Again the militaristic and fascist gang in West Germany presents new aggression against the peace-loving peoples" (Grotewohl 1958a). The statement denounced West German plans to introduce atomic weapons and missiles into the hands of "fascist murderers" and "old Nazi generals." The committee planning the Buchenwald dedication demanded an immediate halt to nuclear weapons tests, the creation of a nuclear weapons–free zone in Central Europe, negotiations for disarmament and détente, and peace (ibid.). The commemoration at Buchenwald was meant to focus attention on present-day politics and to lend the moral prestige of Communist martyrdom to East German foreign policy. As East Germany continued the legacy of the victims in Buchenwald, dissent from that policy was not only a political error; it was also a desecration of their sacred memory. The clear message of the memorials was that East Germany was the successor to the antifascist resistance fighters, whereas West Germany was the successor to the fascists and Nazis (Grotewohl 1964, 7–8). Fighting the cold war was *Vergangenheitsbewältigung*, that is, the way to come to terms with the Nazi past. Yet on this and other occasions, Grotewohl both neglected to mention the persecution of the Jews and expressed East German support for the Arabs in the Middle East conflict.

The most important commemorative event in the history of the German Democratic Republic took place on the occasion of the dedication of the memorial to victims of fascism in Sachsenhausen on April 24, 1961. An estimated two hundred thousand people from East Germany and from twenty-three foreign countries attended. Now-familiar slogans appeared on banners held aloft in the crowd. Walter Ulbricht delivered a classic political funeral oration that connected the national past to the East German present and future:

> With deepest respect we turn to our precious dead, the fighters against war, fascism, and militarism, and to the victims of Nazi terror. This place is dedicated to memory [*Erinnerung*] and warning [*Mahnung*]: to the memory of countless martyrs and heroes of the antifascist resistance struggle and to

warning coming generations never again to allow fascist barbarism to break out among our own people, or among other peoples. Every foot of this earth is soaked with the blood and sweat of ten thousand martyrs from many countries, and of many different worldviews. They were driven and tortured to death, and murdered only because they loved their people, because they loved freedom, peace, and democracy more than their own life, because they were socialists, because they rejected hatred among peoples, and rejected genocide, and because they dedicated their lives to humanism and to friendship among peoples. (Ulbricht 1961)

Neither torture nor terror was able to break the fighters' spirit. The history of the resistance "under inhuman conditions of a factory for the extermination of human beings in Sachsenhausen" was "a painful but honorable chapter of the heroic history" of antifascist struggle by German Communists and other antifascists. Inside and outside the concentration camps and torture chambers, "people of diverse beliefs fought together with unheard of sacrifices against the blood-soaked Hitler regime. *In so doing, they saved the future of the German nation*" (ibid.). Ulbricht then recalled the thousands of Communists, Social Democrats, Soviet prisoners of war, and citizens of Poland, Luxembourg, Yugoslavia, Holland, Belgium, Denmark, Austria, Hungary, Czechoslovakia, and France, as well as British prisoners of war, who had been murdered in Sachsenhausen. Ulbricht did not mention that Jews were killed in Sachsenhausen, or anywhere else. This was so both because the Holocaust did not fit into the narrative of suffering and heroic redemption told in Sachsenhausen and because the East German government linked the Jews, in ways eerily reminiscent of earlier German nationalism, to powerful, international, Western forces threatening Germany.

To be sure, there was some truth in what Ulbricht had to say. There were "martyrs and heroes" who were murdered "only" because of their political convictions and activities. Many died heroic deaths "in struggle" against fascism. Yet the untruths in his statement were even more important. In Sachsenhausen and other concentration camps, the Jews were not murdered because of their political actions or beliefs, but simply because they were Jews. Yet Ulbricht clearly privileged "our precious dead," that minority of Nazism's victims that was composed of political opponents as well as the members of the nations of Europe, especially Eastern Europe and the Soviet Union.

Ulbricht's 1961 Sachsenhausen address was less about mourning past losses than it was a plea for secular redemption for the dead. "Comrades and friends," he continued, "died together in Sachsenhausen so that we, together, could complete their work and secure freedom, democracy, and peace for humanity" (ibid.). After the speeches, political dignitaries led a march out of the memorial. The photo of that march is the defining image of East German memory of the Nazi era. It shows Walter Ulbricht leading the SED leadership out of the memorial in Sachsenhausen. Behind him is the smokestack of the concentration camp, and a crowd of people. Otto Grotewohl, Rosa Thälmann, and other members of the politburo are among those walking next to Ulbricht. On either side, East German soldiers stand at attention. Ulbricht is waving the politician's wave of victory. The photo could be captioned "Communism rises like a phoenix from the ashes of defeat." It was the supremely Hegelian moment, a moment of historical triumph and identification with the past heroes and victors rather than with history's tragic and unredeemed victims. It was a defining moment of the nation in East Germany, establishing that those who belonged were those who fit within the boundaries of antifascist commemoration. The Jews and their memories were outsiders again.

The public controversies in West Germany from the 1960s to 1989 surrounding national identity and the memory of the Holocaust were the topic of considerable discussion. These controversies included parliamentary debates over continued prosecution of Nazi war crimes in the 1960s; the internal leftist debate of the 1970s over anti-Zionism and anti-Semitism; Willy Brandt's bended knee at the Warsaw ghetto memorial in 1970; and the *Historikersstreit* in the 1980s followed by the Bitburg dispute and Richard von Weizsacker's speech on May 8, 1985. The central point I would make about them, and about the emergence of neo-Nazi violence against Jews and refugees in postunification Germany, is that none of the challenges from right or left have managed to displace the tradition within the political establishment of memory of the Holocaust that began in the 1950s and became far more widespread during the 1960s. The rejection of German memory of the Holocaust inherent in East German antifascism collapsed in 1989–90. Indeed, the first act of the first freely elected parliament in eastern Germany was to express regret for forty years of neglect of the Holocaust in the official discourse of antifascism.

In unified Germany, a euphoric and triumphalist nationalism of the right sought, again, to "finally" put the memory of the Holocaust to rest. It too failed, even in the Helmut Kohl era. West German Chancellor Helmut Kohl, who insisted that President Ronald Reagan visit a graveyard in Bitburg, West Germany, in which members of the Waffen SS were buried, turned out in the 1990s to be an heir to both Adenauer and Heuss, surprising his Bitburg critics with his support for a memorial to the murdered Jews of Europe in Berlin. Although in its early months the Gerhard Schröder government, the first German government of 1968ers, indicated a desire to leave the past behind, look to the future, and not build the Berlin monument, this too gave way in the face of criticism. Moreover, the Schröder government succeeded, in the face of considerable conservative opposition, in reforming Germany's citizenship laws so that the legal obstacles to belonging based on ethnic considerations would be displaced. The always criticized and discomforting tradition of coming to terms with the past scored a victory with the decision of the German parliament in 1999 to proceed with construction of the Berlin Holocaust memorial in the same decade in which neo-Nazis and skinheads carried out hundreds of violent attacks on foreigners or those thought to be foreigners and Jews. On the other hand, the distinctive postwar West German, and then German, tradition of memory of the Holocaust continued to make an important contribution to a more inclusive view of the nation, one with a more universalist conception of belonging than, of course either its Nazi predecessor or its antifascist antagonist, the German Democratic Republic. From Schumacher and Heuss on to those who supported construction of the Holocaust memorial in Berlin, the German advocates of honestly facing the crimes of the Nazi past made the historically unusual case that facing the truth about an evil past was an unavoidable and necessary aspect of belonging to the continuities of German history after the Holocaust. Neither fleeing from this past to postnational, European identity nor seeking to revive now-discredited national traditions were viable options. Instead, and contrary to initial expectations, the memory of the Holocaust became an important element in the development of a Germany with increasingly democratic and inclusive notions of belonging and citizenship.

Notes

1 In the immediate postwar years in the west, a reversal of political coordinates concerning the nation occurred. In the nineteenth and twentieth centuries, German nationalism was, on the whole, most deeply rooted on the political right. After 1945, insofar as we are discussing major rather than fringe phenomena, those most comfortable even using the word *nation* were universally on the left, in both its Social Democratic and Communist variants. The nation to which they belonged was "das andere Deutschland" (the other Germany). I have explored this reversal and the emergence of a Western-oriented conservatism in *War by Other Means: Soviet Power, West German Resistance and the Battle of the Euromissiles* (1999).
2 Two important works by German historians have documented the extent to which

the crimes of the Nazi era were forgotten in the early years of the Federal Republic of Germany (see Frei 1996 and Herbert 1996).

3 The argument that public silence and the avoidance of trials for war crimes and crimes against humanity in the 1950s were a precondition for successful democratization goes beyond the evidence by assuming that democratization could not have taken place with an extensive program of trials. The fact that the Federal Republic emerged as a stable democracy does not mean that the failures of justice in its early years made a positive contribution to that outcome or that a different path to democratization was not both conceivable and possible.

4 Many veterans' organizations remained unconvinced and their members, as well as Germans expelled from Eastern Europe in the last phase of the war and in the postwar years, focused on their own "victimization" and attacked advocates of public memory (see Moeller 2001).

5 This is a common theme in the historiography of Nazism. For a classic early analysis of the establishment of belonging to the German nation through differentiation from the Jews, see Mosse 1964.

6 The history of the suppression of the "Jewish question" in East Germany is a chapter in a large story of the "anticosmopolitan purge" throughout the Soviet bloc rooted in policies initiated in Moscow. From the extensive literature, see, among recent works, the discussion in Herf 1997, as well as Vaksberg 1994 and Rubenstein and Naumov 2001.

Works Cited

Adenauer, Konrad. 1975. "Grundsatzrede des 1. Vorsitzenden der Christlich-Demokratishen Union für die Britische Zone in der Aula der Kölner Universität." In Konrad Adenauer: Reden, 1917–1967: Eine Auswahl, 82–107. Stuttgart: Deutsche Verlagsanstalt.

Adorno, Theodor. 1977. "Was bedeutet Aufarbeitung der Vergangenheit." In Theodor Adorno: Gesammelte Schriften, 10:2: 555–72. Frankfurt am Main: Suhrkamp Verlag.

Frankfurter Rundschau. 1952. "Heuss weiht Mahnmal in Belsen ein: Der Bundespräsident gedenkt der Opfer des ehemaligen Kz." December 1, 1.

Frei, Norbert. 1996. Vergangenheitspolitik: Die Anfänge der Bundesrepublik und die NS-Vergangenheit. Munich: C. H. Beck.

Goldmann, Nahum. 1952. "Speech at Bergen-Belsen, November 30, 1952." In Nachlass Theodor Heuss B122 2082, 1–2. Bundesarchiv Koblenz.

Grotewohl, Otto. 1958a. "Aufruf des Komitees für die Einweihung der Mahn- und Gedenkstätte Buchenwald." SAPMO-BA, ZPA NL [Foundation for the Archive of the GDR's Parties and Mass Organizations in the Bundesarchive, Berlin] 90/553: 46.

———. 1958b. "Mahn- und Gedenkstätte Buchenwald." In SAPMO-BA, ZPA NL 90/553 (January 13): 96.

———. 1964. "Buchenwald mahnt! Rede zur Weihe der nationalen Mahn- und Gedenkstätte Buchenwald, 14 September 1958." In Otto Grotewohl, Im Kampf um die Einige Deutsche Demokratische Republik: Reden und Aufsätze, vol. 6, Auswahl aus den Jahren 1958–1960. [East] Berlin: Dietz Verlag.

Herbert, Ulrich. 1996. *Best: Biographische Studien über Radikalismus, Weltanschauung und Vernunft, 1903–1980*. Bonn: J. H. W. Dietz.

Herf, Jeffrey. 1997. *Divided Memory: The Nazi Past in the Two Germanys*. Cambridge: Harvard University Press.

———. 1999. *War by Other Means: Soviet Power, West German Resistance and the Battle of the Euromissiles*. New York: Free Press.

———. 2000. "Abstraction, Specificity and the Holocaust: Recent Disputes over Memory in Germany." *German Historical Institute Bulletin* 22:2 (November): 20–35.

Heuss, Theodor. 1952. "Diese Scham nimmt uns niemand ab! Der Bundespräsident sprach bei der Weihe des Mahnmals in Bergen-Belsen." In *Bulletin des Presse- und Informationsamtes der Bundesregierung* 189 (December 1): 1655–56.

———. 1965. *Der Grossen Reden: Der Staatsmann*. Tübingen: Rainer Wunderlich Verlag.

Moeller, Robert G. 2001. *War Stories: The Search for a Usable Past in the Federal Republic of Germany*. Berkeley and Los Angeles: University of California Press.

Mosse, George L. 1964. *The Crisis of German Ideology*. New York: Grosset and Dunlap.

Reichel, Peter. 1995. *Politik mit der Erinnerung: Gedächtnisorte im Streit um die nationalsozialistische Vergangenheit*. Munich: Hanser Verlag.

Reuter, Ernst. 1973–75. "Ansprache auf der Gedenkfeier des Bezirksamtes Neukölln am 10. Jahrestag der Vernichtung des Warschauer Ghettos am 19. April 1953." In *Ernst Reuter: Schriften, Reden* 4:714–21. Berlin: Propylaen Verlag.

Rubenstein, Joshua, and V. P. Naumov, eds. 2001. *Stalin's Secret Pogrom: The Postwar Inquisition of the Jewish Anti-Fascist Committee*. New Haven: Yale University Press.

Schmid, Carlo. 1951. *Deutscher Bundestag, Stenographische Bericht* 6:4592, 120 Sitzung (February 22). Reprinted as "Zur Wiedergutmachung." In *Bundestagsreden*. Bonn: AZ Studio, 1966.

———. 1966. "Zur Wiedergutmachung." In *Bundestagsreden*, 52–55. Bonn: AZ Studio.

———. 1973. "Wir Deutschen und die Juden." In *Politik als Geistige Aufgabe*, 282–300. Bern, Munich, and Vienna: Scherz.

Schumacher, Kurt. 1985. "Wir verzweifeln nicht." In *Kurt Schumacher: Reden-Schriften-Korrespondenz, 1945–1952*, ed. Willy Albrecht, 203–36. Berlin: J. H. W. Dietz.

Schwartz, Thomas. 1991. *America's Germany: John J. McCloy and the Federal Republic of Germany*. Cambridge: Harvard University Press.

Ulbricht, Walter. 1945. *Die Legende vom Deutschen Sozialismus*. [East] Berlin: Dietz Verlag.

———. 1961. "Von der DDR wird stets der Frieden ausstrahlen: Rede des Genossen Ulbricht, Walter." *Neues Deutschland*, April 24, 1, 3.

Vaksberg, Arkady. 1994. *Stalin against the Jews*. Trans. Antonina W. Bouis. New York: Knopf.

Contributors

SEYLA BENHABIB is distinguished chair in political science and philosophy at Yale University; she was previously professor of government at Harvard University and senior research fellow at the Center for European Studies. She is the author of *Critique, Norm, and Utopia: A Study of the Foundations of Critical Theory; Situating the Self: Gender, Community, and Postmodernism in Contemporary Ethics;* and *The Reluctant Modernism of Hannah Arendt.* She is the editor of *Democracy and Difference: Contesting the Boundaries of the Political.*

JOHN A. HALL is professor of sociology at McGill University. He has published widely in historical sociology and in social theory. Among his books are *Powers and Liberties; International Orders; Liberalism;* and *Civil Society.* He is currently completing an intellectual biography of Ernest Gellner.

ULF HANNERZ is professor of social anthropology at Stockholm University; he has also taught at several American, European, and Australian universities. He is a member of the Royal Swedish Academy of Sciences and the American Academy of Arts and Sciences, and a former chair of the European Association of Social Anthropologists. His research has focused on urban anthropology, media anthropology, and transnational cultural processes. Among his books are *Soulside, Exploring the City, Cultural Complexity,* and *Transnational Connections;* several of these have also appeared in French, Spanish, and Italian. He is anthropology editor for the new *International Encyclopedia of the Social and Behavioral Sciences.*

ULF HEDETOFT is professor of international studies at Aalborg University, Denmark, and founding director of AMID (the Academy for Migration Studies in Denmark). Previously, he was director of SPIRIT (School for Postgraduate Interdisciplinary Research on Interculturalism and Transnationality) at Aalborg University. Among his books are *British Colonialism and Modern Identity; Signs of Nations: Studies in the Political Semiotics of Self and Other in Contemporary European Nationalism; Political Symbols, Symbolic Politics: European Identities in Transformation* (editor); and *The Politics of Multiple Belonging* (forthcoming).

JEFFREY HERF is professor of history at the University of Maryland in College Park, where he teaches modern European and German political and intellectual history. His books include *Divided Memory: The Nazi Past in the Two Germanys* and *Reactionary Modernism: Technology, Culture, and Politics in Weimar and the Third Reich*.

MICHAEL HERZFELD is professor of anthropology at Harvard University and the former editor of *American Ethnologist*. He has written numerous books and articles that deal principally with modern Greek society and culture, the ethnographic dimensions of nationalism and bureaucracy, the history and social context of anthropology, and the analysis of social practice and meaning. His book *Anthropology through the Looking-Glass: Critical Ethnography in the Margins of Europe* was awarded the Rivers Memorial Medal by the Royal Anthropological Institute in London.

METTE HJORT is associate professor of comparative literature and film at the University of Hong Kong and senior lecturer in intercultural studies at Aalborg University, Denmark. She previously taught at McGill University in Canada, where she was director of cultural studies. She is the author of *The Strategy of Letters* and the coauthor (with Ib Bondebjerg) of *The Danish Directors: Dialogues on a Contemporary National Cinema*. She has also edited or coedited *Rules and Conventions, Emotion and the Arts*, and *Cinema and Nation*.

RICHARD JENKINS is professor of sociology at the University of Sheffield. He has undertaken research in Belfast, the English West Midlands, South Wales, and Denmark, and his current areas of interest include social identity theory, European societies, ethnicity and nationalism, and the cultural construction of competence and disability. He is the author of, among other books, *Pierre Bourdieu, Social Identity, Rethinking Ethnicity*, and *Questions of Competence*.

MARK JUERGENSMEYER is professor of sociology and director of global and international studies at the University of California, Santa Barbara. He is the author or editor of twelve books, including *Terror in the Mind of God: The Global Rise of Religious Violence* and *The New Cold War? Religious Nationalism Confronts the Secular State,* which were cited as notable books by the *New York Times,* the *Washington Post,* and the *Los Angeles Times.*

RIVA KASTORYANO is senior researcher at CNRS (National Center for Scientific Research), associated with CERI (Center of Research in International Studies). She also teaches at the Institute for Political Studies in Paris. She is the author of *Être Turc en France: Réflexions sur familles et communauté* and *La France, l'Allemagne et leurs immigrés: Négocier l'identité,* and the editor of *Quelle identité pour l'Europe? Le multiculturalisme à l'épreuve.*

MICHÈLE LAMONT is professor of sociology at Princeton University. A cultural sociologist, she has written widely on issues of cultural membership, evaluation, and community, focusing on boundary-drawing processes. Her books include *The Dignity of Working Men: Morality and the Boundaries of Race, Class, and Immigration; Rethinking Comparative Cultural Sociology: Repertoires of Evaluation in France and the United States* (with Laurent Thévenot); *The Cultural Territories of Race: Black and White Boundaries; Money, Morals, and Manners: The Culture of the French and the American Upper-Middle Class;* and *Cultivating Differences: Symbolic Boundaries and the Making of Inequality* (with Marcel Fournier).

BENJAMIN LEE teaches anthropology at Rice University and is codirector, with Dilip Gaonkar, of the Center for Transcultural Studies in Chicago. He is also codirector of the Center for the Study of Globalization and Culture at the University of Hong Kong. He and Dilip Gaonkar are co-editors of the Public Worlds series at the University of Minnesota Press.

ORVAR LÖFGREN is professor of European ethnology at the University of Lund in Sweden. He is currently working on an interdisciplinary project on transnational regions. His latest books are *On Holiday: A History of Vacationing* and *Invoking a Transnational Metropolis: The Making of the Øresund Region* (coedited with Per Olof Berg and Anders Linde-Laursen).

PHILIP SCHLESINGER is professor of film and media studies at the University of Stirling, Scotland, and director of the Stirling Media Research Institute. He is the author of *Media, State, and Nation* and *Open Scotland?,* and he is an editor of the journal *Media, Culture and Society.*

YASEMIN NUHOĞLU SOYSAL is a senior lecturer in sociology at the University of Essex. She is the author of *Limits of Citizenship: Migrants and Postnational Membership in Europe*. Her current projects concern the changing basis and forms of collective identity and claims-making in Europe, and postwar reconfigurations of nation-state identities as projected in secondary school history and civics textbooks.

RAY TARAS is professor of political science at Tulane University; he has also taught at universities in Canada, England, and Poland. His publications include *National Identities and Ethnic Minorities in Eastern Europe*.

JAMES TULLY is professor and chair of political science at the University of Victoria, British Columbia, Canada. He is the author of *Strange Multiplicity: Constitutionalism in an Age of Diversity*.

Index

Appiah, Kwame Anthony, 231
Arabs, 144, 289
Arendt, Hannah, 86, 109, 150n1, 154, 156
Argyrou, Vassos, 202
Aristotle, 96
Armstrong, Neil, 78
Aron, Raymond, 58
Asian economic crisis (1997), 64, 246
Assimilation, xiii, xxxin1, 159, 161, 164;
   history of, 121; institutional, 125; refus-
   ing, 182, 188, 190; social membership
   and, 183
Associations, 125, 194n24; belonging to,
   126, 152; civil, 233; multinational, 156;
   nation-states and, 103; participation in,
   124. *See also* Political associations
Asylum, 90, 107; policies, 93, 94, 113n11;
   seeking, 92, 111n1, 111–12n3
Asylum seekers, 91, 111nn1, 2; accepting,
   115n16; borders and, 88; standards of
   living and, 108; treatment of, 115n16
Atlantic Alliance, 29
Atlanticists, 279
Audi alteram partem, 156, 167, 172
Aum Shinrikyo, 8, 12
Auschwitz, 281, 285
Ausländische Mitbürger, 130
Aussiedler, 111n2, 129
Authoritarianism, 277, 279
Avoidance: memory and, 276

Bachelard, Gaston, 261
Backlash states, 28
Bailyn, Bernard, 54
Bakhtin, Mikhail: metalinguistics of, 239
Balkans, 20, 23, 28, 199; belonging in,
   202; stereotypes about, 200–201
Ballard, J. G.: on Heathrow, 264
Bank of America, 246
Barber, Benjamin, 7, 53
Barclay Brothers: European Press Holdings
   of, 46
Battaglia, Debbora, 223
Baubock, Rainer, 95, 132
Bauman, Zygmunt: on tourists/vagabonds,
   74
BBC, 47, 48, 59

Beck, Ulrich, 229, 248
Begriff, 238, 244
Belonging, 76, 100, 111n2, 152; border
   crossings and, 251; citizenship and,
   138; collective guilt and, 285–86; concept of, ix, xv, xx, 87, 102, 139, 259;
   cultural, xi, xxv; cultural diversity and,
   152–53; democratic freedom and,
   153–59; disputation and, 164–70; freedom and, 153–57, 171–75; global, xv,
   xvi, xviii, xix; home as, x–xv; imaginary
   of, 153, 159; meanings/images/contexts
   of, vii–x; memories of, viii; multiple,
   134; national, x, xiii, xix, 55, 284; not
   belonging and, 260; participation and,
   174; postnationality and, xv–xx; problem of, 157–59, 252; recognition and,
   174; reimagining, 53, 152–53, 174;
   sense of, xxvii, 25, 59, 153, 171, 278;
   transatlantic, 53, 61, 64
Benhabib, Seyla: on citizenship, xxiv
Bergen-Belsen: memorial ceremonies at,
   281–82
Berger, Sandy, 28
Beurs, 183, 193n12
Bharatiya Janata Party (BJP), 13
Bialistock, 281
Bin Laden, Osama, 4, 10, 11, 14, 27
Bipolarity: nationalism and, 19–23
Bismarck, Otto von, 148
Bitburg, 291
Biterritorialization, xxviii, 220, 221, 223,
   225, 227
BJP. *See* Bharatiya Janata Party
Black, Conrad, 56
Blackness: Frenchness and, 185; racism
   and, 179, 184, 185
Blacks: boundaries against, 184, 188, 189;
   French workers and, 193–94n17
Boer War, 55, 56
Bojinka Plot, 11
Borden, Sir Frederick, 55–56
Border crossings: airports and, 266; mi-
   gration and, 254; practices of, 251, 254,
   257, 258; recalling, 230, 253–55, 256,
   259, 260, 271–72
Borderlands, 251, 252, 261

Communicative space, 37, 39; EU, 43–44, 49–50; Euro-polity and, 40–44

Communism, 78, 88, 291; Holocaust and, 286; Nazi past and, 287; public memory and, 276, 290; Zionists and, 287

Communist Manifesto, The, 78

Communities, 87, 127, 180, 198; cultural, 122, 125; epistemic, 68, 76; ethnic, xiv, xviii; global, 69; identity-based, xxv; imagined, xviii, 179, 191n2, 235, 237; international, 24–25; national, xxv, 125, 146, 181; political, xii, 96, 105, 122, 123, 132, 157; prepolitical, xiii, xiv; religious, 102; transnational, 135

Concentration camps, 277, 288

Confederation of 1867, 55

Conflicts, resolving, 20, 222

Congress for Cultural Freedom, 57

Connaught, Duke of, 55

Conservatism, anti-Western, 279

Consistory, 128

Constitutional democracies: participation in, 158, 165

Constitutionalism, 109, 154, 165; free people and, 157

Consumerism, 74, 79, 130, 212

Convention relating to the Status of Refugees, 109

Copenhagen, 257, 262, 268; airport at, 263; Swedes in, 260, 261, 262

Corporations, 67, 73, 75; as global family, 76, 79; subsidiaries, 72

Corsicans, 21, 199

Cosmopolis, 227–31

Cosmopolitanism, xiii, xvii, 76, 231n2, 255, 270; aesthetic, xxix, 229; bases of, 227, 228; experiential, 229, 230, 231; globalization and, 86; patriotism versus, 230; political, 228, 229, 230

Council of Europe, 90, 140, 142

Council of Ministers, 36, 40, 41; *European Voice* and, 46

Couroucli, Maria, 212

Cowan, Jane, 211

Cox, Robert W.: on transnational managerial class, 69

Crimes against humanity, 110

Crisis of Parliamentary Democracy, The (Schmitt), 108

Crossman, Richard, 57

Cuban-Americans: out-marriage by, 62

Cultural change, 270

Cultural clash, global, 11–12

Cultural community, 122, 125

Cultural convergence, 70, 121, 128

Cultural diversity, 158, 162–63, 170, 172, 228, 229; belonging and, 152–53; citizenship and, 132; fragmentation and, 175; recognition of, 153, 164, 173

Cultural formation, 228, 235

Cultural fundamentalism, xxviii, 200, 202

Cultural power: exercising/resisting, 70

Cultural rights, 130

Cultural Turn, The (Jameson), 248

Culture, xii, xiii, 7, 9; dialogue of, 234; Euro-political, 49; globalization of, 6, 8, 69; national, 60; political, 38, 282; politics and, 122, 132, 134; popular, 6, 182; transnational, xxix, 14, 69; world, 78

Custom officials, 269

Dachau, 281

Daily Telegraph, 56

Danes, 253, 255; Swedes and, 260, 261, 262, 267

Das Handelsblatt, 45

Das Reichs- und Staatsbürgerschaftgesetz, 100

Debray, Régis, 182

Decolonization, 7, 23, 148, 185

Democracy, 165, 284; cosmopolitan, 231n3; parliamentary, 38; reinvention of, 233

Democratic Convention (1968), 74

Democratic legitimacy, 154, 155, 165

Democratization: in Germany, 278–79, 280; war crimes trials and, 293n3

Demos, 153

Derivatives, 246, 247, 248

Der Spiegel, 45

Deterritorialization, xxviii, 220, 231, 271

Deutsch, Karl: on communicative complementarity, 37

Diamandouros, P. Nikiforos: on underdogs/reformers, 207–8

Home, 221, 225; as belonging, x–xv; biterritorialization/multiterritorialization and, 227; concept of, 218–20, 259; generalized version of, 218; immigrants and, 260; leaving, 222; meanings/images/contexts of, vii–x; migrants and, 223, 224; national, 260; returning, 228; separation from, 224; temporary, 266; too little, 222–23

Homecomings, 258–60

Homelessness, 259

Homeness, vii, xix, 222, 223; conditions for, xv; deficit, xxviii

Homeyness, 252, 259

Homogeneity, xv, 4, 60, 70; cultural, xii, xiii, 37, 69, 229; national, ix, xiii, xxiii; nationalizing, 62; sociocultural, 67

Hudson's Bay Company, 55, 71

Human rights, xxvi, 85–86, 89, 105, 144, 146–47, 228, 234; citizenship and, 141; codification of, 140; commitment to, 87; discourses of, 148; fundamental, 107, 109–10; moral principles of, 109; Muslims and, 140; nation-states and, 108–10; naturalization and, 101; perplexities of, 86; personhood and, 142, 143; respect for, 94; self-determination and, 86; universal, xxv, 86, 170; violation of, 107, 108; women and, 145

Huntington, Samuel, 11, 24, 199, 200, 231

Hussein, Saddam, 27

Identification, 71, 160, 180, 240; globalization of, 69; multiple, 134; nation and, 135; political, 134

Identities: alien, 158, 161; alternative, 183; changing, 148, 173, 228; citizen, 126, 127, 156–57, 158, 161, 162; citizenship, 120–23, 124, 125, 132, 134, 148, 149, 155; civic, 92; collective, 35, 78, 79, 94–96, 103, 125, 128, 129, 140, 141, 142, 147, 182, 240; consumption and, 79; corporate, 77–78; cultural, xvi, 104, 158, 169, 172; defining, 159, 161, 180, 255; discourse of, 142; dissolution of, 39, 161, 168; diverse, 163, 170; do-

mestic, 4, 255; dominant, 161, 168; dynamics/distribution of, 139; ethnic, xxvi, 4, 27, 62, 128, 138, 142, 172; exclusion and, 143; expression of, 131; globalization and, xxiv, 15–16; habitual, 172–73; imposed, 161–62; linguistic, 172; Muslim, 15, 22, 140, 144; national, 8, 124, 128, 131, 142, 152, 155, 156, 158, 162, 165, 172, 175, 198, 202–3, 291; negotiated, xvii, 160, 161; new forms of, 236, 270; occupational, 75, 77–78, 80; overlapping, 159, 164, 166–67; passports and, 255–56; political, 38, 49, 53, 102, 124–25, 158, 165; practical, 160, 162, 168, 170, 172; prejudices against, 168; recognition of, 161, 162, 168, 169, 170; religious, 4, 128, 172; rights and, 122, 141–43; shared, 58, 143, 166; spaces and, 218; territoriality and, 133; transatlantic, xxiii, 57, 59, 61, 62, 64; transnational, xxiii, 13, 54; understanding, 169, 170, 236

Identity politics, 149, 174; changes in, 259; characteristics of, 159–64, 172; negotiations and, 162, 164, 166, 167; "we, the people" and, 240

Ideology, 242, 284; globalization of, 4, 6

Ideoscapes, 237

Ignatieff, Michael, 24, 25, 56

Imagination: circulation and, 237–38; lived experience and, 221–22

Imagined communities, xviii, 179, 191n2, 235, 237

Immigrant groups, 125; citizenship and, 101; claims by, 146; mobilization of, 146; social/cultural attributes of, 99; voting rights and, 146

Immigrants, 272; allegiance of, 134; assimilation of, 188; black African, 185; borders and, 88; boundaries and, 179, 184, 189–90, 193n12; citizenship and, 95, 183; experience of, 149; home and, 260; illegal, 107, 116n18, 258; investment projects and, 130; Muslim, 181, 189; naturalization for, 103, 114n14; negative attitudes toward, 189; noncitizen, 142; non-European, 181, 182;

MEPs. *See* Members of European Parliament

Merker, Paul, 277, 287

Mernissi, Fatima, 23

Metalanguage, 238, 239

Middlemass, Keith, 49

Migration: border crossings and, 254; in Germany, 91; home and, 223, 224; labor, 255; mass, 270; Muslim African, 185; population, 257–58; television and, 227; transnationalization and, 95

Milosevic, Slobodan, xxviii, 30, 32

Minima Moralia (Adorno), 137

Minorities, 278; assimilation of, 164; attitudes toward, 184; cultural, 152; ethnic, 22, 129–30; linguistic, 164; national, 129, 131; official, 98; racism and, 130; recognition and, 159, 174; rights of, 152, 163, 168

Mirror Group Newspapers: *The European* and, 46

Mission civilisatrice, 183

MNCs. *See* Multinational corporations

Mobility, x, 264

Mobilization, 126, 128, 133, 135, 144, 146–47

Modernity, 64, 72, 198, 208–9, 263; barriers to, 203; European, 201; foreign, 210; religious, 208; secular, 9; technological/ethical, 211; term, 202; Western notion of, 204

Modernity at Large (Appadurai), 237

Mogadishu line, 27

Money, Morals, and Manners (Lamont), 180

Morality, 16, 27, 108, 120, 179

Morgan Bankers Trust, 246

Mountbatten, Lord, 56

Movement, 95, 269–70; freedom of, 255; place and, 269

Movements: local, 14–15; religious, 4; social, 102, 234; transnational, 255; workers', xxiv

Moynihan, Daniel Patrick, 21

MTV, 9

Muenz, Rainer: on German population, 90

Mugabe, Robert, 32

Muhammad, 3

Multiculturalism, xiii, xvi–xvii, xxiii, 38, 60, 61

Multicultural societies, 7, 14, 38

Multilogues, 167

Multinational corporations (MNCs), 63, 67, 71; origins of, 72; TNCs and, 73

Multinationality, 68, 70, 134, 163

Multipeoples polities, 163

Multiterritorialization, 220, 221, 227, 231

Murdoch, Rupert, 68

Muslim Brotherhood, 11

Muslims, 143, 163, 169, 174, 266; Bosnian, 91; citizenship and, 145–46; discrimination against, 144, 183; in Europe, 145; in France, 179, 181, 183–84; in Germany, 91; mobilization of, 146–47; religious society and, 12; Sunni, 12. *See also* Islam

Mutual respect, 156, 162–63, 170–71

NAFTA. *See* North American Free Trade Agreement

Nagorno-Karabakh, 22, 29

Nairn, Tom: on nationalism, 19

Napoleon, 55, 128

Nasser, Gamal Abdel, 7

National: transnational and, 149

National Advisory Council of Ethnic Minorities, 98

National Committee for a Free Germany, 286

National Federation of Protestant Churches, 128

National identity, xvi, xix, 32, 57; globalization and, xxiii; nationalist identity and, 54; political/prepolitical components of, xx; resurgence of, 3

Nationalism, 26, 32, 54, 58, 149, 153, 237–38, 242, 275, 287; American thinking about, 25; analysis of, 16n1, 239; anti-immigrant, 21; bipolarity and, xxi, 19–23; borders and, 269; civic, xi, xv, xvi, xxix, xxxin5, 229–30; debates over, 18, 229; ethnic, xvi, 3, 7, 8–12, 13, 15, 229; ethnoreligious, xxi, 3, 9; European history and, 53; globalization and,

Socialism, 78, 186; Orthodoxy and, 207
Socialist Unity Party (SED), 277
Socialization, political, 125, 134
Social membership, xvii, 186, 188; assimilation and, 183
Social reality, 128, 242
Social rights, 112n6, 123, 130, 143; claims to, 98; collective identity and, 94–95; described, 97–98
Social welfare, 97–98, 185, 186
Solidarity, xxvii; French cultures of, 181–86; natural, 199–200
Sovereignty, xxii, 32, 107; diffusion of, 141; exercising, 106, 110; nation-states and, 108–10; perplexities of, 86
Soviet Union, 222; collapse of, 19, 20, 233
Soysal, Yasemin Nuhoglu, xxv–xxvi, 98, 123, 132
Space: audiovisual, 42; bounded, 251; civic, 146; communicative, 37, 39, 40–44, 49–50; identities and, 171, 218; movement and, 269; pedagogy of, 251, 271; political, xxii, 24, 42, 46; public, 41–42, 124, 147, 263; social, 219; transit, 264; transnational, 134
SPD. *See* Social Democratic Party
Sphere of publics, 37, 49
Spheres of influence, 20
Staatsangehörigkeit, 129
Staatsbürger, 131
Staatsbürgerschaft, 129
Stalin, Joseph, 207
Standards of living, 107–8
Stateless nation, 39
States, 127; civil society and, 114n13, 132; collapse of, 64; EU and, 135; nations and, 134; participation and, 131; postwar European, 139–41
Steinherr, Alfred: on financial risks, 247
Stereotyping, 169–70, 185, 210, 255, 262; Balkan, 200–201; Danish-Swedish, 260; regimentation and, 211
Stewart, Charles: hegemony and, 209
Stolcke, Verena: on cultural feminism, 199
Strange Multiplicity: Constitutionalism in an Age of Diversity (Tully), xxvi

Struggles, 159–64, 175n5
Subjectivity, 236, 239, 242; capital and, 246, 248; civil society and, 248; nationalist, 240–41
Subjects: citizens and, 157
Summer Holiday in Scandinavia, A (Arnold), 253
Sutton, Donald E., 202
Swart, Warrant Officer, 219, 220, 231
Swedes, 255, 258; border crossings and, 254; Danes and, 260, 261, 262, 267
Symbolic, 207, 208

Taguieff, Pierre-André, 183
Taliban, 13, 31, 115n15
Tampere Council Resolutions, 94, 111
Tariffs, 63; of virtue, 282
Taussig, Michael: state fetishism and, 271
Taylor, Charles, 234, 235, 236
Technology, 44; circulation of, 237; information, 72, 235, 243; integration in, 85; media, 227; redistribution and, 225–27; relationships and, 226–27
Technoscapes, 237
Television, 74, 225, 226; EU, 43, 44, 47; migrants and, 227
Territoriality, 100, 133, 271
Terrorism, 9, 11, 21, 114–15n15; fears of, 258; religious/ethnic, 15; threat of, 31, 258, 270; war on, 18, 30
Thales, 246
Thalmann, Rosa, 291
Thatcher, Margaret, 64n1, 107
Theodicy, 206–7, 208
Third World, 4, 85, 251
Thomas Cook's, 71
Thompson, Frank, 35, 186
"Ties That Fray, The" (Walt), 58–59
Tijuana: as laboratory of the postmodern, 251
Time, Labor, and Social Darwinism (Postone), 244
TNCs. *See* Transnational corporations
Tourism, 61, 71, 74, 102, 218; boundaries and, 270; Danish, 260–61; emergence of, 257, 270; integration in, 85
Tourists: vagabonds and, 74

Toyota Motor Manufacturing North
America (TMMNA), 76–77
Tradition, xviii, 202, 204; invented, 149;
Jewish/German, 283, 285; symbolic
and, 208
Transnational, 6, 54, 68, 70–71, 76, 132,
139; core/periphery and, 74; global and,
75; migration and, 95; national and,
149; shallowness of, 229; social experiment in, 267
Transnational corporations (TNCs), xxiii,
63, 70–75; activities of, 71, 73–74, 80;
global identities and, 68, 80; marketplace
and, 79; MNCs and, 73; modernity and,
80; nominal nationality of, 67; origins of,
72; practices of, 79; science and, 76
Transportation, 71; chaos/disorder of,
266; technological changes in, 225
Travel, 263; air, 268; mass, 264, 270
Travels in Portugal (Saramago), 266–67
Treadmill effect, 244, 245
Treaty of Amsterdam (1997), 111; citi-
zenship/naturalization laws and, 93; im-
migration/asylum and, 94
Treaty of Rome, 109
Treaty of Versailles, 256, 264
Treaty on European Union (1991), 41
Treblinka, 281
Trobrianders: yams and, 223, 224
Trudeau, Pierre, 56
Tully, James, xxvi, 56
Turabi, Hassan, 11
Turks, 21, 140, 144, 147; civil society
and, 130; dual citizenship and, 129; in
France, 145; in Germany, 91; Kurds
and, 22, 111n3
Turner Diaries, The, 14

Ulbricht, Walter, 277, 286;
Sachsenhausen oration by, 289–91
Underdogs: reformers and, 207–8
Unemployment, 181, 185, 187–88
Unequals: equals and, 108
UNESCO, 140, 142
Unfreedom, 169
UNHCR. *See* United Nations High
Commissioner on Refugees

UNICE. *See* Union of Industries in the
European Community
Unification: family, 114n14; German, 88,
92, 275
Unification Church, 78
Union of Industries in the European
Community (UNICE), 41
United Nations, 6, 14, 29, 78, 140, 142,
234
United Nations Fourth World
Conference on Women, 144
United Nations High Commissioner on
Refugees (UNHCR), 109
Universal Declaration of Human Rights,
78
Universalism, xxv, xxvii, 76, 78, 179, 182,
189
Urbain, Jean-Didier, 262
USA Patriot Act (2001), 115n15
USS *Cole*, attack on, 14
Utopias, 78, 222
U2: criticism of, 61

Vagabonds: tourists and, 74
Vajpayee, Atal Bihari, 13
Values: as automatic subject/self-moving
substance, 243; finance capital and, 246
Vergangenheitsbewältigung, xxx, xxxi, 289
Victimization, 284, 288
Victoria, Queen, 55
Victor Verster prison camp, 217–19
Virilio, Paul, 269
Visas, 258, 267, 270; rules about, 254;
scrutiny of, 256
Volatility, 247, 248
Von Weizsacker, Richard, 282, 291
Voting rights, 99, 113n10, 146

Wahid, Abdurrahman, 13–14
Wallpaper (magazine), 269
Wall Street Journal, 45
Walt, Steven, 58–59
Walzer, Michael, 106, 188
War crimes trials, xxx–xxxi, 277, 279,
287, 293n3
Warner, Michael, 234, 241
Warsaw ghetto, 282–83, 291